Learning Hebrew in Medieval England

The fountainhead of theology, a "doorway to wisdom," or a philological riddle: there were many reasons to learn Hebrew for inquisitive Christian minds in the Middle Ages. Although preoccupation with the meanings of the names of the Hebrew letters and their presumed inherent virtues can be traced back to the early Church Fathers, the rediscovery of classical sources and Aristotelian philosophy and the engagement with Graeco-Arabic sciences that marked the renaissance of the twelfth century also brought about an acute awareness of the need for a philological understanding of the Hebrew language.

In England in particular, various factors combined together to encourage and facilitate the study of Hebrew texts, not only among well-known writers such as Andrew of St Victor, Herbert of Bosham, and Alexander Neckam in the twelfth century, and Robert Grosseteste and Roger Bacon in the thirteenth, but also among English scholars whose names have not been preserved. They nevertheless produced bilingual Hebrew-Latin manuscripts in collaboration with Jewish scribes, along with manuals, textbooks, and reference aids to facilitate access to the sources.

Learning Hebrew in Medieval England presents an edition and analysis of one such learning tool: a thirteenth-century grammar written in Hebrew, Latin, and Anglo-Norman French (the vernacular language of the Jews of England) in a complex combination of Hebrew and Latin alphabets. It can be traced to the Benedictine Ramsey Abbey in East Anglia and is preserved in a unique copy in a volume that is today part of the private collection of the Marquess of Bath at Longleat House in Wiltshire.

Studies and Texts 230

Judaism in the Medieval and Early Modern World 2

Edited by
PIET VAN BOXEL
University of Oxford

JOANNA WEINBERG
University of Oxford

Learning Hebrew in Medieval England

Christian Scholars and the Longleat House Grammar

JUDITH OLSZOWY-SCHLANGER

Toronto
PIMS
PONTIFICAL INSTITUTE OF MEDIAEVAL STUDIES

Acknowledgement

The Pontifical Institute of Mediaeval Studies gratefully acknowledges the generous support of Ann M. Hutchison, James P. Carley, and the Janet E. Hutchison Foundation, Toronto.

Library and Archives Canada Cataloguing in Publication

Title: Learning Hebrew in medieval England : Christian scholars and the Longleat House grammar / Judith Olszowy-Schlanger.

Names: Olszowy-Schlanger, Judith, author. | Longleat House (Warminster, England). Manuscript Ms. 21. | Pontifical Institute of Mediaeval Studies, publisher.

Series: Judaism in the medieval and early modern world ; 2. | Studies and texts (Pontifical Institute of Mediaeval Studies) ; 230.

Description: Series statement: Studies and texts ; 230 | Judaism in the medieval and early modern world ; 2 | Includes bibliographical references and indexes. | Text chiefly in English; some text in Hebrew and Latin.

Identifiers: Canadiana (print) 20220457735 | Canadiana (ebook) 20220457840 | ISBN 9780888442307 (hardcover) | ISBN 9781771104234 (PDF)

Subjects: LCSH: Hebrew language, Medieval – Grammar – Study and teaching – England – Early works to 1800. | LCSH: Christian Hebraists – England – History – To 1500. | LCSH: Manuscripts, Hebrew – England – History – To 1500. | LCSH: Longleat House (Warminster, England). Manuscript Ms. 21.

Classification: LCC PJ4547 .O47 2023 | DDC 492.4/5094209022–dc23

Pontifical Institute of Mediaeval Studies
59 Queen's Park Crescent East
Toronto, Ontario M5S 2C4
Canada
pims.ca

PRINTED IN CANADA

Contents

Abbreviations • vii
Tables • viii
Preface • ix

Facsimile of the Longleat House Grammar • *after page* 78

INTRODUCTION • 1

CHAPTER 1
The Manuscript: Its Structure, Texts and Scribes • 11
The Codicological, Textual and Palaeographical Units of LH MS 21 • 12
The Codicological and Textual Composition of the Longleat House Grammar • 17
The Scribes of LH MS 21 • 19
Palaeographical Remarks • 22
Page and Text Layout • 24

CHAPTER 2
The Longleat House Grammar and Hebrew Scholarship at Ramsey Abbey • 29
The Longleat House Grammar Among the Bilingual Hebrew-Latin Manuscripts • 29
The Longleat House Grammar and Ramsey Abbey • 35

CHAPTER 3
The Longleat House Grammar and Different Linguistic Approaches to Hebrew in Medieval England • 41
Through the Latin Lens • 42
Christian Hebrew Grammar and Jewish Linguistic Traditions • 56

CHAPTER 4
The Edition of the Longleat House Grammar • 79
Grammar Textual Unit 1: The Hebrew Grammar in Latin Characters • 81
Grammar Textual Unit 2: The Essay on Hebrew Vowels and Accents • 93
Grammar Textual Unit 3: The Hebrew Grammar in Hebrew Characters • 99
Grammar Textual Unit 4: The Hebrew Verb Paradigms in Latin Characters • 108

CHAPTER 5
Contents and Sources of the Longleat House Grammar • 113
Grammar Textual Unit 1: The Hebrew Grammar in Latin Characters • 113
Grammar Textual Unit 2: The Essay on Hebrew Vowels and Accents • 127
Grammar Textual Unit 3: The Hebrew Grammar in Hebrew Characters • 146
Grammar Textual Unit 4: The Hebrew Verb Paradigms in Latin Characters • 160

Conclusions • 165

Bibliography • 167
Index of Quotations • 185
Index of Manuscripts • 186
General Index • 188

Abbreviations

AHDLMA	*Archives d'histoire doctrinale et littéraire du Moyen Âge*
AND2	*Anglo-Norman Dictionary Online, 2nd edition*
BL	British Library
Bm	Bibliothèque municipale
BnF	Bibliothèque nationale de France
Bodl.	Bodleian Library
CCC	Corpus Christi College
CU	Codicological Unit
DEAF	*Dictionnaire Etymologique de l'Ancien Français*
GTU	Grammar Textual Unit
HEL	*Histoire, Épistémologie, Langage*
HUCA	*Hebrew Union College Annual*
JA	*Journal asiatique*
JHS	*Jewish Historical Studies*
JQR	*Jewish Quarterly Review*
LH	Longleat House, Library of the Marquess of Bath
mF	modern French
MT	Masoretic Text
REJ	*Revue des études juives*
RTAM	*Recherches de théologie ancienne et médiévale*
TCBS	*Transactions of the Cambridge Bibliographical Society*
TU	Textual Unit

Tables

Table 1.1 Textual and codicological units of LH MS 21 • 12
Table 1.2 The structure of the Longleat House Grammar • 17
Table 1.3 The scribes of the different texts of LH MS 21 • 21
Table 1.4 Comparison of selected letters in Longleat House Grammar, LH MS 21 Psalter scribe 1, LH MS 21 Psalter scribe 2 and Oxford, Bodl., MS Or. 62 • 24
Table 2.1 Manuscripts of the "*enek.*" group and their scribes • 32
Table 5.1 The structure and order of the grammatical categories in the paradigm of the verb *Ḳal* in GTU 1, fol. 193r • 120
Table 5.2 The structure of the presentation of the *Ḳal* verb with object suffixes of the 1st person singular and plural • 123
Table 5.3 Designations of the grammatical persons • 125
Table 5.4 List and description of vowels in GTU 2 and their comparison to the list in Hebrew in GTU 3 • 130
Table 5.5 Joseph Kimhi's classification of vowels • 144
Table 5.6 Form of שמר translated into French written in Hebrew characters • 150
Table 5.7 The mapping of the verb paradigms in GTU 4 • 162

Preface

It was in 2003 that I began the study of the manuscript of a grammar of Hebrew written for Christian scholars in the Middle Ages, a study which is finally published in this book. Later, with a group of medieval historians and philologists from the Institut de Recherche et d'Histoire des Textes of the CNRS in Paris, I worked on preparing the publication of a trilingual Hebrew-Latin-Old French dictionary bound in the same miscellaneous volume Longleat House, Library of the Marquess of Bath, MS 21 that includes the grammar edited here. My own work on this grammar had been encouraged by discussions with the late Professor Raphael Loewe who was kind enough to join our research team in Paris and to share his erudition with us all. This is a fitting opportunity to pay homage to his pioneering contribution to the study of medieval Christian Hebraism in England, as well as to his great generosity and kindness.

It is a pleasure to acknowledge the kind permission of the Marquess of Bath to publish the manuscript and its facsimile, and to thank Dr Kate Harris, the Librarian of the Longleat House, for her assistance. I also thank the Bodleian Library, and especially Dr César Merchán-Hamann, and Corpus Christi College, Oxford, its President Helen Moore and its Librarians Joanna Snelling and Julian Reid, as well as the Bibliothèque nationale de France and the Head of the Oriental Collections, Mr Laurent Héricher in particular, for their assistance and encouragement.

My special thanks go to my home academic institutions, which have inspired and supported my research. In Paris, the École Pratique des Hautes Études, PSL, and its research laboratory Savoir et Pratiques depuis l'antiquité jusqu'au XIXe siècle (SAPRAT), and the Institut de Recherche et d'Histoire des Textes (IRHT) of the Centre national de la recherche scientifique (CNRS). In Oxford, since 2018, the University of Oxford and its Centre for Hebrew and Jewish Studies, as well as Corpus Christi College, whose magnificent collections contain several bilingual Hebrew-Latin manuscripts. Over the years, I have had the opportunity to present preliminary results of my studies at several venues where I benefitted from questions, comments, and discussions with the learned audience. I thank my friend, Anne Grondeux of the CNRS, Paris, for her precious advice on medieval Latin and its script. I thank James Carley and Ann Hutchison for their friendship, erudite advice and invitation to publish this book in the series of the Pontifical Institute of Mediaeval Studies. I thank Fred Unwalla, the Institute's editor in chief, and series editors Joanna Weinberg and Piet van Boxel for their advice, kindness and patience with the book which has been too long in the making. I thank Jaclyn Piudik for her careful editing of this book. Last but not least, special thanks go to my family, my husband Nathan, always my first and most demanding reader, and my three daughters, Tali, Ada and Eva, who have now grown to be informed critics of their mother's writings.

Introduction

The fountainhead of theology, a "doorway to wisdom"[1] or a philological riddle – there were many good reasons to learn Hebrew for inquisitive Christian minds in the Middle Ages. Theologically relevant as the language of the prophets, ideologically potent as a means to convert the Jews "through the powers of their mother tongue,"[2] Hebrew featured strongly among the intellectual preoccupations of Christian scholars, just as the exotic shapes of the unfamiliar alphabet captured their imagination. From the days of the early Church Fathers, Christian scholarship had been pondering the meanings of the names of the Hebrew letters and their presumed inherent virtues.[3] Acquiring even a rudimentary grasp of Hebrew grammar and vocabulary was believed to lead to a new understanding of the sacred texts. The general growth in cultural curiosity and literacy during the "Twelfth-Century Renaissance" prompted transformations in the needs and methods of learning. This included the study of languages and their grammar.[4] Alongside the rediscovery of classical sources and Aristotelian philosophy, followed by the engagement with Greco-Arabic sciences, this intellectually fertile period had also brought about an acute awareness of the need for a philological understanding of the Hebrew language.

It cannot be said that the study of Hebrew was at the centre of Western scholarship at that time.[5] Yet, recent and ongoing research, reinforced by a closer

1. Roger Bacon, *Opus Tertium*, in *Opera quaedam hactenus inedita*, ed. J.S. Brewer (London, 1859), 102.

2. As advocated, for example, by Odo, the author of the *Ysagoge*, an introduction to theology, written in England around 1150 (Cambridge, Trinity College, MS B.14.33), Artur Landgraf, *Écrits théologiques de l'école d'Abélard: Textes inédits* (Louvain, 1934), 127. For the manuscript, see Montague Rhodes James, *The Western Manuscripts in the Library of Trinity College, Cambridge: A Descriptive Catalogue* (Cambridge, 1900), 1: 431. For Odo's attitude to conversion, see Avrom Saltman, "Odo's *Ysagoge:* A New Method of Anti-Jewish Polemic," *Criticism and Interpretation* 13–14 (1979): 265–280 (Hebrew); Avrom Saltman, "Gilbert Crispin as a Source of the Anti-Jewish Polemic of the *Ysagoge in theologiam,*" in *Confrontation and Coexistence*, ed. Pinḥas Artzi (Ramat Gan, 1984), 89–99.

3. J. Cornelia Linde, "Notandum duas hic litteras, phe et ain, ordine praeposteratas esse: Rupert of Deutz, Guibert of Nogent and the Glossa Ordinaria on the Incorrect Order of the Hebrew Alphabet," *Archa Verbi* 7 (2010): 68–78.

4. Rodney M. Thomson, "England and the Twelfth-Century Renaissance," *Past & Present* 101 (1983): 3–21.

5. Roger Bacon was probably not far from the truth in observing that barely four of his contemporaries (unfortunately unspecified) knew the Hebrew grammar well enough to be

reading of previously neglected sources and unpublished manuscripts, shows that Hebrew learning was far less marginal and eccentric than previously thought. In England in particular, some twelfth- and thirteenth-century monks and friars mastered the rules of the Hebrew language and Jewish commentaries and could therefore competently compare the Latin Vulgate with the Hebrew Bible.[6] A new Latin translation of the Bible was undertaken; its text has been preserved in several manuscripts, written as a gloss between the Hebrew lines (*superscriptio*).[7] This investigation of Hebrew joined an ancient tradition of philological study in the monasteries and schools of England. At another level, close everyday business contacts between Christians and Jews in main English towns provided opportunities for learning Hebrew, as did cases of conversions of impoverished and threatened Jewish individuals, frequent from the mid-thirteenth century onwards.[8]

---

able to teach it. *Opus Tertium*, in *Opera quaedam hactenus inedita*, ed. Brewer, 33–34: "Nam non sunt quatuor Latini, qui sciant grammaticam Hebraeorum, et Graecorum, et Arabum: bene enim cognosco eos, quia et citra mare et ultra diligenter feci inquiri, et multum in his laboravi. Multi vero inveniuntur, qui sciunt loqui Graecum, et Arabicum, et Hebraeum, inter Latinos, sed paucissimi sunt qui sciunt rationem grammaticae ipsius, nec sciunt docere eam."

6. On the *correctoria* (lists of textual emendations) of the Paris Bible in general, see Heinrich Denifle, "Die Handschriften der Bibel-Correctorien des 13. Jahrhunderts," *Archiv für die Literatur- und Kirschengeschichte des Mittelalters* 4 (1888): 263–311 and 471–601; Laura Light, "Versions et révisions du texte biblique," in *Le Moyen Âge et la Bible*, ed. Pierre Riché and Guy Lobrichon (Paris, 1984), 55–93; J. Cornelia Linde, *How to Correct the Sacra Scriptura?: Textual Criticism of the Latin Bible between the Twelfth and Fifteenth Century* (Oxford, 2012).

7. A complete or partial *superscriptio* appears in seven Psalters (Oxford, CCC, MS 10; Oxford, CCC, MS 11 [Psalter]; Cambridge, Trinity College, MS R. 8. 6; London, Westminster Abbey Library, MS 2; Paris, BnF, MS hébreu 113; LH MS 21 [Psalter] and London, Lambeth Palace Library, MS 435), as well as in the Bible manuscripts Oxford, CCC, MS 5; Oxford, CCC, MS 8; Oxford, CCC, MS 9; Oxford, St John's College, MS 143; Oxford, Bodl., MS Or. 46 and Oxford, Bodl., MS Or. 62. More sporadic interlinear and marginal translations are also found in the commentary of Rashi, Oxford, CCC, MS 6, and in a maḥzor for Yom Kippur, Oxford, Bodl., MS Arch. Selden A. 3. The comparison of the *superscriptio* for the Psalters shows that despite some minor textual variations the translations in LH MS 21, Oxford, CCC, MS 10 and Cambridge, Trinity College, MS R. 8. 6 represent essentially the same text. This translation is also mentioned under the title of "*iudeus*," "the Jew," as one of the sources of the collation in the Psalter in Oxford, CCC, MS 11. For the study of the *superscriptio* and its attribution (still unconfirmed) to Robert Grosseteste, see Beryl Smalley, *Hebrew Scholarship among Christians in XIIIth Century England as Illustrated by Some Hebrew-Latin Psalters* (London, 1939); Raphael Loewe, "The Medieval Christian Hebraists of England: The Superscriptio Lincolniensis," *HUCA* 28 (1957): 205–252; Raphael Loewe, "Latin Superscriptio MSS on Portions of the Hebrew Bible Other than the Psalter," *Journal of Jewish Studies* 9 (1958): 63–71; Judith Olszowy-Schlanger, *Les manuscrits hébreux dans l'Angleterre médiévale: Étude historique et paléographique* (Louvain and Paris, 2003).

8. See especially Robert. C. Stacey, "The Conversion of Jews to Christianity in Thirteenth-Century England," *Speculum* 67 (1992): 263–283.

All these factors combined together to encourage and facilitate the study of Hebrew texts. Englishmen such as Andrew of Saint-Victor (d. 1175),[9] Herbert of Bosham (c. 1120–1194)[10] and Alexander Neckam (c. 1157–1217)[11] in the twelfth century, or Robert Grosseteste (c. 1175–1253),[12] Roger Bacon (c. 1214–

9. Andrew, the canon of Saint-Victor and since 1147 the abbot of Wigmore, had only a smattering of Hebrew but referred many times to "*Iudei*" or "*Hebrei*" in his Bible commentaries written c. 1153–1163, see Beryl Smalley, "Andrew of Saint Victor, Abbot of Wigmore: A Twelfth-Century Hebraist," *RTAM* 10 (1938): 358–373; Beryl Smalley, *The Study of the Bible in the Middle Ages* (Notre Dame, 1964), 154–172; Loewe, "The Medieval Christian Hebraists of England: The Superscriptio Lincolniensis," 208. A century later, Roger Bacon praised Andrew for his calls for a comparison of the Vulgate with Hebrew but reported that his Hebraist zeal brought on Andrew accusations of "judaizing." See *Compendium Studii Philosophiae*, in *Opera quaedam hactenus inedita*, ed. Brewer, 480–483. See Rainer Berndt, *André de Saint-Victor (1175): Exégète et théologien* (Turnhout, 1991), 108–163.

10. On Herbert of Bosham's Hebraism, see Beryl Smalley, "A Commentary on the Hebraica by Herbert of Bosham," *RTAM* 18 (1951): 29–65; Raphael Loewe, "Herbert of Bosham's Commentary on Jerome's Hebrew Psalter," *Biblica* 34 (1953): 44–77, (II) 159–192, (III) 275–298; Raphael Loewe, "The Medieval Christian Hebraists of England: Herbert of Bosham and Earlier Scholars," *Transactions of the Jewish Historical Society of England* 17 (1953): 225–249; Deborah L. Goodwin, *Take Hold of the Robe of a Jew: Herbert of Bosham's Christian Hebraism* (Leiden, 2006); Eva De Visscher, *Reading the Rabbis: Christian Hebraism in the Works of Herbert of Bosham* (Leiden, 2014); Eva De Visscher, "Cross-religious Learning and Teaching: Hebraism in the Works of Herbert of Bosham and Contemporaries," in *Crossing Borders: Hebrew Manuscripts as a Meeting-place of Cultures*, ed. Piet van Boxel and Sabine Arndt (Oxford, 2009), 123–132; Eva De Visscher, "Putting Theory into Practice?: Hugh of St Victor's Influence on Herbert of Bosham's Psalterium cum commento," in *Bibel und Exegese in der Abtei Saint-Victor zu Paris: Form und Funktion eines Grundtextes im europäischen Rahmen*, ed. Rainer Berndt (Münster, 2009), 491–502; Eva De Visscher, "'Closer to the Hebrew': Herbert of Bosham's Interpretation of Literal Exegesis," in *The Multiple Meaning of Scripture: The Role of Exegesis in Early-Christian and Medieval Culture*, ed. Ienje Van't Spijker (Leiden, 2009), 249–272.

11. Alexander Neckam was a theologian, philosopher and abbot of Cirencester. Neckam's references to Hebrew were subservient to his theological argumentation but showed considerable familiarity with Hebrew vocabulary and with Jewish interpretation techniques. They were studied by Raphael Loewe, "Alexander Neckam's Knowledge of Hebrew," in *Hebrew Study from Ezra to Ben-Yehuda*, ed. William Horbury (Edinburgh, 1999), 207–223.

12. The towering theologian, natural philosopher, and Hellenist, appointed in 1235 bishop of Lincoln, Robert Grosseteste, is also credited with Hebrew learning. Roger Bacon underplayed Grosseteste's proficiency, reporting that his level of Hebrew and Greek was not sufficient for him to translate alone but that he had many proficient helpers who assisted him in his labours, see *Compendium Studii Philosophiae*, in *Opera quaedam hactenus inedita*, ed. Brewer, 472: "Graecum et Hebraicum non scivit sufficienter ut per se transferret, sed habuit multos adiutores." See J.C. Russell, "The Preferments and 'Adiutores' of Robert Grosseteste," *Harvard Theological Review* 26 (1933): 161–172. However, later sources such as the Dominican Nicolas Trivet (1258–1334) admired Grosseteste as proficient in Latin, Greek

1292)[13] and William de Mara (fl. 1270s–1280s)[14] in the thirteenth century are all known to have been involved in Hebrew studies. Some of them, notably Herbert of Bosham, achieved good linguistic proficiency. Other English scholars and monks whose names have not been preserved produced bilingual Hebrew-Latin manuscripts in collaboration with Jewish scribes.[15] They also consulted freely,

and Hebrew, see Nicholas Trivet, *Annales sex regum Angliae, qui a comitibus andegavensibus originem traxerunt*, ed. Thomas Hog (London, 1845), 243: "Doctor vero in triplici lingua eruditus, Latina Hebraea et Graeca, multa de glossis Hebraeorum extraxit, et de Graeco multa transferri fecit." On Grosseteste's Hebraism and his possible involvement in the new Latin translation of the Psalter from Hebrew (*superscriptio Lincolniensis*), see Smalley, *Hebrew Scholarship Among Christians*; David J. Wasserstein, "Grosseteste, the Jews and Medieval Christian Hebraism," in *Robert Grosseteste: New Perspectives on His Thought and Scholarship*, ed. James McEvoy (Turnhout, 1995), 357–376.

13. An Oxford Franciscan and natural philosopher, Roger Bacon, advocated the study of Hebrew and referred to Hebrew in several places scattered through his works: *Operis maioris partes I–VI* (new edition), ed. John Henry Bridges (Turnhout, 2010); *Opus Tertium*, in *Opera quaedam hactenus inedita*, ed. Brewer; *Compendium Studii Philosophiae* in *Opera quaedam hactenus inedita*, ed. Brewer; *Grammatica Graeca*, in *The Greek Grammar of Roger Bacon and a Fragment of His Hebrew Grammar*, ed. Edmond Nolan and S.A. Hirsch (Cambridge, 1902). He is also credited with a page-long note on Hebrew grammar, see "Cambridge Hebrew Grammar," in *The Greek Grammar*, ed. Nolan and Hirsch, 199–208. Another work attributed to Roger Bacon or to someone of his circle (such as William de Mara) are the remarks on Hebrew in the *Notabilia extraordinaria*, see Samuel Berger, *Quam notitiam linguae Hebraicae habuerint Christiani medii aevi temporibus in Gallia* (Paris, 1893), 45; Etienne Anheim, Benoît Grévin and Martin Morard, "Exégèse judéo-chrétienne, magie et linguistique: Un recueil de Notes inédites attribuées à Roger Bacon," *AHDLMA* 68 (2001): 95–154, at 98–107. For Bacon's interest in Hebrew grammar, see Irène Rosier-Catach, "La Grammatica practica du ms. British Museum V A IV: Roger Bacon, les lexicographes et l'étymologie," in *L'étymologie de l'Antiquité à la Renaissance*, ed. Claude Buridant (Lille, 1998), 97–125; Benoît Grévin, "L'hébreu des Franciscains: Nouveaux éléments sur la connaissance de l'hébreu en milieu chrétien au XIIIe siècle," *Médiévales* 41 (2001): 65–82.

14. A Franciscan, William de Mara, was the author of the *Correctorium Vaticanum*, composed around 1280, in which he often referred to the Hebrew Bible and Jewish exegesis. For his correctorium, see Denifle, "Die Handschriften der Bibel-Correctorien," 295–298. On William de Mara's somehow elusive biography, see D.A. Callus, "William de la Mare," in *New Catholic Encyclopaedia* 14 (New York, 1967), 928B–929A; John Marenbon, "Mare, William, de la" (William de Mara), in *Oxford Dictionary of National Biography Online*, 2011, https://doi.org/10.1093/ref:odnb/18025; Raymond Creytens, "Autour de la littérature des correctoires," *Archivum Fratrum Praedicatorum* 12 (1942): 313–330; Palémon Glorieux, *Répertoire des maîtres en théologie de Paris au XIIIe siècle* (Paris, 1934), 99–101; Ephrem Longpré, "la Mare, Guillaume de," in *Dictionnaire de théologie catholique* 8 (Paris, 1924), 2467–2470; Hans Kraml, "Guillaume de la Mare, theologian," in *Lexikon des Mittelalters* 9 (Munich, 1998), 174–175. On his Hebrew learning, see Berger, *Quam notitiam*, 32–36.

15. See esp. Berger, *Quam notitiam*; Smalley, *Hebrew Scholarship among Christians*; Loewe, "The Medieval Christian Hebraists of England: The Superscriptio Lincolniensis";

both with the help of Jewish teachers and through independent reading, such Jewish works as the Aramaic version of the Bible (Targum), Bible commentaries of the renowned exegete of Troyes, Rabbi Solomon ben Isaac, known by the acronym Rashi, (1040–1105), or the dictionary *Maḥberet he-ʿArukh* composed around 1160 in Salerno by Solomon ben Abraham ibn Parḥon. To study and translate the Hebrew Bible, to collate it with the Latin Vulgate, and to be able to read Jewish exegesis, Christian scholars needed to master the Hebrew language. While in the previous centuries Christian interest in Jewish interpretation was usually satisfied by (often vague) information provided by their more or less learned Jewish neighbours, the twelfth- and thirteenth-century scholars in England appreciated the importance of the Hebrew language as a path towards the knowledge of the sources. It was becoming increasingly evident that the correct understanding of the founding texts of Christianity required the comprehension of the "properties," the "inner meanings," of their original Hebrew words and language structures.[16]

To access these original texts and grasp the *proprietas* of their language, Christian scholars undoubtedly required the help of Jewish teachers, but first and foremost they needed Hebrew books. While some were lucky enough to come across Jewish manuscripts, others complained about the difficulty of procuring Hebrew bibles, dictionaries and grammar manuals. The most adventurous and innovative of these scholars, inspired and helped by their Jewish teachers, actually undertook to create their own manuals and textbooks with which to gain access to Hebrew and its literary treasures.

This book presents an edition and analysis of such a learning tool: a succinct Hebrew grammar written in Hebrew in Hebrew characters, but also in Hebrew in Latin characters, in Anglo-Norman French (the vernacular language of the Jews of England) in Hebrew characters, and in Latin in Latin characters. Its script, codicological context and some elements of its grammatical terminology indicate

Loewe, "Latin Superscriptio MSS"; Malachi Beit-Arié, "The Valmadonna Pentateuch and the Problem of Pre-expulsion Anglo-Hebrew Manuscripts – MS London, Valmadonna Trust Library 1: England (?), 1189," in *The Makings of the Medieval Hebrew Book: Studies in Palaeography and Codicology*, ed. Malachi Beit-Arié (Jerusalem, 1993), 129–151; Colette Sirat, "Notes sur la circulation des livres entre juifs et chrétiens au Moyen Âge," in *Du copiste au collectionneur: Mélanges d'histoire des textes et des bibliothèques en l'honneur d'André Vernet*, ed. Donatella Nebbiai-Dalla Guarda and Jean-François Genest (Turnhout, 1999), 383–403; Olszowy-Schlanger, *Les manuscrits hébreux*.

16. See Roger Bacon's discussion on the importance of grammar and language study in his *Operis maioris* III, ed. Bridges, 3: 80: "Nam totus textus sacer a Graeco et Hebraeo transfusus est, et philosophia ab his et Arabico deducta est; sed impossibile est quod proprietas unius linguae servetur in alia. (...) Et ideo nullus Latinus sapientiam sacrae scripturae et philosophiae poterit ut oportet intelligere, nisi intelligat linguas a quibus sunt translatae."

that this grammar book was composed in England, in the thirteenth century. It was compiled, copied and studied by Christian scholars who had access to the works of Jewish grammarians and relied to some extent on the help of Jewish informers. As the grammar itself has it, these *interpretes* notably provided information on how Hebrew should be pronounced (fol. 197r).[17]

The unique known copy of this grammar is preserved in a slim and modest booklet of twelve slightly irregular, yellow and damaged parchment folios, bound together with other medieval works. These works include a substantial Latin and Anglo-Norman French dictionary of biblical Hebrew[18] and a Hebrew Psalter translated and glossed in Latin, still awaiting a comprehensive edition. These three works together constitute a perfect learning set of linguistic aids for Christian Hebraists – dictionary and grammar, bound with the perfect textbook, the Psalter. Christian scholars indeed had excellent knowledge of the Latin Psalms which were a part of the daily liturgy, and this familiarity made learning Hebrew Psalms easier than other texts. This volume comprising the grammar and other works is today a part of the private collection of the Marquess of Bath at Longleat House in Wiltshire and will be henceforth referred to as LH MS 21.

The Hebraists' "dossier" in LH MS 21 is an accomplished example of a distinctive "school" of Christian Hebraism in medieval England. The main characteristic of this "school" is its ready and systematic reliance on Jewish sources. These sources included the Hebrew Bible but also the Bible commentaries of Rashi and several Jewish works on grammar and lexicography. The "Longleat House Grammar" (as we shall from now refer to the component of LH MS 21 which is the focus of this book) was intended as a primary tool for mastering the rudiments of the Hebrew language. This teaching objective was expressed in the manuscript itself, through the ambitious claim that the booklet's contents are "all one needs to

17. On the role of "living Jews" in the study of Hebrew in the Middle Ages, see for example, David Kaufmann, "Les juifs et la Bible de l'abbé Etienne de Cîteaux," *REJ* 18 (1889): 131–133; Aryeh Grabois, "The Hebraica Veritas and Jewish-Christian Intellectual Relations in the Twelfth Century," *Speculum* 50 (1975): 613–634; Gilbert Dahan, "Juifs et chrétiens en occident médiéval: La rencontre autour de la Bible," *Revue de Synthèse* 110 (1989): 3–31; Gilbert Dahan, "L'enseignement de l'hébreu en occident médiéval (XIIe–XIVe siècles)," *Histoire de l'éducation* 57 (1993): 3–22; Michael A. Singer, "Polemic and Exegesis: The Varieties of Twelfth-Century Hebraism," in *Hebraica Veritas?: Christian Hebraists and the Study of Judaism in Early Modern Europe*, ed. Alison P. Coudert and Jeffrey S. Shoulson (Philadelphia, 2004), 21–32 at 22–23; Rebecca Moore, *Jews and Christians in the Life and Thought of Hugh of St Victor* (Atlanta, 1998); Jeremy Cohen, *The Friars and the Jews: The Evolution of Medieval Anti-Judaism* (Ithaca, 1984); Jeremy Cohen, *Living Letters of the Law: Ideas of the Jew in Medieval Christianity* (Berkeley, 1999); De Visscher, "Cross-religious Learning and Teaching."

18. Judith Olszowy-Schlanger and Anne Grondeux, eds., *Dictionnaire hébreu-latin-français de la Bible hébraïque de l'Abbaye de Ramsey (XIIIe s.)* (Turnhout, 2008).

master Hebrew" (fol. 200v). Exaggerated as this claim undoubtedly is, the Longleat House Grammar remains, to the best of our current knowledge, the most accomplished linguistic tool for the study of Hebrew produced during the Christian Middle Ages.

The Longleat House Grammar was conceived to facilitate access to Hebrew for Christian students. Composed of three self-contained small fascicles containing four different texts over twelve parchment folios, this grammar provides the morphological paradigms of Hebrew verbs, notes on nouns and prepositions and a short tractate on Hebrew pronunciation and vowels. The codicological and palaeographical aspects of this unique grammar, its contents, sources of linguistic concepts, its intellectual and institutional context of production and its subsequent history are all explored in the successive chapters of this book, alongside the edition of the text and a facsimile of the manuscript.

This study of the Longleat House Grammar begins with a description of the manuscript itself. Chapter One analyses its codicological composition, scribal hands and the structure of its textual units. Unfortunately, the manuscript itself does not contain any information regarding its origin and provenance. However, its material aspects, and in particular the handwriting analysis of the different scribes and glossators who intervened across both the Longleat House Grammar and the entire bound volume LH MS 21, pave the way for tentative identification of the manuscript's place of production.

Indeed, unique as it is, the Longleat House Grammar is not an isolated accomplishment. It belongs to a distinct tradition of Christian Hebraism which flourished in twelfth- and thirteenth-century England. The most remarkable feature of this medieval English Hebraism was its production and use of unusual Bible manuscripts written in Hebrew and Latin in parallel columns on the page. These bilingual and bi-alphabetical manuscripts, the earliest of which date to the middle of the twelfth century, were jointly created by scribes respectively trained in Christian and Jewish traditions. Eleven such custom-made bilingual Psalters and other parts of the Bible in parallel columns, produced for a convenient comparison of the texts, have been preserved.[19] To these Psalters several Hebrew manuscripts with interlinear and marginal Latin glosses can be added, as well as the aforementioned trilingual Bible dictionary in LH MS 21. The part of the

19. Berger, *Quam Notitiam*; Smalley, *Hebrew Scholarship among Christians*; Smalley, *The Study of the Bible*, 342–346; Loewe, "The Medieval Christian Hebraists of England: The Superscriptio Lincolniensis"; Loewe, "Latin Superscriptio MSS"; Malachi Beit-Arié, *Hebrew Manuscripts of East and West: Towards a Comparative Codicology* (London, 1992); Sirat, "Notes sur la circulation des livres"; Gilbert Dahan, "Deux psautiers hébraïques glosés en latin," *REJ* 158 (1999): 61–87; Olszowy-Schlanger, *Les manuscrits hébreux*; Olszowy-Schlanger and Grondeux, *Dictionnaire hébreu-latin-français*.

Longleat House Grammar in Hebrew script was written by a scribe who was evidently trained in Jewish scribal tradition, whereas the Hebrew entries in the dictionary in LH MS 21 were copied by a Christian scribe who mastered Hebrew calligraphy.

The English origin of this corpus of bilingual manuscripts is well established on palaeographical and linguistic grounds since some of them contain passages and notes in Anglo-Norman French and even in Middle English. The Longleat House Grammar notably contains a translation of the paradigms of the verb שמר, "to guard," into a Northern dialect of the *langue d'oïl*, written in Hebrew characters. The dictionary in LH MS 21, for its part, includes hundreds of Anglo-Norman words and four translations into Middle English. The production and study of these multilingual and bi-alphabetical manuscripts spanned several generations of scholars – from the earliest Psalter from Canterbury, datable to c. 1150, to the trilingual dictionary in LH MS 21, copied in the third quarter of the thirteenth century.[20] Beyond these broad indications, a more specific place of production and study proves less easy to establish. Nor is it clear whether all the bilingual Hebrew-Latin manuscripts from medieval England stem from the same milieu, or whether they were produced by and for different institutions. That said, one particular group among the thirteenth-century manuscripts, with its typical interlinear *superscriptio*, is closely related also in palaeographical terms. The trilingual dictionary in LH MS 21 and the Longleat House Grammar belong to this subgroup of manuscripts. In Chapter Two, I discuss the possible relationship of this group, and in particular of LH MS 21 and the Longleat House Grammar, with the East Anglian Benedictine Abbey of Ramsey.

In truth, it is difficult to assess just how exceptional the Longleat House Grammar was.[21] It has survived in one exemplar only, and no other Hebrew

20. Leiden, Bibliotheek der Rijksuniversiteit, MS Or. 4725, see Gerard I. Lieftinck, "The Psalterium Hebraycum from St Augustine's Canterbury Rediscovered in the Scaliger Bequest at Leyden," *TCBS* 2 (1955): 97–104; Loewe, "The Medieval Christian Hebraists of England: The Superscriptio Lincolniensis," 223; Albert Van der Heide, *Hebrew Manuscripts of Leiden University Library* (Leiden, 1977), 62; Margaret T. Gibson, *The Bible in the Latin West* (Notre Dame, 1993), 66–67, no. 20; Beit-Arié, *Hebrew Manuscripts of East and West*, 18; Sirat, "Notes sur la circulation des livres," 392; Olszowy-Schlanger, *Les manuscrits hébreux*, 205–211, no. 11.

21. It is possible that more Christian grammars of Hebrew circulated among scholars in England in the Middle Ages. Richard of Bury (1287–1345), in the conclusion to chapter X of his *Philobiblon* (Love of Books), stated that he had provided the scholars with a Greek and Hebrew grammar "with certain additions" to give them some help in their study of the Bible while warning that it is only through the active hearing the language that one can learn it. See Richard de Bury, *Ricardi de Bury Philobiblon ex optimis codicibus recensuit versione anglica necnon et prolegomenis adnotationibusque auxit Andreas Fleming West*, ed. Andrew Fleming West (New York, 1889), 1: 86–87: "Quamobrem grammaticam tam Hebraeam

grammars of similar nature, scope and quality are known to us prior to the development of Christian Hebraism of the sixteenth century. It is equally difficult to establish whether the grammar had successfully served its pedagogical purpose and whether it had any influence beyond a small elite of thirteenth-century scholars, although a few marginal notes in later Latin handwritings testify to its subsequent readership.

The authors of the Longleat House Grammar remain anonymous, and the manuscript provides little information on their identity. Some passages of one of the units of the Grammar are subjectively formulated by the author addressing his readers in the 1st person. This work is not a faithful copy of any known grammatical treatise but rather an independent composition which draws on and echoes preexisting linguistic writings. It is certain, however, that its grammatical approach crossed the boundaries of the standard medieval Christian curriculum. The Longleat House Grammar relies almost exclusively on Jewish linguistic tradition at a time when "grammar" was paramount to the Latin *grammatica* of Donatus and Priscian. To better appreciate the grammatical theory underlying the Longleat House Grammar, Chapter Three offers an overview of various grammatical approaches to Hebrew attested in medieval England among both Christian Hebraists and Jews.

Chapter Four is the core of the book: it contains the edition of the Longleat House Grammar and its facsimile. This edition proved complex, with different layouts and editorial techniques required for the different codicological and textual components of the Grammar. Indeed, parts of the text in Hebrew and Latin script follow each other, sometimes in the same quire, raising problems with the direction of reading. Some portions of the grammar are arranged as a text with an interlinear gloss (*superscriptio*), with a very tight graphic relationship between the source word written in the line and its interlinear translation or annotation. For their medieval scribes, this bilingual and bi-alphabetical text certainly represented a challenge: the present edition is designed to reflect their work, the difficulties they encountered and the solutions they found. This is why the edition in Chapter Four reproduces the texts and the relationship between their different components as faithfully as possible, and resorts to corrections only in the rare cases of obvious *lapsus calami*. It reproduces the complicated tabular layout of the glossed parts of the grammar. My editorial interventions

---

quam Graecam nostris scholaribus providere curavimus, cum quibusdam adjunctis, quorum adminiculo studiosi lectores in dictarum linguarum scriptura, lectura necnon etiam intellectu plurimum poterunt informari, licet proprietatem idiomatis solus auditus aurium animae repraesentet." In Ramsey Abbey, Laurence Holbeach is reported to have created a Hebrew dictionary sometime around 1400 (see below, p. 37).

are relegated to the copious critical apparatus, according to the editorial norms explained in the opening paragraph of Chapter Four.

A detailed analysis of the contents of the Longleat House Grammar follows in Chapter Five. Different grammatical topics, including phonetics, vocalization and morphology, are discussed in detail. Through the identification of specific Jewish grammatical approaches and the analysis of its terminology, an attempt is made to identify the possible Jewish linguistic sources of the Longleat House Grammar.

The Longleat House Grammar was first mentioned by Raphael Loewe in his 1966 seminal paper on the extant manuscript witnesses of medieval Christian Hebraism in England.[22] Its subsequent, more detailed description appeared in a paper I published in 2014.[23] However, the entire text of this remarkable medieval grammar book has not been published so far, and its implications for the history of Christian Hebraists and their contacts with Jewish intellectual tradition have remained insufficiently known among today's scholars. Making this unique text and manuscript better known should therefore contribute to the study of medieval intellectual history, and the role played in it by Jewish authors and by Hebrew language and texts.

22. Raphael Loewe, "Hebrew Books and 'Judaica' in Mediaeval Oxford and Cambridge," in *Remember the Days, Essays on Anglo-Jewish History presented to Cecil Roth*, ed. John M. Shaftesley (London, 1966), 23–48.

23. Judith Olszowy-Schlanger, "'With That, You Can Grasp all the Hebrew Language': Hebrew Sources of an Anonymous Hebrew-Latin Grammar from Thirteenth-Century England," in *A Universal Art: Hebrew Grammar across Disciplines and Faiths*, ed. Nadia Vidro, Irene E. Zwiep and Judith Olszowy-Schlanger (Leiden and Boston, 2014), 179–195.

CHAPTER ONE

The Manuscript: Its Structure, Texts and Scribes

The Longleat House Grammar is a part of a miscellaneous volume held today in the private collection of the Marquess of Bath at Longleat House in Wiltshire under catalogue number 21 (LH MS 21).[1] In the seventeenth century, this whole volume, composed of 204 parchment folios, was the property of the humanist, legal historian and antiquarian, Henry Spelman (1561–1641). Spelman, whose ex-libris appears on fol. 1v, is probably also the one who had the volume bound together. The manuscript was acquired in 1709 or 1710 by Thomas Thynne, 1st viscount of Weymouth at a sale of Spelman's collection.[2]

The volume contains six different texts. They include three Latin works: a commentary on Aristotelian logic, which in the manuscript is misleadingly entitled *Predicamenta Augustini*, and two medical tractates of the school of Salerno,[3] as well as three works of Christian Hebraism: a Hebrew Psalter with Latin translation and glosses, the Hebrew–Latin–Old French dictionary and, finally, the Longleat Hebrew Grammar, the object of the present study. These six works were copied as four distinct codicological units. These different codicological and textual components of LH MS 21 are palaeographically or textually related. While the present binding dates from Spelman's time, it is probable that the four

1. Raphael Loewe, "Jewish Scholarship in England," in *Three Centuries of Anglo-Jewish History*, ed. Vivian D. Lipman (Cambridge, 1961), 125–148, at 133; Judith Olszowy-Schlanger, *Les manuscrits hébreux dans l'Angleterre médiévale: Étude historique et paléographique* (Leuven and Paris, 2003), 88–196, no. 8; Judith Olszowy-Schlanger and Anne Grondeux, eds., *Dictionnaire hébreu-latin-français de la Bible hébraïque de l'Abbaye de Ramsey (XIIIe s.)* (Turnhout, 2008).

2. Kate Harris, "An Augustan Episode in the History of the Collection of Medieval Manuscripts at Longleat House," in *The English Medieval Book: Studies in Memory of Jeremy Griffiths*, ed. Anthony Stockwell Garfield Edwards, Vincent Gillespie and Ralph Hanna (London, 2000), 233–247, at 240–244.

3. For the identification of these texts, see François Dolbeau, "Les textes latins du volume," in *Dictionnaire hébreu-latin-français*, ed. Olszowy-Schlanger and Grondeux, xiv–xv.

codicological units have been kept together since the Middle Ages. Essential indication as to the origins of the Longleat House Grammar is provided by the codicological structure and the overlap between different scribal hands intervening across LH MS 21.

The Codicological, Textual and Palaeographical Units of LH MS 21

The volume is composed of twenty-two quires of parchment. It contains six main texts (textual units, TU) copied as four discrete codicological units (CU), some arranged from left to right and others from right to left, like any Hebrew book. The Longleat House Grammar, which itself contains four different parts, will be referred to as CU 4.[4]

Table 1.1 Textual and codicological units of LH MS 21

CU	TU	Folios	Dimensions (mm)	Text direction	Quires
1	1. *Predicamenta Augustini*	1r–19r	260 × 190	Left to right	I^{12}, II^{10}, III^{5+1}, IV^{8-1}
	2. *Tractatus de urinis*	19v–23rb			
	3. *Liber de virtute simplicis medicine*	23rb–28v			
2	4. Hebrew-Latin-Anglo-Norman Bible dictionary	29r–143v (text begins on 143v)	260 × 190	Right to left but columns left to right	XIII^{12}, XII^{12}, XI^{12}, X^{12}, IX^{12}, VIII^{12}, VII^{12}, VI^{12}, V^{12}, IV^{8-1}
3	5. Hebrew Psalter with Latin *superscriptio* and glosses	144r–192r (text begins on 192r)	265 × 180	Right to left	XIX^{8}, XVIII^{8}, XVII^{8}, XVI^{8}, XV^{8}, XIV^{8}

4. The codicological and palaeographical description of the manuscript here benefits from a detailed analysis by Patricia Stirnemann, "Le manuscrit," in *Dictionnaire hébreu-latin-français*, ed. Olszowy-Schlanger and Grondeux, x–xiv.

CU	TU	Folios	Dimensions (mm)	Text direction	Quires
4	6. Hebrew grammar: Hebrew in Latin characters	193r–196r	255 × 180	Left to right	XX^{4}, XXI^{6}, XXII^{2}
	Hebrew grammar: note in Latin on Hebrew pronunciation	196v–197r	255 × 180	Left to right	
	Hebrew grammar: Hebrew in Hebrew characters	197v–202r	255 × 180	Right to left	
	Hebrew grammar: Hebrew conjugation paradigms in Latin characters (incomplete)	203r–204r	255 × 180 (irregular)	Right to left	

The Quires

As illustrated in Table 1.1, the 204 parchment folios of the volume are structured in twenty-two quires. The composition of the quires differs according to the texts and highlights the originally heterogeneous nature of the bound volume LH MS 21. While the numbers of bifolios per quire in CU 1 and CU 4 vary a great deal, CU 2 and CU 3 display a more regular quire composition. CU 2 (Dictionary) is built of ten quires, all of which but the last contain six bifolios. Only the last, Quire IV, is smaller: an original quaternion whose last leaf was cut off. Indeed, the length of the text to copy at the end of the unit did not require a larger quire. CU 3 (Hebrew Psalter) is composed of six quaternions. Folios 158 and 155 (one bifolio in Quire XV) of CU 3 were damaged or lost and were replaced with matching folios written by a different scribe, without disturbing the structure of the quires or the flow of the text. CU 4 (Grammar) is copied in three irregular quires.

The Texts of LH MS 21

LH MS 21 is a miscellany of six different textual units (TU), which belong to two groups from the point of view of their subjects. Group one contains three medieval

Latin scientific compositions (TU 1–3), all a part of the same CU 1. Group two (TU 4–6) is a comprehensive dossier of Christian Hebrew studies. Each TU of this second group was conceived independently, as a separate codicological unit (CU 2–4).

The three Latin texts (TU 1–3) have been identified and described by François Dolbeau.[5] TU 1, beginning with the title *Incipiunt Predicamenta Augustini* written in the upper margin of fol. 1r, is a medieval commentary on the Categories of Aristotle, unrelated to the Augustinian corpus and different from the Pseudo-Augustinian *Categoriae decem*. The title, *Predicamenta Augustini*, appears in medieval catalogues, including two copies listed in the medieval catalogue of the library of Ramsey Abbey, relevant to our study.[6] TU 2, beginning with an incipit "*Quinque perita* (for *Quinquepertita*) *est urine consideratio*" and a title, *De urinis* penciled by a modern hand in the upper margin of fol. 19v, is a non-identified medical tractate.[7] The last tractate of this part of the volume, TU 3, begins by "*Incipit liber de uirtute simplicis medicine*," and is a copy of John of Saint Paul's *Liber de simplicium medicinarum uirtutibus*.[8] Codicologically coherent, this part was copied by two different scribes: *Predicamenta Augustini* by Scribe A and the two medical works by Scribe C (see below).

The second theme, Hebrew learning, includes TU 4–6 contained in CU 2–4. TU 4 (= CU 2) is a trilingual dictionary of the Hebrew Bible compiled and copied by Christian scholars in the last quarter of the thirteenth century.[9] This unique comprehensive work of Hebrew lexicography by medieval Christians contains 3682 Hebrew entries in two sections: verbs (1392 entries) and nouns and other parts of speech (2290 entries). The entries cover 2120 Hebrew roots attested in the Bible. Only 106 biblical roots have been omitted in this work. The Hebrew lemmata are transliterated in Latin characters, translated into Latin and in more than 1000 cases also in Anglo-Norman French. Four entries contain translations

5. Dolbeau, "Les textes latins du volume," xiv–xv.

6. Richard Sharpe, J.P. Carley, R.M. Thomson and A.G. Watson, *English Benedictine Libraries: The Shorter Catalogues* (London, 1996), 403.

7. As pointed out by François Dolbeau, a similar incipit appears in a medical anthology of the Salerno school, copied in the fourteenth century (London, BL, MS Royal 12 D. XIII, fol. 211v–222r); see George F. Warner and Julius P. Gilson, *Catalogue of Western Manuscripts in the Old Royal and King's Collections* (London, 1921), 2: 46–47; see Dolbeau, "Les textes latins du volume," xv.

8. See Georg Heinrich Kroemer, *Johanns von Sancto Paulo: Liber de simplicium medicinarum virtutibus und ein anderer Salernitaner Traktat; quae medicinae pro quibusmorbis donandae sunt nach dem Breslauer Codex herausgegeben* (Borna-Leipzig, 1920); see Dolbeau, "Les textes latins du volume," xv.

9. For the edition of the trilingual dictionary in LH MS 21, and its detailed commentary, see Olszowy-Schlanger and Grondeux, eds., *Dictionnaire hébreu-latin-français*.

in Middle English, introduced by "*anglice*," which further confirm the English origin of the work.[10] The lemmata are contextually illustrated by the quotations from Jerome's Vulgate according to the Parisian recension, introduced by "*nos habemus*." In most entries, the Vulgate translation is confronted with the Hebrew Bible and/or Jewish sources, introduced by "*sed ebreus dicit*." In addition to the Hebrew Bible, the dictionary refers hundreds of times to the Bible commentary of Rashi. It also mentions the Talmud ("*Talamut*," probably quoted after Rashi rather than consulted independently), as well as the book of *Gamaliel* – an unidentified anthology of talmudic and rabbinic texts mentioned in several medieval Christian sources.[11] The dictionary also quotes the biblical Hebrew lexicon, *Maḥberet he-ʿArukh*, of Solomon ibn Parḥon (see below, p. 67), and three medieval Jewish belles-lettres pamphlets: the *Liber dierum Mose* (Chronicles of Moses),[12] the "*Bensara*," which can be identified with the *Alphabet of Ben Sira*, and the "*Se(n) debar*," which most probably refers to the Hebrew *Sindbad/Sindebar* tales.[13] In more than 320 instances, the dictionary refers to the Aramaic translation of the Bible. Among the sources of the dictionary the literal Latin translation of the Bible can be identified, the *superscriptio*, attested in several extant Hebrew-Latin manuscripts from medieval England.

One of the Hebrew manuscripts with *superscriptio* is the Psalter bound within LH MS 21. The consonantal text of this Psalter was written by Jewish scribes, or

10. Richard Marsden, "L'anglais du dictionnaire," in *Dictionnaire hébreu-latin-français*, ed. Olszowy-Schlanger and Grondeux, xli–xlvii.

11. The book entitled *Gamaliel* and its price are mentioned in the records of the Jewish Exchequer, ed. James Macmullen Rigg, *Select Pleas, Starrs and Other Records from the Rolls of the Exchequer of the Jews, AD 1220–1284* (London, 1902), 18. See Cecil Roth, *The Intellectual Activities of Medieval English Jewry* (London, 1949), 9. On the mention of "Gamaliele suo" by Ralph Niger, see George B. Flahiff, "Ralph Niger: An Introduction to His Life and Works," *Mediaeval Studies* 2 (1940): 104–126, at 120–121. According to Raphael Loewe, "Alexander Neckam's Knowledge of Hebrew," in *Hebrew Study from Ezra to Ben-Yehuda*, ed. William Horbury (Edinburgh, 1999), 207–233, at 214–216, the book of *Gamaliel* designates the Gemara. Similarly, Frans van Liere considers that it is a reference to the Talmud in "Gamaliel, Twelfth-Century Christian Scholars, and the Attribution of the Talmud," *Medieval Perspectives* 17.2 (2002): 93–104; Chenmelech Merchavia, *The Church versus Talmudic and Midrashic Literature (500–1248)* (Jerusalem, 1970), 208–212 (Hebrew), considers that it is a rabbinic anthology translated into Latin. For *Gamaliel* as an aggadic anthology, see also Judith Olszowy-Schlanger, "Christian Hebraism in Thirteenth-Century England: The Evidence of Hebrew-Latin Manuscripts," in *Crossing Borders: Hebrew Manuscripts as a Meeting-place of Cultures*, ed. Piet Van Boxel and Sabine Arndt (Oxford, 2009), 115–122, at 121.

12. See Avigdor Shinan, "Divrei ha-Yamim shel Moshe Rabbenu: Contribution to the Question of the Date, Sources and Nature of the Hebrew Tale in the Middle Ages," *Hasifrut* 24 (1977): 100–116 at 114.

13. For the sources of the dictionary in LH MS 21, see Olszowy-Schlanger and Grondeux, eds., *Dictionnaire hébreu-latin-français*, lxxxvi–lxxxvii.

at least by scribes trained in Jewish tradition, in the early thirteenth century. The vowels were added later, most probably by a Christian scholar, since they follow a simplified system different from the standard Tiberian vocalization but similar to the vocalization attested in several Christian texts in Hebrew script from medieval England.[14] This Psalter was probably created for Jewish readers: it is written from right to left, structured according to the Jewish tradition (Psalms 9 and 10 are distinct units, whereas the Christian Psalter considers them as one Psalm) and its original consonantal text is copied by two proficient individuals whose handwritings reveal a Jewish scribal training. The first three quires (Quires XIX to XVII, fols. 192v–168v) are copied in a highly calligraphic square script of large dimensions. There are on average 16 lines of text per page, and the margins are broad. The further three quires (Quires XVI to XIV) are written in a typologically similar but less calligraphic script of smaller dimensions. The margins are narrow and there are around 28 lines of the Hebrew text per page. Shortly after it was copied, probably as early as the 1230s–1240s, the Psalter came into possession of Christian scholars. It was studied and heavily annotated by several individuals but the overwhelming majority of the notes are the work of one exceptional Hebraist, whom we will designate as "Scribe D" (see below, p. 19), as we have no clear indication of his identity. Scribe D provided the entire text with an interlinear Latin translation (*superscriptio*) which differs from the Vulgate. This translation follows the Hebrew text of the Psalms as closely as possible and relies on Jewish exegetical and lexicographical sources. This remarkable Christian scholar not only provided an original and competent translation but proceeded to justify his semantic choices in the copious glosses which cover the margins of the book. After the manuscript was annotated in Latin and French, its Christian owners were still in contact with a Jewish or at least Jewish-trained scribe. Indeed, one bifolio in Quire XV (fols. 158 and 155) was lost and had to be replaced. The replacement folios are written by a professional Jewish hand and vocalized with the standard Jewish Tiberian vowels rather than the simplified Christian system used in the rest of the Psalter. As these added folios do not contain the *superscriptio* or Latin glosses, the manuscript must have been repaired after the remarkable Christian glossator, Scribe D, covered the volume with philological notes and interlinear translation in his characteristic spidery handwriting of a scholar.[15]

Last but not least, the final work of the Hebraists' learning kit, TU 6 (=CU 4), is our Longleat House Grammar, which contains four different parts. Textually and codicologically independent, the Grammar is nonetheless related to the other

14. See Olszowy-Schlanger, *Les manuscrits hébreux*, 137–140; Judith Olszowy-Schlanger, "A Christian Tradition of Hebrew Vocalization in Medieval England," in *Semitic Studies in Honour of Edward Ullendorff*, ed. Geoffrey Khan (Leiden and Boston, 2005), 126–146.

15. Olszowy-Schlanger, *Les manuscrits hébreux*, 189.

texts of the volume by the recurrence of the same main scribal hands and of the same annotators.

The Codicological and Textual Composition of the Longleat House Grammar

The Longleat House Grammar, CU 4 and TU 6, is composed of three fascicles made of 12 folios of poor-quality parchment. There is a clear distinction between flesh (whitish-gray) and hair sides (dark yellow). The text is written in brown iron-gall ink. On fols. 203r–204v, the initials are drawn in bright red pigment.

CU 4 has a complex codicological, palaeographical and textual structure, with four distinct textual units (henceforth GTU 1–4) written over three small quires (Quires XX to XXII of the volume as a whole) (Table 1.1, 4). It was certainly considered as a coherent booklet in the Middle Ages, as it is today, and its different parts are palaeographically related. However, it is not certain that all of its four texts were conceived and produced as the same codicological unit from the start. Different parts of the Longleat House Grammar might have originally been self-contained independent pamphlets. Indeed, GTU 1, 3 and 4 are written on separate quires, with blank initial and final pages. Only GTU 2 bridges the gap between two different quires, since it was written on the blank last pages of GTU 1 (copied from left to right, Quire XX) and GTU 3 (copied from right to left, Quire XXI) (Table 1.2).

Table 1.2 The structure of the Longleat House Grammar

Grammar Textual Unit	Text	Folios	Direction of copy	Relationship of the text to the quires
GTU 1	Hebrew grammar: Hebrew in Latin characters	193r–196r	Left to right	Quire XX (fols. 193r–196v), last page, 196v, was left blank
GTU 2	Hebrew grammar: note in Latin on Hebrew pronunciation	196v–197r	Left to right	Written at a later stage on the last blank page of Quire XX (fol. 196v) and the last blank page of Quire XXI (197r)
GTU 3	Hebrew grammar: Hebrew in Hebrew characters	197v–202r	Right to left	Quire XXI (fols. 197r–202v) Fol. 202v is blank

Grammar Textual Unit	Text	Folios	Direction of copy	Relationship of the text to the quires
GTU 4	Hebrew grammar: Hebrew conjugation paradigms in Latin characters (incomplete)	203r–204r	Left to right	2 folios, Quire XXII (203r–204v)

The collation in Table 1.2 shows that GTU 1, the Hebrew grammar in Latin script, and GTU 3, the Hebrew grammar in Hebrew script, differ in the direction of their writing: GTU 1 is written from left to right whereas GTU 3 is written from right to left, like any Hebrew book. GTU 1 begins abruptly with the verbal conjugation, without any title or introduction, at the beginning of a new quire. It originally ended on fol. 196r, with the last page, fol. 196v, left blank. GTU 3 begins on fol. 202v, with the recto left blank, and ends on fol. 197v. The verso of the last folio, fol. 197r, was originally left blank. These two units are written on different quires, by different scribes, in different alphabets and different directions. Although they are similar in their grammatical approach and contents, these two works are not two versions of the same text, one is not a transliteration or translation of the other. They were, however, studied together in the Middle Ages. GTU 2, a short tractate on Hebrew vowels, was written in the late thirteenth century on the blank final folios of the GTU 1 and 3. This text bridges the gap between the two units, spreading respectively from left to right on the last and first pages of two different quires. The text of GTU 2 refers to and comments on the last section of GTU 3.

As to the fourth part of the grammar, GTU 4, the tables of conjugation in Latin script, its codicological relationship to the other texts is difficult to ascertain. Indeed, this part is poorly preserved. Fol. 203 is damaged, torn, and was detached from the volume. It was restored and put back with the rest of the book at a later date. It seems that during the restoration, this leaf was turned and bound in the wrong direction. The contents suggest that the text began on what is now fol. 203v and was followed by what is now fol. 203r. In addition to the contents, the state of the leaf indicates such an order. Fol. 203v is damaged, and the text is partly erased. This type of damage is consistent with the placement of the page on the outside of a volume or booklet, where the text was constantly exposed to mechanical rubbing. Our text edition below follows the reconstructed original order of the pages of fol. 203.

Despite this complicated codicological structure of the twelve folios of the Longleat House Grammar and a strong possibility that the different units were not originally copied as a part of the same booklet, there is a connection between them both at the level of production (recurring scribal hands) and subsequent use (recurring hands of annotators). Moreover, the Longleat House Grammar shows palaeographical affinities with the other units of the composite volume LH MS 21.

The Scribes of LH MS 21

Indeed, despite the discrepancy in codicology and subject matters, five out of six textual units of LH MS 21 are related from the point of view of their copyists. Building upon their palaeographical identification,[16] a pattern of overlapping scribes emerges both at the level of the manuscript's production and its subsequent use.

All in all, five different Christian scribes (henceforth A, B, C, D, E) contributed to the copy of the different parts of LH MS 21.

Scribe A copied:
- CU 1: TU 1 *Predicamenta Augustini* (fols. 1r–19r)
- CU 2: TU 4 Latin script of a part of Dictionary (fols. 29r–143v)
- CU 4: TU 6 Grammar:
  - GTU 1: Hebrew grammar in Hebrew in Latin script
  - GTU 4: Verb paradigms in Hebrew in Latin script

Scribe B copied:
- CU 1: TU 1 corrections in *Predicamenta Augustini*
- CU 2: TU 4 Latin script of another part of Dictionary (12 folios: 44v–55v, 1 col. on fol. 73v, two lines on fol. 74r)
- CU 2: TU 4 Most Hebrew words within the Latin text of the entries of the Dictionary

Scribe C copied:
- CU 1: TU 2 *De urinis*
- CU 1: TU 3 *De uirtute simplicis medicine*
- CU 4: TU 6 Grammar:
  - GTU 2: Note on pronunciation (fols. 197v–196r)

Scribe D copied:
- CU 3: TU 5 Latin *superscriptio* and most of the glosses in the Psalter
- CU 3: TU 5 Hebrew words within the marginal Latin glosses to the Psalter
- CU 3: TU 5 correction of the Hebrew text and collation with another Psalter
- CU 3: TU 5 most probably this scribe added Hebrew vowels in the Psalter

Scribe E copied:
- CU 2: Lemmata of the dictionary in calligraphic Hebrew characters

16. See Stirnemann, "Le manuscrit," x–xiv.

The Christian scribes A–E copied the Latin parts of LH MS 21, and scribes B, D and E wrote passages in Hebrew characters as well. Most often correct and, in the case of scribe E, highly calligraphic, their Hebrew letters follow a different ductus than that practised by Jewish scribes, or scribes who acquired Hebrew literacy early in their life.

Four scribes who intervened in different parts of LH MS 21 were trained in Jewish scribal tradition (Scribes א, ב, ג, ד).

Scribe א copied:
CU 3: TU 5 Psalter, scribe of the consonantal text (fols. 192v–168v)

Scribe ב copied:
CU 3: TU 5 Psalter, scribe of the consonantal text (fols. 167r–144v except for 1 bifolio, fols. 158 and 155)

Scribe ג copied:
CU 3: TU 5 Psalter, scribe of the replacement bifolio (fols. 158 and 155), probably both consonants and vowels

Scribe ד copied:
CU 4: TU 6 Grammar:
GTU 3: Hebrew grammar in Hebrew script

The distribution of the nine different scribes shows that whereas the four Jewish scribes copied one well-defined portion of the manuscript each, at least three Christian scribes (A, B and C) contributed to the copy of two or three different textual units each (Table 1.3). Scribe A, who worked on CU 1 = TU 1 *Predicamenta*, CU 2 = TU 4 Dictionary and CU 4 = TU 6 Grammar: GTU 1 and 4, overlaps with Scribe C in CU 1 who copied both medical tractates (TU 2 and 3) and in CU 4 = TU 6, GTU 2 (note on pronunciation). Scribe A also overlaps with Scribe B who copied parts of CU 2 = TU 4, Dictionary, and they both overlap with Scribe E, who executed calligraphically the Hebrew lemmata of the Dictionary.

The overlap of the scribes of the Longleat House Grammar with those of other parts of LH MS 21 confirms a close "genetic" relationship between these different codicological and textual units. There is little doubt that the Longleat House Grammar is a product of the same medieval scriptorium or workshop as the Latin texts on logic and medicine and the dictionary in LH MS 21. Moreover, the Grammar was kept and transmitted with the other parts of the volume, as confirmed by the glosses written by the same hands, which appear in different parts of the manuscript. In addition to the scribes who copied parts of the main

Table 1.3 The scribes of the different texts of LH MS 21

Scribe	CU 1 TU 1–3			CU 2 TU 4	CU 3 TU 5	CU 4 TU 6			
	Predicamenta	*De urinis*	*De uirtute*	Dictionary	Psalter	Grammar in Latin	Note on pronunciation	Grammar in Hebrew script	Paradigms
A	•			•		•			•
B	•			•					
C		•	•				•		
D					•				
E				•					
א					•				
ב					•				
ג					•				
ד								•	

text and a systematic *superscriptio*, the Longleat House Grammar indeed contains occasional marginal glosses. GTU 3 (Hebrew grammar in Hebrew characters) contains glosses by five Christian hands, whose dating ranges from the thirteenth to the sixteenth century:

Glossator 1, Latin hand of the thirteenth century, wrote marginal annotations on fols. 197v, 198r and 199r and v.

Glossator 2, Latin hand of the thirteenth century, wrote a gloss in the inner margin of fol. 199v.

Glossator 3, Latin *textualis* hand of the thirteenth century, wrote a gloss in the inner and upper margin of fol. 199r and in the inner margin of fol. 198v. This hand is similar but not identical to that of TU 1 and 4.

Glossator 4, Latin hand of the thirteenth century, wrote interlinear and marginal glosses in fols. 197v, 198r–v, 199r–v.

Glossator 5, Latin hand of the sixteenth century, wrote three interlinear glosses on fol. 197v. The same hand left eighteen glosses in the dictionary LH 21. The handwriting can be identified as that of Robert Wakefield (see below).

As we saw, the hand of GTU 1 and GTU 4 is identical to the one which occurs in the other parts of the LH MS 21 (trilingual dictionary and Latin compositions), and dates most probably from the third quarter of the thirteenth century. The same scribe also copied a part of another Ramsey manuscript, Cambridge, CCC, MS 468 (see p. 36). A similar hand had annotated GTU 3. The hand which copied GTU 2, the note on vowels, of course, intervenes later, since it appears on the blank versos of GTU 1 and GTU 3, but is also datable to later part of the thirteenth century.

Palaeographical Remarks

Latin Script

The Latin script of the main text of GTU 1 and GTU 4, the work of Scribe A, is a Gothic *textualis* which can be attributed to thirteenth-century England, and more precisely to Ramsey. This attribution is founded on the palaeographical comparison with Cambridge, CCC, MS 468.

A remarkable scribal feature of the Longleat House Grammar is its occasional use of Hebrew elements in Latin. In GTU 1 fol. 195v, l. 24, the Hebrew word transliterated in Latin is provided with Hebrew vowels: *niseteret* (see Figure 1) for נִסְתֶּרֶת. And inversely, some Latin graphic devices are applied to the words in transliterated Hebrew. Thus, Hebrew words in Latin transliteration are often abbreviated according to Latin conventions. For example, on fol. 194v, l. 8, *medab'* (see Figure 2) for *medaber*, מְדַבֵּר, with the standard abbreviation for *er*, or, on fol. 193r, l. 23, *behasemā* (see Figure 3), with a line above the *a* to indicate the *m* (*mem*) of the transliterated בְּעַצְמָם. It is noteworthy that in some cases the scribe renders the *alef* at the beginning of a word by an *a* with an apostrophe in the form of a *spiritus lenis*, e.g., fol. 194v, l. 8, *a'had* for אֶחָד. This transliteration of the *alef* is also found in the Dictionary in LH MS 21, in the part copied by the same Scribe A.

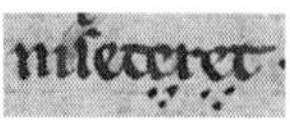

Figure 1

Figure 2

Figure 3

The contemporary Scribe C who copied GTU 2 (note on pronunciation) wrote in a more cursive style. He was also the scribe of the medical compositions in CU 1 (TU 2 and 3).

Hebrew Script

TU 3 is written in Hebrew square Ashkenazi script with calligraphic features such as small serifs on the extremities of the horizontal bars of *dalet, heh, ḳuf, resh, tav,* occasionally a small decorative flag on the ascender of the *lamed,* diamond-shaped heads of *gimel, zayin* and *nun,* additional roofs on the arms of the *shin,* a decorative foot at the end of the left-hand stroke of the *alef,* a drop-shaped right-hand downstroke of the *gimel* and left-hand downstroke of the *heh.* The script lacks the pronounced gothic stylistic features such as very strong shading, the presence of long and thin hairline serifs and prominent fish-tail forking on the extremities of the horizontal strokes. The script is compact and regular. Its characteristic feature is the regularity of the baseline: the letters whose descender is usually long (final *kaf,* final *peh, ḳuf*) barely descend below the baseline, especially the final *peh.* Final *nun*'s descender is slightly longer than the baseline. The writing leans slightly to the left. Some letters have a detached aspect: the right-hand part of the *alef,* the nose of the *peh* or the foot of the *gimel* in some cases do not touch the main stroke of the letter.

The ductus and the morphology of the Hebrew letters of TU 3 indicate that its scribe was trained in the Jewish scribal tradition. His handwriting shares common characteristics with other manuscripts from medieval England written in square script, and especially with the manuscripts belonging to the bilingual Hebrew-Latin corpus. These features include the inclination to the left, the tendency to detaching parts of the letters and some aspects of the letters' morphology, which can be compared here with the Hebrew script of the Psalter in LH MS 21 and with the bilingual book of Ezekiel, Oxford, Bodl., MS Or. 62 (see Table 1.4). For example, a characteristic wavy shape of the main stroke of the *alef* in GTU 3 is also attested in Oxford, Bodl., MS Or. 62, and in the other manuscripts copied by the same scribe (Oxford, Bodl., MS Or. 46; Oxford, St John's College, MS 143 and Oxford, CCC, MS 9, see pp. 30–31 and Table 2.1). However, the scribe of GTU 3 is different from the two Hebrew scribes of the Psalter in LH MS 21 and from those of the other bilingual manuscripts.

Table 1.4 Comparison of selected letters in Longleat House Grammar, LH MS 21 Psalter scribe 1, LH MS 21 Psalter scribe 2 and Oxford, Bodl., MS Or. 62

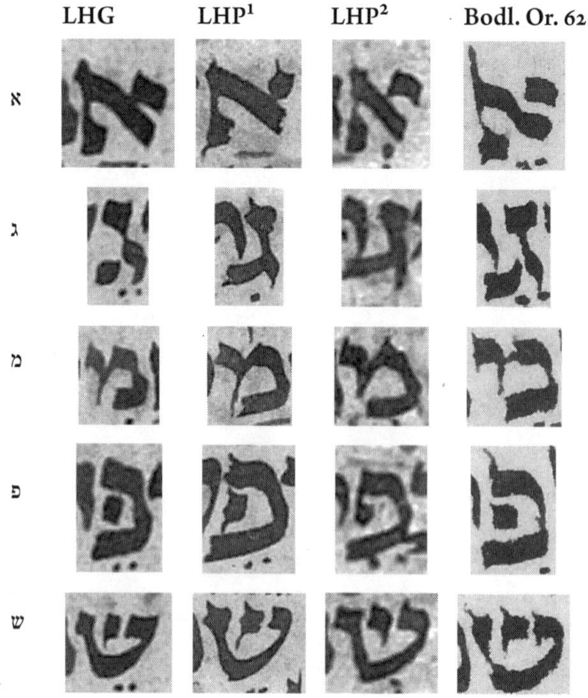

Page and Text Layout

Each textual unit of the Longleat House Grammar has a different page and text layout. They are described below in separate sections.

Grammar Textual Unit 1: The Hebrew Grammar in Latin Characters

The Hebrew grammar in Hebrew rendered in Latin characters is written in a tabular layout, in four columns per page. The length of the lines in each column can be irregular, and the tabular effect is sometimes blurred. The parchment was ruled before the writing with a brown metal hard point. The columns are separated by a single vertical ruled line. There is also a similar vertical line on the outer sides of the columns marking the outer and inner margins. There are thus five vertical lines per page. As for the horizontal lines, their number varies from one folio to another. There are, however, two longer parallel lines at the head of the page, and one long line at its foot. The text does not always respect the ruled lines.

The text of GTU 1 is to be read like a Latin codex, from left to right. Such is also the reading order of the columns. The columns contain Hebrew verb paradigms arranged according to the verbal stems (*binyanim*). The grammatical classification is reflected in the page and text layout of the GTU 1. Separate *binyanim* are usually introduced by a heading written in the same handwriting and letter size as the rest of the text, in a line left blank, either at the beginning of the line (fol. 193r, l. 19; fol. 193v, l. 9, l. 24) or in its middle (fol. 194r, l. 10). Similar headings introduce other grammatical subdivisions such as past, present, future, passive and imperative. In many cases, the paragraphs end with the Hebrew explicit formula סליק. In addition, a Christian reader provided the text with paragraph signs for new subdivisions. The first 18 lines of fol. 193r, four lines on fol. 193v and fol. 195r, l. 15 to fol. 196r contain an interlinear Latin translation written by the same hand and ink as the main text but in smaller Latin characters.

To make the reading of this complicated Hebrew text in Latin characters set in a tabular layout easier, the scribe provided it with systematic punctuation. It consists of a dot placed after each separate phrase. The main scribe has also provided the text with diacritics – short horizontal *rafeh*-like lines above abbreviations and above certain consonants to indicate their correct Hebrew pronunciation (see below), and short slanted strokes over the letter *i*. However, the use of the diacritics, and especially the stroke over the *i*, is inconsistent. It was corrected by another hand which added large and crude strokes in light brown, slightly watery ink.

Grammar Textual Unit 2: The Essay on Hebrew Vowels and Accents

This short note on Hebrew vowels and accents by a different but contemporary thirteenth-century hand is copied in Latin order from left to right. It is laid out in two regular columns per page. The columns are guided by the ruling made with a hard point. It includes four vertical lines, one on each side of the column, and horizontal lines to guide the written lines of the text. There are 27 ruled lines for 26 written lines on fol. 196v and 27 ruled lines for as many as 33 and 35 lines of written texts in the two respective columns of the facing folio 197r. This short note occupies the blank verso of the last folio of Quire XX (and TU 1) and the blank verso of the first folio of Quire XXI, corresponding to the end of TU 3 (copied from right to left). This note was written at a later stage, filling the blank space between GTU 1 and GTU 3. The text fills up the two pages completely. The necessity to accommodate the text in this restricted available space led to the increase of density on fol. 197r. Furthermore, the last word, for which there was no place in the last line, was written below the line with a paragraph sign.

Grammar Textual Unit 3: The Hebrew Grammar in Hebrew Characters

The part in Hebrew characters is written from right to left, like a Hebrew codex. The beginning of the unit is missing, but its last page corresponds to the end of the work; indeed, the last column does not fill all the available space, and the verso of the folio was blank before it was reused for writing GTU 2. The unit is written in two parallel columns per page. The page layout is guided by the ruling made with a hard point. The pattern of the ruling consists of four vertical lines, one on each side of the column, and of horizontal lines. The first and the last horizontal lines go across the full page. There are 18–19 lines of text per page.[17] The top, bottom and side margins are broad. The text is fully vocalized. Grammatical subdivisions are introduced each in a new line. The scribe, whose handwriting reveals Jewish education, followed the practices of the Jewish scribes in justification of the margins. The left-hand margins are kept even by the use of extended letters or by the anticipation of the abbreviated beginning of the first word of the next line to fill the space left at the end of the line. Some corrections, as well as signs to mark the beginning of new paragraphs and other text subdivisions, were probably introduced by the same hand as the one in GTU 1 and 2, in light brown ink and were traced with a thick and crude pen-nib. In addition, there are interlinear and marginal glosses and comments by several Christian scribes in Hebrew and Latin.

Grammar Textual Unit 4: The Hebrew Verb Paradigms in Latin Characters

The table of Hebrew verb paradigms in Latin characters is written in regular columns, in the direction of a Latin codex, from left to right. The text on fol. 203 is badly preserved and partly rubbed off. There are four columns per page, arranged following the ruling traced with a hard point. When visible (e.g., fol. 204), the ruled grid is composed of eight vertical lines: there are two parallel lines 4 mm apart on the left side of each column. The inner line is used for the justification of the verbal forms, written one per line of the column. The outer line is used for the justification of the textual subdivisions (e.g., "past," "future," "present," "imperative"), whose first letter is put well in evidence by being written ahead of the column. The horizontal lines were traced for all four columns simultaneously. There are 33 ruled lines for 32 lines of the text. The text is written in brown ink, but the first letter of each line of every column is traced in red pigment and decorated with dots.

17. For the ruling patterns, see Olszowy-Schlanger, *Les manuscrits hébreux*, 195.

In sum, the four different textual parts of the Longleat House Grammar were created as independent units, three of them as separate booklets and one (GTU 2) "recycling" the available blank space at the interstice of two of these booklets. While the layout of GTU 3, the Hebrew grammar in Hebrew characters, and of GTU 2, a note on vowels, follow a simple layout in two columns of running text per page, GTU 1, verb morphology, and GTU 4, verbal paradigms, both written in Hebrew in Latin characters, follow a complex tabular layout with, in the case of GTU 1, an additional textual layer of the interlinear translation of grammatical terms and examples. This layout, as well as the enhancement of the initials with red pigments in GTU 4, aims to guide reading and navigating in this complicated text and thus to facilitate learning of the Hebrew grammar. The identification of the Latin scribes of the units of the Longleat House Grammar with those who copied other passages in the works bound today in the same LH MS 21 confirms the common origin of these units. To consider the history of the volume as a whole will allow us, in the next chapter, to argue that the origin of the Longleat House Grammar and its codicological context can be traced to Ramsey Abbey.

CHAPTER TWO

The Longleat House Grammar and Hebrew Scholarship at Ramsey Abbey

The Longleat House Grammar does not contain any scribal colophons or direct mentions regarding the time and place of its compilation and copy. Its author(s) remain anonymous, and so do its scribes. Nevertheless, its codicological context and palaeography show that it is a part of a wider undertaking by thirteenth-century Christian scholars, whose goal was to produce books and teaching aids for learning the Hebrew language. In this respect, the Longleat House Grammar is directly related to the other codicological and textual units of LH MS 21. It is also related – as we will see – to a group of eight extant manuscripts from an even larger corpus of bilingual Hebrew-Latin manuscripts produced in medieval England. The history of LH MS 21 provides arguments in favour of the production and study of our Longleat House Grammar in the Benedictine Abbey of Ramsey, in East Anglia.

The Longleat House Grammar Among the Bilingual Hebrew-Latin Manuscripts

As we saw, LH MS 21 includes among its textual units a unique "dossier" of medieval Christian Hebraism. In addition to the Longleat House Grammar, this "dossier" contains a Hebrew Psalter annotated in Latin, and a Hebrew-Latin-Old French dictionary of the Hebrew Bible. The Latin *superscriptio* translation is explained by the glossator in abundant marginalia which rely heavily on Jewish sources. Together with arguments and examples contextually derived from other parts of the Hebrew Bible, the glossator explicitly quoted the commentary of Rashi, as well as the dictionary *Maḥberet he-ʿArukh* by Solomon ibn Parḥon, the latter under a slightly corrupted form of "Piraam" or "Pirhaam." Most importantly, the glosses also quote the Aramaic Targum, and refer to it by an unusual abbreviation "*enek*." This abbreviation is now been recognized as a corrupted version of "*Onkelos*," itself probably a Hebrew rendition of the name of its presumed author, the Roman convert to Judaism, Aquila.[1]

The same Jewish sources inspired the Hebrew-Latin-Old French biblical dictionary in LH MS 21. In addition to an impressive array of medieval Jewish sources (see p. 15), the dictionary refers more than 320 times to the Aramaic translation of the Bible, which, like in the gloss on the Psalter, is referred to by the term "*enek*." This idiosyncratic abbreviation constitutes a link between LH MS 21 and six other bilingual manuscripts, in which the marginal notes are written by the same Christian glossator, Scribe D, who annotated the Psalter in LH MS 21 (see Table 2.1). These manuscripts include four parts of the same bilingual Bible set: Oxford, CCC, MS 9 (two codicological units, Samuel and Chronicles);[2] Oxford, Bodl., MS Or. 46 (Ezra, Nehemiah, Job, Lamentations, Esther, and

1. J.P. Rothschild, "Enek: targum araméen?," in *Dictionnaire hébreu-latin-français de la Bible hébraïque de l'Abbaye de Ramsey (XIIIe s.)*, ed. Judith Olszowy-Schlanger and Anne Grondeux (Turnhout, 2008), lxxxi–lxxxv; Judith Olszowy-Schlanger, "The Study of the Aramaic Targum by Christians in Medieval France and England," in *A Jewish Targum in a Christian World*, ed. Alberdina Houtman, Eveline van Staalduine-Sulman and Hans-Martin Kirn (Leiden, 2014), 233–249.

2. Oxford, CCC, MS 9a contains an incomplete book of Samuel (1 Sam. 1 – 1 Sam. 20:16) written from left to right, like a Latin book (fols. 1r–56v [or rather 56v–1r]). It contains the Latin Vulgate in a parallel lateral column on the outside of the page, as well as an alternative *superscriptio* translation, which does not cover all the text. Oxford, CCC, MS 9b contains the books of Chronicles, written in the Hebrew fashion, from right to left (fols. 57r–226r). The book of Chronicles has no Latin parallel column but contains the *superscriptio* and marginal annotations. The Hebrew text of both codicological units of Oxford, CCC, MS 9 was copied by the same scribe, and their *superscriptio* and marginal glosses are also the work of the same Latin hands. However, the presence of the column of the Vulgate in Oxford, CCC, MS 9a and the fact that each of the units was copied in a different direction show that they were not originally destined to be bound in one volume. See Adolf Neubauer, *Catalogue of the Hebrew Manuscripts in the Bodleian Library and in the College Libraries in Oxford* (Oxford, 1886–1906), no. 2435; Malachi Beit-Arié, *Catalogue of the Hebrew Manuscripts in the Bodleian Library: Supplement of Addenda and Corrigenda to Vol. 1 (A. Neubauer's Catalogue)* (Oxford, 1994), no. 2435; Raphael Loewe, "Latin Superscriptio MSS on Portions of the Hebrew Bible Other than the Psalter," *Journal of Jewish Studies* 9 (1958): 63–71 at 66–67; Malachi Beit-Arié, "The Valmadonna Pentateuch and the Problem of Pre-expulsion Anglo-Hebrew Manuscripts – MS London, Valmadonna Trust Library 1: England (?), 1189," in *The Makings of the Medieval Hebrew Book: Studies in Palaeography and Codicology*, ed. Malachi Beit-Arié (Jerusalem, 1993), 129–151, at 134; Judith Olszowy-Schlanger, *Les manuscrits hébreux dans l'Angleterre médiévale: Étude historique et paléographique* (Leuven and Paris, 2003), 212–219, no. 12; Peter E. Pormann, *A Descriptive Catalogue of the Hebrew Manuscripts of Corpus Christi College* (Oxford, 2015), 57–65.

incomplete Ruth);[3] Oxford, Bodl., MS Or. 62 (Ezekiel)[4] and Oxford, St John's College, MS 143 (Joshua, Judges, Song of Songs, Kohelet)[5], all four small (20 × 14 cm) and similarly laid-out books copied by the same Hebrew scribe[6] and a volume of Rashi commentary on the Prophets and Hagiographa, Oxford, CCC, MS 6.[7] A similar hand annotated the liturgical Oxford, Bodl., MS Arch. Selden A.

3. The books of Ezra and Nehemiah contain the *superscriptio* and a gloss, whereas the other books do not contain any Latin writing. See Beit-Arié, *Supplement*, no. 101; Olszowy-Schlanger, *Les manuscrits hébreux*, 234–237, no. 16.

4. The Hebrew text of Ezekiel is accompanied by the Vulgate in a parallel column on the outer side of each page. In addition, the Hebrew text contains a *superscriptio* which differs from the Vulgate, as well as marginal annotations. The initial and final flyleaves contain various texts, including a thematic list of passages of the book of Ezekiel (fol. 131r), grammatical notes, a Hebrew text on biblical chronology (fols. 1–2) and its Latin translation, and a Hebrew translation of the beginning of the Pater Noster, written twice, in a square and then in a calligraphic non-square bookhand Hebrew script (fol. 3r). See Beit-Arié, *Supplement*, no. 88; Colette Sirat, "Notes sur la circulation des livres entre juifs et chrétiens au Moyen Âge," in *Du copiste au collectionneur: Mélanges d'histoire des textes et des bibliothèques en l'honneur d'André Vernet*, ed. Donatella Nebbiai-Dalla Guarda and Jean-François Genest (Turnhout, 1999), 383–403, at 393; Olszowy-Schlanger, *Les manuscrits hébreux*, 229–233, no. 15; Judith Olszowy-Schlanger, "Rachi en latin: Les gloses latines dans un manuscrit du commentaire de Rachi et les études hébraïques parmi des chrétiens dans l'Angleterre médiévale," in *Héritages de Rachi*, ed. René-Samuel Sirat (Paris, 2006), 137–150, at 141–147.

5. See Loewe, "Latin Superscriptio MSS," 64–65; Beit-Arié, "The Valmadonna Pentateuch," 134; Olszowy-Schlanger, *Les manuscrits hébreux*, 224–228, no. 14; Peter E. Pormann, "Hebrew Manuscripts," in *A Descriptive Catalogue of Oriental Manuscripts at St John's College, Oxford*, ed. Emilie Savage-Smith (Oxford, 2005), 98–103.

6. The square Gothic script is careful and well trained, and its ductus suggests that the scribe was a "native" Jewish scribe, that he trained in Jewish scribal tradition. It is impossible to ascertain whether he was a convert or a Jew commissioned by a Christian Hebraist or institution. The Latin scribe who wrote the text of the parallel column (where a parallel Latin translation was included) was the same in most manuscripts of this group. Since most of its codicological units were copied from left to right like a Latin book, this "cycle" was most probably conceived and produced for the use of Christian Hebraists. See Judith Olszowy-Schlanger, "Christian Hebraism in Thirteenth-Century England: The Evidence of Hebrew-Latin Manuscripts," in *Crossing Borders: Hebrew Manuscripts as a Meeting-place of Cultures*, ed. Piet van Boxel and Sabine Arndt (Oxford, 2009).

7. Oxford, CCC, MS 6, the commentary of Rashi on the Prophets and Hagiographa (Joshua, Samuel, Kings, Ezekiel, Lamentations, Kohelet, Esther, Song of Songs, Jeremiah, Isaiah and the Minor Prophets, in this order). It is written in Ashkenazi square script of small size, similar to the script used for masoretic annotations. Some sporadic sections of the text have been vocalized by a Christian reader who used a simplified vowels system as attested in other Hebrew texts vocalized by Christians in medieval England; see Judith Olszowy-Schlanger, "A Christian Tradition of Hebrew Vocalisation," in *Semitic Studies in Honour of Edward Ullendorff*, ed. Geoffrey Khan (Leiden and Boston, 2005). Some passages contain a Latin *superscriptio* and a few marginal notes. See Beit-Arié, *Supplement*, no. 2435;

3, but without using the term *"enek."* In addition, Oxford, CCC, MS 6 is related to Oxford, Bodl., MS Or. 62 because it contains on fol. 1r (beginning of the book of Joshua) a literal translation of a Hebrew text on biblical chronology found on fols. 1v–2r of Oxford, Bodl., MS Or. 62.[8] In addition, the same anonymous glossator corrected the Latin *superscriptio* translations in yet another Hebrew-Latin Psalter, Oxford, CCC, MS 10. Although it does not contain the term *"enek.,"* it is likely that a thirteenth-century maḥzor – a prayer book containing liturgical poems (piyyutim) for festivals – in Oxford, Bodl., MS Arch. Selden A. 3[9] annotated by a Christian scholar in Latin, French and transliterated Hebrew, is also related to this group of bilingual manuscripts. Less directly connected with the group is the glossed Hebrew Psalter in London, Lambeth Palace Library, MS 435, whose first folio was at some point bound with Oxford, St John's College, MS 143.[10] London, Lambeth Palace Library, MS 435; Oxford, Bodl., MS Arch. Selden A. 3 and the Longleat House Grammar, as well as the trilingual dictionary in LH MS 21 share one more characteristic: all four of them seem to contain notes in the sixteenth-century hand of Robert Wakefield, an eminent Christian Hebraist, the chaplain of Henry VIII and the first instructor of Hebrew in Tudor England.[11]

Table 2.1 Manuscripts of the *"enek."* group and their scribes

MS	Same Hebrew hand	Same Latin hand	Same Latin glossator	Textual connection	MSS transmitted together	Wakefield's notes
Oxford, CCC, MS 9a (Samuel)	•	•	Glossator Scribe D			

Loewe, "Latin Superscriptio MSS," 68; Beit-Arié, "The Valmadonna Pentateuch," 134; Olszowy-Schlanger, *Les manuscrits hébreux*, 283–288, no. 26; Olszowy-Schlanger, "Rachi en latin," 137–150; Pormann, *A Descriptive Catalogue*, 43–48.

8. Olszowy-Schlanger, "Rachi en latin," 137–150.

9. Beit-Arié, *Supplement*, no. 1159.

10. Montague Rhodes James and Claude Jenkins, *A Descriptive Catalogue of the Manuscripts in the Library of Lambeth Palace*, vol. 1 (Cambridge, 1930–1932), p. 607.

11. Olszowy-Schlanger and Grondeux, eds., *Dictionnaire hébreu-latin-français*, xxii–xxiii. See further the following essays: Judith Olszowy-Schlanger, "Robert Wakefield and the Medieval Background of Hebrew Scholarship in Renaissance England," in *Hebrew to Latin Latin to Hebrew: The Mirroring of Two Cultures in the Age of Humanism*, ed. Giulio Busi (Berlin, 2006), 61–87; "Robert Wakefield and His Hebrew Manuscripts," *Zutot* 6.1 (2009): 25–33; "'My Silent Teachers': Hebrew Manuscripts as the Source of Robert Wakefield's Hebraism," in *Hebraism in Sixteenth-Century England: Robert and Thomas Wakefield*, ed. Charles Burnett and James P. Carley (Toronto, forthcoming).

MS	Same Hebrew hand	Same Latin hand	Same Latin glossator	Textual connection	MSS transmitted together	Wakefield's notes
Oxford, CCC, MS 9b (Chronicles)	•		Glossator Scribe D			
Oxford, Bodl., MS Or. 46 (Hagiographa)	•	•	Glossator Scribe D			
Oxford, Bodl., MS Or. 62 (Ezekiel)	•	•	Glossator Scribe D	Text on chronology		
Oxford, St John's College, MS 143 (Joshua, Judges, Song of Songs, Kohelet)	•	•	Glossator Scribe D		Contained fol. 1 of Lambeth Palace, MS 435	
Oxford, CCC, MS 6			Glossator Scribe D	Text on chronology		
Longleat House, MS 21 (Psalter)			Glossator Scribe D		Bound together	
Longleat House, MS 21 (Dictionary)		Main scribe B			Bound together	•
Longleat House, MS 21 (Grammar)		Main scribe B			Bound together	•
London, Lambeth Palace, MS 435 (Psalter)					Fol. 1 was bound with Oxford, St John's College, MS 143	•

MS	Same Hebrew hand	Same Latin hand	Same Latin glossator	Textual connection	MSS transmitted together	Wakefield's notes
Oxford, CCC, MS 10		Scribe of the Prologue	*super-scriptio* corrected by Scribe D			One short note in a similar hand
Oxford, Bodl., MS Arch. Selden A. 3			Glossator Scribe D			•

Although the Longleat House Grammar, the trilingual dictionary and the Psalter bound together in LH MS 21 are originally independent compilations, they (and the other manuscripts annotated by the "*enek.*" glossator) are related and were probably transmitted together already in the thirteenth century. Indeed, the comparison of some selected samples of the marginal glosses of the Psalter in LH MS 21 with the entries in the dictionary reveals that many of the glosses were a source for the dictionary. The glossator, reading the Psalter (and the other parts of the Bible in the "*enek.*" corpus) "quill in hand," left a trail of notes which at some point, situated on palaeographical grounds in the third quarter of the thirteenth century, had been integrated into the alphabetically arranged dictionary in LH MS 21. The entries of the dictionary follow the same structure as the relevant marginal glosses and quote the same sources. The wording of the entries of the dictionary is often similar to the glosses and the *superscriptio*, even if the dictionary often modifies and expands their contents.[12]

While the Psalter was probably created for Jewish readership and included post facto in the heterogeneous LH MS 21, the other textual units of this volume, both its Latin texts and the works of Christian Hebraism, are "genetically" related. Indeed, as we saw, the same scribes intervened in their different parts: out of the five different Christian scribes involved in the copy of the four codicological units of the volume, three copied passages in more than one unit, including two scribes of the Longleat House Grammar (see p. 19 and Table 1.3). Both the dictionary and the Longleat House Grammar were moreover transmitted together at a later stage; they were both undeniably annotated in the sixteenth century by the same scholar identified as Robert Wakefield.

12. See Olszowy-Schlanger and Grondeux, eds., *Dictionnaire hébreu-latin-français*, xciv–xcvii.

The Longleat House Grammar and Ramsey Abbey

The study of the Longleat House Grammar together with the other works copied in the volume LH MS 21 provides arguments for its place of compilation and copying. The comparison of the manuscript with the extant medieval monastic catalogues, the palaeographical analysis of its Latin scripts and later historical accounts provide grounds to suggest that the manuscript once belonged to the medieval library of Ramsey Abbey – and that it might have been produced for its monks.[13]

The first clue as to the book's provenance from Ramsey is provided by the unusual mixture of philosophical, medical and Hebrew texts in one volume. Two fragmentarily preserved fourteenth-century catalogues of the books of Ramsey Abbey (London, Lambeth Palace, MS 585, two leaves, pp. 661–664 and London, BL, MS Cotton Rolls II 16/3) contain a list of Hebrew books, including several Bible manuscripts and Jewish exegetical works, which is quite impressive for the period.[14] In these catalogues, the books are inventoried under the names of the individuals who had bequeathed them to the library. The Hebrew items appear under the names of two individuals, Prior Gregory, active in the middle of the thirteenth century and Robert Dodeford, who compiled the cartulary of Ramsey Abbey after 1246, and was involved in the administration of the Abbey in the 1260s.[15] Neither Prior Gregory nor Robert Dodeford is mentioned in connection with Hebrew learning in medieval accounts, but the contents of their quite specialized libraries leave no doubt that they studied both Hebrew and Greek, and were interested in lexicography and grammar, as well as theology and exegesis.

The item B67.53 = B68.529 of the catalogue of the books of Prior Gregory is of particular relevance for the provenance of LH MS 21 and the Longleat House Grammar. Its description as "*Predicamenta Augustini cum exposicionibus nominum hebraicorum, et ars loquendi in lingua hebraica. in j uolumine*" seems to reflect quite precisely the contents of LH MS 21. Indeed, despite the brevity of this medieval catalogue description, and a similarity of the title of the second work, "Expositions of the Hebrew Names" with the patristic dictionaries of Hebrew etymologies, this entry is similar to the contents of LH MS 21. Indeed, the first codicological unit of the volume bears on its initial page the title *Predicamenta Augustini* penned

13. Judith Olszowy-Schlanger, "Provenance et histoire du dictionnaire," in *Dictionnaire hébreu-latin-français*, ed. Olszowy-Schlanger and Grondeux, xvi–xxiii; Olszowy-Schlanger, "Christian Hebraism."

14. These two fragments of the catalogues of Ramsey have been printed under the sigla B67 and B68 respectively in Richard Sharpe, J.P. Carley, R.M. Thomson and A.G. Watson et al., *English Benedictine Libraries: The Shorter Catalogues* (London, 1996), 327–417.

15. Sharpe, Carley, Thomson and Watson, *English Benedictine Libraries*, 403.

in red ink. The presence in the same volume of the Latin composition with the title corresponding to the catalogue and of two works dedicated to Hebrew, one clearly a work on lexicography and the other which could be a language manual, as is the Longleat House Grammar – cannot be a coincidence.

The Ramsey connection of LH MS 21 can be further substantiated by the palaeographical identification of one of its two main scribes with one of the scribes of Cambridge, CCC, MS 468.[16] This miscellaneous volume contains among other works a calendar of Ramsey Abbey, copied in the middle of the thirteenth century, which argues strongly that the manuscript emanates from Ramsey scriptorium.[17] Another text of Cambridge, CCC, MS 468 is a Greek Psalter with Latin translation. The Greek text is transliterated in Latin characters. This Psalter likely corresponds to one of the two Greek Psalters mentioned in the catalogue of Ramsey Library among the books of Prior Gregory (B67.55–56 = B68.531–532) or to the Greek and Latin Psalter belonging to Robert Dodeford (B68.502). The hypothesis of Prior Gregory's ownership of Cambridge, CCC, MS 468 is reinforced by the presence of a partially erased ex-libris inscription on fol. IIr: "*Psalterium grecum (prioris) gregorii*," where the word "*prioris*" had been intentionally scraped off and is barely legible. The flyleaves of the volume (fols. II–III) contain notes on Greek grammar, and more precisely on Greek prepositions, with Greek words transcribed in Latin characters. The same scribe left several marginal notes in other parts of Cambridge, CCC, MS 468. His handwriting has affinities with one of the two main scribes of the dictionary in LH MS 21 (Scribe B). Among the texts of Cambridge, CCC, MS 468, there is a poem on natural phenomena and prognostics (fol. VII) as well. Its scribe seems identical to Scribe A of LH MS 21. This scribe copied a part of the trilingual dictionary, as well as the *Predicamenta Augustini* and two textual units of the Longleat House Grammar (GTU 1 and GTU 4) (see p. 19 and Table 1.3).

Further corroboration of the connection of LH MS 21 with Ramsey comes from the annotations of eighteen entries in the dictionary[18] and of three words in Longleat House Grammar by Robert Wakefield. His identity could be established based on the palaeographical comparison of the glosses with the autographs of Robert Wakefield. Several books with his marginalia are known to us, as well as

16. Montague Rhodes James, *A Descriptive Catalogue of the Manuscripts in the Library of Corpus Christi College, Cambridge* (Cambridge, 1912), 2: 399–403; Nigel Wilkins, *Catalogue des manuscrits français de la bibliothèque Parker (Parker Library)* (Cambridge, 1993), 143.

17. On the dating and attribution of this calendar, see Keith V. Sinclair, "The Manuscript Evidence for the 'Dedicatio Ecclesie' of Ramsey Abbey: A Re-examination," *Scriptorium* 38 (1984): 305–309.

18. For the list, see Judith Olszowy-Schlanger, "Le dictionnaire, Ramsey et Robert Wakefield," in *Dictionnaire hébreu-latin-français*, ed. Olszowy-Schlanger and Grondeux, xxii–xxiii, at xxii n39.

his two autograph quitclaims for travel expenses, still kept today in the archive of Wakefield's alma mater, St John's College, Cambridge (D.56.140 and D.56.180).[19]

The fact that Robert Wakefield annotated LH MS 21, including the Longleat House Grammar, is relevant for the reconstruction of its earlier history. According to Wakefield's contemporary, the antiquarian and man of letters John Leland, Robert Wakefield visited Ramsey Abbey before Leland's tour of monastic libraries between 1533 and the Dissolution in 1537 and appropriated a Hebrew dictionary produced at the Abbey. Leland's account contains some inconsistencies but provides an essential clue for the history of Ramsey Hebraism and of the Longleat House Grammar.

According to Leland's account, the dictionary purloined by Wakefield was a work of a certain Lawrence Holbeach, a Cambridge man who became a monk at Ramsey at the turn of the fourteenth and fifteenth centuries, rather than the evidently thirteenth-century work included in LH MS 21:

> The author (Holbeach) carried off a great prize as the reward of his work, having elegantly prepared a Hebrew dictionary, a work as polished as it was learned. It was snatched away a few years ago by the excessive zeal of that rapacious fellow, Robert Wakefield. John Faunte (Iohannes Infantius), a former monk of Ramsey, who also saved some Hebrew books from destruction when the monastery, including its noble library, was falling into ruin, told me these facts about Lawrence, who flourished in the reign of Henry IV. They stick in my mind so memorably at this time that they will never suffer any oblivion on my account.[20]

It is difficult to ascertain whether there were two different Hebrew dictionaries or whether the account of Leland takes a thirteenth-century book for a later work – after all, Leland repeated information that was given to him orally and did not see the volume itself, since it had been already "snatched" by Wakefield. However, in this account, Leland, quoting Iohannes Infantius, also makes a connection between Holbeach and the earlier Ramsey Hebraists. Indeed, the work of Holbeach is presented as motivated by a "pious envy" to emulate and surpass the

19. On Robert Wakefield's library, see especially James P. Carley, "Religious Controversy and Marginalia: Pierfrancesco di Piero Bardi, Thomas Wakefield, and Their Books," *TCBS* 12 (2002): 206–245 at 210, 236–242; James P. Carley, "Thomas Wakefield, Robert Wakefield and the Cotton Genesis," *TCBS* 12 (2002): 246–265; Olszowy-Schlanger, "Robert Wakefield and the Medieval Background of Hebrew Scholarship"; Olszowy-Schlanger, "Robert Wakefield and His Hebrew Manuscripts"; Olszowy-Schlanger, "My Silent Teachers." See also *Hebraism in Sixteenth-Century England*, ed. Burnett and Carley.

20. For the edition and translation see John Leland, *De uiris illustribus (On Famous Men)*, ed. and trans. James P. Carley (Toronto and Oxford, 2010), no. 553, 756–759.

Hebraist achievements of Prior Gregory. Holbeach became an assiduous student of Hebrew; he discovered at Ramsey the Hebrew manuscripts that had been saved from destruction by Prior Gregory more than a century earlier and "wished to complete more fruitfully the work that Gregory had fruitfully begun on the Hebrew language."[21] Thus, Leland reveals that Prior Gregory was remembered as a founder of Hebrew studies at Ramsey Abbey long after the time of his activity.

Indeed, when we consider Prior Gregory's ownership of the Greek Psalter in Cambridge, CCC, MS 468, the identification of the handwriting of one of its scribes with Scribe A, and possibly of another with Scribe B of LH MS 21, and finally the account of John Leland recording the living memory of the early Hebraism at Ramsey, the figure of Prior Gregory emerges as one of the leading Hebraists and Hellenists of medieval England. John Leland discussed Prior Gregory again in a separate entry where he called him Gregory of Huntingdon. He described Gregory, a monk at Ramsey, as an assiduous student of languages, and especially of Hebrew, who needed Hebrew books. The opportunity to acquire such books arose when

> the synagogues of Huntingdon and Stamford were desecrated and all their furniture put up for sale at auction, including their stores of precious books. Gregory lived nearby and he had ready money; when he heard that this auction was to take place, he hurried to it. Paying the price he easily acquired gold for brass, and returned home very well pleased.[22]

Leland continues the account of Gregory's feat describing how he studied these Hebrew manuscripts "night and day, until he had drunk in a deep knowledge of the language from its very fountainheads." Gregory had also left annotations on the manuscripts (*multa egregie calamo annotata*) for the future generation of his fellow monks and scholars. As stated, Leland was no longer able to see Gregory's Hebrew books themselves. He concluded his account by a mention of the entries on his Hebrew books in the catalogue of Ramsey Abbey, together with the Hebrew books of Robert Dodeford.

Leland's entry is the most complete information on Gregory of Huntingdon, on his manuscripts and the study of Hebrew at Ramsey. Leland is however also the source of chronological confusion which has caused the dating of Prior Gregory's activities to c. 1300.[23] Indeed, he associated the aforementioned acquisition of the Hebrew books by Prior Gregory with the expulsion of the Jews from England at

21. Leland, *De uiris illustribus*, ed. and trans. Carley, 757–759.

22. Leland, *De uiris illustribus*, ed. and trans. Carley, no. 323, 538–539.

23. See Marios Costambeys, "Gregory [Gregory of Huntingdon]," in *Oxford Dictionary of National Biography Online*, 2011, https://doi.org/10.1093/ref:odnb/11454.

the time of Edward I (1 November 1290). The books were acquired, according to Leland, at the destruction of the synagogues in Huntingdon and Stamford in 1290, and they were consequently studied and annotated after this date. Such a late dating is inconsistent with the palaeography of LH MS 21, of the palaeography and calendar of Cambridge, CCC, MS 468 and with the dates of Robert Dodeford who was active in the 1240s–1260s and who is listed after Gregory in the list of the books' donors. Indeed, as stated, LH MS 21 except the Psalter, still earlier, can be situated in the third quarter of the thirteenth century. It is possible that the oral tradition transmitted to Leland was problematic even if it contained a kernel of truth. Gregory's acquisition of Hebrew books might have occurred at an earlier and less final confiscation of the goods in the East Anglian Jewish communities. Although I have not found any record of such a book auction, we know that in 1222 several Jews of Stamford were arrested because of a play or joke (*ludum*) mocking Christianity[24] and that they suffered again in 1255 at the occasion of the sadly famous ritual murder accusation when the Jews in nearby Lincoln were accused of killing a little boy, Hugh, who was soon after declared a martyr and a saint.[25]

To sum up, the snippets of evidence gleaned from the manuscripts themselves and from a few medieval and renaissance sources reveal that scholars from the Benedictine Abbey of Ramsey achieved an unprecedented proficiency in Hebrew.[26] The Longleat House Grammar is a product of this particular milieu of Christian students. Their interest in Hebrew went beyond biblical exegesis and led them to grapple with the intricacies of the very structure of the Hebrew

24. Thomas D. Hardy, ed., *Rotuli litterarum clausarum in Turri Londinensi asservati* (London, 1833–1844), 1: 491 (25 March 1222); see Robert C. Stacey, "The Conversion of Jews to Christianity in Thirteenth-Century England," *Speculum* 67 (1992): 263–283 at 265.

25. For the story of "Little Saint Hugh" of Lincoln, see especially Gavin I. Langmuir, "The Knight's Tale of Young Hugh of Lincoln," *Speculum* 47 (1972): 459–482.

26. Another trace of the knowledge of Hebrew and Jewish exegetical literature at Ramsey is the iconographic programme of the "Ramsey Psalter," created at the beginning of the fourteenth century and today, incomplete and split in two, kept at New York, Pierpont Morgan Library (MS M. 302) and in the Carinthian Abbey of St Paul in Lavantthal (Stiftsbibliothek, MS Cod. XXV/2.19); see Lucy Freeman Sandler, "The Historical Miniatures of the Fourteenth-Century Ramsey Psalter," *Burlington Magazine* 111 (1969): 605–611. Lucy Freeman Sandler argued that some illustrations of this Psalter, for example of the Psalm 109, rely on Jewish literalistic and historical exegesis rather than on Christological and allegorical understanding of the text, and have affinities with the exegesis of Herbert of Bosham's commentary on the Hebraica; see her "Christian Hebraism and the Ramsey Abbey Psalter," *The Journal of the Warburg and Courtauld Institutes* 35 (1972): 123–134. The author follows Leland's chronology of Prior Gregory and claims that he was directly responsible for the Hebrew knowledge underlying the iconography. In any case, the iconography of the Ramsey Psalter shows that the interest in Hebrew and Jewish interpretation at Ramsey Abbey continued at least into the early fourteenth century.

language. As attested in LH MS 21 and throughout the corpus of the related Hebrew-Latin manuscripts, the main distinctive feature of this Ramsey Hebraism was an unprecedented interest in Jewish sources. The Longleat House Grammar is a perfect example of such reliance on Jewish learning: the grammatical approach followed in this pedagogical work is wholly indebted to the Hebrew language description as developed by medieval Jewish grammarians and lexicographers.

CHAPTER THREE

The Longleat House Grammar and Different Linguistic Approaches to Hebrew in Medieval England

Challenged by the unfamiliar and exotic Hebrew language, a medieval Christian scholar who aspired to reach beyond the old patristic genre of etymology and alphabet as expressed in such works as the *Interpretation of Hebrew Names*[1] could

1. Jerome, "Liber interpretationis nominum hebraicorum," in *Hebraicae Quaestiones in Libro Geneseos* [...], ed. Paul de Lagarde (Turnhout, 1959), 57–161. For the structure of Jerome's lists and their mnemonic role, see Mary Carruthers, *The Book of Memory: A Study of Memory in Medieval Culture* (Cambridge, 2008), 144–146. For the partial lists of the manuscripts, see Bernard Lambert, *Bibliotheca Hieronymiana Manuscripta: La tradition manuscrite des oeuvres de Saint Jérôme* (Steenbrugis, 1969–1972), 3B: 260–268 and Friedrich Stegmüller and Nikolaus Reinhardt, *Repertorium Biblicum Medii Aevi* (Madrid, 1950–1980) (digital version: http://repbib.uni-trier.de/cgi-bin/rebihome.tcl), no. 7708–7709 (lists attributed to Stephen Langton), no. 7192; Samuel Berger, *Quam notitiam linguae Hebraicae habuerint Christiani medii aevi temporibus in Gallia* (Paris, 1893), 20–25; Matthias Thiel, *Grundlagen und Gestalt der Hebräischkenntnisse des Frühen Mittelalters* (Spoleto, 1973), 159–175; Amaury d'Esneval, "Le perfectionnement d'un instrument de travail au début du XIIIe siècle: Les trois glossaires bibliques d'Etienne Langton," in *Culture et travail intellectuel dans l'occident médiéval*, ed. Geneviève Hasenohr and Jean Longère (Paris, 1981), 163–175; Olivier Szerwiniack, "Des recueils d'interprétations des noms hébreux chez les Irlandais et le wisigoth Théodulf," *Scriptorium* 48 (1994): 187–258; Olivier Szerwiniack, "Les interprétations des noms hébreux dans le Liber glossarum," *HEL* 36.1 (2014): 83–96; Gilbert Dahan, "Lexiques hébreu-latin?: Les recueils d'interprétations des noms hébraïques," in *Les manuscrits des lexiques et glossaires de l'Antiquité à la fin du moyen âge*, ed. Jacqueline Hamesse (Louvain-la-Neuve, 1996), 481–526; Giovanna Murano, "Chi ha scritto le Interpretationes Hebraicorum Nominum?," in *Étienne Langton, prédicateur, bibliste, théologien*, ed. Louis-Jacques Bataillon, Nicole Bériou, Gilbert Dahan and Riccardo Quinto (Turnhout, 2010), 353–371. For the lists appended to the manuscripts of the Parisian Bible, see Laura Light, "The New Thirteenth-Century Bible and the Challenge of Heresy," *Viator* 18 (1987): 275–288, at 280; Eyal Poleg, "The Interpretations of Hebrew Names in Theory and Practice," in *Form and Function in the Late Medieval Bible*, ed. Eyal Poleg and Laura Light (Leiden and Boston, 2013), 217–236; Laura Light, "French Bibles, c. 1200–30: A New Look at the Origin of the

follow two distinct paths. He could try to understand the Hebrew language through the grammatical categories of his own learned tradition – the Latin grammar that he acquired early on, at the beginning of his *trivium* training, and learned to consider as universal and applicable to any language. Alternatively, leaving behind the familiar path of *grammatica,* he could try to follow the language descriptions offered by Jewish grammarians and lexicographers. Both approaches were fraught with practical and epistemological challenges. On the one hand, Latin categories did not necessarily provide adequate tools for describing Hebrew linguistic phenomena. On the other hand, recourse to the categories of the Hebrew grammatical tradition required access, by no means easy, to Jewish learning. These two different approaches, both of which can be found among Christian Hebraists in twelfth- and thirteenth-century England, are discussed in this chapter. The question of the Jewish sources available locally for those who opted for the Jewish grammatical approach is further addressed. This discussion should provide a broader context for understanding the grammatical theories applied in the Longleat House Grammar. Indeed, this exceptional work is not only the most comprehensive medieval Christian presentation of the Hebrew grammar known to us so far; it is also the one which reveals the closest acquaintance with Jewish linguistic thought.

Through the Latin Lens

The use of Latin grammatical categories for describing Hebrew was an obvious choice for a medieval Christian mind. In the thirteenth century, *grammatica* and its theoretical study were paramount to Latin grammar. In England, Roger Bacon admitted that while the "Latins" have a great deal to gain from the ancient wisdom of the Hebrews and Greeks, they surpass them in one particular aspect: the capacity to "theorize" the language and to think about it through the "causes and reasons as exposed in the books of Priscian."[2] The thirteenth century was indeed the time when various languages, including Europe's vernaculars, began to be analyzed using the concepts of Latin grammar. This process of "grammatization"[3]

Paris Bible," in *The Early Medieval Bible; Its Production, Decoration and Use,* ed. Richard Gameson (Cambridge, 1994), 156.

2. Roger Bacon, *Opus Tertium,* in *Opera quaedam hactenus inedita,* ed. J.S. Brewer (London, 1859), 34: "Nam Hebraei et Graeci amiserunt sapientiam Dei et sapientiam philosophiae, ita quod paucissimi eorum sciunt docere grammaticam veraciter, cum causis et rationibus reddendis, sicut nos Latini scimus per libros Prisciani."

3. For this term, its origins, definition and use by the historians of linguistic thought, see Sylvain Auroux, "Grammatisation," *HEL* 11.1 (1995): 5–6.

through Latin categories was particularly easy for those vernaculars considered to be mere dialects (*idiomata*) of Latin, as they display small variations within a linguistic continuum spanning "from Apulia to Spain." The differences observed locally were not deemed sufficient to affect the common substance of this "pan-European" language.[4] In contrast, the application of Latin categories to Hebrew of course posed a far more serious challenge.

The Hebrew language has grammatical features which differ from the familiar *grammatica*, for instance, the definite article, the dual or possessive and object suffixes. To grasp some of these elements absent from Latin, a thirteenth-century scholar could turn to another classical model, the Greek grammar. Indeed, the revived study of Greek and the newly gained access to Greek manuscripts was one of the acknowledged achievements of the Twelfth-Century Renaissance. Hellenism and Hebraism often developed in the same learned circles, especially in England (then the most flourishing center of Hellenism outside of Italy), thanks to the efforts of Robert Grosseteste, his teacher and friend, John of Basingstoke (d. 1252), and other scholars working with them.[5] The study of Greek and its grammar is also attested among the monks of Ramsey Abbey, alongside that of Hebrew.

4. Bacon, *Opus Tertium*, in *Opera quaedam hactenus inedita*, ed. Brewer, 90: "Idioma est proprietas alicujus linguae distincta ab alia, ut picardicum, et gallicum, et provinciale, et omnia idiomata a finibus Apuliae usque ad fines Hispaniae. Nam lingua latina est in omnibus una et eadem secundum substantiam, sed variata secundum idiomata diversa."

5. According to the contemporary chronicler Matthew Paris, Basingstoke learned Greek in Athens from Constantina, a daughter of a Greek archbishop, before he became the archdeacon of Leicester in 1235; see Matthew Paris, *Chronica Majora*, in *Monachi Sancti Albani Chronica Majora*, ed. H.R. Luard (London, 1880), 5 (A.D. 1248 to A.D. 1259): 286. Basingstoke is said to have translated and adapted into Latin a Byzantine Greek grammar, maybe the work of Dionysius Thrax. See Roberto Weiss, "The Study of Greek in England during the Fourteenth Century," *Rinascimento* 2 (1951): 209–239; Bernhard Bischoff, "The Study of Foreign Languages in the Middle Ages," *Speculum* 36 (1961): 209–224; Pascal Boulhol, *La connaissance de la langue grecque dans la France médiévale, VIe–XVe s.* (Aix-en-Provence, 2008), 79–80. A "Donatus in Greek" (*Donatus grece*) is mentioned in the library catalogue of Christ Church, Canterbury, but is not preserved; see Montague Rhodes James, *The Ancient Libraries of Canterbury and Dover: The Catalogues of the Libraries of Christ Church Priory and St Augustine's Abbey at Canterbury and St Martin's Priory at Dover* (Cambridge, 1903), LXXXV, 7. Roberto Weiss suggested that scholastic notes on grammar quoting Greek in London, BL, MS Arundel 165, associated in the manuscript with Robert Grosseteste, may be identified with the lost work of Basingstoke. For Grosseteste's translations, see Ruth Nisse, *Jacob's Shipwreck: Diaspora, Translation, and Jewish-Christian Relations in Medieval England* (Ithaca, 2017), 142–147. The manuscript from which Grosseteste and his helpers worked on the translation is still in existence; it is Cambridge, University Library, MS Ff. 1. 24. On the Greek manuscripts of Pseudo-Dionysius copied in thirteenth-century England, see Ruth Barbour, "A Manuscript of Ps.-Dionysius Areopagita Copied for Robert Grosseteste," *The Bodleian Library Record* 6.2 (1958): 401–416.

The aforementioned Cambridge, CCC, MS 468 from Ramsey Abbey, which belonged to Prior Gregory, contains *inter alia* a Greek Psalter in Latin characters, as well as notes on Greek prepositions and their different grammatical functions.[6] Indeed, scholars, such as Roger Bacon, used some comparisons with Greek in their discussions of Hebrew.[7] As for the compilers of the Longleat House Grammar, it seems that, despite the well-documented interest in both Greek and Hebrew at Ramsey Abbey, they turned directly and exclusively to Hebrew books and scholarship for their methodological framework of grammatical description.

Hebrew, Latin and the Universal Grammar

The most famous proponent of the understanding of the structure of the Hebrew language through the Latin grammatical tradition was the leading natural philosopher of his time, Roger Bacon. This was in line with Bacon's broader interest in the theories of language in general. Early in his career, between 1240 and 1250, he authored the *Summa Grammatica,* a tractate on speculative grammar and Aristotelian logic expounding views on universal features underlying linguistic phenomena.[8] His concept of grammar in general and of Hebrew grammar in particular was based on the classics: Donatus and Priscian.[9] A more advanced level of the acquisition of Hebrew (as of Greek) was defined by Bacon by the learner's capacity to define the parts of speech "according to the model of Donatus."[10]

Roger Bacon's later works, *Opus Maius* (1268), *Opus Tertium* (1266–1268) and *Compendium Studii Philosophiae* (1272), include many passages on Hebrew words, their meaning and etymology, as well as some rudimentary information on grammar. A short note on basic rules of the Hebrew language in Cambridge, University Library, MS Ff. 6. 13, has also been attributed to Bacon because it is copied in this anthological manuscript together with his Greek grammar (fols.

6. Montague Rhodes James, *A Descriptive Catalogue of the Manuscripts in the Library of Corpus Christi College, Cambridge* (Cambridge, 1912), 399–403; Judith Olszowy-Schlanger and Anne Grondeux, eds., *Dictionnaire hébreu-latin-français de la Bible hébraïque de l'Abbaye de Ramsey (XIIIe s.)* (Turnhout, 2008), xxi.

7. In his Greek Grammar written c. 1268, Roger Bacon, *The Greek Grammar of Roger Bacon and a Fragment of His Hebrew Grammar,* ed. Edmond Nolan and Samuel A. Hirsch (Cambridge, 1902).

8. See Irène Rosier-Catach, "Roger Bacon and Grammar," in *Roger Bacon and Sciences: Commemorative Essays,* ed. Jeremiah Hackett (Leiden and New York, 1997), 67–102.

9. Horst Weinstock, "Roger Bacon's Polyglot Alphabets," *Florilegium* 11 (1992): 60–178, at 162.

10. *Compendium Studii Philosophiae,* in *Opera quaedam hactenus inedita,* ed. J.S. Brewer (London, 1859), 433: "Et ut secundum formam Donati sciat accidentia partium orationis."

67r–69ra), and because some of its contents match the quotations in his other works.[11] Widely known under the ambitious title of the *Hebrew Grammar of Roger Bacon* since its publication by Samuel Abraham Hirsch as an appendix to the edition of the *Grammatica Graeca* by Edmond Nolan in 1902, this modest leaf has been long considered to be the utmost grammatical achievement of the Christian Hebraism in the Middle Ages. Very basic, in fact, this text is an excellent example of an attempt to explain Hebrew through Latin grammatical categories without any reference to the Jewish grammatical concepts. Even if, on the whole, these efforts to describe Hebrew through the template of the Latin categories fall short of a proper understanding of its nature, they do reflect a conscious attempt to "grammatize" this unfamiliar language.[12]

The note begins with a list of the Hebrew consonants. In the manuscript, the names of these letters are transliterated in Latin. Their Latin phonetic equivalents are marked above their names. The list is written in a disorderly manner which shows that the copyist did not know Hebrew, even as little as the sequence of the Hebrew alphabet. Groups of three or four letters follow an internal alphabetical order, from right to left, but these blocks are misplaced. Thus, line one begins with the block *ṭet – yod – kaf* written from right to left and is followed by what should be the first block *alef – bet – gimel – dalet – heh,* and so on. This arrangement indicates most probably that in the exemplar used as a model for the copy the alphabet must have been written in a tabular form, in parallel columns. The scribe of the Cambridge manuscript copied the two parallel rows in long lines, and from left to right.[13]

The list of the alphabet is followed by a lengthy discussion of the Hebrew vowels. This discussion represents an intricate attempt to make sense of the Hebrew vocalic system and match it to the Latin concept of the vowels. According to the grammar and a parallel text, with slightly different wording, in the *Opus*

11. Roger Bacon, "Cambridge Hebrew Grammar," in *The Greek Grammar of Roger Bacon and a Fragment of His Hebrew Grammar,* ed. Edmond Nolan and Samuel A. Hirsch (Cambridge, 1902), 199–208.

12. Benoît Grévin, "L'hébreu des Franciscains: Nouveaux éléments sur la connaissance de l'hébreu en milieu chrétien au XIIIe siècle," *Médiévales* 20.41 (2001): 65–82.

13. Bacon, "Cambridge Hebrew Grammar," ed. Nolan and Hirsch, 202. Hirsch quotes other examples of such an irregular presentation of the Hebrew alphabet in Latin manuscripts. See also Berger, *Quam notitiam,* 7 and 39; Arsène Darmesteter, (review of J. Bonnard, "Un alphabet hébreu-anglais au XIVe siècle, I") "Même sujet, II," *REJ* 4.8 (1882): 259–268. Horst Weinstock sought to explain the layout of the alphabet in the Cambridge fragment through the medieval propensity to use mnemonics and to group letters according to *connexiones;* see Weinstock, "Roger Bacon's Polyglot Alphabets," 65, but a scribal misunderstanding of the layout is more plausible.

Maius, Hebrew has six vowels which are *alef, heh, vav, ḥet, yod* and *ʿayin*.[14] While *yod* corresponds only to the Latin *i* sound and *vav* to *u* or *o*, all the other "vowels" can have any Latin vocalic sound, with *alef* and *ʿayin* pronounced respectively "in the mouth and in the throat without aspiration," and *heh* and *ḥet* respectively "in the mouth and in the throat with aspiration."[15] The Hebrew alphabet at the head of the folio indeed contains equivalents for all the Latin vocalic sounds (*a, e, i, o, u*[16]) written above the letters *alef, heh, ḥet* and *ʿayin*. A similar equivalence is found in the *Opus Maius*.[17]

Bacon was aware that the Jews used a system of graphic symbols to mark the vowels. Indeed, he provided a list of ten Hebrew vowels (with *alef* as the example) corresponding, from left to right, to *pataḥ, ḳamaẓ, ẓere, shva, segol, ḥaṭaf segol, ḥaṭaf pataḥ, ḥireḳ, ḥolam* and *ḳubbuẓ*.[18] According to Bacon, these "points" serve to modify the pronunciation of the six "vowels." Four "vowels," i.e., *alef, heh, ḥet* and *ʿayin*, can be pronounced as any of the five Latin vowels, according to the "points."[19] Of course, the author could not deny the evidence of the use of the "points" under all the other Hebrew consonants in the vocalized Hebrew manuscripts. Faced with this contradiction, he resorted to cryptology and claimed that the Jews write the signs, which normally should accompany only the six "vowels," under all the consonants to confuse the non-Jewish readers:

> It is known that they [the Jews] point not only the vowels with the sounds of different vowels that they should have but also the consonants because they

14. Bacon, "Cambridge Hebrew Grammar," ed. Nolan and Hirsch, 202: "Et sunt sex, ut aleph, he, vav, heth, iod, ain." For the parallels, see Roger Bacon, *Operis maioris* III (new edition), ed. John Henry Bridges (Turnhout, 2010), 3: 89.

15. Bacon, "Cambridge Hebrew Grammar," ed. Nolan and Hirsch, 204: "Aleph sonat in ore sine aspiracione, ain in gutture sine aspiratione. Set he et heth habent aspirationem; he unam, heth dupplicem, et he sonat in ore, heth in gutture." For the parallels see Bacon, *Operis maioris* III, ed. Bridges, 3: 89: "he et heth aspirantur, ut he in principio, heth non solum in primo sed in fine, et generatur in gutture, he in ore; aleph similiter in ore; ain in gutture."

16. Bacon considered that the five Latin vowels are the basic number of vowels necessary for the pronunciation of the consonants in any language, as explained in his Greek Grammar, *The Greek Grammar*, ed. Nolan and Hirsch, 4.

17. Bacon, *Operis maioris* III, ed. Bridges, 3: 89.

18. In this list, the *ḥaṭaf ḳamaẓ* is missing, and *ḥaṭaf pataḥ* is written mistakenly with three dots instead of two.

19. Bacon, "Cambridge Hebrew Grammar," ed. Nolan and Hirsch, 202: "Sciendum quod sunt ille vocales, super quas vocales nostre scribuntur [it refers to the list of the letters with Latin equivalents]. Et sunt sex, ut aleph, he, vav, heth, iod, ain, set quatuor, scilicet aleph, he, heth, ayn, sonant omnes vocales nostras sicut supra notatum est, set vav non valet nisi v et o, iod i tantum." A similar description of the "six vowels" appears in the *Operis maioris* III, ed. Bridges, 3: 89.

> write rarely with the vowels and usually only with the consonants. It also happens that they place under consonants the signs that should be under the vowels because they do not want the other nations to read their books.[20]

Bacon pushed this logic to create forms of Hebrew words which do not exist. He described the word "son" with a possessive suffix of the 2nd person singular as spelled with an *alef*: "... with an added final *kaf*, as *benakh* with alpha is 'your son' (*et addito caph secundo ut benach*[21] *cum alpha est filius tuus*)." If we transliterate his words back into Hebrew, this would give בנאך instead of the required בנך. Indeed, since Bacon claimed that Hebrew, like Latin, had vowels (which he identified with the six aforementioned consonants), it logically follows that any of these six "vowels" – *alef* in the case of "your son" – should be added to "vocalize" a word, even if such "vowels" do not appear in the actual Hebrew texts.

Bacon explained this absence of the "vowels" as a technique of cryptography, another field in which he had gained a scholarly reputation. The *Epistle on the Secrets of the Art and of Nature and on the Invalidity of Magic,* for which Bacon's authorship has been strongly argued,[22] states:

> The third way of concealing secrets through the modes of writing is writing with consonants only so that no one can read unless he knows the word; this is how the Hebrews, Chaldeans, Syrians and Arabs write their secrets.[23]

This mention of cryptography is surprisingly absent in the parallel text in the *Opus Maius*. Rather than polemicizing with the Jewish writing and reading practices, the *Opus Maius* states in a matter-of-fact way that the diversity of vocalic sounds is expressed by "points and lines," and describes in detail the shapes of the Tiberian vowels applied to the *alef*. Bacon adds that the same application of the points and lines to express the five vocalic sounds also concerns the *'ayin,*

20. Bacon, "Cambridge Hebrew Grammar," ed. Nolan and Hirsch, 205: "Sciendum quod non solum punctant vocales pro sonis diversarum vocalium habendarum, set consonantes, quia raro scribunt per vocalem, set in pluribus per consonantes. Et ideo oportet quod signa vocalium habendarum ponantur sub consonantibus, quia noluerunt quod alie gentes legerent libros suos."

21. Edited as "*benath*" (c and t are often very similar in manuscripts).

22. For the authorship of this work, see Lynn Thorndike, *A History of Magic and Experimental Science* (New York, 1923–1958), 2: 688–691 (Appendix II).

23. See *Epistola fratris Rogerii Baconis de Secretis Operibus Artis et Naturae, et de Nullitate Magiae*, in Bacon, *Opera quaedam hactenus inedita*, ed. Brewer, 544: "Tercio modo occultaverunt per modos scribendi, scilicet per consonantes tantum, ut nemo posset legere, nisi sciat significata dictionum, sicut Hebraei, et Chaldaei, et Syri, et Arabes scribunt secreta." See Benoît Grévin, "Systèmes d'écriture sémiotique et langage chez Roger Bacon," *HEL* 24.2 (2002): 75–111, at 97–98, on Bacon's view on Hebrew consonantal writing as semi-cryptic.

heh and *ḥet*, the other "vowels." While he still considers *alef, heh, ḥet* and *ʿayin* as vowels, he accepts that the graphic signs can be placed with other consonants to create the syllables. Instead of a negative judgement on the Jewish vowels as a means of encoding, the passage in the *Opus Maius* ends, on the contrary, with a statement that the misunderstanding of this system is a common error because of the lack of knowledge of Hebrew and Aramaic.[24] Incidentally, another example of cryptography, the *atbash*[25] – writing code which replaces the first letter of the alphabet (*alef*) by the last (*tav*), the second (*bet*) by the penultimate (*shin*), and so forth – is presented in Bacon's Grammar polemically, as a way the contemporary Jews teach their children to read to conceal secrets,[26] whereas a parallel text in the *Opus Minus* focuses of the use of the *atbash* as a technique of interpretation, following Jerome on Jeremiah 25:26.[27]

A similar approach to certain consonants which are considered as vowels is found in the rudimentary Hebrew lexical lists in Paris, BnF, MS hébreu 113.[28] The flyleaves (front, fols. I–V) of this calligraphic Hebrew Psalter glossed in Latin

24. Bacon, *Operis maioris* III, ed. Bridges, 3: 89–91: "Et hanc diversitatem sonorum signant per puncta et tractus. Nam si sub aleph trahatur linea sine puncto sic, אַ, vel cum puncto, אָ sonatur a. Si vero duo puncta fiant jacentia sub aleph e transverso אֵ, vel duo stantia אְ, vel tria in modum trianguli אֶ, vel quinque puncta hoc modo אֱ, sonatur e. Si vero tria puncta iaceant sub aleph ex obliquo descendentia sic אֻ sonatur u. Si vero unus punctus fiat supra sonatur o, sic אֹ. Et ita est de ain, et he, et heth, quae habent hos quinque sonos per istorum signorum diversitatem. [...] Ideo oportet quod ad consonantes ponantur haec signa, ut sciatur sonus vocalis syllabicandus cum consonante: ut si volo designare ba, be, bi, bo, bu, scribam sic: בָּ, בֵּ, בִּ, בֹּ, בֻּ. [...] Manifestus ergo et vilis est error omnium in hac parte propter ignorantiam harum linguarum."

25. The acrostic of *alef-tav-bet-shin*, את"בש.

26. Bacon, "Cambridge Hebrew Grammar," ed. Nolan and Hirsch, 206; Bacon, *Opus Minus*, in *Opera quaedam hactenus inedita*, ed. Brewer, 350–351.

27. Bacon, *Opus Minus*, in *Opera quaedam hactenus inedita*, ed. Brewer, 350–351: "Similiter cum Jeremias prophetavit contra Babel, non ausus fuit ponere hoc verbum, ne suscitaret furorem Caldaeorum contra ipsum et populum Dei; sed posuit Sesach pro Babel. Cujus nominis ratio nullo modo potest sciri, nisi homo sciat alphabetum Hebraeum." This interpretation of Jeremiah 25:26 is implicit in the Targum Jonathan: וּמַלְכָּא דְבָבֶל, in bMegillah 6a, and is employed in the Bible commentaries, such as that of Rashi: ששך הוא בבל באת"בש.

28. Hermann Zotenberg, *Catalogue des manuscrits hébreux et samaritains de la Bibliothèque Impériale* (Paris, 1866), 12; Michel Garel, *D'une main forte: Manuscrits hébreux des collections françaises* (Paris, 1992), 90–91; Malachi Beit-Arié, *Hebrew Manuscripts of East and West: Towards a Comparative Codicology* (London, 1992), 109; Malachi Beit-Arié, "The Valmadonna Pentateuch and the Problem of Pre-expulsion Anglo-Hebrew Manuscripts – MS London, Valmadonna Trust Library 1: England (?), 1189," in *The Makings of the Medieval Hebrew Book: Studies in Palaeography and Codicology*, ed. Malachi Beit-Arié (Jerusalem, 1993); Gabrielle Sed-Rajna and Sonia Fellous, *Les Manuscrits hébreux enluminés des bibliothèques de France* (Leuven, 1994), 147–149; Gilbert Dahan, "Deux psautiers hébraïques glosés en latin," *REJ* 158 (1999): 61–87.

and French, copied and annotated in medieval England in the thirteenth century, contain a draft of a Hebrew lexicon arranged in two lists; one follows the order of the Hebrew alphabet and the other arranges the Hebrew entries according to the Latin alphabetical order. In the second list, a Latin letter is written at the beginning of each section (only letters *a* to *i* are preserved), and these sections contain Hebrew words whose first letter could be transcribed by the corresponding Latin letter. Thus, the letter *a* is followed by Hebrew words beginning with both *alef* and ʿ*ayin* (from left to right: עִיר, *ciuitas*, אֵמוּט, [*...*]*ebo*, עָם, *populus*, עֹז, *fort*[*itudo*], אֵשׁ, *ignis*, אָז, *tunc*, עִם, *cum*, עַן [for יען] *propter*, עוֹד, [?], עוֹף, *uolatilis*). To consider the two guttural consonants *alef* and ʿ*ayin* as equivalent to the Latin *a* does not imply that the words were all pronounced with the sound *a* at the beginning – the examples given are actually vocalized with a variety of Hebrew vowel-points. Defining both these consonants as equivalent to *a* simply means that they were both considered as vowels rather than consonants.

The preface to the *Interpretation of Hebrew Names* in Paris, BnF, MS latin 36 presents a compromise approach. On the one hand, the gutturals (*alef*, *heh*, *ḥet* and ʿ*ayin*) are included among the consonants (unlike *vav* and *yod*), and the consonants are said not to have a sound, but to become "speech" only by the addition of "points and strokes which, by an ancient institution, have the value of the vowels."[29] On the other hand, like in the grammar of Roger Bacon, the gutturals are described as vowels.[30] For example, when discussing "Gomorrah" (e.g. Genesis 18–19), the text states that the initial *G* in the Greek and Latin translations is not a part of this word in Hebrew. It rightly states that in Hebrew "Gomorrah" begins with an ʿ*ayin* (עֲמֹרָה) and defines this ʿ*ayin* as a vowel (*per uocalem aym*).[31]

Bacon's Cambridge grammatical notes deal further with a double pronunciation of *t*, called respectively "simple" (*ṭet*) and "aspirated" (*tav*), and examine the letters with a double graphic form, pointing out correctly that *kaf*, *mem*, *nun*, *peh* and *ẓadi* have a different shape when written at the end of a word. In a comment on the double pronunciation of *peh* as "*feh*," *p*, or *f*, the notes closely follow Jerome's inexact remark in his commentary on Daniel 11:45, that in only one word, *Apedno* (for אַפַּדְנוֹ, "balcony, canopy"), the letter *peh* was pronounced *p*, whereas, in all other instances, it was pronounced *f*.[32] Bacon added an interesting observa-

29. Berger, *Quam notitiam*, 22.

30. See Judith Olszowy-Schlanger, "The Knowledge and Practice of Hebrew Grammar Among Christian Scholars in Pre-expulsion England: The Evidence of 'Bilingual' Hebrew-Latin Manuscripts," in *Hebrew Scholarship in the Medieval World*, ed. Nicholas De Lange (Cambridge, 2001), 107–128, at 124.

31. Berger, *Quam notitiam*, 21.

32. On the pronunciation of this word, see Richard C. Steiner, "Emphatic p in the Massoretic Pronunciation of ʾappaḏno (Dan. 11:45)," in *Hebrew and Arabic Studies in Honour*

tion that since the time of Jerome, his contemporary Jews abandoned this original absence of *p*, and pronounce it just like their Christian neighbours "because they live among us since the destruction of Jerusalem." Bacon's grammar is not the first to comment on the difference between Jerome's view that *p* does not exist in Hebrew and the contemporary Jews' pronunciation. More than half a century earlier, in his rewriting of the *Interpretation of Hebrew Names* entitled *Philippicus*, the archdeacon of Gloucester, Ralph Niger (c. 1149–1199),[33] commented on the contemporary Jewish pronunciation of *peh*:

> The letter *peh*, as Jerome said, does not exist among the Hebrews. But modern Jews say that they have both *peh* and *feh* for our (Latin) *p* because they put a strong *f* everywhere for *p*. I indeed observe in our times that at the beginning (of a word) always occurs *p*, whereas *feh* occurs at the end (of a word). But *p* is often put instead of *feh* also at the beginning.[34]

In an even simpler way, the author of *Notabilia*,[35] a gathering of notes and letters concerning Hebrew, identified differently by scholars either with William de Mara or with Roger Bacon,[36] expressed his doubts about the pronunciation of *p*, because, he observed, according to Jerome, that *peh* (*p*) does not exist in Hebrew, but his contemporary Jews pronounced it.[37]

---

of Joshua Blau, ed. Moshe Bar Asher, Z. Ben Hayyim, M.J. Kister, A. Levin, S. Shaked and A. Tal (Tel Aviv and Jerusalem, 1993), 551–561.

33. George B. Flahiff, "Ralph Niger: An Introduction to His Life and Works," *Mediaeval Studies* 2 (1940): 104–126; Avrom Saltman, "Supplementary Notes on the Works of Ralph Niger," in *Bar-Ilan Studies in History*, ed. Pinhas Artzi (Ramat-Gan, 1978), 103–113.

34. Lincoln, Cathedral Library, MS 15, fol. 61v: "Apud Hebreos, ut dicit Jeronimus, P littera non est. Moderni Hebrei dicunt habere Pe et Phe pro nostro P; ponit autem F forte ubique pro P. Ego vero tempora nostra sequor quia P habere semper in principio, Phe autem in fine; Pe autem pro Phe etiam plerumque ponitur principio." Flahiff, "Ralph Niger," 121. See *Patrologiae cursus completus, Series Latina*, ed. J.-P. Migne (Paris, 1844–1855), 23: 889.

35. This important work, preserved in three manuscripts, Toulouse, Bm, MS 402, fol. 233ra–278vb, Florence, Biblioteca Laurenziana, MS Santa Croce Pl. XXV sin. 4, fol. 82r–213vb, and a part of the text, the "Lexicon," in Einsiedeln, Stiftsbibliothek, MS 28, has been described by Berger, *Quam notitiam*, 45 and more recently by Étienne Anheim, Benoît Grévin and Martin Morard, "Exégèse judéo-chrétienne, magie et linguistique: Un recueil de *Notes* inédites attribuées à Roger Bacon," *AHDLMA* 68 (2001): 95–154, but still awaits a full edition. For the manuscripts' description, see Anheim, Grévin and Morard, "Exégèse judéo-chrétienne," 100–109. For Einsideln, Stiftsbibliothek, MS 28, see https://www.e-codices.unifr.ch/de/list/one/sbe/0028. The title *Notabilia* is based on the incipit "extraordinaria notabilia" on fol. 233ra in Toulouse, Bm, MS 402.

36. See Berger, *Quam notitiam*, 45; Anheim, Grévin and Morard, "Exégèse judéo-chrétienne," 98–107.

37. Toulouse, Bm, MS 402 (fol. 271r); Berger, *Quam notitiam*, 38: "Item de hac littera p nescio quid sentiam uel quid dicam, quia secundum Ieronimum in libro Interpretationum

Unlike Ralph Niger or the author of the *Notabilia,* Bacon's Grammar problematizes the fact that this contemporary pronunciation of *peh* does not correspond to the graphic form of the initial/medial versus the final letter form.[38] A similar remark concerns *kaf*; according to Bacon, the "natural" pronunciation of both final and medial *kaf* was originally identical but these two graphic forms are pronounced differently by contemporary Jews.[39] It is evident from this remark on the double pronunciation that the author has a vague notion of the rules of the masoretic Hebrew grammar concerning the letters בגדכפת (*bet, gimel, dalet, kaf, peh* and *tav*) whose pronunciation differs according to the place these letters occupy in a word. In the case of three of these letters, *bet, kaf* and *peh,* the difference of pronunciation is considerable: *b* or *v, k* or a guttural *kh, p* or *f*. As is well known to all Hebraists, in the Tiberian Masoretic Hebrew, all six of these letters bear a dot called *dagesh* when they open a new syllable when the preceding syllable is a "closed" syllable (ended by a vowel-less consonant). When they appear at the end of a syllable or after a syllable ending with a vowel, in some manuscripts these letters may bear above them a thin horizontal stroke called *rafeh.* The letters *kaf* and *peh* in the final position in a word close a syllable and are therefore pronounced *rafeh* (even when some manuscripts omit to insert the *rafeh* strokes). Bacon knew about this graphic differentiation by a dot or a stroke:

> It should be noted that the consonants sometimes keep their strong sound. This is marked with a dot within or below. But sometimes the sound is weakened, and it is marked with a line above the letter, such as, when I say David, the first *d* sounds stronger and the second weaker. This is why when they write Adam, they put a fine stroke above the *dalet,* and it sounds like *zz,* as in *adamas.*[40]

---

hebraicorum nominum super Lucam dicit quod p littera apud hebreos non habetur [...] Unde mirror quomodo uos dicatis uel etiam iudei quod ipsi predictam litteram habeant uel quomodo hoc defendi possit."

38. Bacon, "Cambridge Hebrew Grammar," ed. Nolan and Hirsch, 203–204: "Et tamen hebrei dicunt phe in una figura et in alia pe, set hoc non est hebraicum nisi in Apethno ut in XIo Danielis, sicut dicit Jeronimus. Judei vero sonant nunc p sicut nos, quia conversati sunt inter nos a destructione Ierusalem. Sed hoc non est secundum formam eorum naturalem, et hoc etiam patet quia non habent diversum sonum."

39. Bacon, "Cambridge Hebrew Grammar," ed. Nolan and Hirsch, 204: "Caph tamen secundum diversificant a primo in nomine set non in sono secundum modum eorum antiquum, licet tamen moderni Iudei diversificant aliquantulum in sono caph primi a secundo, set hoc est contra naturam."

40. אדֿם : the Hebrew is written mistakenly in the manuscript as אםדֿ. As noted by Hirsch, Bacon, "Cambridge Hebrew Grammar," ed. Nolan and Hirsch, a similar passage is found in *Operis maioris* III, ed. Bridges, 3: 91: "Unde quando super Dalet ponitur tractus sic דֿ tunc debilem sonum reddit ut nostri z, et cum dico adamas."

Similarly, he discussed the *kaf*, and stated confusedly that the final *kaf* (lit. "second *kaf*," *caph secundum*) sounds stronger when it bears a line and weaker when it has a dot. Surely, the distinction should be made, first and foremost, for the *kaf* in the initial or non-final position, the *caph primum* according to the terminology of the notes, since the final *kaf* is by definition *rafeh*.[41] The author mentions in the same breath the diacritical point of the letter *sin/shin*, which is placed respectively on the left or on the right, within the letter.[42] It is clear from these examples that the author understands that Hebrew manuscripts use a dot or a thin horizontal stroke to mark variant pronunciation of the same consonant. However, he does not grasp at all the grammatical differences related to the syllable structures underlying these phonetic principles and the use of these signs on different letters. The dot on *sin/shin* differentiates between two different consonants, whereas the *dagesh* or *rafeh* on the letters *begadkefat* marks an allophone, an alternative pronunciation of these letters according to the phonetic rules depending on the syllabic structure. Nor does the author realize that the different pronunciation of the final letters *kaf* and *peh* is linked to the *begadkefat* rules. Finally, the author does not explicitly make a connection between the presence of the *dagesh* versus *rafeh* and the group of letters *begadkefat*, although the examples he quotes concern precisely these letters.

In contrast to the relatively detailed discussion of the alphabet in Bacon's Grammar, the presentation of morphology is disappointingly short. There is no mention of the verbal system at all. A short reference is made to the relative pronoun spelled "*esser*" (for אֲשֶׁר, "*asher*"). A few lines concern the noun; they mention the formation of the masculine and feminine plural and the definite article and attempt to apply to Hebrew the system of case declension, similar to Latin and Greek. Indeed, Bacon's Grammar is explicit about the presence in Hebrew of the noun categories of gender (*genera*), case (*casus*) and number (*numerus*), the latter, like in Greek, covering three categories (the text does not specify it, but most probably refers to singular, plural and dual). The reference to Greek is relevant: as we saw, since the Hebrew grammar differs from Latin by the presence of the dual, another "classical" equivalent is needed to elucidate the Hebrew forms. This concerns the definite article as well.

41. There are a few instances in the Bible when the final *kaf* contains a *dagesh*, not for phonetic but rather grammatical reasons, but I doubt that the author was referring to these exceptions.

42. Although most frequently the diacritic point of *sin* and *shin* is placed above the letter, in some manuscripts from medieval France and England the dot appears indeed inside the letter, as described here, see Olszowy-Schlanger, "A Christian Tradition of Hebrew Vocalisation in Medieval England," in *Semitic Studies in Honour of Edward Ullendorff*, ed. Geoffrey Khan (Leiden and Boston, 2005), 126–146.

The definite forms are described as declined: the form with the article *ha-* (ה) marks the Nominative and Genitive case, *la-* (the preposition ל, "to, for, towards" with the assimilated definite article) is the Dative, *et* (the particle את) introduces the Accusative. The Vocative does not have an article, but an *"adverbium vocandi" oi* (exclamation הוי), whereas the Ablative is expressed by the preposition *mi* or *mo* (should be *me*) or *ma* (again probably for *me*) (Hebrew preposition מן, "of, from" with *nun* assimilated with the following letter).[43]

An association of the prepositions (which in Hebrew are written jointly with the word that follows them) with the grammatical cases appears in the works of other scholars, including those more familiar with the Jewish tradition. William de Mara in the *Correctorium Vaticanum* (fol. 154v) compared the Hebrew article to the French *le* and discussed its use to express the Dative and Genitive cases.[44] The remarkable twelfth-century Hebraist, Herbert of Bosham, for his part, noted in his *Commentary on the Hebraica Psalter* the absence of grammatical case designations in Hebrew, and the use of what he called "articles" (which for him include particles or prepositions) to express them:

> Since the Hebrews lack the oblique cases, they distinguish the cases only by the article. With this procedure the error can easily arise that one case is mistakenly put for another one.[45]

Thus, for example, when commenting on למנצח on fol. 5r, Herbert of Bosham correctly identified the three radicals, *nun*, *ẓadi* and *ḥet* and commented that they are preceded by the *"articulus lamed."* The designation of the Hebrew prepositions as *articulus*, "article," is a constant feature across the different traditions of English medieval Hebraism. The *superscriptio* in manuscripts associated with the Ramsey school also refers to the definite article ה, to the preposition ל, and the direct object particle את as *articulus*. The abbreviation *ar* for *articulus* indeed appears in the *superscriptio* above these different categories of words. The notion that the Hebrew preposition ל designates a Dative case is also discussed in the gloss to the opening lines of Psalm 24 (Vulg. 23), in the bilingual Psalter Oxford, CCC, MS 11 (fol. 39r–v):

43. Grévin, "L'hébreu des Franciscains," 69–70. Benoît Grévin understands this discussion in the Grammar as Bacon's attempt to elaborate a coherent linguistic theory.

44. Berger, *Quam notitiam*, 33 (Deuteronomy 33:7): "Hic ponit quod hebreus habet in datiuo, sed sciendum, quod hic ponitur articulus sicut est le uel al in gallico, quod non solum datiuo sed genetiuo seruit, sicut diceremus la chape le mestre siue al mestre."

45. Herbert of Bosham, *Commentary on the Hebraica Psalter*, fol. 98r: "Et nota quod Hebrei cum careant obliquis, distinguunt varietates casuum solum per articulos. In quo error facilis suboriri potest, in eronee ponatur casus pro casu"; see Eva De Visscher, *Reading the Rabbis in the Works of Herbert of Bosham* (Leiden, 2014), 33.

> ledavid [...] the letter *lamed* is prefixed to a letter of the case; it sometimes has the sound *la*, sometimes *le* and sometimes *li*, according to the custom of Hebrew pronunciation, and it is the article of the Dative.[46]

A note in Bacon's Grammar on the addition of suffixes to בן, "son," shows how the author tried to grasp the way Hebrew expresses possession. He does not present the full list of the possessive suffixes and gives only three forms without describing or defining them. These forms are the singular of בן, "son," with the possessive suffixes of the 1st person singular ("beni addito iod est filius meus," "*beni*, with an added *yod*, is 'my son'"), 2nd person masculine singular ("addito caph secundo ut benach[47] cum alpha est filius tuus," "with an added final *kaf*, like *benakh*, with an alpha, is 'your son'"), and 3rd person masculine singular ("et dicunt beno, unde scribunt sic: בנוֹ," "and they say beno, that they write thus: בנוֹ"). There is no attempt to explain that these additions are possessive suffixes or to compare them to the Latin system of possessive pronouns. Rather than presenting in detail the intricate system of Hebrew possessive suffixes and object suffixes attached to the verb, the author stated bluntly that the use of suffixes accounts for an over-simplicity of Hebrew grammar:

> And thus (by addition of suffixes) they make many distinctions in nouns and in verbs, and in other (parts of speech), because they have a minimal grammar with very few rules.[48]

This is why Bacon considered that the Hebrew grammar was easy to learn, at least at the initial stages. In his *Compendium Studii Philosophiae*, he distinguished three levels of the knowledge of Hebrew and other "sapiential languages" (Greek, Arabic and Aramaic in this case): a native level as the mother tongue, a level allowing to translate from Hebrew into one's "native" Latin, and finally, a rudimentary level which would enable scholars to understand references to Hebrew in the works of the Church Fathers. It is this third elementary and accessible level that was Bacon's target. He criticized those who disparage this initial stage as too easy and try to achieve the second and third proficiency levels too fast. Their efforts will be in vain; only the mastering of the basics would allow them to progress further.[49] Bacon claimed that to teach elementary Hebrew, three days would be

46. Oxford, CCC, MS 11, fol. 39r: "Ledavid [...], nam littera lamed preposita littera casuali; sonat aliquando la aliquando le aliquando li pro more loquationis hebree et est articulus dative casus."

47. In the edition, *benath*.

48. Bacon, "Cambridge Hebrew Grammar," ed. Nolan and Hirsch, 205: "et sic distinguunt in nominibus multa, et in verbis, et in aliis quia modicum habent grammaticam et paucas regulas."

49. Bacon, *Compendium Studii Philosophiae*, in *Opera quaedam hactenus inedita*, ed. Brewer, 433–434: "Prima igitur est scientia linguarum sapientialium a quibus tota latinorum

sufficient provided that the student be diligent.[50] It may be the case that such a modest basic goal explains the brevity and oversimplification of the notes in Cambridge, University Library, MS Ff. 6. 13, unless what was preserved is only a fragment or a draft of what was supposed to be a more extensive treatise.[51]

Be it as it may, Bacon's Hebrew Grammar and the passages on Hebrew in his other works all reveal a strong reliance on the Latin *ars grammatica* and a lack of references to the works of Jewish grammarians and their linguistic concepts. After all, Bacon himself complained that he did not possess either a Greek or Hebrew Bible, or a Hebrew dictionary he needed for the study of Jewish texts.[52] The use of Latin grammatical categories to describe Hebrew probably also had some deeper intellectual reasons. A passage in his Greek Grammar explains that Bacon was aware of a pedagogical need to use a familiar Latin system as a point of reference to describe other languages (Greek in that particular passage). After all, in the aforementioned paragraph of the *Compendium Studii Philosophiae,* Bacon described basic Hebrew knowledge as the familiarity with the "accidents of the parts of speech according to the manner of Donatus."[53] More importantly, as a grammarian conversant with the tradition of Priscian, Bacon reflected on the universality of grammar underlying all human languages and on the potential of the Latin grammar to capture this essential unity:

> When I desire to expound the Greek grammar for the use of the Latins, I find it necessary to compare it to the Latin grammar, either because I need to

sapientia translata est; cujusmodi sunt Graecum, Hebraeum, Arabicum, et Chaldaeum. Non tamen intelligo quid quilibet sciat has linguas sicut maternam in qua natus est, ut nos loquimur Anglicum, Gallicum, et Latinum; nec ut sciamus tantum de his linguis ut quilibet fiat interpres, et transferre possit in linguam maternam Latinam scientiam de linguis illis. Sed tertius gradus hic eligendus est, qui facillimus est habendi doctorem, scilicet ut sciamus de his quantum sufficit ad intelligendum quae requirit Latinitas in hac parte. Et vis hujus rei stat in hoc; ut homo sciat legere Graecum, et Hebraeum, et caetera. Et ut secundum formam Donati sciat accidentia partium orationis. Nam his notis, constructio et intellectus vocabulorum linguarum illarum, quantum latinis sufficit, de facili habentur per modos quos inferius assignabo. Stulti enim homines et imperiti, quum adiunt loqui de scientia linguarum, aestimant se obligari primo gradui et secundo, et ideo desperant, et contemnunt tertium gradum facillimum; quamvis si considerarent et diligentes essent a juventute, etiam post triginta annos possent pertingere ad omnes gradus dictos, et saltem ad secundem cum tertio. Nam tota difficultas consistit in primo gradu; ut nos qui talibus insistimus experimur."

50. Bacon, *Opus Tertium,* in *Opera quaedam hactenus inedita,* ed. Brewer, 65: "Sed certum est mihi quod infra tres dies ego quemcumque diligentem et confidentem docerem Hebraeum, ut sciret legere et intelligere quicquid sancti dicunt, et sapientes antiqui, in expositione sacri textus, et quicquid pertinent ad illius textus correctionem et expositionem . . ."

51. Olszowy-Schlanger, "The Knowledge and Practice of Hebrew Grammar."

52. Quoted in Bacon, *The Greek Grammar,* ed. Nolan and Hirsch, lix.

53. Quoted in Bacon, *The Greek Grammar,* ed. Nolan and Hirsch, lix.

> explain it in Latin, since the general public does not speak Greek, or because grammar is one and the same in substance, and only varies among languages by accident, or because the Latin grammar is derived in a special way from the Greek grammar, as testified by Priscian and taught by other grammarians.[54]

Bacon was therefore confident about the capacity of the Latin grammatical tradition to describe other languages. Thus, the apparent misunderstanding of the system of the Hebrew vowels and the attempt to reconstruct the declension of Hebrew nouns on the model of the Latin case system likely results from the reluctance to abandon the familiar grammatical framework of Latin and its rich theoretical tradition more than of a lack of Hebrew proficiency as such.

Christian Hebrew Grammar and Jewish Linguistic Traditions

Finding parallels between Hebrew and the familiar Latin grammatical rules can be a useful pedagogical approach. However, the structure of Semitic languages with their complex verbal system, the intricacies of the morphological derivation from the base that is conceptualized as an abstract consonantal "root," the lack of notation of the vowels or marking them as a secondary graphic system added above and below the consonants or the possessive and object pronouns attached as suffixes to nouns and verbs must have puzzled Christian grammarians trained in the Latin *trivium*. However, when Roger Bacon and many other scholars strove to force Hebrew into the "straitjacket" of Latin categories, others did venture to understand the Jewish linguistic approach on its own terms. Together with their study of the Bible and rabbinic commentaries in the original Hebrew, some scholars in medieval England, and especially those related to the aforementioned "Ramsey school," also turned to Hebrew grammar books by medieval Jewish lexicographers and grammarians. References to medieval Jewish tractates, glosses in Hebrew linguistic manuscripts left by Christian readers, various Latin annotations which reflect Jewish grammatical theory and last but not least the linguistic concepts and sources behind the Longleat House Grammar all indicate that at least some Christian individuals did approach the Hebrew language through its unfamiliar Jewish description.

54. Bacon, *The Greek Grammar*, ed. Nolan and Hirsch, 27: "Cupiens igitur exponere grammaticam grecam ad vtilitatem latinorum necesse est illam comparari ad grammaticam latinam, tum quia latine loquor vt in pluribus, sicut necesse est, cum linguam grecam nescit vulgus loqui, tum quia grammatica una et eadem est secundum substantiam in omnibus linguis, licet accidentaliter varietur, tum quia grammatica Latina quodam modo speciali a greca tracta est, testante Prisciano, et sicut auctores grammatice docent euidenter."

Jewish Grammar and Lexicography in Medieval England

At the time when Christian scholars in England began to study it, Hebrew had long possessed its own grammatical tradition. The "grammatization" of Hebrew goes back to the tenth century in the Muslim East.[55] Jewish scholars, such as Saʿadiah Gaon[56] and the Karaites: Yūsuf ibn Nūḥ or his disciple Abū al-Faraj Hārūn ibn al-Faraj, applied to Hebrew the theoretical concepts and practical categories devised by Arab grammarians, who were in turn inspired by Greek grammar and logic. They combined this new scientific approach with the Masorah, the text-critical description of the biblical language and its anomalies devised in the early Middle Ages, based on the oral transmission and liturgical recitation of the Bible.[57] The Oriental tradition of grammar soon reached the Muslim West.[58] In the tenth century, such Andalusian authors as Menaḥem ben Saruḳ and his opponent Dunash ibn Labrāṭ composed lexicographical works and grammatical pamphlets. The most salient feature of the early Spanish grammatical school and its Oriental precursor is the definition of the derivational base of the words, the "root," as composed of a varying number of consonants, ranging from one to four. This early approach was widely accepted by Jewish audiences in Northern Europe.

At the turn of the tenth and eleventh centuries in Muslim Spain, Abū Zakariyyā Yaḥyā ibn Daʾūd (Judah) Ḥayyūj (c. 945–1010) revised the concept of the morphological derivation of words. In his view, the actual conjugated forms result from changes at the level of an underlying derivational base. The derivational base of all Hebrew words is an abstract consonantal "root," which is not a

55. For an overview, see Judith Olszowy-Schlanger, "The Science of Language Among Medieval Jews," in *Science in Medieval Jewish Cultures*, ed. Gad Freudenthal (Cambridge, 2011), 359–424.

56. Aron Dotan, "De la Massora à la grammaire: Les débuts de la pensée grammaticale dans l'hébreu," *JA* 278 (1990): 13–30; Aron Dotan, *The Dawn of Hebrew Linguistics: The Book of Elegance of the Language of the Hebrews by Saadia Gaon* (Jerusalem, 1997) (Hebrew); Aron Dotan, "Saadia Gaon: A Master Linguist," in *Jewish Studies at the Turn of the Twentieth Century: Proceedings of the 6th European Association of Jewish Studies Congress, I: Biblical, Rabbinical and Medieval Studies, Toledo, July 1998* (Leiden, 1999), 26–30.

57. Rina Drory, *The Emergence of Jewish Arabic Literary Contacts at the Beginning of the Tenth Century* (Tel Aviv, 1988) (Hebrew); Aron Dotan, "The Origins of Hebrew Linguistics and the Exegetic Tradition," in *History of the Language Sciences: An International Handbook on the Evolution of the Study of Language from the Beginnings to the Present*, ed. Sylvain Auroux, E.F.K. Koerner, Hans-Josef Niederehe and Kees Versteegh (Berlin, 2000–2006), 1: 215–244; Aron Dotan, *The Awakening of Word Lore: From the Massora to the Beginnings of Hebrew Lexicography* (Jerusalem, 2005) (Hebrew).

58. Ilan Eldar, "The Andalusian School of Grammar: The First Period," *Peʿamim* 38 (1989), 21–33 (Hebrew).

form that actually occurs in the language. This "root" is composed of three consonants even if one or two consonants may drop out and become "invisible" in some conjugated forms. This structural uniformity of the derivational base and the definition of the transformation patterns during conjugation make the method of Ḥayyūj applicable to all verbs by analogy, which in turn makes it possible to conceive of the verb conjugation in terms of analogical model paradigms or constructions (*binyanim*).[59] The Spanish approach of Ḥayyūj and his followers has been the foundation of the study of Hebrew among the Jews in Europe until today and, since the Renaissance, also among the Christians.[60]

As for the French and English communities, their knowledge and interest in language are attested through the remarks of linguistic nature in various biblical and talmudic commentaries, as well as through independent linguistic works.[61] Although the towering scholar Rashi of Troyes (d. 1104) is not known to have written a linguistic treatise, his commentaries bear testimony to his keen interest in grammar and lexicography. They contain thousands of translations of Hebrew and Aramaic words into French and references to the early Hebrew Spanish grammarians, Menaḥem ben Saruḳ and Dunash ibn Labrāṭ.[62] Rashi used grammatical terminology akin to the masoretic tradition. His designations for "nouns" or "construct state" are found in the works of his followers, as well as in the Longleat House Grammar. The French school also elaborated a tradition of glossaries of the Bible, in which selected words and expressions, arranged according to their order of appearance in the text or, less often, in alphabetical order, are commented upon and translated into vernacular French dialects.[63]

59. Ilan Eldar, "Ḥayyūj's Grammatical Analysis," *Leshonenu* 54 (1990): 169–181; Ilan Eldar, "Hebrew Philology Between the East and Spain: The Concept of Derivation as a Case Study," *Journal of Semitic Studies* 43 (1998), 49–61.

60. Sophie Kessler-Mesguich, *Les études hébraïques en France de François Tissard à Richard Simon (1508–1680)* (Geneva, 2013); Sophie Kessler-Mesguich, "L'étude de l'hébreu et des autres langues orientales à l'époque de l'humanisme," in *History of the Language Sciences*, ed. Auroux, Koerner, Niederehe and Versteegh, 1: 673–680.

61. For an overview of Hebrew grammatical thought in Ashkenaz, see esp. Ilan Eldar, "The Grammatical Literature of Medieval Ashkenazi Jewry," in *Hebrew in Ashkenaz: A Language in Exile*, ed. Lewis Glinert (New York, 1993), 26–45; Ilan Eldar, "The Grammatical Literature of Medieval Ashkenazi Jewry," *Massorot* 5–6 (1991): 1–34 (Hebrew).

62. See Henry Englander, "Rashi's View on the Weak ʿayin-ʿayin and peh-nun Verbs: With Special Reference to the Views of Menaḥem b. Saruk and Dunash b. Labrat," *HUCA* 7 (1930): 399–437; Henry Englander, "Grammatical Elements and Terminology in Rashi's Biblical Commentaries," Part I: *HUCA* 11 (1936): 367–389, Part II: *HUCA* 12/13 (1937–1938): 505–521, Part III: *HUCA* 14 (1939): 387–429; Jonathan Kearney, *Rashi Linguist Despite Himself: A Study of the Linguistic Dimension of Rabbi Solomon Yishaqi's Commentary on Deuteronomy* (New York, 2010).

63. Nine more or less complete glossaries and numerous fragments, many found in European book bindings, are known today. For a list, see Raphael Levy, *Trésor de la langue*

Scholars north of the Alps and Pyrenees had access to the Oriental tradition of language and Masorah studies. One of the works included in an anthology in Oxford, Bodl., MS Or. 135, copied in the first half of the thirteenth century in Normandy or England (and glossed in Latin),[64] is a Hebrew reworking of the

des juifs français au moyen âge (Austin, 1964); Marc Kiwitt, "Les glossaires hébreu-français du XIIIe siècle et la culture juive en France du nord," in *Cultures et Lexikographies (sic!): Actes des "Troisièmes Journées Allemandes des Dictionnaires" en l'honneur d'Alain Rey* (Berlin, 2010), 113–125. See Mayer Lambert and Louis Brandin, *Glossaire hébreu-français du XIIIe siècle: Recueil de mots hébreux bibliques avec traduction française* (Paris, 1905); Menahem Banitt, "Fragments d'un glossaire judéo-français du moyen âge," *REJ* 120 (1961): 259–296; Menahem Banitt, "L'étude des glossaires bibliques des juifs de France au moyen âge: Méthode et application," in *Proceedings of the Israel Academy of Sciences and Humanities*, (Jerusalem, 1967), 2.10: 189–190; Menahem Banitt, *Le glossaire de Bâle* (Jerusalem, 1972); Menahem Banitt, *Le Glossaire de Leipzig* (Jerusalem, 1995–2005); Marc Kiwitt, *Les gloses françaises du glossaire biblique B.N. hébr. 301* (Heidelberg, 2010).

64. Oxford, Bodl., MS Or. 135 is an anthology of various works of linguistics and belles-lettres copied as a single codicological unit by a scribe named Samuel, as can be deduced from the fact that he decorated this name whenever it appeared in the text (fols. 33v, 62r and 99r). The manuscript can be dated to the thirteenth century: see Malachi Beit-Arié, "Manuscript Oxford, Bodl. Or. 135," *Tarbiz* 54 (1985): 629–634 (Hebrew). See also Malachi Beit-Arié, *Catalogue of the Hebrew Manuscripts in the Bodleian Library: Supplement of Addenda and Corrigenda to Vol. 1 (A. Neubauer's Catalogue)* (London, 1994), no. 1466; Eli Yassif, "Sefer ha-Maʿasim: Character, Origins and Influence of a Collection of Folktales from the Time of the Tosaphists," *Tarbiz* 53 (1984): 409–429, at 428 (Hebrew); Eli Yassif, "'Leisure' and 'Generosity': Theory and Practice in the Creation of Hebrew Narratives in the Late Middle Ages," *Kiryat Sefer* 62 (1990): 887–905 (Hebrew); Judith Olszowy-Schlanger, *Les manuscrits hébreux: Étude historique et paléographique* (Leuven and Paris, 2003), 33–34, no. 21.

The manuscript contains: (**fols. 1r–6r**) a note on pronunciation attributed in the manuscript to a certain Abraham ha-Bavli, but probably a Hebrew translation of the introductory sections of the *Kitāb jāmiʿ al-ʾalfāẓ*, a Hebrew-Arabic dictionary by the Karaite author David ben Abraham al-Fāsī; see Adolf Neubauer, "Abraham ha-Babli: Appendice à la notice sur la lexicographie hébraïque," *JA* (6e série) 2 (1863): 195–216. See Hartwig Hirschfeld, *Literary History of Hebrew Grammarians and Lexicographers Accompanied by Unpublished Texts* (London, 1926), 53; (**fols. 6r–10v and 232r–237v**) a list of homonyms from Moses ibn Ezra's *Sefer he-ʿAnak* or *Sefer ha-Tajnis* – a glossary of rhymed ends of words for the use of poets. Here it was translated into Old French written in Hebrew characters (**fols. 6r–9v and 232r–239v**); Adolf Neubauer, "Un vocabulaire hébraïco-français," *Romanische Studien* 1.2 (1872): 163–196; Eduard Boehmer, "De vocabulis Francogallicis Judaice transcriptis," *Romanische Studien* 1.2 (1872): 197–220; David S. Blondheim, "Le glossaire d'Oxford," *REJ* 57 (1909): 1–18; (**fols. 11r–230v**) Dictionary *Maḥberet he-ʿArukh* by Solomon ben Abraham ibn Parḥon, intercalated between the two parts of the glossary [Salomo Gottlieb Stern's edition, *Maḥberet he-ʿArukh, Salomonis ben Abrahami Parchon Aragonensis Lexicon Hebraicum* (Pressburg, 1844), is based on a different manuscript]; (**fols. 237v–255r**) *Alphabet of Ben Sira*; (**fols. 256r–290r**) *Mishlei Shuʿalim* (Fox Fables) by the twelfth-century Anglo-Norman author Berekhiah ben Natronai ha-Nakdan. On Berekhiah and his works, see esp. Tamás Visi, "Berechiah ben Naṭronai's Dodi ve-Nekdi and the Transfer of Scientific Knowledge from Latin to Hebrew in the Twelfth introductory sections on the pronunciation of the *Kitāb jāmiʿ al-ʾalfāẓ* (Comprehensive Book of Words) of a tenth-century Karaite lexicographer from Jerusalem, David ben Abraham al-Fāsī.[65] The abridgement of the *Hidāyat al-Qāriʾ* (Guide for the Reader) by yet another Karaite, Abū al-Faraj Hārūn, active in Jerusalem in the first half of the eleventh century,[66] was translated into Hebrew in Mainz in

---

Century," *Aleph* 14.2 (2014): 9–73; (**fols. 290v–291v and 300r–339v**) sixty-nine tales and fabliaux entitled *Maʿasim* (Tales); Rella Kushelevsky, *Tales in Context: Sefer ha-Maʿasim in Medieval Northern France* (Detroit, 2017); (**fols. 292r–300r**) Oriental tales known as *Mishlei Sendebar* intercalated between the *Maʿasim*; (**fols. 340r–346v**) *Divrei ha-yamim le-Mosheh Rabenu* (The Chronicles of Moses); (**fols. 346v–352r**) *Midrash ʿAseret ha-Dibrot* (Midrash on the Ten Commandments) [the version here differs from the version edited by Anat Shapira, *Midrash ʿAseret ha-Dibrot: Text, Sources and Commentary* (Jerusalem, 2005) (Hebrew)]; (**fols. 352r–356r**) *Midrash va-Yoshaʿ*; (**fols. 356r–358v**) *ʾIggrot shel Dibrot* (The Letters of the Ten Commandments); (**fols. 358v–361r**) *Otot ʿEser Milḥamot Melekh ha-Mashiaḥ* (The Signs of the Ten Wars of the Messiah); (**fols. 361r–363v**) a short account of the pilgrimage to the holy places in the land of Israel, followed by fantastic travel fables, by a certain Menaḥem ben Pereẓ ha-Ḥebroni. Oxford, Bodl., MS Or. 135 seems to be the only attested version of this travelogue. The text was edited and catalogued as a "letter" although nothing indicates its epistolary nature or even that it was a literary text of the epistolary genre. On the contrary, it is presented in the text as a report after the voyage took place. A.M. Luncz, *Hameamer: Letters of Travellers, Inscriptions on Graves, Testimonials, Rules, Memorials and Other Documents concerning the Middle Ages*, vol. 3 (Jerusalem, 1919), 36–46 (Hebrew). See S. Klein, "The Letter of Rabbi Menaḥem of Hebron," *Bulletin of the Jewish Palestine Exploration Society* 6 (1939): 19–30 (Hebrew); Elchanan Reiner, "'Oral versus written': The Shaping of Traditions of Holy Places in the Middle Ages," in *Ve-Zot le-Yehudah: Studies in the History of Eretz Israel presented to Yehuda ben Porat*, ed. Yehoshua Ben-Arieh and Elchanan Reiner (Jerusalem, 2003), 308–345 (Hebrew); Elchanan Reiner, "A Travelogue and Its Fate: The Lost Travel Account of Menahem Ha-Hebroni, 'The Knowledge of the Land,' and the Beginning of the Jewish Research on the Land of Israel," *Gilyon* 133–134 (2016): 33–46 (Hebrew).

65. Fols. 1r–6r. In the manuscript, this text is attributed to a certain Abraham ha-Bavli. Some scholars believed that Abraham was indeed a grammarian from Iraq. See Neubauer, "Abraham ha-Babli"; Hartwig Hirschfeld, *Literary History of Hebrew Grammarians and Lexicographers Accompanied by Unpublished Texts* (London, 1926), 53.

66. A Hebrew version of the *Hidāyat al-Qāriʾ*, preserved in Paris, BnF, MS hébreu 1221, copied in 1285–86, under the title *Sefer Ṭaʿamei ha-Mikraʾ*, claims that its author was Yehudah ibn Balʿam (active in Toledo in the eleventh century). It is with this attribution that the manuscript was printed in 1556 and 1565 in Paris by Jean Mercier, ספר טעמי המקרא. *Liber de accentibus scripturae autore R. Iuda filio Balaam*, at the printing house of Robert Estienne. Questioned by more recent scholars [see Giulio Busi, *Horayat ha-Qoreʾ: Una grammatica ebraica del secolo XI* (Frankfurt am Main and New York, 1984), 18–20; Ilan Eldar, "È davvero Yehudah ibn Balʿam l'autore della Hidāyat al-Qāriʾ?," *Henoch* 7 (1985): 301–324], the authorship of the original Arabic *Hidāyat al-Qāriʾ* was finally established by Ilan Eldar, based on new manuscript evidence: a colophon in Manchester, John Rylands Library, MS A 694 mentions explicitly Abū al-Faraj Hūrūn as the author; see Ilan Eldar, *The Art of the Correct Reading of the Bible* (Jerusalem, 1994), 40–42 (Hebrew). See Geoffrey Khan, *The*

the twelfth century as *Horayat ha-Ḳore'* and also circulated in Italy under the title of *Tokhen Ezra* or *Sefer Ṭa'amei ha-Miḳra'*.[67] These translations were the main source of *'Ein ha-Ḳore'* by Yeḳutiel ha-Kohen ben Judah and of *Darkhei ha-Niḳḳud ve-ha-Neginot* written around 1250 by a leading rabbi, Masorete and grammarian, member of a prominent London family, Moses ben Yom Tov (d. 1268).[68] As we shall see in Chapter Five, the work of Moses ben Yom Tov in particular had an impact on the Longleat House Grammar.

In the twelfth century, Northern-French rabbis developed their own grammatical methods and terminology. This French school is represented by two main authors, both Rashi's grandsons and pupils, Samuel ben Me'ir, known as Rashbam (c. 1080–after 1158), and his brother Jacob ben Me'ir, known as Rabbenu Tam (c. 1100–1171). In addition to his Bible commentaries and legal enactments, Rashbam authored a work entitled *Dayyḳot* (or *Dayyaḳut*) *le-R. Shemuel* (Grammatical Details of R. Samuel), which includes a grammar and a grammatical commentary on biblical words.[69] The part on grammar focuses on vocalization and verb morphology. In its approach to the Hebrew root, Rashbam took as deriva-

---

Tiberian Pronunciation Tradition of Biblical Hebrew: Including a Critical Edition and English Translation of the Sections on Consonants and Vowels in the Masoretic Treatise Hidāyat al-Qārī' 'Guide for the Reader' (Cambridge, 2020), 2: 1.

67. Eldar, *The Art of the Correct Reading*. For the edition and translation, see Khan, *The Tiberian Pronunciation Tradition*. For the Hebrew translations and adaptations in medieval Europe, see Busi, *Horayat ha-Qore'*. See Ilan Eldar, "Mukhtaṣar (an Abridgment) of Hidāyat al-Qārī': A Grammatical Treatise Discovered in the Genizah," in *Genizah Research after Ninety Years: The Case of Judaeo-Arabic*, ed. Joshua Blau and Stefan C. Reif (Cambridge, 1992), 67–73, at 71. On the influence of the Oriental tradition on the Ashkenazi grammatical tradition, see Olszowy-Schlanger, "The Science of Language," 393–394.

68. Moses ha-Naḳdan, *Tractatio de punctis et accentibus quae a Moyse Punctatore scripta dicitur*, ed. Samuel Löwinger (Budapest, 1929) (Hebrew). See David Kaufmann, "Three Centuries of the Genealogy of the Most Eminent Anglo-Jewish Family Before 1290," *JQR* 3 (1891): 550–566; Adolf Neubauer, "Analecta I – English Massorites," *JQR* 2 (1890): 322–333, at 325.

69. J.T. Stein, "The Grammar of R. Shemuel and His Grammatical Commentary on the Torah," in *Jahrbuch des Traditionstreuen Rabbinerverbandes in der Slowakei* (Trnava, 1923), 33–59 and i–vii (Hebrew); Samuel ben Me'ir, *Dayyaqut me-Rabbenu Shemuel [Ben Meir (Rashbam)]: Critical Edition with an Introduction and a Detailed Table of Contents*, ed. Ronela Merdler (Jerusalem, 1999) (Hebrew). See Eldar, "The Grammatical Literature," *Massorot*, 6, n16. The *Dayyḳot* is preserved in a unique, relatively late, manuscript (Berlin, Deutsche Staatsbibliothek zu Berlin, MS Or. Qu. 648, dated from 1470), which also contains a masoretic poem by Rabbenu Tam and fragments of the dictionary of Solomon ibn Parḥon; see Moritz Steinschneider, *Verzeichnis der hebräische Handschriften der Königlichen Bibliothek zu Berlin* (Berlin, 1878–1897), no. 118. On the life of Moses ben Yom Tov ha-Naḳdan, or Moses of Milk Street in London, see esp. Joe and Caroline Hillaby, *The Palgrave Dictionary of Medieval Anglo-Jewish History* (Basingstoke, 2013), 253–255.

tional base the 3rd person of the masculine perfect *Ḳal* (e.g., כָּתַב), and, just like Judah Ḥayyūj in Spain, considered that almost all Hebrew verbs are composed of three consonants. Rashbam identified verbs in which the tri-consonantal structure is not always apparent in the attested forms. He called these verbs חטופים, lit. "taken away, snatched," (which in Ḥayyūj's system correspond to the "weak verbs" *peh-yod, peh-nun* and *lamed-heh*) and remarked that certain consonants of these verbs disappear in the conjugation (נחטפים, "are taken, seized, snatched"). The only verbs he described as "bi-consonantal" (הפעלים השניים) are the *ʿayin-vav/yod* verbs (verbs whose second radical is a *vav* or a *yod*) because they have only two consonants in the 3rd person sg. masc. perfect *Ḳal* (e.g., קָם). It seems that Rashbam had elaborated the theory of the "weak verbs" without relying on Ḥayyūj's works.[70]

The second French grammarian is Rashbam's younger brother, the leading Tosafist and Talmudist, Jacob ben Meʾir (Rabbenu Tam) of Ramerupt.[71] Rabbenu Tam's only known grammatical work, *Hakhraʿot* (Decisions), is a set of discussions on selected difficulties of biblical grammar which were a point of contention between the two leading tenth-century Spanish grammarians, Menaḥem ben Saruḳ and Dunash ibn Labrāṭ. Rabbenu Tam analysed the disputed passages and argued in favour of one opinion, usually but not always that of Menaḥem ben Saruḳ. He also reported the views of Rashi in his observation on language scattered through his commentaries and proposed solutions of his own. Rashi's remarks included short theoretical comments, such as the division of verbs into groups (*gezerot*).[72] Some conclusions of the *Hakhraʿot* were criticized by Joseph Kimhi (c. 1111–1170), Rabbenu Tam's contemporary and the proponent of the Spanish school, in his *Sefer ha-Galui*, written c. 1165, after Kimhi left his native Andalusia for Narbonne in the wake of the Almohads' persecutions.[73] The written polemics between Joseph Kimhi and the members of the Northern-French school show the easy flow of writings and ideas between the communities of the South and the North.

Grammar, lexicography and Masorah were particularly popular in medieval England. The professional title ha-naḳdan, "the punctator, Masorete," appears

70. Eldar, "The Grammatical Literature," *Massorot*, 8.

71. Henry Englander, "Rabbenu Jacob ben Meir Tam as Grammarian," *HUCA* 15 (1940): 485–495.

72. Dunash ibn Labrāṭ, *Sefer Teshuvot Dunash ben Labrat: ʿIm Hakhraʿot Rebbenu Yaʿakov Tam*, ed. Herschell Filipowski, Leopold Dukes and Raphael Kircheim (London and Edinburgh, 1855). For the description of the approach of Rabbenu Tam and its comparison with Rashbam's grammar, see Eldar, "The Grammatical Literature," *Massorot*, 10. Englander, "Rabbenu Jacob ben Meir Tam," 485, considered that Rabbenu Tam followed closely Menaḥem ben Saruḳ's approach to the Hebrew root, and argued that Rabbenu Tam did not propose the tri-letter roots for the weak verbs. Englander's arguments, based on an incorrect interpretation of the term נחטף, are not convincing.

73. Joseph Kimhi, *Sefer ha-Galui*, ed. H.J. Matthews (Berlin, 1887).

as the nickname of several individuals. Unsurprisingly, like many other aspects of Jewish culture, the early grammatical works in England initially followed the Northern-French lead. Thus, the grammatical debates of Rabbenu Tam with Joseph Kimhi were studied with attention across the English Channel. Benjamin, a disciple of Rabbenu Tam, rose in defense of his teacher's views. This Benjamin was identified by Joseph Jacobs with Magister Benjamin of Cambridge mentioned in the Pipe Rolls of the fifth year of King John (1204) and with a certain Benjamin quoted by Berekhiah ben Natronai ha-Naḳdan in his commentary on Job preserved in a manuscript of Anglo-Norman origin (Cambridge, University Library, MS Dd. 8. 53).[74] His rejoinder in the form of short comments on specific linguistic and lexicographical points is preserved in Vatican City, Biblioteca Apostolica Vaticana, MS Vat. ebr. 402.[75] In addition to the *Hakhraʿot* (fols. 2r–23r) and the *Sefer ha-Galui* (fols. 24v–79v) with Benjamin's comments, this thirteenth-century anthology of poetry and masoretic and linguistic texts includes a Hebrew version of the aforementioned Masoretic Guide for the Reader (*Horayat ha-Ḳoreʾ*) (fols. 80r–89v). As we shall see, the phonetic description of the Hebrew vowels in the *Horayat ha-Ḳoreʾ* is reflected in the short tractate on Hebrew vowels in the Longleat House Grammar. The presence in Vatican City, Biblioteca Apostolica Vaticana, MS Vat. ebr. 402 of the elegy on the death of Menaḥem ben Pereẓ Vardimas, a scholar from Rouen (fol. 24r)[76] whose offspring seem to have settled in England,[77] and of the poems of Meʾir ben Elijah of Norwich

74. According to this commentary, Benjamin was Berekhiah's uncle. For the manuscript and the commentary on Job, see Berekhiah ben Natronai, *A Commentary on the Book of Job from a Hebrew Manuscript in the University Library, Cambridge*, ed. William Aldis Wright (London, 1905); Samuel Poznański, "Un commentaire sur Job de la France septentrionale," *REJ* 32 (1906): 51–70 and 198–214; Banitt, *Le glossaire de Leipzig*, 4: Introduction, 46–47 and 48–52; Visi, "Berechiah ben Natronai ha-Naqdan's Dodi ve-Neḳdi," 18–19.

75. Benjamin Richler, *Hebrew Manuscripts in the Vatican Library* (Vatican City, 2008), 348–350. This manuscript, including Benjamin's comments, was used for the edition of *Sefer ha-Galui* by Mathews.

76. Adolf Neubauer, "Menahem Vardimas," *REJ* 17 (1888): 151–154. Reprinted and discussed by Norman Golb, *The History of the Jews in Rouen in the Middle Ages* (Tel Aviv, 1976), 97–98 (Hebrew) and, with a French translation, in his *Les juifs de Rouen au moyen âge: Portrait d'une culture oubliée* (Mont Saint-Aignan, 1985), 298–299.

77. In a deed of sale of a property drawn up in Nottingham, on 28 June 1257, London, Westminster Abbey Muniments 6799, the buyer is Jacob ben Menaḥem ha-Vardimasi, most probably the son of the Tosafist of Rouen, Menaḥem Vardimas ben Pereẓ ben Menaḥem. For the charter, see Myer David Davis, *Hebrew Deeds of English Jews before 1290* (London, 1888), no. 116; Judith Olszowy-Schlanger, *Hebrew and Hebrew-Latin Documents from Medieval England: A Diplomatic and Palaeographical Study* (Turnhout, 2015), 1: no. 68. For Menaḥem Vardimas of Rouen, see Norman Golb, *The Jews in Medieval Normandy: A Social and Intellectual History* (Cambridge, 1998), 387–395.

(fols. 114v–117r),[78] together with the manuscript's palaeographical features, suggest that it was copied in an Anglo-Norman setting. In this manuscript, the comments of Benjamin of Cambridge are intercalated into the text of the *Sefer ha-Galui* and introduced by ואני בנימן אומר, "And I, Benjamin, say." The glosses of Benjamin show a good grasp of grammar and of diverging opinions of Hebrew scholars on problematic issues of the biblical text. A salient feature of Benjamin's approach is his reluctance to accept some of the key methods of the Spanish school. He notably shows a marked hostility towards the use of Arabic language and Arabic science to understand difficult passages of the Hebrew Bible. Whereas comparison between Hebrew, Aramaic and Arabic was the point of honour for the Spanish school's linguistic approach,[79] Benjamin questioned its utility and advocated the contextual understanding of the terms and forms as they occur within the Hebrew Bible. Thus, for example, he rejected Joseph Kimhi's interpretation of the hapax expression יְפֵה נוֹף found in Psalm 48:3. In the relevant entry in the *Sefer ha-Galui*,[80] Kimhi disagreed with the derivation of this word from עָנָף, "tree branch," proposed by Dunash ibn Labrāṭ. He preferred the interpretation by Menaḥem ben Saruḳ, which was also accepted by Rabbenu Tam, and which compared נוֹף with הַנָּפֶת, "region, country" (Joshua 17:11).[81] Joseph Kimhi considered, however, that Menaḥem's and Rabbenu Tam's understanding was incomplete and offered his own interpretation based on the theory of seven climes – seven parallel latitudinal bands of the inhabited world whose environmental conditions (temperature, humidity, length of the day and night) are responsible for different physical, mental and social characteristics of their human inhabitants. The Arab geographers, mathematicians and astronomers and their Jewish followers inherited this description of the *oikumene* from the Greek tradition transmitted by Ptolemy's *Almagest*.[82] Kimhi followed the Arab authors, and chief among them al-Kindi,

78. Edited by A. Berliner, Meʾir ben Elijah of Norwich, *Haruzim: Hebräische Poesien des Meir ben Elia aus Norwich*, ed. Abraham Berliner (London, 1887), and again by A.M. Habermann, together with a piyut by Meir ben Elijah of Norwich, in the Hebrew section of Vivian David Lipman, *The Jews of Medieval Norwich* (London, 1967), 1–45. See Susan Einbinder, "Meir b. Elijah of Norwich: Persecution and Poetry Among Medieval English Jews," *Journal of Medieval History* 26 (2000): 145–162.

79. On the "comparative linguistics" in medieval Hebrew grammatical tradition, see Aharon Maman, *Comparative Semitic Philology in the Middle Ages from Saʿadiah Gaon to Ibn Barūn* (Leiden and Boston, 2004).

80. Vatican City, Biblioteca Apostolica Vaticana, MS Vat. ebr. 402, fol. 31v; Joseph Kimhi, *Sefer ha-Galui*, ed. Mathews, 24–25.

81. Menaḥem ben Saruḳ is quoted by Rashi in his commentary on Psalm 48:3, together with the interpretation of Dunash and bRosh ha-Shanah 26a (deriving נוף from ננפי, "a bride", from Greek). Rashi translates הנפת in Joshua 17:11 as קונטריאה, "*contrée*," "region," in Old French.

82. Marina Tolmacheva, "Ptolemaic Influence on Medieval Arab Geography," in *Discovering New Worlds: Essays on Medieval Exploration and Imagination*, ed. Scott D.

when he linked this classical division into seven climes with the humoral pathology and argued that the climes have such an influence on their inhabitants' constitution that moving from one clime to another can prove dangerous for one's health. The exception is the Land of Israel and Jerusalem: moving into this geographical zone can only be beneficial:

> I said: Know that the Creator divided his world into seven parts called in Arab sciences *ʾaqālim* and by Christian scholars "climes." The sages of the Hebrew language call them seven נופות, "regions." It is said that the air is different in every clime. When a man leaves his native clime and enters another, if he was healthy, he will become ill, and if he has been ill, his illness will become even worse because of the change of the air. This is not so with the land of Israel and Jerusalem. If a sick man enters it from another clime, he will recover, and if he had been healthy, his health will further improve. This is why the verse says: "the beautiful clime is the joy of all the earth" (Psalm 48:3) because there is joy there for all people coming hither from different climes.[83]

Joseph Kimhi's interpretation of the word נוף as "clime" is indicative of the Provençal Jewish adoption of Arabic scientific discourse. It remains in the same semantic field as Menaḥem ben Saruḳ's understanding as "region" (Rashi, Psalm 48:3, "*contrée*"), but adds to it a scientific dimension: not just a geographical "region" or "country" but a "clime" with its scientific implications as a possible Hebrew translation of the Arabic concept. Indeed, one of the challenges for medieval Jewish transmitters of the Arabic sciences was how to translate scientific terms into Hebrew. "Clime," Arabic *ʾiqlim* derived from Greek κλίμα, "inclination" (of the sunrays in a specific zone), was translated into Hebrew in many ways: through the loan word אקלים, for example by Abraham bar Ḥiyya, or by the term גבול, lit. "border, limit," by Abraham ibn Ezra.[84] In his *ʾIggeret ha-Shabbat* (The Letter of the Sabbath) written in London in 1158, this remarkable Andalusian polymath described England, unflatteringly, as situated in the seventh clime – the most remote from the optimal temperate zone.[85] Joseph Kimhi's interpretation

---

Westrem (New York, 1991), 125–151; J.T. Olsson, "The World in Arab Eyes: A Reassessment of the Climes in Medieval Islamic Scholarship," *Bulletin of the School of Oriental and African Studies* 77 (2014): 487–508; Resianne Fontaine, "Between Scorching Heat and Freezing Cold: Medieval Jewish Authors on the Inhabited and Uninhabited Parts of the Earth," *Arabic Sciences and Philosophy* 10 (2000): 101–137, at 103.

83. Vatican City, Biblioteca Apostolica Vaticana, MS Vat. ebr. 402, fol. 31v; Joseph Kimhi, *Sefer ha-Galui*, ed. Mathews, 124.

84. Shlomo Sela, *Abraham ibn Ezra and the Rise of Medieval Hebrew Science* (Leiden and Boston, 2003), 111.

85. Abraham ibn Ezra, "ʾIggeret ha-Shabbat," ed. M. Friedlander, *Transactions of the Jewish Historical Society of England* 2 (1894–1895): 61–75.

in the *Sefer ha-Galui* is the earliest attestation of the use of נוף in the sense of "clime."[86]

Benjamin of Cambridge reacted to this meridional learning with an outright rejection of this and any other interpretation taken out of its biblical context and based on Arabic:

> And I, Benjamin, wonder why the Reader (= Joseph Kimhi) needs to explain most words via his Arabic language or the language of the Mishnah, as in the passage on the Masters of the Assemblies (יכרסמנה bḤagigah 3b)? What do we need them for if we can find the proof in the Bible itself? The meaning is like the explanation of R. Samuel (=Rashbam): נוף means "height," it is a noun (*shem davar*) derived from תנופה, "lifting" and הנפה, "hoisting" [...]. Thus, the interpretation of יפה נוף is "of beautiful height" (יפה גובה).[87]

Similarly, in the entry on בצלם, Benjamin passionately refuses Joseph Kimhi's interpretation of "darkness" based on Arabic *ḍilm*: "as I, Benjamin, have already said, all the Reader's (= Kimhi's) interpretations derived from his Arabic are not pleasing and will never uplift one's heart." When Kimhi discusses מן הוא in the episode of the manna in Exodus 16:15 and criticizes Dunash for comparing it with Arabic *man*, "who," because *man*, "who," refers to people whereas the context requires "what," Benjamin exclaims insultingly that "the Reader's (= Kimhi's) response to Dunash is vain and empty and of no avail because who would now go to Egypt to check that *man* in the language of the Egyptians is really 'who' and applies only to beings endowed with intellect and not 'what?'" Benjamin's repetitive use of the possessive pronoun referring to Kimhi, "*his* Arabic language," (לשון ערבי שלו), is meant to pour even stronger scorn and convey a sense of distance and lack of solidarity with this "foreign" interpretation. Benjamin's almost fundamentalist attachment to the language of the Bible clashes with the superiority of Arabic and of the Andalusian *adab* proclaimed by the Spanish Jews who settled in Provence. Joseph Kimhi's contemporary Judah ibn Tibbon, who like him fled from the Almohads, wrote in the preface to his translation of Baḥya ibn Paḳuda's *Sefer Torat Ḥovot ha-Levavot* (The Duties of the Heart):

> Every matter is better expressed in Arabic than in Hebrew because the only Hebrew that has come down to us is what is found in the books of the Bible and that is not enough for a speaker.[88]

86. Eliezer Ben-Yehuda, *Thesaurus totius Hebraitatis et veteris et recentioris (Milon ha-Lashon ha-ʿIvrit)* (Berlin and Jerusalem, 1908–1959), 7: 3582.

87. Vatican City, Biblioteca Apostolica Vaticana, MS Vat. ebr. 402, fol. 31v; Joseph Kimhi, *Sefer ha-Galui*, ed. Mathews, 123.

88. Baḥya ibn Paḳuda, *Sefer Torat Ḥovot ha-Levavot* (The Duties of the Heart), ed. Joseph Kafih (repr. New York, 1984), 8 (Hebrew).

As hostile as the comments of Benjamin of Cambridge are, they are perfect proof that in twelfth-century England Jewish scholars were familiar with the Hebrew grammatical approaches rooted in the learning of the Arabs, as developed in the Iberian Peninsula and propagated north of the Pyrenees by nostalgic Andalusian émigrés.

For Benjamin of Cambridge, the pride of the Andalusian tradition, its closeness to Arabic, was clearly unwelcome, but the hostility towards the grammatical and scientific approaches from Iberia was not general. After all, Abraham ibn Ezra spent the last years of his life in Rouen and London, and although his own impressions of the North were not always flattering, his works were very well received among the Norman and English Jews. Ibn Ezra's linguistic comments in particular were included in the works written in the Anglo-Norman territories. He is quoted extensively in the aforementioned commentary on Job by Berekhiah ha-Naḳdan (Cambridge, University Library, MS Dd. 8. 53) and in the Hebrew dictionary *Sefer ha-Shoham* (The Onyx Book) written in England around 1260. The Hebrew-Norman French Bible glossary, composed at the end of the thirteenth century and preserved in Leipzig, Universitätsbibliothek, MS Vollers 1099, refers to Abraham ibn Ezra dozens of times and shows how well his teachings were integrated into the Jewish intellectual landscape of the North.[89] Copies of the biblical dictionary *Maḥberet he-ʿArukh*, a Hebrew rewriting of the Arabic dictionary of Jonah ibn Janāḥ, written in Salerno in 1161 by another Spanish émigré, Solomon ibn Parḥon, a disciple of Judah ha-Levi and of Abraham ibn Ezra,[90] circulated among Northern-French and English Jews. The *Maḥberet he-ʿArukh* was notably copied in the aforementioned Oxford, Bodl, MS Or. 135 and in another Northern French anthology, Oxford, Bodl., MS Oppenheim 625.[91] Solomon ibn Parḥon was cited by the leading rabbi and Masorete from London, Moses ben

89. Bannit, *Le glossaire de Leipzig*, 4: Introduction, 414–415.

90. Salomon ben Abraham ibn Parḥon, *Mahberet he-ʿArukh*, ed. Stern. See Wilhelm Bacher, "Salomon Ibn Parhon's hebräisches Wörterbuch: Ein Beitrag zur Geschichte der hebräischen Sprachwissenschaft und der Bibelexegese" (Part I), *Zeitschrift die Alttestamentliche Wissenschaft* 10 (1890): 120–156; Wilhelm Bacher, "Aus Salomon Ibn Parchon's Machberet," *Zeitschrift für hebräische Bibliographie* (1896): 57–61. This work is for a large part a Hebrew adaptation of Ḥayyūj and ibn Janāḥ. It contains, however, many original interpretations. It was written to supersede the two main linguistic sources used by Italian Jews: the *Maḥberet* of Menaḥem ben Saruḳ and the Talmudic lexicon *he-ʿArukh* of Nathan ben Yeḥiel of Rome, and it bears an evocative title of *Maḥberet he-ʿArukh*. While proposing a new approach and structuring his dictionary according to the triliteral roots (with separate lists of four- and more lettered roots at the end of each alphabetical chapter), Ibn Parḥon addressed the ideas of Menaḥem ben Saruḳ and Nathan ben Yeḥiel, and extensively used rabbinic sources in his explanation of biblical roots.

91. Several entries of the *Maḥberet he-ʿArukh* in Oxford, Bodl., MS Or. 135 were annotated by a Latin hand of thirteenth-century England.

Yom Tov, nick-named ha-Naḳdan, in his *Darkhei ha-Niḳḳud ve-ha-Neginot* (Ways of the Vocalization and Cantillation), written c. 1250.[92] Moses of London quoted other Iberian and Provençal authors, such as Menaḥem ben Saruḳ, Dunash ibn Labrāṭ, Judah Ḥayyūj, Jonah ibn Janāḥ and Joseph Kimhi, alongside compositions by Ashkenazi scholars and exegetes, Rashi, Rashbam and Moses Roti (a Masorete whose work is not preserved[93]). He also integrated the teachings of the *Horayat ha-Ḳore*ʾ also known as *Sefer Ṭaʿamei ha-Miḳra*ʾ (The Book of the Biblical Cantillation), a Hebrew translation of the *Hidāyat al-Qāriʾ* (The Guide of the Reader). Concerned primarily with the tradition of vocalizing and liturgical performance of the Bible, the *Darkhei ha-Niḳḳud ve-ha-Neginot* includes a fair number of discussions on grammatical matters. Far from rejecting the methods of the Spanish school, Moses of London's verb morphology follows the system of Ḥayyūj. Indeed, according to his disciple, Moses ben Isaac ha-Nessiʾah, Moses ben Yom Tov was the first grammarian of Northern Europe to accept Ḥayyūj's system. Moses ben Yom Tov of London was also credited with detailed comments on Joseph Kimhi's grammar of biblical Hebrew, the *Sefer Zikkaron*, comments transmitted in two extant manuscripts.[94]

The linguistic tradition from al-Andalus left a particularly strong mark on the most accomplished work on the Hebrew language written in medieval England: the comprehensive biblical dictionary titled *Sefer ha-Shoham* (The Onyx Book) by Moses ben Isaac ha-Nessiʾah. Written c. 1260 most probably in London, this work is preserved in two manuscripts, St Petersburg, National Library of Russia, MS Firkovicz Evr II A 34 and Oxford, Bodl., MS Oppenheim 152.[95] This grammatical and lexicographical compendium opens with an overview of Hebrew grammar; it contains a detailed description of the consonants according to their phonetics and their function, as well as a section on the role of grammar in biblical interpretation. The main part of the work is organized as a dictionary subdivided into sections according to the three parts of speech (verb, noun and preposition). It follows an original and unusual arrangement, combining alphabetical order with a grammatical classification of the words. The entries on verbs of the

92. Moses ha-Naḳdan, *Tractatio de punctis*, ed. Löwinger. See Aron Dotan, "Moses ben Yom Tov," in *Encyclopaedia Judaica* (Jerusalem, 1971), 12: cols. 427–428.

93. See Michel Wilensky, "R. Moshe al-Roṭi (אלרוטי)," *HUCA* 11 (1936): 647–649.

94. Wilhelm Bacher, "Moïse ha-Nakdan, glossateur de la grammaire de Joseph Kimchi," *REJ* 12 (1886): 73–79.

95. Beit-Arié, *Supplement*, no. 1484. A large part of the first section (on verbs) of the dictionary was edited twice: by George Wolseley Collins, Moses ben Isaac ha-Nessiʾah, *A Grammar and Lexicon of the Hebrew Language entitled Sefer Hassoham* (London, 1882), from St Petersburg, National Library of Russia, MS Firkovitch Evr II A 34, and again by Benjamin Klar, Moses ben Isaac ha-Nessiʾah, *The Sefer ha-Shoham* (The Onyx Book) (London, 1947) (Hebrew), collated with the manuscript, Oxford, Bodl., MS Oppenheim 152.

Sefer ha-Shoham are arranged alphabetically, according to the roots, and according to the derivational structures (*binyanim*) in which they are actually attested in the biblical text. Following the Spanish approach, Moses ben Isaac distinguishes eight *binyanim*: *Pa'al, Nif'al, Pi'el, Pu'al, Hif'il, Huf'al, Hitpa'el* and *Meruba'* (for the verbs containing four radical consonants). The different types of weak roots are also considered separately. The nouns section is divided into groups according to the *mishkalim* (noun patterns), and alphabetically within these groups. The section on the prepositions is also arranged as an alphabetic dictionary. The last section of the *Sefer ha-Shoham* is devoted to the vowels and biblical accents. The Hebrew part is followed by an appendix containing a dictionary of biblical Aramaic. While some of Moses ben Isaac's terminology echoes that of the French scholars Rashbam and Rabbenu Tam (for example, the weak verbs are called נחטפים), the structure of the *Sefer ha-Shoham*, and especially the listing according to the nominal formations, follows the *Sefer Mikhlol* (The All-Encompassing Book), a grammar by David Kimhi (c. 1160–c. 1235), the younger son of Joseph.[96]

The *Sefer ha-Shoham* is clearly one of the most comprehensive and important medieval descriptions of the Hebrew language. It offers an original structure and in-depth analysis of the linguistic phenomena and draws from an impressive array of scholars. Moses ben Isaac ha-Nessi'ah was of course familiar with French commentators and grammarians such as Rashi, Joseph Kara, Eliezer of Beaugency, Rashbam, Rabbenu Tam, Moses Roti, as well as the scholars from the Anglo-Norman area, such as Berekhiah ha-Naḳdan and his teacher Moses ben Yom Tov of London. He also mentioned a certain Jacob of Tchernichov, a Jew from Russia, and a Christian convert to Judaism, Yoḥannan, whom he described as an excellent grammarian.[97] The St Petersburg manuscript also contains a large number of glosses introduced by the scribe, Aharon, who incorporated grammatical interpretations of an eminent physician, Talmudist and exegete, Eliyahu Menaḥem son of Moses ben Yom Tov and Moses ben Isaac's fellow pupil.[98] Like most North-French authors, Moses ben Isaac often used vernacular translations in his native Anglo-Norman French to better convey the meanings of the biblical words. But the main source of the structure and terminology of the *Sefer ha-Shoham* is the Iberian school. The dictionary refers to such grammarians and lexicographers as Menaḥem ben Saruḳ, Judah Ḥayyūj, Abraham ibn Ezra, Solomon ibn Parḥon, Solomon ibn Gabirol, Joseph Kimhi and his two sons, Moses and David, as well

96. David Kimhi, *Sefer Mikhlol*, ed. Isaac Rittenberg (Lyck, 1842).

97. See Cecil Roth, "Introduction," in *The Sefer ha-Shoham*, ed. Klar, viii.

98. Judith Olszowy-Schlanger, "Sefer ha-Shoham ('Le Livre d'Onyx'): Dictionnaire de l'hébreu biblique de Moïse ben Isaac ben ha-Nessiya (Angleterre, vers 1260)," in *En Mémoire de Sophie Kessler-Mesguich*, ed. Jean Baumgarten, José Costa, Jean-Patrick Guillaume and Judith Kogel (Paris, 2012), 183–198.

as two grammarians whose works are not preserved, Isaac ha-Levi[99] and Abraham ben Ḳamniel[100] And finally to the *Sefer ha-Hassagah* – a Hebrew translation by ʿOvadiah ha-Sefaradi of the *Kitāb al-mustalḥaq* of Jonah ibn Janāḥ. The main lexicographical source of the *Sepher ha-Shoham* was undoubtedly the *Sefer Shorashim*[101] of David Kimhi, whereas David Kimhi's grammar, *Sefer Mikhlol*, provided the model for the structure of the dictionary. Moses ben Isaac probably did not know Arabic but he explained several Hebrew words through Arabic.[102] He was acquainted with the works of the Spanish grammarians writing in Arabic through the books of Ibn Parḥon and Kimhi, but his *Sefer ha-Shoham* constitutes the most remarkable Hebrew adaptation of the grammatical tradition of the Arabic speaking Iberian Jews in England. In addition to his mature *Sefer ha-Shoham*, Moses ben Isaac ha-Nessi'ah, by his own account, wrote a Hebrew grammar in his youth called *Leshon Limmudim*, but it is not preserved.

This brief survey reveals that the study of Hebrew lexicography and grammar was vibrant and popular among English Jews in the late twelfth and thirteenth centuries. In addition to their adherence to the North-French school, the English grammarians also had an excellent knowledge of the Hebrew linguistic literature from Arabic-speaking Iberia which they were able to access through the Hebrew adaptations, and especially via the works of Solomon ibn Parḥon and Joseph and David Kimhi. The Longleat House Grammar was created within this context of the syncretic linguistic approach elaborated by thirteenth-century English grammarians and Masoretes who drew inspiration from both the French and the Iberian schools of Hebrew grammar.

English Christian Scholars and Jewish Linguistic Works

Jewish linguistic works of various origins were indeed a part of the Jewish readers' "bookshelf" in twelfth- and thirteenth-century England. However, while Roger Bacon reported that Jews possessed grammars and dictionaries in abundance, it is still likely that such books were less popular among the Jews than the bibles or prayer books. Any statistical extrapolation from the numbers of medieval codices

99. See Joseph Kimhi, *Sefer Zikkaron/Sefer Sikkaron: Grammatik der hebräischen Sprache von R. Joseph Kimchi*, ed. Wilhelm Bacher (Berlin, 1888), 3 and xiii n23, on the author's possible identity.

100. See Joseph Kimhi, *Sefer Zikkaron/Sefer Sikkaron*, ed. Bacher, xiii n27.

101. David Kimhi, *Sefer ha-Shorashim: Radicum Liber sive Hebraeum Bibliorum Lexicon cum animadversionibus Eliae Levitae*, ed. Fürchtegoff Lebrecht and Johann Heinrich Raphael Biesenthal (Berlin, 1847).

102. For example, Oxford, Bodl., MS Oppenheim 152, fols. 71r, 72v, 73r, 74r and 81v.

still in existence is, of course, likely to be misleading but it is the case that, all in all, only 2% or less of the extant medieval Hebrew manuscripts concern grammar and lexicography. It must have been even more difficult for a Christian Hebraist to get hold of a copy of a dictionary or grammar than of a Hebrew Bible codex.

It is known, however, that a few linguistic manuscripts did find their way into Christian ownership in the Middle Ages. Ralph Niger in his *Philippicus* praised a Jewish convert, Philip, thanks to whose assistance he was able to use Jewish sources when updating the patristic etymological lexicon *De Interpretationibus nominum hebreorum.* He mentioned in particular that Philip was his *magister et interpres,* "teacher and translator (informer)" when reading the "*Machuere*" and "*ʿAruch.*"[103] These two titles may refer respectively to the two biblical dictionaries, the *Maḥberet* of Menaḥem ben Saruḳ and the *Maḥberet he-ʿArukh* of Solomon ibn Parḥon (rather than, as suggested by Raphael Loewe, to the *Sefer he-ʿArukh,* the talmudic dictionary of Nathan ben Yeḥiel of Rome).

The *Maḥberet he-ʿArukh* of Solomon ibn Parḥon had some impact on Christian Hebraists in the thirteenth century. As we saw, the anthology of belles-lettres and linguistics in Oxford, Bodl., MS Or. 135 includes Ibn Parḥon's dictionary together with two other works on language, a note on Hebrew pronunciation and Masorah excerpted and translated from the dictionary of David ben Abraham al-Fāsī, and a dictionary of the rhymes by Moses ibn Ezra, *Sefer Tajnis.* The *Sefer Tajnis* and *Maḥberet he-ʿArukh* are annotated by at least three different Christian hands. The first four folios of the *Sefer Tajnis* contain a list of words in alphabetical order. Their Latin notes consist only of the running titles and the names of the Hebrew consonants at the beginning of each alphabetical section. The copy of the *Sefer Tajnis* continues from fol. 232r. Here, the alphabetical lists of Moses ibn Ezra are written by the same Hebrew hand, but in this second part, they are accompanied by a translation in Old French written in Hebrew characters.[104] A Latin scholar, different from the writer of the titles in part one, translated the French entries into Latin.

The copy of the *Maḥberet he-ʿArukh,* inserted between the two parts of the *Sefer Tajnis* in Oxford, Bodl., MS Or. 135 contains thirteen marginal annotations in Latin. Most of the glosses are concerned with "natural sciences": astronomy, zodiac and planets (fols. 55v, 116v, 130v, 135v), natural phenomena such as thunder (fols. 57r, 166v), hot springs (fol. 64r) and the human body (fol. 61r). Only one

103. Flahiff, "Ralph Niger," 120–121. Lincoln, Cathedral Library, MS 15, fol. 59v: "in lectionem Machuere et Aruch magister et interpres meus fuit." See Saltman, "Supplementary Notes," 109.

104. Neubauer, "Un vocabulaire hébraïco-français"; Boehmer, "De vocabulis Francogallicis Judaice transcriptis."

gloss bears on theological issues (fol. 132r: "diuersi modi apparitionis domini," "different ways of the apparition of the Lord"), and another refers to a specific religious custom of the Jews, the phylacteries (fol. 93r). The hand of the glosses in Ibn Parḥon's dictionary is different from the two Latin scribes who annotated the *Sefer Tajnis*. None of the Latin glossators of Oxford, Bodl., MS Or. 135 is to be identified with the owners who left their ex-libris marks in the volume: John Grandisson (1328–1369), bishop of Exeter and famous bibliophile (ex-libris on fols. 1r and 363v: "Johannis Exoniensis episcopi quem dedit ecclesie sue Exonie")[105] or a certain "Johannes Marti" (March?) whose name in a fifteenth-century script is written twice on fol. 1r. Although the notes left by Christian Hebraists in Oxford, Bodl., MS Or. 135 concern lexicography rather than grammar as such, they show that their authors owned and read native Jewish philological works. The dictionary of Ibn Parḥon was quoted by the glossator of the Psalter LH MS 21 and by the compilers of the trilingual dictionary bound together with it.[106]

Notes of a very different nature appear in the Hebrew Psalter London, Lambeth Palace, MS 435. The margins and the flyleaves at the beginning of the volume were covered in annotations by different Christian individuals in Latin and Anglo-Norman French. They reflect the readers' thoughts and understanding of the Hebrew text. Most glosses are translations and brief notes on the semantics of specific words but several of them deal with grammar and morphological analysis. For example, on fol. 1v, the verb תְּנַפְּצֵם, "you shall shatter them," in Psalm 2:9 is analyzed above the line: "tenapez est dictio per se mem faciat eos," "*tenapez* is the word itself, *mem* makes 'them.'" This laconic note remarks correctly on the fact that the object pronoun of the 3rd person plural is expressed by the final *mem* suffixed to the verb. Next to דֹּבְרֵי כָזָב, "the liars," in Psalm 5:7, the glossator's note shows

105. See James, *The Ancient Libraries of Canterbury and Dover*, xlvi. We have no direct information on Grandisson's knowledge of Hebrew, but in addition to this anthology, his personal library also included a bilingual Hebrew Psalter with Latin glosses, London, Westminster Abbey Library, MS 1 (see J. Armitage Robinson and M.R. James, *The Manuscripts of Westminster Abbey* [Cambridge, 1909], 63–64; Olszowy-Schlanger, *Les manuscrits hébreux dans l'Angleterre médiévale: Étude historique et paléographique* [Leuven and Paris, 2003], 253–357), a copy of the commentary on Jerome's Hebraica with references to the Hebrew text by the Oxford Dominican Nicholas Trivet (Oxford, Bodl., MS 738) and a copy of the commentary on Psalms by Nicolas of Lyre (see Arduin Kleinhaus, "Nicholas Trivet OP Psalmorum interpres," *Angelicum* 20 [1943]: 219–236). On Nicholas Trivet's commentary and the Hebrew Psalter, see esp. Hubert M. Stadler, *Textual and Literary Criticism and Hebrew Learning in English Old Testament Scholarship, as Exhibited by Nicholas Trevet's Expositio Litteralis Psalterii and by MS. Corpus Christi College (Oxford) 11*, MLitt Thesis (University of Oxford, 1990).

106. Olszowy-Schlanger and Grondeux, eds., *Dictionnaire hébreu-latin-français*, lxxx–lxxxviii. Ibn Parḥon, under a corrupted name of *Piraam* or *Piraham* is referred to six times in the dictionary: nGimel 52, nṭet 23, nMem 16, nSamekh 45, nSamekh 69, nPe 14.

his understanding of the common derivational base for nouns and verbs: "davar loquela dovere loquentes," *davar* (דָּבָר), "speech," *dovere* (דּוֹבְרֵי), "the ones who speak."[107] Singular and plural noun formation is mentioned in a gloss on דַּרְכֵי in Psalm 18:22: "derechz iter derachzim itinera," *derekh* (דֶּרֶךְ), "way," *derakhim* (דְּרָכִים), "ways." Verb conjugation features in several marginalia. When commenting Psalm 18:4, the glossator lists conjugated forms of the root ישע, "to save": "osea tosea iosea nosea quod (est) salvabo –bis –bit –bimus," "*osea* (אוֹשִׁיעַ), *tosea* (תּוֹשִׁיעַ), *iosea* (יוֹשִׁיעַ), *nosea* (נוֹשִׁיעַ), that is I will save you will [. . .], he will [. . .], we will [. . .]."[108] On fol. 14v, on the upper margin, the gloss gives a full conjugation of the verb קום, "stand up," transliterated in Latin characters and translated into Latin: "cam leuauit, camu leuauerunt / camti leuaui, camtim leuastis / cama leuauit, uel camezas / camenu leuauimus," "*cam* (קָם), he stood up, *camu* (קָמוּ), they stood up, *camti* (קַמְתִּי) I stood up, *camtim* (קַמְתֶּם) you (pl. masc.) stood up, *cama* (קָמָה) she stood up, or *camezas* (?), *camenu* (קַמְנוּ) we stood up." Indeed, the verb קום, "to stand up," appears in the text on this page, in 1st person plural קַמְנוּ, "we stood up," in Psalm 20:9. It seems that the study of the Psalm has allowed the reader to learn/revise all the forms of this verb in perfect tense. On the same page, prompted by מִמְּךָ, "from you," in Psalm 21:5, the same annotator wrote in the right-hand lower margin the forms of the preposition מִן, "from," with suffixes, occasionally writing the relevant suffix in Hebrew, and commenting with precision on the different pronunciation – with or without a *dagesh* – of the otherwise similar suffix of the 3rd sg. masc. and 1 pl.: "mimecha ך, de te / mimeni de me / mimenu נו tangendo grauiter de illo / mimenu laxe de nobis / mikim de uobis / mihem de illis," "*mimecha* (מִמְּךָ) ך, from you / *mimeni* (מִמֶּנִּי), from me / *mimenu* (מִמֶּנּוּ) נו, pronounced stronger, from him / *mimenu* (מִמֶּנּוּ) weak, from us / *mikim* (מִכֶּם) from you (2 pl. masc.) / *mihem* (מֵהֶם), from them."

Further grammatical material appears in the notes on the flyleaves of the same London, Lambeth Palace Library, MS 435. These are informal and unstructured notes on various subjects. A few contain names of Christian individuals, probably from Norfolk (fol. IV). But most of the notes concern Hebrew. They appear in multiple layers, written as an entangled palimpsest of information, taken in shorthand maybe during a Hebrew lesson. An earlier hand's writing in a metallic pencil is partly covered by notes written by a hand similar to that of the main glossator of the Psalter. Very difficult to read due to their informal and overlapping writing, many of these remarks concern Hebrew vocabulary in Latin characters translated into Latin and French (e.g., "tihilla laus loange/ Tihillim

107. Gilbert Dahan, "L'enseignement de l'hébreu en occident médiéval (XIIe–XIVe siècles)," *Histoire de l'éducation* 57 (1993): 3–22, at 18.

108. Dahan, "L'enseignement de l'hébreu," 19.

laudes lohanges," "*tihilla* [תְּהִלָּה], praise, praise / *Tihillim* [תְּהִלִּים], praises, praises," on fol. Vr), words grouped according to their semantic fields (coins, animals, synonyms for "man," fol. VIr), mentions of the Aramaic Targum (fol. VIr). Specific grammatical points are interspersed with more general linguistic explanations. These notes are remarkable in their dynamic dimension as a record of a learning session, as well as in their focus on Hebrew language and grammar. Even more importantly, the description of Hebrew, as much as it can be reconstructed from these hardly legible notes, seems to rely on Jewish grammatical tradition.

The treatment of the consonants and vowels is a good example of the reliance of the Christian glossator of London, Lambeth Palace Library, MS 435 on Jewish sources. The presentation of the consonants in the notes actually reflects the way the Jewish grammarians grouped them according to various criteria. The consonants forming Hebrew prepositions are listed together as a mnemonic compound בְּכָּלָמָה, transliterated as *bechalama,* and illustrated by the example of *dor* (דוֹר), *generatio,* "generation": *bador, kador, lador, midor, hador* ("in the generation, like the generation, to the generation, from a generation, the generation"). The strong and weak pronunciation of some consonants is the subject of several notes. Their author is conversant with the Jewish classification of consonants. He writes the Hebrew alphabet in Hebrew letters on the top of fol. IIIr and discusses in detail the groups of consonants. Like Jewish grammarians, he treats the consonants *alef, heh, vav* and *yod* as a coherent group (the so-called *matres lectionis* of contemporary Hebrew grammars) and designates them by the mnemonic *iehu,* יֱהוּא, reading, however, the grouping of these letters from left to right, in the Latin direction. He also uses the mnemonic term *begadkefat* to designate the group of letters with strong or weak pronunciation depending on whether they are provided with a *dagesh* or a *rafeh* (fol. Vr):

> Iehu habet in origine lingue quatuor litteras ioz י, he ה, vaf ו, alef א
> Begazkefat habet vi litteras, bez ב, ג gimel, ד dalet, caf כ, פ pe, taf ת et hoc est magnum secretum apud hebreos

> *Iehu* has in the origin of the language four letters, *yod* י, *heh* ה, *vav* ו, *aleph* א. *Begadkefat* has six letters, *bet* ב, ג *gimel,* ד *dalet, kaf* כ, פ *peh, tav* ת, and this is a great secret among the Jews.

The author is even aware of the masoretic rule that if a letter *begadkefat* follows a word which ended by one of the *matres lectionis,* the *begadkefat* has a weak pronunciation (without the *dagesh*) (fol. Vr): "Precedente iehu יֱהוּא begazkefaz sonant grammata postreme vocis laxata videntur," "When *iehu,* יֱהוּא, come before them, the *begadkefat* letters sound weak at the end of the word."

Unlike in the grammatical approach of Roger Bacon, the consonants are not treated as vowels. On the contrary, the gutturals *ḥet* and *ʿayin* are described as "letters" which do not exist in Latin (fol. Vr): "Due littere sunt apud ebreos quas nos non habemus ח et ע," "There are in Hebrew two letters which we don't have, *ḥet* and *ʿayin*." A large portion of the notes concerns the Hebrew vowels, their graphic aspect and phonetic realization. The vowels are designated by their Hebrew names. In addition to the basic seven vowels, the notes describe the *ḥaṭaf* vowels which are composed of a full vowel and a *shva* and are placed under guttural consonants.

The names and graphic shapes of the Hebrew vowels are also listed on a flyleaf of another Hebrew Psalter annotated in Hebrew and French in early thirteenth-century England, Paris, BnF, MS hébreu 113 (fol. Ir). As discussed earlier, the flyleaves of this manuscript contain a draft of a Hebrew-Latin lexicon which treats the vowels in a similar way as the Latin-oriented approach of Roger Bacon. The notes on the vowels for their part follow the Jewish tradition and are written by a different scribe from that of the draft of the lexicon.

Further important evidence of the knowledge of Jewish linguistic tradition is to be found in the notes by two Christian scribes, inscribed on the flyleaves of the bilingual book of Ezekiel in Oxford, Bodl., MS Or. 62. On fol. 131r, one of the scribes records peculiarities of the pronunciation of some letters in a final position in the word: "א et ה ponita in fine dictionis non sonant," "*alef* and *heh* placed at the end of a word are silent," and "ב . ד . ת ponita in fine dictionis [...]," "*bet, dalet, tav* placed at the end of a word [are weakened ?])." Particularly interesting glosses appear on fol. 132r. They consist of a list of consonants arranged in groups corresponding to their place of articulation:

Col. 1
Iste littere formantur in gutture אֲ חְ הֲ ע
Iste littere formantur in palato ג י כ ק
Iste formantur in dentibus ד ל ט נ ת
Iste formantur in lingua ז ש ס ר ץ

Col. 2
Iste formantur labiis בּ ו מ פ

While articulatory phonetics was not a well-studied branch of grammar in the medieval Latin West, some descriptions of the individual letter-sounds as produced by the flow of the air passing through the different organs of speech are attested, notably in the *Etymologies* of Isidore of Seville or in Geoffrey of Ufford's *Scutum Bede*.[109] In the Jewish linguistic tradition, on the other hand, the phonetics

109. Isidore of Seville, in the chapter on grammar in his *Etymologies*, defined vowels as "letters that are released in various ways through the straightforward opening of the throat, without any contact," and consonants as "letters that are produced by various motions of

approach and notably grouping of the consonants according to their place of articulation is attested early on. It first appears in the *Sefer Yeẓirah* (The Book of Creation) whose date is uncertain, some scholars placing its composition in late antiquity whereas others date it to the early Islamic period.[110] This phonetic classification of the consonants was later included in most of the works on Hebrew grammar and lexicography. The linguistic works mentioned above which were available among the Jews in medieval England contain these phonetic categories in various configurations. The division mentioned by Menaḥem ben Saruḳ contains four groups rather than five,[111] Dunash ibn Labrāṭ mentions five groups but does not specify the organ of speech.[112] The *Sefer ha-Shoham* and its source of inspiration, the *Sefer Mikhlol* of David Kimhi, contain five groups.[113] Oxford, Bodl., MS Or. 62 defines the group ד ל ט נ ת as dentals and the group ז ש ס ר ץ as linguals whereas for Moses ben Isaac ha-Nessi'ah and David Kimhi, letters ז ש ס ר ץ are dentals and ד ל ט נ ת are lingua-dentals. The long version of the *Hidāyat al-Qāri'* describes the five groups of consonants in detail and defines them as pronounced at the back of the throat (א ה ח ע), in the middle of the tongue (ג י כ ר ק), on "the extremity of the tongue touching the flesh of the teeth," (ד ט ל נ ת) between the teeth (ז ס צ ש) and with lips (ב ו מ ף).[114] Despite some discrepancies, there is no doubt that the phonetic division of Hebrew consonants by the Hebraist who annotated Oxford, Bodl., MS Or. 62 is borrowed from Jewish grammar.

An attempt to present the verb conjugation is found on the flyleaves of Oxford, Bodl., MS Arch. Selden A. 3.[115] This thirteenth-century *maḥzor* containing mostly *seliḥot* for Yom Kippur reflects the French rite and may have been copied in England. A Christian scholar studied several piyyutim in this volume, and left his notes in transliterated Hebrew, Latin and Anglo-Norman French, in the margins or between the lines on fols. 3r, 6r–v, 16r–v, 17r–v. The handwriting of the glossator,

---

the tongue or a compression of lips," see Isidore of Seville, *The Etymologies*, ed. and trans. S.A. Barney, W.J. Lewis, J.A. Beach and O. Berghof (Cambridge, 2014), 40. In Geoffrey of Ufford's twelfth-century compilation *Scutum Bede*, whose unique exemplar is London, BL, MS Stowe 57, all the letters of the Latin alphabet are described from the point of view of their organ of articulation (fol. 5r).

110. "A Preliminary Critical Edition of *Sefer Yezira*," ed. Ithamar Gruenwald, *Israel Oriental Studies* 1 (1971): 135–177, at 147.

111. Menaḥem ben Saruḳ, *Maḥberet: Edición crítica e introducción*, ed. Ángel Sáenz-Badillos (Granada, 1986), 8*–9*.

112. Dunash ben Labrat, *Teshuvot*, ed. Ángel Sáenz-Badillos (Granada, 1980), 5b.

113. Moses ben Isaac ha- Nessi'ah, *The Sefer ha-Shoham*, ed. Klar, 6; David Kimhi, *Mikhlol*, ed. and trans. William Chomsky (New York, 1952), 11.

114. Khan, *The Tiberian Pronunciation Tradition*, 48–55.

115. Beit-Arié, *Supplement*, no. 1159.

as well as his method of annotations, links this manuscript to the Ramsey group.[116] The initial blank bifolio of the volume was used to write the conjugated forms of the roots אבב, אבד and אבה. These verbs are written in Hebrew characters and are vocalized following the simplified Christian tradition of Hebrew vocalization, which does not use either *ḳamaẓ* or *segol*. The scribe who wrote them did not train as a Jewish scribe, although his handwriting is clear and aesthetically pleasing. The three roots in this order appear at the beginning of Jewish dictionaries, for example the *Maḥberet he-ʿArukh* of Ibn Parḥon, where they are preceded by אב. However, while אבד, "to lose," and אבה, "to desire" are frequent verbs, the root אבב is not attested as a verbal form but only in nouns, such as אָבִיב, "fresh barley ears" (Exodus 9:31), which, by extension from חֹדֶשׁ הָאָבִיב, "the month of the new harvest" (Exodus 13:4), came to mean "spring." The unrealistic conjugated forms of אבב, translated here as "primiciare," "to begin," are artificially created by analogy with existing conjugated verbs. They attempt to reflect the Hebrew *binyanim Ḳal, Polel* (by analogy with geminate verbs whose second and third radical letters are identical), forms with a *dagesh* in the second radical resembling *Piʿel* and *Puʿal*, and forms with inserted *yod* resembling *Hifʿil*. The vocalization is often wrong, not only for the non-existent verb אבב, but also for the two other verbs.

It is relevant that the root אבב appears vocalized as an imperative as the first lemma of the dictionary in LH MS 21. In LH MS 21, this root is also considered as a verb. The translation in the dictionary corresponds to the one in Oxford, Bodl., MS Arch. Selden A. 3: "primicia," "iniciare."[117] The incorrect understanding of אבב as a verb and its similar translation in both manuscripts confirms the relationship between the two manuscripts. Although the grammar LH MS 21 was composed by someone who was much better acquainted with Hebrew morphology than Oxford, Bodl., MS Arch. Selden A. 3, they are both rare witnesses of the attempts to grasp the Hebrew verbal system by Christian scholars in the Middle Ages.

In conclusion, both the Latin-based description of Hebrew and the knowledge of Jewish native tradition are attested in the works and glosses left by medieval Hebraists in England. It is difficult to ascertain at this stage of research whether these two different methods correspond to different milieux of Christian scholars. It appears however that the universal use of Latin categories is represented in the works of Roger Bacon, whereas evidence of the knowledge of the native Jewish grammar is attested in the body of bilingual manuscripts, some linked with Ram-

116. Judith Olszowy-Schlanger, "Christian Scholarship and Jewish Prayer in Thirteenth-Century England: Oxford, MS Arch. Selden A.3," in the forthcoming Festschrift for Gary Rendsburg, ed. Vincent Beiler and Aaron D. Rubin (Leiden, in print).

117. Olszowy-Schlanger and Grondeux, eds., *Dictionnaire hébreu-latin-français*, 1 (vAleph 1). Like in the dictionary of Ibn Parḥon, this entry in LH MS 21 follows אב, which is, however, written in the upper margin, in lieu of a running title.

sey Abbey. Elaborated and studied in the same context as these bilingual manuscripts, the Longleat House Grammar relies on the Jewish linguistic tradition. Chapter Five will discuss its grammatical approach in more detail and reveal the specific Jewish sources and concepts which inspired the Christian compilers of the Longleat House Grammar.

Facsimile of the Longleat House Grammar

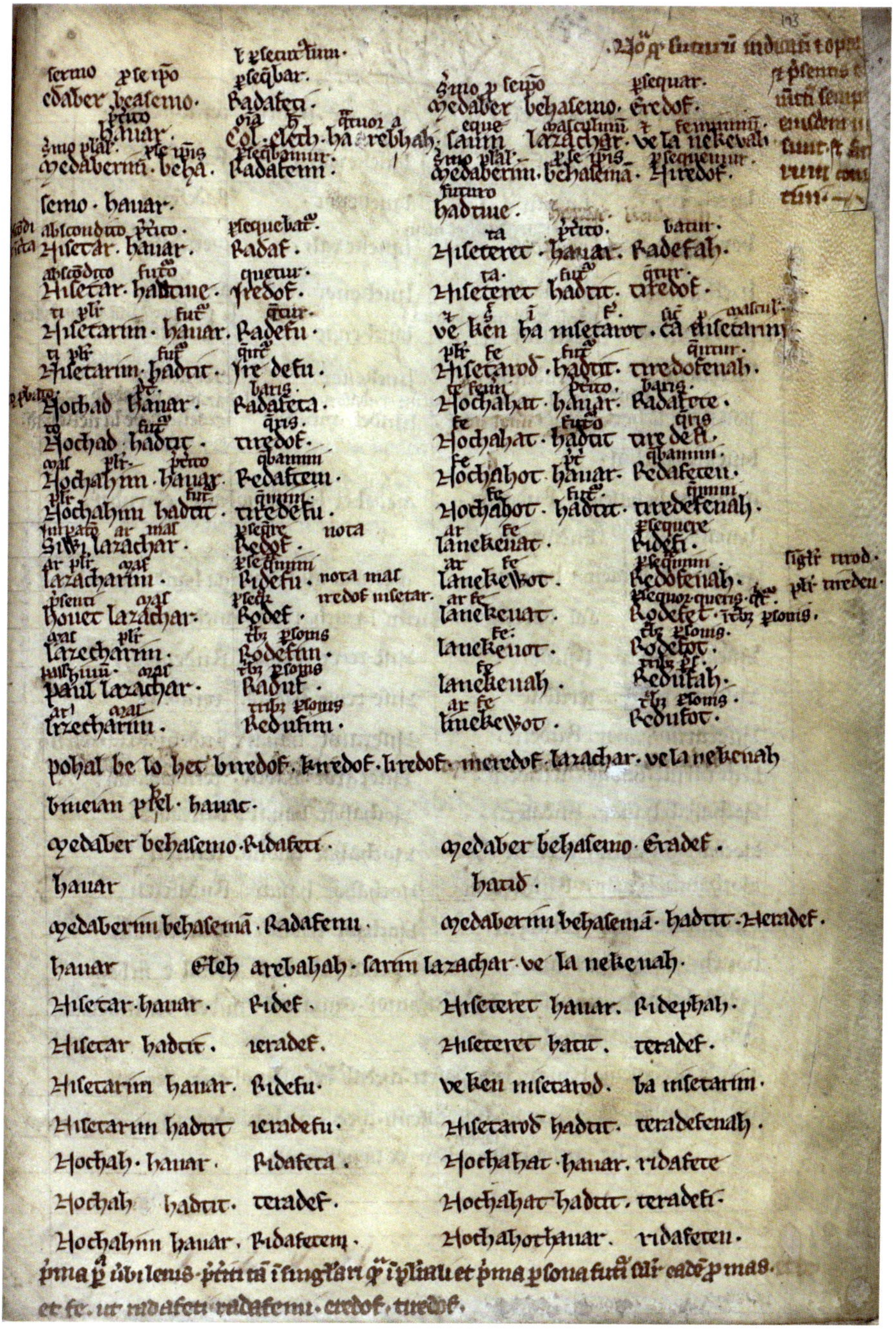

Longleat House, Library of the Marquess of Bath, MS 21, fol. 193r. All images in this section are used by the kind permission of the Marquess of Bath.

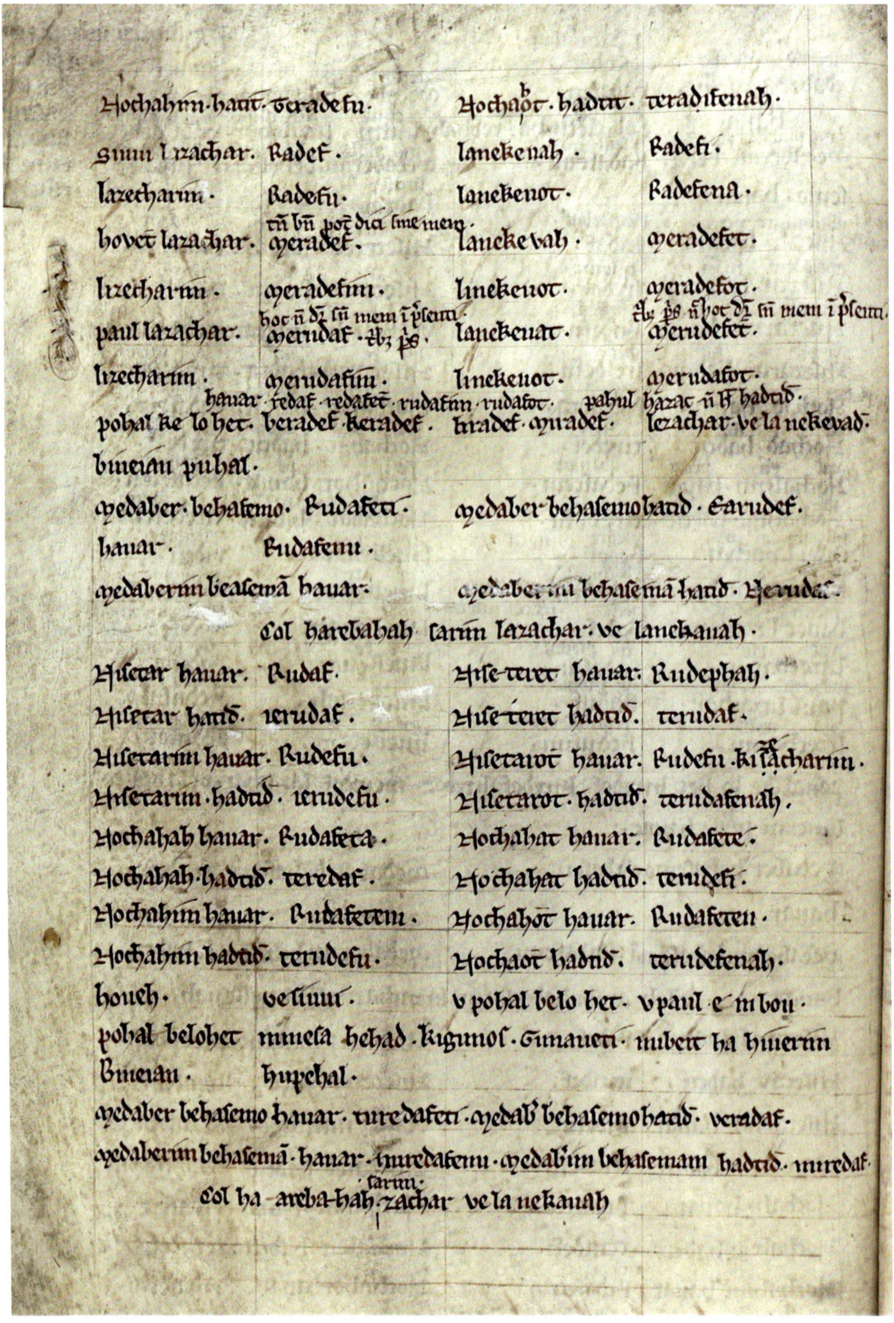
Hochalhem · hauit · Teradefu · Hochaot · hadtit · teradifenah ·
Suuu l tzachar · Radef · lanekenah · Radefi ·
lazecharim · Radefu · lanekenot · Radefena ·
tu bu poz dici sine mem ·
hovet lazachar · meradef · lanekevah · meradefet ·
lizecharim · meradefim · linekenot · meradefot ·
hot u dz su mem i plenit · ... ps u hot dz su mem i plenit ·
paul lazachar · merudaf · ... ps · lanekenat · merudefet ·
lizecharim · merudafim · linekenot · merudafot ·
hauar · redaf · redafet · rudafim · rudafot · pahul hazac u ... hadtid ·
pohal ke lo het · beradef · keradef · leradef · meradef · lezachar · ve la nekevad ·
bineian puhal ·
medaber · behasemo · Rudafeti · medaber behasemo hatid · Eradef ·
hauar · Rudafenu ·
medaberim beasema hauar · medaberim behasema hatid · Nerudaf ·
Col harebahah sarim lezachar · ve lanekanah ·
Hisetar hauar · Rudaf · Hise teret hauar · Rudephah ·
Hisetar hatid · ierudaf · Hise teret hadtid · terudaf ·
Hisetarim hauar · Rudefu · Hisetarot hauar · Rudefu · ki ... charim ·
Hisetarim · hadtid · ierudefu · Hisetarot · hadtid · terudafenah ·
Hochahah hauar · Rudafeta · Hochahat hauar · Rudafete ·
Hochahah · hadtid · teredaf · Hochahat hadtid · terudefi ·
Hochahim hauar · Rudafetem · Hochahot hauar · Rudafeten ·
Hochahim hadtid · terudefu · Hochaot hadtid · terudefenah ·
houeh · ve sinut · v pohal belo het · v paul e m bou ·
pohal belohet mitesa hehad · kiguinos · Ginaueti · nubert ha hinerim
Bineian · hupehal ·
medaber behasemo hauar · turedafeti · medab behasemo hatid · veradaf ·
medaberim behasema · hauar · hiuredafenu · medabim behasemam hadtid · nuredaf ·
Col ha areba hah sarim zachar ve la nekanah

LH MS 21, fol. 193v.

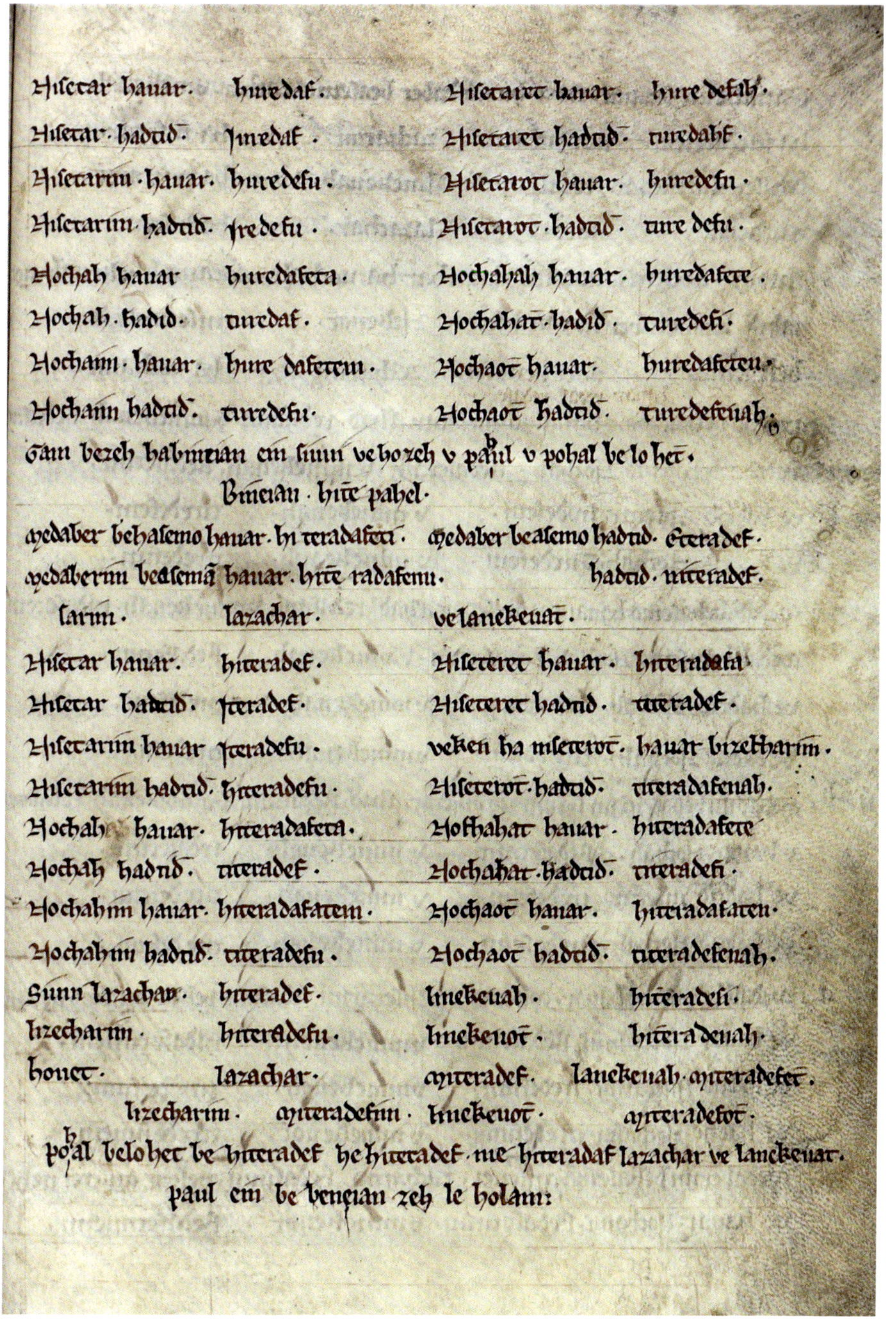

Hisetar hauar. hitedaf. Hisetaret hauar. hite defah.
Hisetar. hadtid. Jitedaf. Hisetaret hadtid. titedahf.
Hisetarim. hauar. hitedefu. Hisetarot hauar. hitedefu.
Hisetarim. hadtid. Jtedefu. Hisetarot. hadtid. tite defu.
Hochah hauar hitedafeta. Hochahah hauar. hitedafete.
Hochah. hadid. titedaf. Hochahat. hadid. titedefi.
Hochahm. hauar. hite dafetem. Hochaot hauar. hitedafeten.
Hochahm hadtid. titedefu. Hochaot hadtid. titedefenah.
Gam bezeh habinian em sium ve hozeh v pahul v pohal be lo het.
Binian. hite pahel.
Medaber behasemo hauar. hi teradafeta. Medaber beasemo hadtid. eteradef.
Medaberim beasemam hauar. hite radafenu. hadtid. niteradef.
Sarim. lazachar. ve lanekeuat.
Hisetar hauar. hiteradef. Hiseteret hauar. hiteradefi.
Hisetar hadtid. Jteradef. Hiseteret hadtid. titeradef.
Hisetarim hauar Jteradefu. veken ha miseterot. hauar bizekharim.
Hisetarim hadtid. hiteradefu. Hiseterot. hadtid. titeradafenah.
Hochah hauar. hiteradafeta. Hochahat hauar. hiteradafete
Hochah hadtid. titeradef. Hochahat. hadtid. titeradefi.
Hochahim hauar. hiteradafatem. Hochaot hauar. hiteradafaten.
Hochahim hadtid. titeradefu. Hochaot hadtid. titeradefenah.
Sium lazachar. hiteradef. linekeuah. hiteradefi.
lizecharim. hiteradefu. linekeuot. hiteradenah.
houet. lazachar. miteradef. lanekeuah. miteradefet.
lizecharim. miteradefim. linekeuot. miteradefot.
pohal belohet be hiteradef he hiteradef. ne hiteradaf lazachar ve lanekeuat.
paul em be benian zeh le holam:

LH MS 21, fol. 194r.

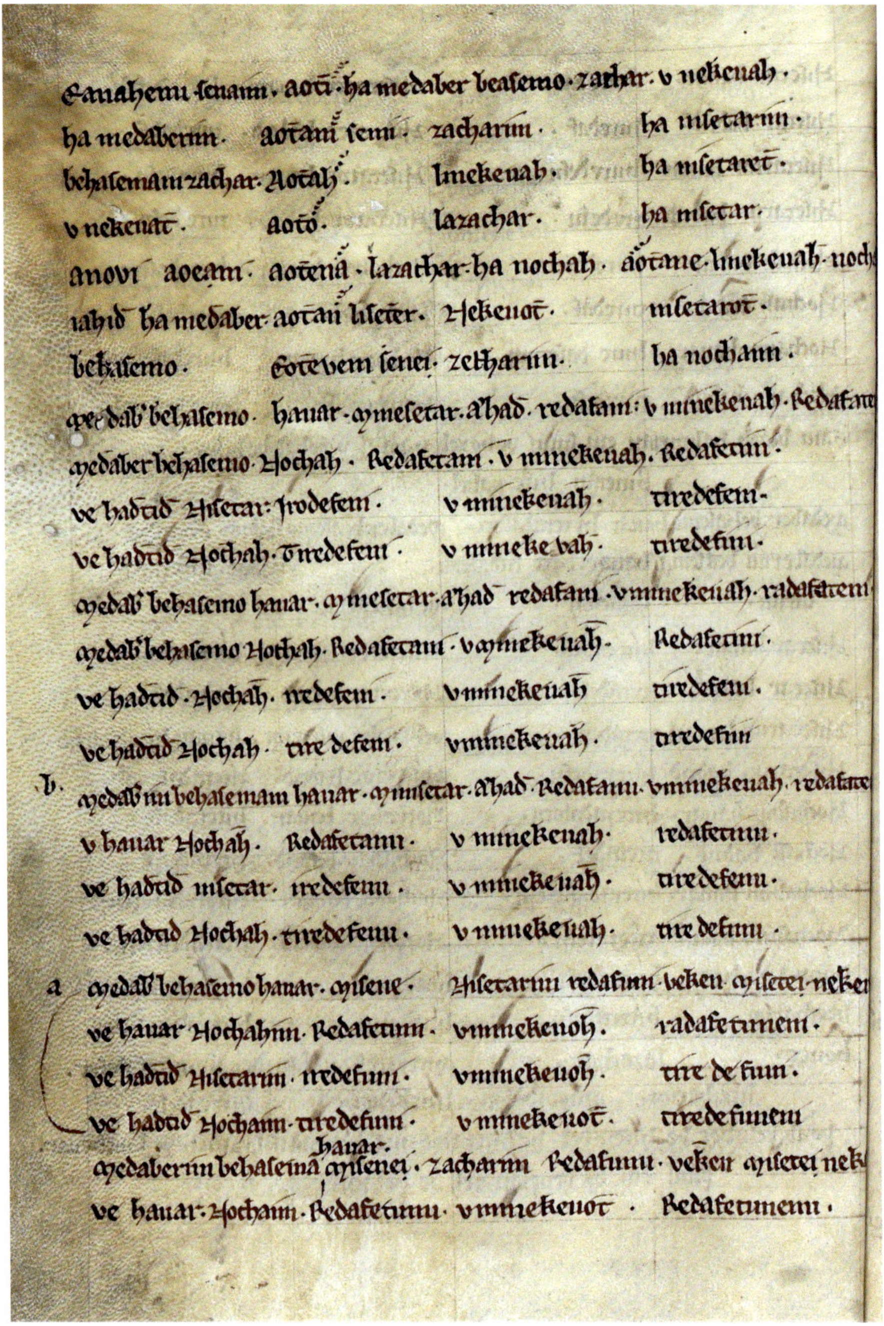

LH MS 21, fol. 194v.

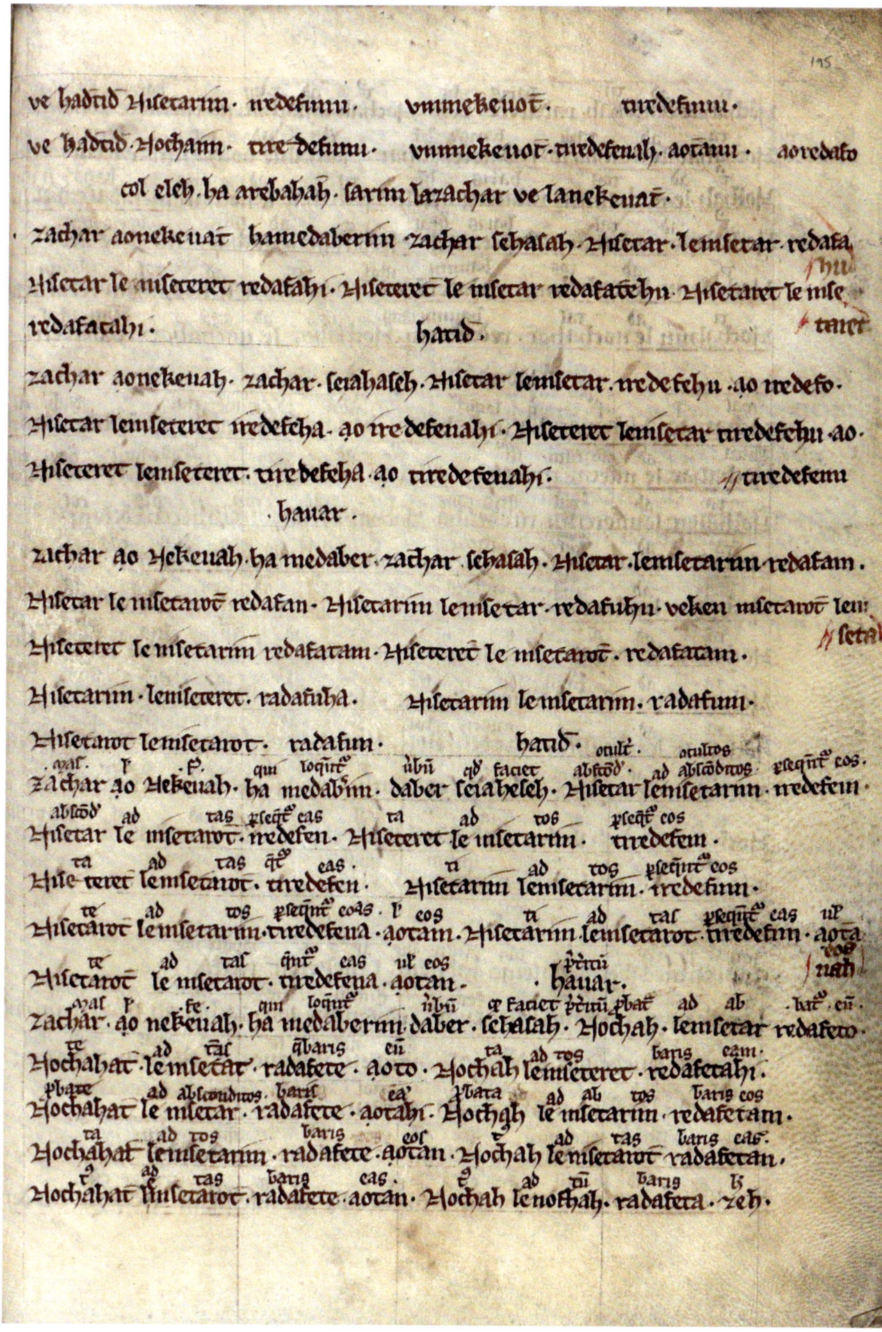
ve hadud Hisetarim · tredefimu · vimmekenot · tiredefimu ·
ve hadud · Hocham · tire defimu · vimmekenot · tiredefenuh · aotam · aoredafo
col eleh ha arebahah · sarim lazachar ve lanekenat ·
zachar aonekenat hamedaberim zachar sehalah · Hisetar · lemsetar · redafa ·
Hisetar le misetaret redafahi · Hisetaret le misetar redafatehu · Hisetaret le mise
redafatahi · hatid · taret
zachar aonekenah · zachar · seiahaseh · Hisetar lemisetar · tredefehu · ao tredefo ·
Hisetar lemisetaret tredefeha · ao tredefenahi · Hisetaret lemisetar tiredefehu · ao ·
Hisetaret lemisetaret · tiredefeha ao tiredefenahi · tiredefenu
· hanar ·
zachar ao Nekenah · ha medaber · zachar sehalah · Hisetar · lemisetarim redafam ·
Hisetar le misetarot redafan · Hisetarim lemisetar · redafuhu · veken misetarot lem
Hisetaret le misetarim redafatam · Hisetaret le misetarot · redafatam ·
Hisetarim · lemisetaret · radafuha · Hisetarim lemisetarim · radafum ·
Hisetarot lemisetarot · radafun · hatid ·
zachar ao Nekenah · ha medabrim · daber seiahaseh · Hisetar lemisetarim · tredefem ·
Hisetar le misetarot · tredefen · Hisetaret le misetarim · tiredefem ·
Hisetaret lemisetarot · tiredefen · Hisetarim lemisetarim · tredefum ·
Hisetarot lemisetarim · tiredefena · aotam · Hisetarim lemisetarot · tiredefun · aota
Hisetarot le misetarot · tiredefena · aotan · · hanar · nah
zachar · ao nekenah · ha medaberim · daber · sehalah · Hochah · lemisetar redafeto ·
Hochahat · lemisetar · radafete · aoto · Hochah lemisetaret · redafetahi ·
Hochahat le misetar · radafete · aotahi · Hochah le misetarim · redafetam ·
Hochahat lemisetarim · radafete · aotan · Hochah le misetarot radafetan ·
Hochahat lemisetarot · radafete · aotan · Hochah le nochah · radafeta · zeh ·

LH MS 21, fol. 195r.

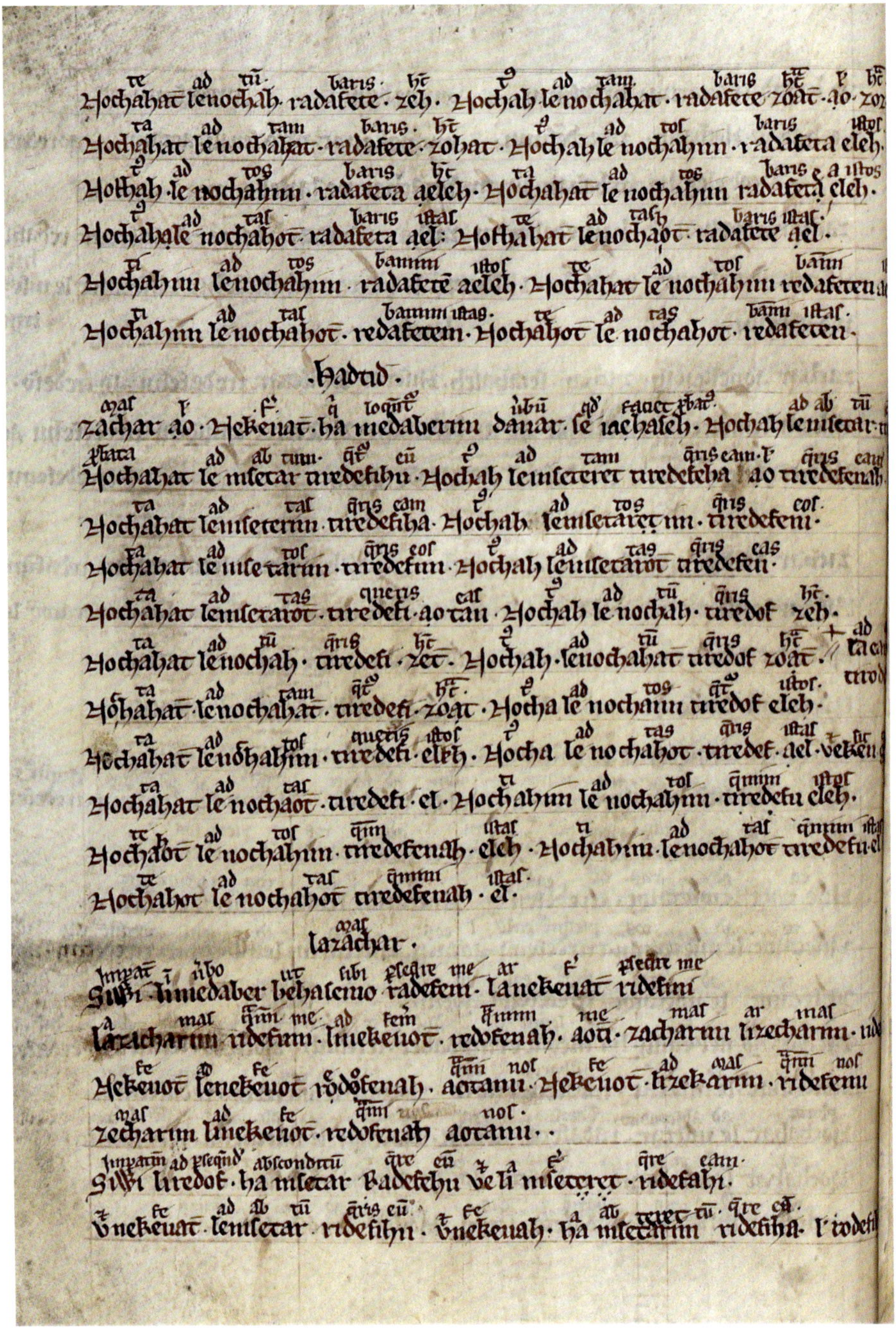

LH MS 21, fol. 195v.

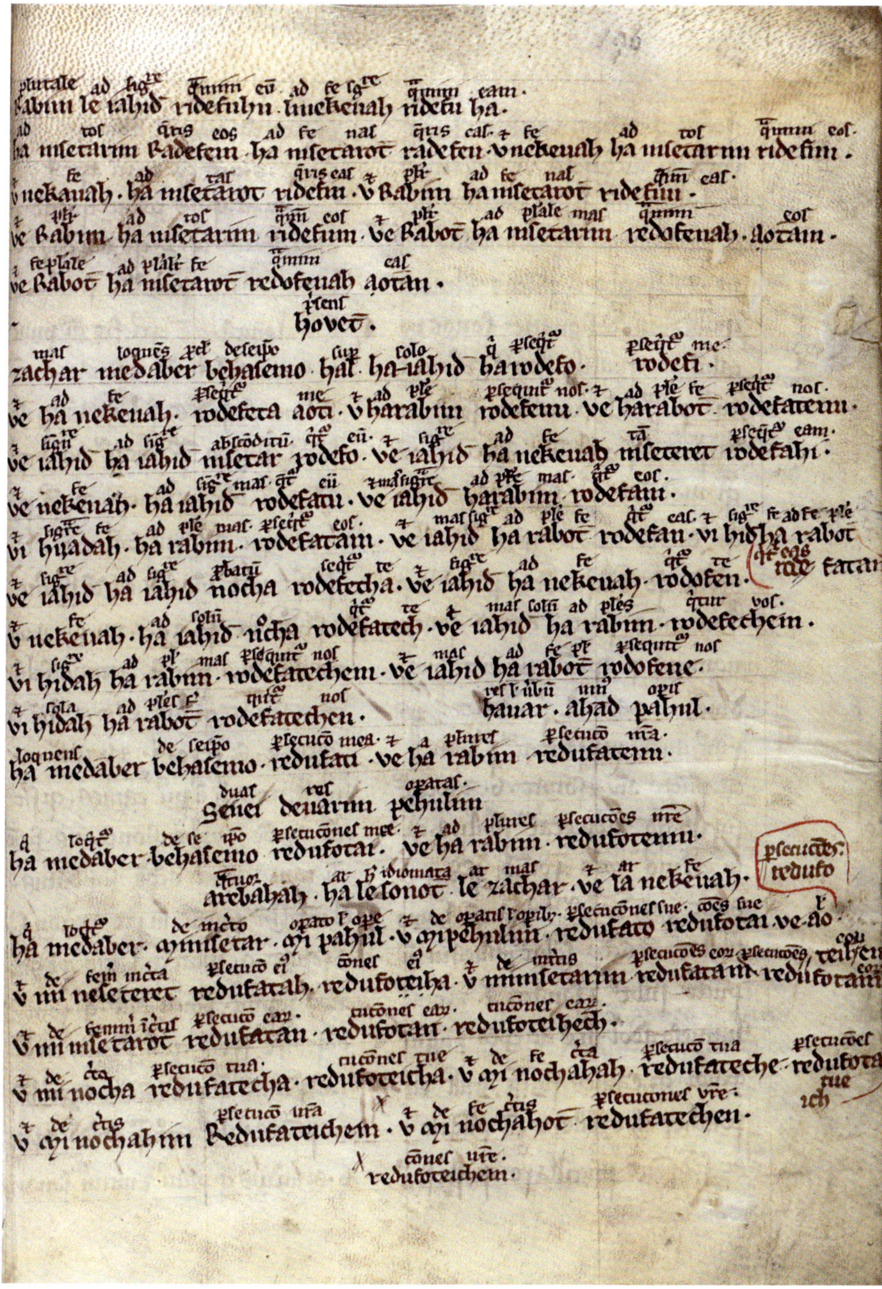

LH MS 21, fol. 196r.

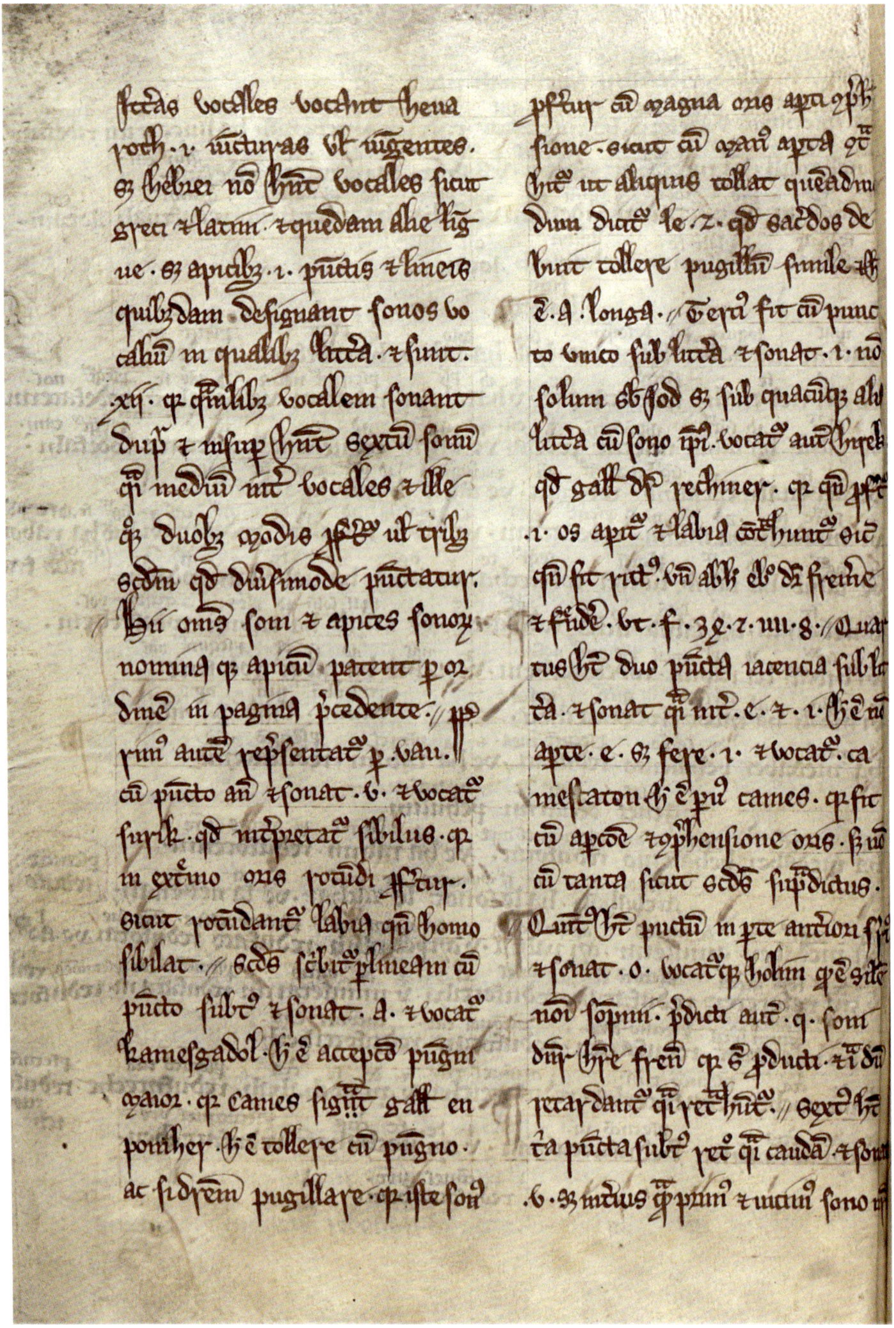

LH MS 21, fol. 196v.

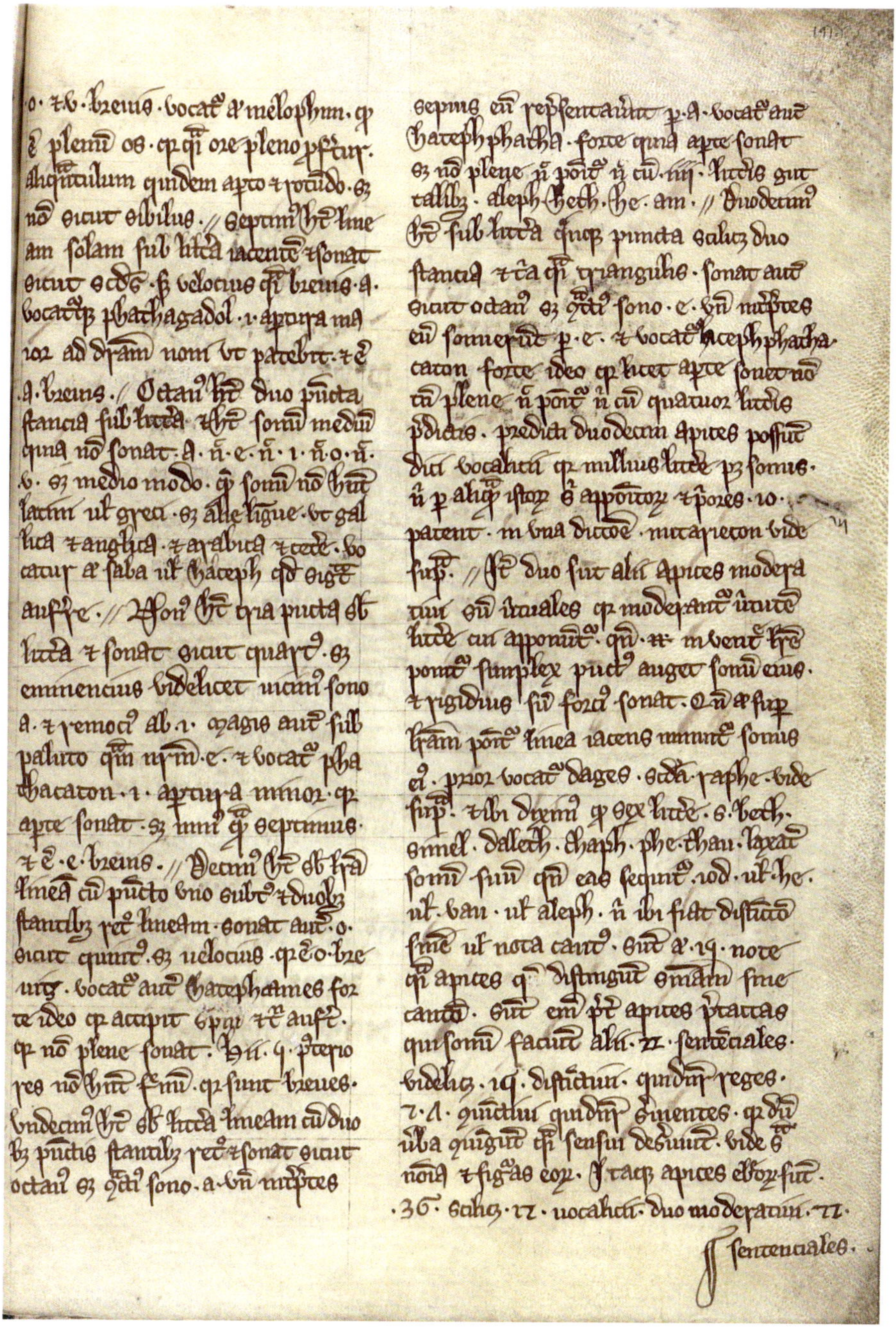
.o. ꝛ u. breuis. vocatur a melophum. quia
est plenum os. quia quasi ore pleno profertur.
Aliquantulum quidem apto ꝛ rotundo. sed
non sicut sibilus. // Septima habet line
am solam sub littera iacentem ꝛ sonat
sicut secundus. sed velocius quam breuis a.
vocaturque phathagadol. i. apertura ma
ior ad distanciam nominis vt patebit. ꝛ est
a. breuis. // Octaua habet duo puncta
stancia sub littera. ꝛ habet sonum medium
quia non sonat. a. uel. e. uel. i. uel. o. uel.
u. sed medio modo. qui sonum non habet
latinus uel greca. sed alie lingue. vt gal
lica ꝛ anglica. ꝛ arabica ꝛ cetere. vo
catur a saba ul chateph quod significat
auferre. // Nona habet tria puncta sub
littera ꝛ sonat sicut quartus. sed
eminencius videlicet vicini sono
a. ꝛ remocior ab i. magis autem sub
paluto quam nostrum. e. ꝛ vocatur pha
thacaton. i. apertura minor. quia
apte sonat. sed minus quam septimus.
ꝛ est. e. breuis. // Decima habet sub littera
lineam cum puncto vno subtus ꝛ duobus
stantibus recte lineam. sonat autem. o.
sicut quintus. sed uelocius. quia est o. bre
uis. vocatur autem chatephatmes for
te ideo quia accipit spiritum ꝛ ratione aufert.
quia non plene sonat. hi. 4. priorio
res non habent finem. quia sunt breues.
Vndecima habet sub littera lineam cum duo
bus punctis stantibus recte ꝛ sonat sicut
octaua sed quasi sono. a. vel interpretes
sepius eum representauit per. a. vocatur autem
chateph phatha. forte quia apte sonat
sed non plene non ponitur nisi cum. iiij. litteris gut
turalibus. aleph. heth. he. ain. // Duodecima
habet sub littera quinque puncta scilicet duo
stancia ꝛ tria quasi triangulis. sonat autem
sicut octaua sed quasi sono. e. vel interpretes
eum sonuerunt per. e. ꝛ vocatur hateph phatha
caton forte ideo quia licet apte sonet non
tum plene non ponitur nisi cum quatuor litteris
predictis. predicti duodecim apices possunt
dici vocalici quia nullius littere per sonus.
non per aliquos istorum secundum appositorum ꝛ pores io.
patent. in una dictione. mitapreton vide
supra. // Sunt duo sunt alii apices modera
tiui siue itriales quia moderantur uirtute
littere cui apponuntur. quorum in vent habet
ponitur simplex punctum auget sonum eius.
ꝛ rigidius sic forci sonat. Alter aute sup
litteram ponitur linea iacens minuitur sonus
ei. prior vocatur dages. secunda raphe. vide
supra. ꝛ ubi dicitur quod sex littere. s. beth.
gimel. daleth. chaph. phe. thau. habeat
sonum suum quando eas sequitur. iod. ul. he.
ul. vau. ul aleph. non ibi fiat distinctio
fine ul nota cantus. sunt a. 19. note
que apices qui distingunt sermonem sine
cantu. sunt enim preter apices predictos
qui sonum faciunt alii. 22. sentenciales.
videlicet 19. distinctiui. quando reges.
ꝛ. 3. quietiui quando seruientes. quia denotant
ubi quiescit quasi sensu desinunt. vide supra
nomina ꝛ figuras eorum. Itaque apices ebreorum sunt.
.36. scilicet. 12. uocalici. duo moderatiui. 22.
sentenciales.

LH MS 21, fol. 197r.

אין מתג נוטריקון
אותיות הגרון החיך אח
הע גיכק בין שנים
הלשון זש סרץ דטלנת
אותיות שפתים בומף
אלה חמש מוצאות כל אותיות
המוציא מתחלפה לפעמים
כל אות בחברו והוא
כגד כפת דגש כ רפה כ
כשאותיות יהוא באות לפני
בגד כפת מרפים בגד כפת אם
לא שיש על האות של בגד
כפת אחד מטו מלכים
הפורקים חוץ אותיות יהוא וא
ואלה הם
אתנחתא זקף גדול
זקף קטן זרקא
יתיב טרחא טפחא

לגרמיה סגרל
סגת פסוק רביע
פזר פשטא שר
שלשלת תבירה
תלישא גדולה
כל אלו מבדילים בין טעם
לטעם ואלה המשרתים
שמחברים הטעם והניגון
מהפך מונח דרגא
מירכא מאיילה
תלישא קטנה
קדמה

LH MS 21, fol. 197v.

LH MS 21, fol. 198r.

וכן הרכבה ואחר על
אורות הדיבוק כמקום
שהתיבה נרכבת כמו
חכמה במקום שאינו
נרכב לתיבה של אח
אחריו אני משים ה
בתיבה הי' לאחריה
וכשהוא דבוק לתיבה
של אחריו כמו אדם
שאמר חכמת אדם
אז אני משים הי' ל
בסופה וכן הרבה
כמו בהמה בהמת
האדם בינה בינת הא
האדם דיעה דעת ה
האדם גבורה גבורת
האדם וכן הרבה אבל
אין אתה אומר בהמה

האדם מפני שיהא
נראה שהאדם יהיה
בהמה וכן חכמה
האדם אם תכתבה ב
בלא הי' בסוף התיבה
נראה שיהיה האדם
שם החכמה וכן בינה
אם תשים הי' בסוף
התיבה נראה שיהיה
האדם שם הבינה כ
כאשר הדבקנו לתיבה
של אחריו בלא הה'
וכן גבורה אם תדבקנו
לתיבה של אחריו בלא
הה' יהיה נראה שה
שהאדם הוא שם ה
הגבורה כלו אורות
הדיבוק

et quando ille

LH MS 21, fol. 198v.

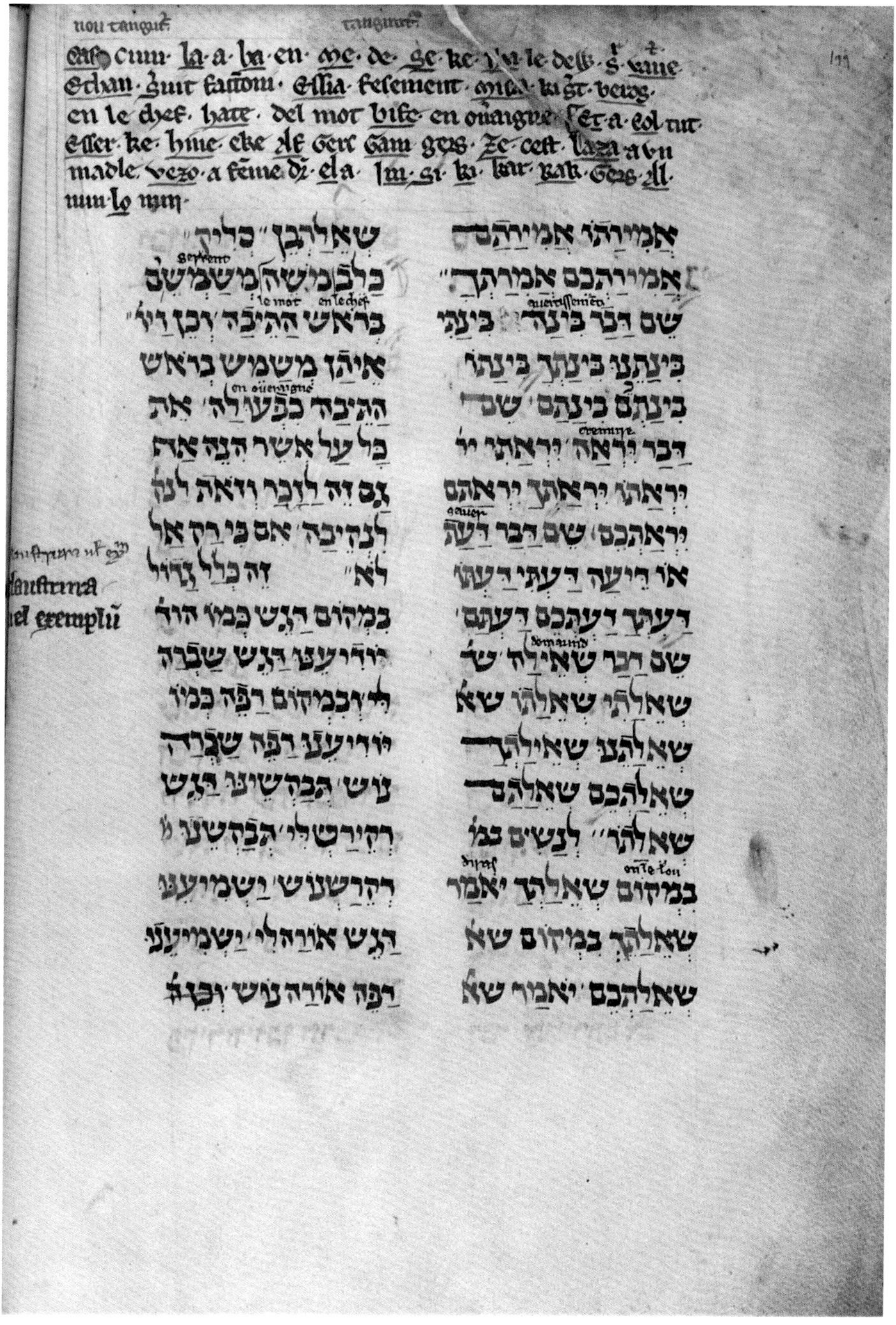

LH MS 21, fol. 199r.

LH MS 21, fol. 199v.

LH MS 21, fol. 200r.

וילכו וישנו וישכבו ויח
רחכמו וילבשו וישאו
ישכבו׳ וכן לשתי נשים
לנסתרות׳׳ לנוכח לשני
אנשים לשון עתיד הע
העשו תאכלו השתו׳
הקומו הלכו השנו הש
השכבו החכמו הלבשו
השאו הינאו השאו׳׳
ויש דברים ששמותם
נוסח׳ אסח כמו הוסית׳
האביד כמו אבד׳ הפקיד
כמו פקד׳ האזין כמו א
אוזן׳ השיב כמו שב׳
הבאיש כמו באש׳ וכן
הרבה׳ והנה נקרא הנוסח׳
ויש נוסח שהמים נוספה׳
מדבר כמו דובר׳ כיהלך

כמו הולך מאסה
כמו אוכה מעקר כמו
בקר׳ יציר קונט׳׳ וכן
הרבה׳ ויש חברים
שנקראים משקל כבד
ומשקל קל פעל׳ אבד
כמו אבד׳ דבק כמו ד
דבק׳ גבר כמו גבר׳ ש
שבר כמו שבר׳ זרד׳ כמו
זרד׳ שמר כמו שמר׳
צרך כמו צרך׳ וכן ה
הרבה׳ כזה תוכל להבין
כל לשון עברי׳ אשמר
גרדרי׳ ישמר גרדרה׳
השמר גרדרש׳ נשמר
גרדרומש׳ שמור גרד
גרדא׳ שמר כמו כן לא
אלא שזה ממשקל

כמו פעל׳

LH MS 21, fol. 200v.

לאחד עשית אל
אכלת שתית קמת
הלכת ישנת שכבת
חמית לבשת נשאת
נשאת שכבת | עבר
לנוכח לשנים עש
עשיתם אכלתם
שתיתם קמתם לכתם
ישנתם שכבתם
חמיתם לבשתם
נשאתם שכבתם
עבר לאשה אחת
לנכחת עשית אל
אכלת שתית קמת
הלכת ישנת שכבת
חמית לבשת נשאת
שכבת עבר לנכח
לשתי נשים עשיתן

אכלתן שתיתן קמתן
הלכתן ישנתן שכבתן
חמיתן לבשתן נשא
נשאתן שכבתן עבר
לשני אנשים לנסתרים
עשו אכלו שתו קמו
הלכו ישנו שכבו חמו
חמו לבשו נשאו ג
שכבו וכן לשתי נשים
לנסתרות לשון עתיד
לאיש אחד אעשה
אוכל | וכן הרבה כשמ
כשמדבר מעצמו
לשון עתיד לאחר יע
יעשה יאכל ישתה
יקום ילך לרבים לשון
עתיד לנסתרים יעשו
יאכלו ישתו יקומו יל

LH MS 21, fol. 201r.

אכל שתה קם הלך
ישן שכב חמם לבש
נשא שב' עבר לא
לאשה אחד' עשה
אכלה שתה קמה
דברה הלכה ישנה
שכבה חממה לבשה
נשאה שבה' עבר
לעינמי אחר' עשי
עשיני אכלני שתי
שתיני קמני דברנ
הלכני ישנני שכבני
חממני לבשני נשא
נשאני שבני' ולכן ל'
לאשה' דבר הוה ל'
לאחר' אוכל שותה
עושה מדבר דובר
מהלך הולך ישן ש
שוכב מחמם לובש
נושא' דבר הוה ל'
לשנים' עושים א'
אוכלים שותים מת
מדברים הולכים יש
ישנים שוכבים' מחמ'
מחממים לובשים'
נושאים' לנקיבה'
אוכלת שותה עושה
מדברת הולכת שוכב
מחממת לובשת נוש
נושאת' דבר הוה
לנקיבות' אוכלות ש'
שותות עושות מדב'
מדברות הולכות שוכ
שוכבות מחממות לוב
לובשות נושאות ש'
שבות' עבר לנקבה לא

LH MS 21, fol. 201v.

תעשה תאכל תש
תשתה תקום תלד
תבא תישן תשכב
תחמם תלבש
נאכל נעשה נשתה
נקום נלד נבא נישן
נשכב נחמם נלבש
נצא נשב
יצווי לאחד אכול
שתה עשה קום
בא ישן שכב חמם
לבש יצא שב
יצווי לאשה אחת
עשי אכלי שתי
קומי לכי באי ישני
שכבי חמי לבשי יצאי
שבי יצווי לשני
אנשים עשו אכלו
שתו קומו לכו באו
ישנו שכבו חמו
לבשו יצאו שבו
יצווי לשתי נשים
עשינה אכלנה
שתינה קומנה לכנה
ישנה שכבנה
חממנה לבשנה
שאנה שבנה
לאיש אחד עשה

LH MS 21, fol. 202r.

LH MS 21, fol. 202v.

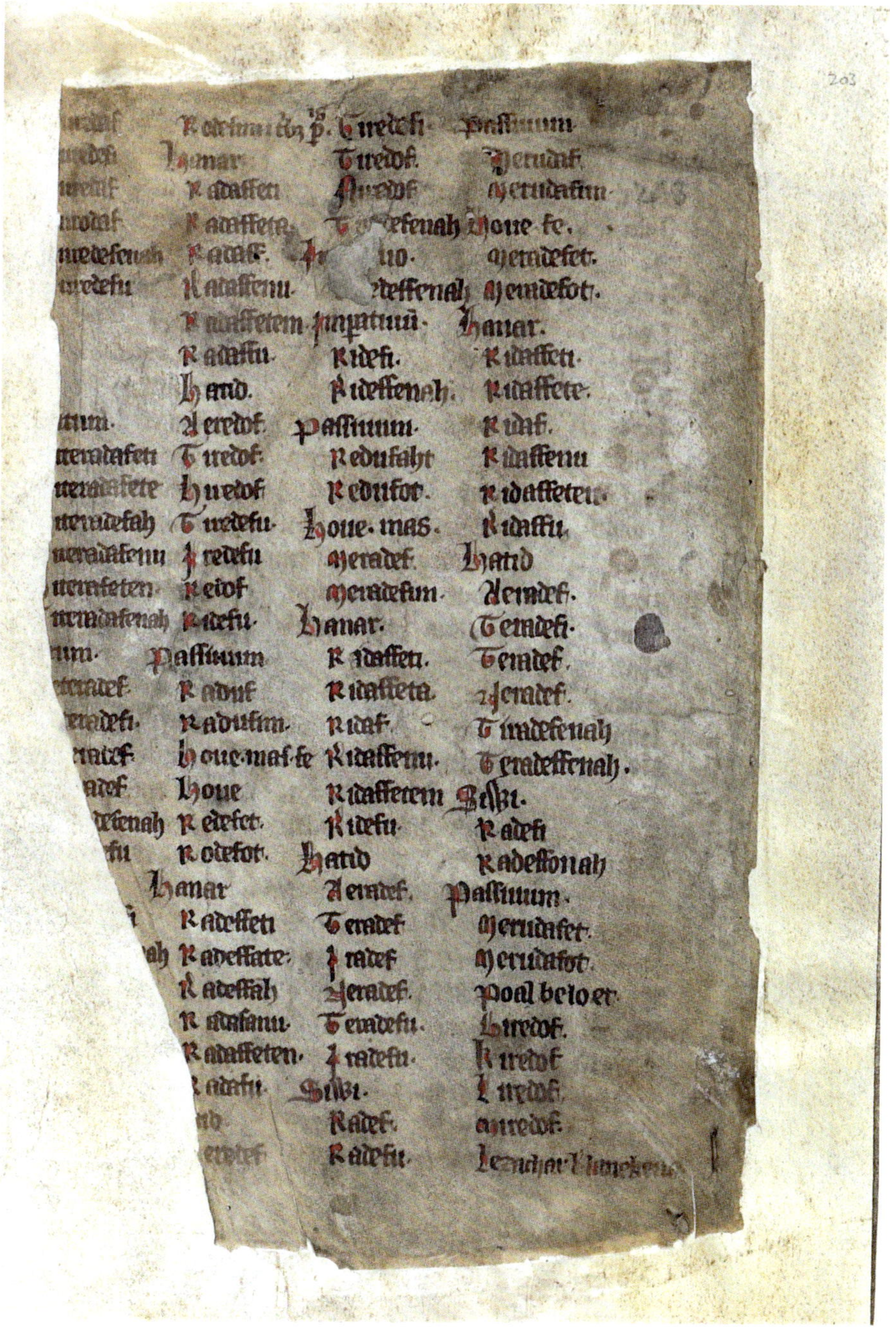

LH MS 21, fol. 203r.

LH MS 21, fol. 203v.

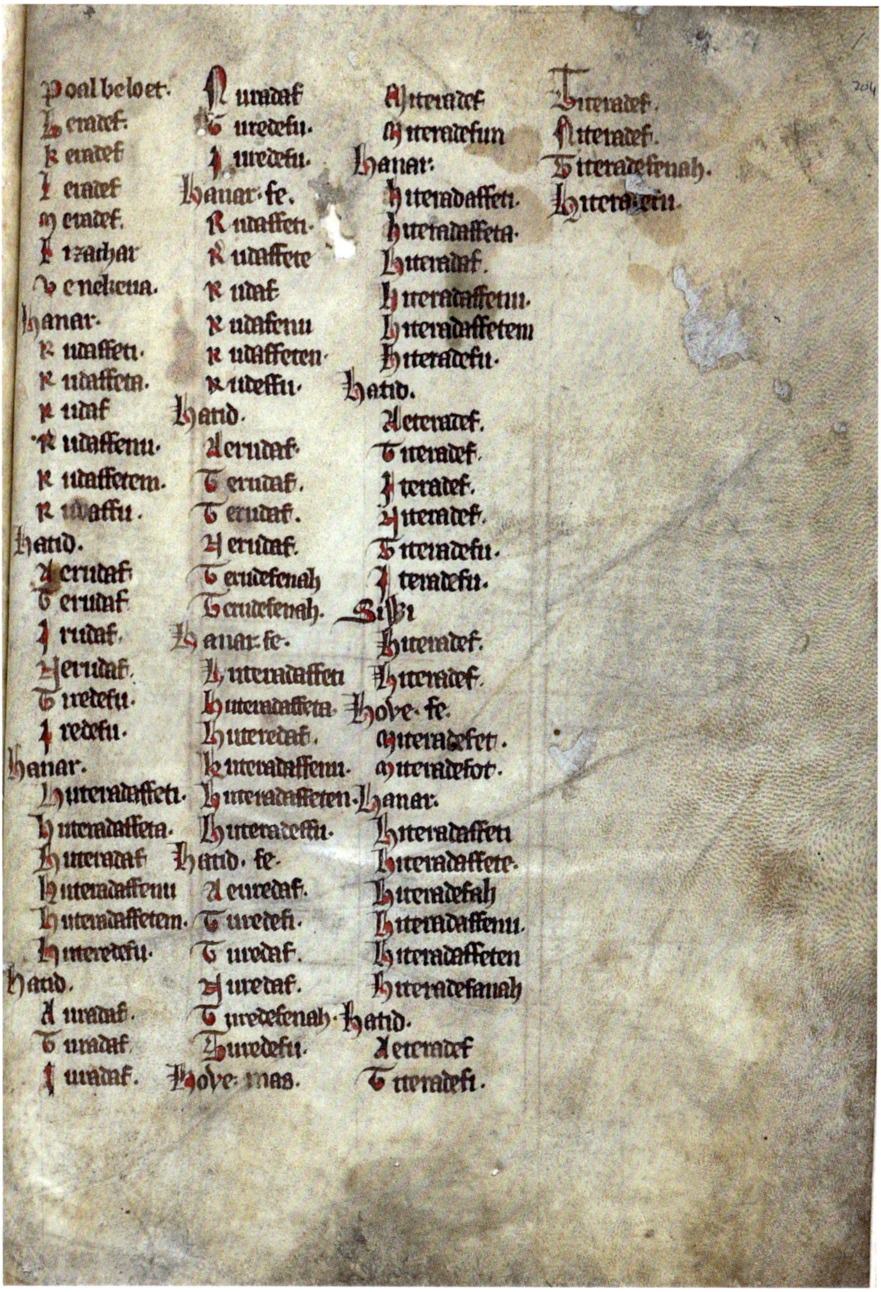

204

Poal beloet.
Leratef.
Keratef
Jeratef
Meratef.
Lizachar
Venekeua.
Hanar.
Rudaffeti.
Rudaffeta.
Rudaf
Rudaffenu.
Rudaffetem.
Rudaffu.
Hatid.
Aerudaf.
Terudaf
Jrudaf.
Herudaf.
Turedefu.
Jredefu.
Hanar.
Huteradaffeti.
Huteradaffeta.
Huteradaf
Huteradaffenu
Huteradaffetem.
Hmteredefu.
Hatid.
Auradaf.
Turadaf.
Juradaf.

Nuradaf
Turedefu.
Juredefu.
Hanar. fe.
Rudaffeti.
Rudaffete
Rudaf
Rudafenu
Rudaffeten.
Rudeffu.
Hatid.
Aerudaf.
Terudaf.
Terudaf.
Herudaf.
Terudefenah
Terudefenah.
Hanar. fe.
Huteradaffeti
Huteradaffeta.
Huteredaf.
Huteradaffenu.
Huteradaffeten.
Huteradeffu.
Hatid. fe.
Aeuredaf.
Turedefi.
Turedaf.
Huredaf.
Turedefenah.
Huredefu.
Hove. mas.

Miteradef
Miteradefun
Hanar.
Hiteradaffeti.
Huteradaffeta.
Huteradaf.
Hiteradaffetiu.
Hiteradaffetem
Hiteradefu.
Hatid.
Aeteradef.
Titeradef.
Jteradef.
Hiteradef.
Titeradefu.
Jteradefu.
Sibi
Hiteradef.
Hiteradef.
Hove. fe.
Miteradefet.
Miteradefot.
Hanar.
Hiteradaffeti
Hiteradaffete.
Hiteradefah
Hiteradaffenu.
Hiteradaffeten
Hiteradefanah
Hatid.
Aeteradef
Titeradefi.

Titeradef.
Niteradef.
Titeradefenah.
Hiteradefu.

LH MS 21, fol. 204r.

LH MS 21, fol. 204v.

CHAPTER FOUR

The Edition of the Longleat House Grammar

The edition of the Longleat House Grammar follows the order of its textual units numbered in the Latin direction, from left to right, even if this order does not reflect the order or chronology of the copy and the relationship between the units. The specificity of the manuscript's layout makes the edition particularly difficult. In GTU 1 in particular, the grammatical contents in Hebrew in Latin characters are provided with an interlinear translation, which is highly abbreviated and, like a typical *superscriptio* gloss, cannot be understood if visually dissociated from the source words. I have therefore followed in this edition the tabular layout of the original to keep the *superscriptio* translations in their original places.

The edition of the text follows the manuscript as closely as possible, but it is not a "diplomatic edition." The facsimile appended to the edition will allow the readers to get a taste of the manuscript itself. The graphic elements such as space fillers have not been transcribed in the edited text. Corrections have sometimes proved necessary for a better understanding of this difficult and highly technical text. I have, however, intervened very rarely, keeping the corrections to the evident cases of a slip of the pen, and commenting on the editorial changes in the apparatus in the footnotes. In most cases, the readings of the manuscript, even if "incorrect" from the grammatical or palaeographical point of view, have been considered as relevant for the understanding of the scribe's work and his engagement with the text he copied, and as such are maintained in the edition. These readings are explained and corrected in the apparatus, the correct or suggested reading introduced by "*lege*" ("read!").

Similarly, this edition follows the vocalization of the Hebrew words as provided by the manuscripts, in GTU 3. The vocalizer of the manuscript employed a simplified vocalization system, often omitting and confusing the standard symbols of the Tiberian Masoretic system. I have systematically supplied the standard Tiberian forms in the apparatus but reproduced the original vowels unchanged in the edition, judging their "non-conformity" to be relevant for the Christian understanding of the Hebrew vocalization and phonetics.

Corrections and additions above the line and in the margins by the main scribes or later readers are edited in curly brackets { }. Square brackets [ ] were used when erased or otherwise illegible text was reconstructed. When the main scribes corrected their own text, the corrected version appears in the edited text, and the version before the correction is quoted in the note, provided with the abbreviation *a.c.* (*ante correctionem*, "before correction").

The text is mostly composed of paradigms and examples, and the Hebrew grammatical terms and examples are often translated into Latin. The Latin is strongly abbreviated, and the abbreviations are developed in full in the edition.

The paradigmatic nature of the text does not justify a full literal English translation. It was provided only when it was judged relevant, either together with the edition or as quotations in the comments in Chapter Five. Thus, I have provided a full translation for the running text of GTU 2. For the other, more paradigmatic parts of the grammar, I provide comments and partial translations of the relevant passage, in the unit's analysis in Chapter Five.

Grammar Textual Unit 1: The Hebrew Grammar in Latin Characters

fol. 193r

			Nota quod futurum indicatiui et opta[tiui] et presentis co[n-] -iunctiui semp[er] eiusdem m[odo] sunt. Et fu[tu-] -rum coniunctiui.
sermo pro se ipso ed̄aber beasemo	*uel persecutus sum* *persequebar* **Radafeti**	*sermo pro se ipso* Medaber behasemo	*persequar* **Eredof**
preterito hauar	*Omnia hec quatuor eque masculinum et femininum* col eleth ha areb{a}hah sauin lazachar ve la nekevah		
sermo pluralis pro se ipsis medaberim beha-| -semo hauar	*persequebamur* **Radafenu**	*sermo pluralis pro se ipsis* Medaberim behasemam	*persequemur* **Niredof**
		futuro hadtiue	
{[ab]scondi- | [-ta in-]-certa}			
abscondito preterito Nisetar hauar	*persequebatur* **Rad̄af**	*-ta preterito* Niseteret hauar	*-batur* **Radefah**
abscondito futuro Nisetar hadtiue	*-quetur* **Yredof**	*-ta futuro* Niseteret hadtit	*-quetur* **tiredof**
-ti plurale futuro Nisetarim hauar	*-quetur* **Radefu**	*et sic in feminino sicut pro masculino* ve ken ha nisetarot ca nisetarim	
-ti plurale futuro Nisetarim hadtid	*-quentur* **Yredefu**	*plurale fe. futuro* Nisetarod̄ hadtit	*-quentur* **tiredofenah**

1–7 Nota... coniunctiui] *add. in margine* 10 ed̄aber] *lege* medaber (מדבר) 13 eleth] *lege* eleh (אלה) areb{a}hah] arebhah *a.c.* (ארבעה) | a *scr. s. l.* 16–17 behasemo] *lege* behasemam (בעצמם) 19 hadtiue] *lege* hadtid (עתיד) 20–21 {[ab]scondi[ta in]certa}] *scr. in margine* 22 -ta preterito] hauar *scr. supra et corr.* | hadtit *scr. a. c.* -batur] radefah *scr. supra et corr.* 25 hadtiue] *lege* hadtit (עתיד) 26 futuro] *lege* preterito -quetur] *lege* (perse)quebantur

[...]to probato

preteriito Nochad hauar	*-baris* **Radafeta**	*-te femin. preterito* Nochahat hauar	*-baris* **Radafete**
-to futuro nochad hadtit	*-queris* **tiredof**	*fe. futuro* nochahat hadtit	*-queris* **tiredefi**
mas. plurale preterito Nochahim hauar	*-quebamini* **Redaftem**	*fe. preterito* Nochahot hauar	*-quebamini* **Redafeten**
plurale futuro Nochahim hadtit	*-quemini* **tiredefu**	*fe. futuro* Nochahot hadtit	*-quemini* **tiredefenah**
imperatiuo ar. mas. Siwi lazachar	*persequere {nota}* **Redof**	*ar. fe.* lanekeuat	*persequere* **Ridefi**
ar. plurale mas. lazacharim	*persequamini* **Ridefu** {nota mas. **iredof** nisetar}	*ar. fe.* lanekewot	*persequamini* **Redofenah** {singularis **tirod.** / pluralis **tiredeu**}
presenti mas. houet lazachar	*persequor* **Rodef**	*ar. fe.* lanekeuat	*persequor -queris –quitur* **Rodefet** in tribus personis
mas. pluralis lazecharim	*tribus personis* **Rodefim**	*fe.* lanekeuot	*tribus personis* **Rodefot**
passiuum mas. pa{h}ul lazachar	*tribus personis* **Raduf**	*fe.* lanekeuah	*tribus personis* **Redufah**
ar. mas. lizecharim	*tribus personis* **Redufim**	*ar. fe.* linekewot	*tribus personis* **redufot**

pohal be lo het biredof kiredof liredof meredof lazachar ve la nekeuah

bineian pi{h}el hauac

Medaber behasemo	**Ridafeti**	Medaber behasemo	**Eradef**
hauar		hatid	
Medaberim behasemam	**Radafenu**	Medaberim behasemam hadtit	**Neradef**
hauar	Eleh arebahah sarim lazachar ve la nekeuah		
Nisetar hauar	**Ridef**	Niseteret hauar	**Ridephah**
Nisetar hadtit	**ieradef**	Niseteret hatit	**teradef**

30 *fortasse legendi*: (preteri)to 32 nochad] *lege* nochah 34 nochad] *lege* nochah 39 nota] *scr. in margine* 40 lanekeuat] *lege* lanekeuah 42–43 nota... nisetar] *scr. in margine* singularis... tiredeu] *add. in margine* 43 tirod.] *lege* tiredof (תרדוף) sive tiredefi (תרדפי) tiredeu] *lege* tiredefu (תרדפו) 45 houet] *lege* houe 49 pa{h}ul] h *add. s. l.* 53 pi{h}el] h *add. s. l.* hauac] *lege* hauar (עבר) 57 radafenu] *lege* ridafenu 60 sarim] *lege* sauim (שוים)

Nisetarim hauar	**Ridefu**	ve ken nisetarod	ba nisetarim
Nisetarim hadtit	**ieradefu**	Nisetarod̄ hadtit	**teradefenah**
Nochah hauar	**Ridafeta**	Nochahat hauar	**ridafete**
Nochah hadtit	**teradef**	Nochahat hadtit	**teradefi**
Nochahim hauar	**Ridafetem**	Nochahot hauar	**Ridafeten**

Prima persona uerbi lenis preteriti tam in singulari quam in plurali et prima persona futuri similiter eadem pro mas. et fe. ut **radafeti radafenu eredof tiredof**

fol. 193v

Nochahim hatit	**teradefu**	Nocha{h}ot hadtit	**teradifenah**
siuui lazachar	**Radef**	lanekeuah	**Radefi**
lazecharim	**Radefu**	lanekeuot	**Radefena**
hovet̄ lazachar	*tamen bene potest dici sine mem* **Meradef**	lanekevah	**Meradefet**
lizecharim	**Meradefim**	linekeuot	**Meradefot**
paul lazachar	*hoc non dicitur sine mem in presenti tribus personis* **Merudaf**	lanekeuat	*tribus personis nec hoc dicitur sine mem in presenti* **Merudefet**
lizecharim	**Merudafim**	linekeuot	**Merudafot**
hauar	**redaf redafet̄ rudafim rudafot**	pahul hazac non habet hadtid̄	
pohal ke lo het	**beradef keradef liradef miradef**	lezachar ve la nekevad̄	
bineian puhal			
Medaber behasemo	**Rudafeti**	Medaber behasemo hatid	**Earudef**
hauar			
Medaberim beasemam hauar	**Rudafenu**	Medaberim behasemam hatid̄	**Nerudaf**

63 nisetarod] *lege* nisetarot ba] *lege* ka 64 nisetarod̄] *lege* nisetarot 67 nochahot hauar] nochahothauar *scr. ms* 68–69 prima…tiredof] *scr. alia manus* 70 nocha{h}ot] h *add. s. l.* 75 hovet̄] *lege* houe 80 lanekeuat] *lege* lanekeuah 82–83 hauar…hadtid̄] *scr. inter l.* 84 nekevad̄] *lege* nekevah

col harebahah sarim lazachar ve lanekauah

Nisetar hauar	**Rudaf**	Niseteret hauar	**Rudephah**
Nisetar hatid̄	**ierudaf**	Niseteret hadtid̄	**terudaf**
Nisetarim hauar	**Rudefu**	Nisetarot̄ hauar	**Rudefu** kizecharim
Nisetarim hadtid̄	**ierudefu**	Nisetarot hadtid̄	**terudafenah**
Nochahah hauar	**Rudafeta**	Nochahat hauar	**Rudafete**
Nochahah hadtid̄	**teredaf**	Nochahat hadtid̄	**terudefi**
Nochahim hauar	**Rudafetem**	Nochahot̄ hauar	**Rudafeten**
Nochahim hadtid̄	**terudefu**	Nochaot̄ hadtid̄	**terudefenah**

houeh ve siuui vpohal belo het vpaul ein bou

pohal belohet nimesa hehad kigunos gunaueti mibeit ha hiuerim

Bineian hupehal

Medaber behasemo hauar	**turedafeti**	Medaber behasemo hatid̄	**veradaf**
Medaberim behasemam hauar	**huredafenu**	Medaberim behasemam hadtid̄	**nuredaf**

col ha areba-hah {sarim} zachar ve la nekauah

fol. 194r

Nisetar hauar	**huredaf**	Nisetaret hauar	**huredefah**
Nisetar hadtid̄	**Iuredaf**	Nisetaret hadtid̄	**turedaf**
Nisetarim hauar	**huredefu**	Nisetarot hauar	**huredefu**
Nisetarim hadtid̄	**Iredefu**	Nisetarot hadtid̄	**turedefu**
Nochah hauar	**huredafeta**	Nochahah hauar	**huredafete**
Nochah hadid	**turedaf**	Nochahat̄ hadid̄	**turedefi**

92 sarim] *lege* sauim lanekauah] *lege* lanekeuah 96 kizecharim] kisacharim *ms a. c.* 98 nochahah] *lege* nochah 99 nochahah] *lege* nochah teredaf] *lege* terudaf 102 nochaot̄] *lege* nochahot̄ 104 kigunos] *lege* kigunov 106 turedafeti] *lege* huredafeti veradaf] *lege* ueradaf 110 sarim] *lege* sauim | *add. s. l.* nekauah] *lege* nekeuah 111 nisetaret] *lege* niseteret 112 nisetaret] *lege* niseteret turedaf] turedahf *ms* 114 iredefu] *lege* iuredefu 115 nochahah] *lege* nochahat

Nochaim hauar	**huredafetem**	Nochaot̄ hauar	**huredafeten**
Nochaim hadtid̄	**turedefu**	Nochaot̄ hadtid̄	**turedefenah**

Gam bezeh habineian ein siuui vehozeh v pa{h}ul v pohal be lo het̄

bineian hit̄epahel

Medaber behasemo hauar	**hiteradafeti**	Medaber beasemo hadtid	**Eteradef**
Medaberim beasemam hauar	**hit̄eradafenu**	hadtid	**niteradef**
sarim	lazachar	velanekeuat̄	
Nisetar hauar	**hiteradef**	Niseteret hauar	**hiteradafa**
Nisetar hadtid̄	**Iteradef**	Niseteret hadtid	**titeradef**
Nisetarim hauar	**Iteradefu**	veken ha niseterot̄ hauar	bizecharim
Nisetarim hadtid̄	**hiteradefu**	Niseterot̄ hadtid̄	**titeradafenah**
Nochah hauar	**hiteradafeta**	Nochahat hauar	**hiteradafete**
Nochah hadtid̄	**titeradef**	Nochahat hadtid̄	**titeradefi**
Nochahim hauar	**hiteradafatem**	Nochaot̄ hauar	**hiteradafaten**
Nochahim hadtid̄	**titeradefu**	Nochaot̄ hadtid̄	**titeradefenah**
Siuui lazachar	**hiteradef**	linekeuah	**hit̄eradefi**
lizecharim	**hiteradefu**	linekeuot̄	**hit̄eradenah**
houet lazachar	**Miteradef**	lanekeuah	**Miteradefet̄**
lizecharim	**Miteradefim**	linekeuot̄	**Miteradefot̄**

po{h}al belohet **behiteradef hehiteradef mehiteradaf** lazachar ve lanekeuat

paul ein be beneian zeh le holam:

117 nochaim] *lege* nochahim huredafetem] hure dafetem *ms* nochaot̄] *lege* nochahot̄ 118 nochaim] *lege* nochahim nochaot̄] *lege* nochahot̄ 119 vehozeh] *lege* vehoueh pa{h}ul] h *scr. s.l.* 120 hit̄epahel] hit̄e pahel *ms* 121 hiteradafeti] hi teradafeti *ms* 123 hit̄eradafenu] hit̄e radafenu *ms* 125 sarim] *lege* sauim velanekeuat̄] *lege* velanekeuah 128 bizecharim] *lege* kizecharim 131 nochah] nochahah *ms a. c.* nochahat] noshahat *a.c.* 133 nochaot̄] *lege* nochahot̄ 134 nochaot̄] *lege* nochahot̄ 136 hit̄eradenah] *lege* hit̄eradefenah 137 houet] *lege* houeh 139 po{h}al] h *add. s. l.* hehiteradef] *lege* lehiteradef *vel* kehiteradef mehiteradaf] *lege* mehiteradef lanekeuat] *lege* lanekeuah

fol. 194v

Eanahenu senaim	**aot̄i**	hamedaber beasemo	zachar v nekeuah
ha medaberim	**aot̄am**	senii zacharim	ha nisetarim
behasemam zachar	**aot̄ah**	linekeuah	ha nisetaret̄
v nekeuat̄	**aot̄o**	lazachar	ha nisetar
anoui aoeani	**aot̄ena**	lazachar ha nochah	**aot̄ane** linekeuah noch[ahat]
iahid̄ ha medaber	**aot̄an**	lisēter Nekeuot̄	nisetarot̄
behasemo	**Eot̄evem**	senei zecharim	ha nochaim
Medaber behasemo hauar minesetar a'had̄	**redafani**	v minekeuah	**Redafate**[**ni**]
Medaber behasemo Nochah	**Redafetani**	v minekeuah	**Redafetini**
ve hadt̄id̄ Nisetar	**Irodefeni**	v minekeuah̄	**tiredefeni**
ve hadt̄id̄ Nochah	**Tiredefeni**	v minekevah̄	**tiredefini**
Medaber behasemo hauar minesetar a'had̄	**redafani**	vminekeuah	**radafateni**
Medaber behasemo Nochah	**Redafetani**	vminekeuah̄	**Redafetini**
ve hadt̄id̄ Nochah̄	**iredefeni**	vminekeuah̄	**tiredefeni**
ve hadt̄id̄ Nochah	**tiredefeni**	vminekeuah̄	**tiredefini**
{a} medaber behasemo hauar misene nisetarim	**redafuni**	veken misetei nekeu[ot̄]	
ve hauar nochahim	**Redafetuni**	vminekeuoh̄	**radafetuneni**
ve hadt̄id̄ nisetarim	**iredefuni**	vminekeuoh̄	**tiredefuni**
ve hadtid̄ nochaim	**tiredefuni**	vminekeuot̄	**tiredefuneni**
{b} medaberim behasemam hauar minisetar a'head	**Redafanu**	vminekeuah	**redafate**[**nu**]

144 nisetaret̄] *lege* niseteret̄ 145 nekeuat̄] *lege* nekeuah 147 anoui] *lege* anoki aoeani] *lege* ao eani (או אני) 149 lisēter] *lege* lisetei 150 eot̄evem] *lege* eot̄ekem? nochaim] *lege* nochahim 151–152 minesetar] *lege* minisetar 154 irodefeni] *lege* iredefeni 156–157 minesetar] *lege* minisetar 159 nochah̄] *lege* nisetar 161–165 medaber…tiredefuneni] *scr. infra et corr. cum* a *et linea* medaber behasemo…tiredefuneni] *scr. post* medaberim behasemam… tiredefinu *et corr. cum a et b* 163 vminekeuoh̄] *lege* vminekeuot̄ radafetuneni] *lege* redafetuni 164 vminekeuoh̄] *lege* vminekeuot̄ 165 nochaim] *lege* nochahim

v hauar Nochah̄	**Redafetanu**	v minekeuah	**redafetinu**
ve hadt̄id̄ nisetar	**iredefenu**	v minekeuah̄	**tiredefenu**
ve hadtid̄ Nochah	**tiredefenu**	v minekeuah	**tiredefinu**
Medaberim behasemam {hauar} misenei zacharim	**Redafunu**	vek̄en misetei nek[euot̄]	
ve hauar Nochaim	**Redafetunu**	vminekeuot̄	**Redafetunenu**

fol. 195r

ve hadt̄id̄ Nisetarim	**iredefunu**	vminekeuot̄	**tiredefunu**
ve hadt̄id̄ Nochaim	**tiredefunu**	vminekeuot̄	**tiredefenah aot̄anu ao redafo**

col eleh ha arebahah̄ sarim lazachar ve lanekeuat̄

zachar aonekeuat̄ hamedaberim zachar sehasah Nisetar lenisetar **redafa{hu}**

Nisetar le niseteret **redafahi** Niseteret̄ le nisetar **redafat̄ehu** Nisetaret lenise{taret} **redafatahi**

hatid̄

zachar aonekeuah zachar seiahaseh Nisetar lenisetar **iredefehu** ạo **iredefo**

Nisetar leniseteret **iredefeha** ạo **iredefenahi** Niseteret lenisetar **tiredefehu** ao **tiredefenu**

Niseteret leniseteret **tiredefeha** ạo **tiredefenahi**

hauar

zachar ạo Nekeuah ha medaber zachar sehasah Nisetar lenisetarim **redafam**

Nisetar le nisetarot̄ **redafan** Nisetarim lenisetar **redafuhu** veken nisetarot̄ leni{seta}

Niseteret le nisetarim **redafatam** niseteret̄ le nisetarot̄ **redafatam**

Nisetarim leniseteret **radafuha** Nisetarim lenisetarim **radafum**

Nisetarot lenisetarot **radafun**

171 hauar] *add. s. l.* 173 nochaim] *lege* nochahim 175 nochaim] *lege* nochahim 177 sarim] *lege* sauim lanekeuat̄] *lege* lanekeuah 178 aonekeuat̄] *lege* ao nekeuah | *signum corr. infra* ao redafa{hu}] hu *add. infra* 179 nisetaret] *lege* niseteret lenise{taret}] *lege* leniseteret | -taret *add. infra* 182 aonekeuah] *lege* ao nekeuah | *signum corr. infra* ao ạo] *punctum infra a* 183 ạo] *punctum infra a* 185 ạo] *punctum infra a* 187 ạo] *punctum infra a* 188 leni{seta}] *lege* lenisetar | seta *scr. alia manus infra*

hatid̄

mas.	*uel fem.*	*qui loquuntur*	*uerbum*	*quod faciet*	*ocultus absconditus*	*ocultos ad absconditos*	*perse-quentur eos*
zachar ạo	nekeuah	ha medaberim	daber	seiaheseh	Nisetar	lenisetarim	**iredefem**

absconditus	*ad -tas*	*persequetur eas*	*-ta*	*ad -tos*	*persequetur eos*
Nisetar	le nisetarot̄	**iredefen**	Niseteret	le nisetarim	**tiredefem**

-ta	*ad -tas*	*-quetur eas*	*-ti*	*ad -tos*	*persequentur eos*
Niseteret̄	lenisetarot̄	**tiredefen**	Nisetarim	lenisetarim	**iredefum**

-te	*ad -tos*	*persequentur eos*	*uel eos*	*-ti*	*ad -tas*	*persequentur eas*	*uel eos*
Nisetarot̄	lenisetarim	**tiredefena**	**ạotam**	Nisetarim	lenisetarot	**tiredefun**	**ạota{nah}**

-te	*ad -tas*	*-quentur eas*	*uel eos*
Nisetarot̄	lenisetarot	**tiredefena**	**ạotan**

preteritum
hauar

mas.	*uel*	*fe.*	*qui*	*loquentur*	*uerbum*	*quod faciet preteritum*	*probatus*	*ad*	*ab.*	*-batur eum*
zachar	ạo	nekeuah	ha	medaberim	daber	sehasah	nochah	lenisetar	**redafeto**

-te	*ad -tas*	*-quebaris*	*eum*	*-ta*	*ad -tos*	*-baris eam*
Nochahat̄	lenisetar	**radafete**	**ạoto**	Nochah	leniseteret	**redafetahi**

probate	*ad absconditos*	*-baris*	*eam*	*probata*	*ad ab…-tos*	*-baris eos*
Nochahat̄	lenisetar	**radafete**	**ạotahi**	Nochah	lenisetarim	redafetam

-ta	*ad -tos*	*-baris*	*eos*	*-tus*	*ad -tas*	*-baris eas*
Nochahat̄	lenisetarim	**radafete**	**ạotan**	Nochah	lenisetarot̄	**radafetan**

-tus	*ad -tas*	*-baris*	*eas*	*-tus*	*ad -tum*	*-baris*	*hoc*
Nochahat̄	l{e}nisetarot̄	**radafete**	**aotan**	Nochah	lenochah	**radafeta**	**zeh**

195 ạo] *punctum infra a* daber] *lege* dabar (דבר) 201 eos[1]] eoas *ms* uel eos[2]] *lege* uel eas 202 ạotam] *punctum infra a* ạota{nah}] *lege* aotan | *punctum infra a* | -nah *add. infra* 204 ạotan] *punctum infra* a 208 probatus] probatur *ms* 209 ạo] *punctum infra* a daber] *lege* dabar (דבר) 210 -te] *lege* -ta -tas] *lege* -tum -ta] *lege* -tus -tos] *lege* -tam 211 ạoto] *punctum infra* a redafetahi] *lege* radefateha 212 probate] *lege* probata absconditos] *lege* absconditam probata] *lege* probatus 213 lenisetar] *lege* leniseteret ạotahi] *lege* ạotah | *punctum infra* a 214 -baris[1]] eos *add. alia manus* 215 ạotan] *lege* ạotam | *punctum infra* a 216 -tus[1]] *lege* -ta hoc] *lege* hunc 217 l{e}nisetarot̄] e[1] *add. s. l.* lenochah] lenoshah *ms a. c.*

fol. 195v

-te ad -tum -baris hec -tus ad -tam -baris hanc uel hanc
Nochahat̄ lenochah **radafete zeh** Nochah lenochahat **radafete zoat̄** ạo **zo**[**u**]

-ta ad -tam -baris hec -tus ad -tos -baris istos
Nochahat lenochahat **radafete zohat** Nochah lenochahim **radafeta eleh**

-tus ad -tos -baris hec -ta ad -tos -baris istos
Nochah lenochahim **radafeta ạeleh** Nochahat̄ lenochahim **radafete** {a}**eleh**

-tus ad -tas -baris istas -te ad -tas -baris istas
Nochah le nochahot̄ **radafeta ạel** Nochahat̄ lenocha{h}ot̄ **radafete ạel**

-ti ad -tos -bamini istos -te ad -tos -bamini ist[os]
Nochahim lenochahim **radafetem aeleh** Nochahat lenochahim **redafeten ae**[**le**]

-ti ad -tas -bamini istas -te ad -tas -bamini istas
Nochahim lenochahot̄ **redafetem** Nochahot̄ lenochahot̄ **redafeten**

hadtid̄

mas. uel fem. qui loquuntur uerbum quod faciet probatus ad ab…-tum […]
zachar ạo Nekeuat̄ ha medaberim dauar se iahaseh Nochah lenisetar ti […]

probata ad ab…-tum -quetur eum -tus ad -tam -queris eam uel -queris eam
Nochahat lenisetar **tiredefihu** Nochah leniseteret **tiredefeha** ạo **tiredefenah**

-ta ad -tas -queris eam -tus ad -tos -queris -eos
Nochahat leniseterim **tiredefiha** Nochah lenisetarim **tiredefem**

-ta ad -tos -queris eos -tus ad -tas -queris eas
Nochahat lenisetarim **tiredefim** Nochah lenisetarot̄ **tiredefen**

-ta ad -tas -queris eas -tus ad -tum -queris hec
Nochahat lenisetarot̄ **tiredefi** ạotan Nochah lenochah **tiredof zeh**

-ta ad -tum -queris hec -tus ad -tum -queris hanc {+ ad -ta eam […]
Nochahat lenochah **tiredefi zet̄** Nochah lenochahat̄ **tiredof zoat̄ tirod**[…]}

218 -te] *lege* -ta hec] *lege* hunc 219 ạo] *punctum infra* a 220 hec] *lege* hanc 223 nochah] noshah *ms a. c.* ạeleh] *punctum infra* a radafete] radafeta *ms a. c.* {a}eleh] a *add. s. l.* 224 -te] *lege* -ta 225 nochah] nochaha *ms a. c.* ạel[1]] *lege* ạele | *punctum infra* a nochahat̄] noshahat̄ *ms a. c.* lenocha{h}ot̄] h[2] *add. s. l.* ạel[2]] *lege* ạele | *punctum infra* a 227 nochahat] *lege* nochahot 232 ạo] *punctum infra* a se iahaseh] se iaehaseh *ms a. c.* 234 ạo] hạo *ms a. c.* | *punctum infra* a 235 -tas] *lege* -tam 236 leniseterim] *lege* leniseteret lenisetarim] lenisetaret *ms a. c.* 239 hec] *lege* hunc 240 ạotan] *punctum infra* a 241 hec] *lege* hunc 241–242 + ad…tirod[…] *add. alia manus* 242 zet̄] *lege* zeh

-ta *ad -tam* *-quetur* *hanc* *-tus* *ad -tos* *-quetur* *istos*
No{c}hahat̄ lenochahat̄ **tiredefi** **zoạt** Nocha lenochaim **tiredof** **eleh**

-ta *ad -tos* *-queris* *istos* *-tus* *ad -tas* *-queris* *istas* *et sic [...]*
Nochahat̄ leno{c}hahim **tiredefi** **eleh** Nocha lenochahot **tiredef** **ạel** veken [...]

-ta *ad -tas* *-ti* *ad -tos* *-quemini* *istos*
Nochahat lenochaot̄ **tiredefi** el Nochahim lenochahim **tiredefu** **eleh**

-te *ad -tos* *-quemini* *-istas* *-ti* *ad -tas* *-quemini* *istas*
Nocha{h}ot̄ lenochahim **tiredefenah** **eleh** nochahim lenochahot̄ **tiredefu** **el**

-te *ad -tas* *-quemini* *istas*
Nochahot lenochahot̄ **tiredefenah** **el**

mas.
lazachar

imperat. *in uerbo* *ut sibi* *persequere me* *ar.* *fem.* *persequere me*
Siwi limedaber behasemo **radefeni** lanekeuat̄ **ridefini**

a *mas.* *-quamini me* *ad fem.* *-quamini* *me* *mas.* *ar.* *mas.*
lazacharim **ridefuni** linekeuot̄ **redofenah** **aot̄i** zacharim lizecharim **ride[fum]**

fe. *ad* *fe.* *-quamini* *nos* *fe.* *ad* *mas.* *-quamini nos*
Nekeuot̄ lenekeuot̄ **redofenah** **aotanu** Nekeuot̄ lizekarim **ridefenu**

mas. *ad* *fe.* *-quamini* *nos*
zecharim linekeuot̄ **redofenah** **aotanu**

Imperatiuum *ad persequendum* *absconditum* *-quere eum* *et a fem.* *-quere eam*
Siwi **liredof** hanisetar **Radefehu** veliniseteṛeṭ **ridefahi**

et fe. *ad* *ab...-tum* *-queris eum* *et fe.* *a ab...-tum* *-quere eam*
vnekeuat̄ lenisetar **ridefihu** vnekeuah ha niseteret **ridefiha** **uel rodefih[a]**

244 no{c}hahat̄] c *add. s. l.* zoạt] *punctum infra* a nocha] *lege* nochah lenochaim] *lege* lenochahim 245 -queris[1]] *lege* -quetur 246 leno{c}hahim] c *add. s. l.* nocha] *lege* nochah ạel] *lege* ạele | *punctum infra* a 248 lenochaot̄] *lege* lenochahot̄ el] *lege* eleh 250 nocha{h}ot̄] h[2] *add. s. l.* el] *lege* eleh 252 el] *lege* eleh 256 lanekeuat̄] *lege* lanekeuah 257 a] *lege* ad 259 -quamini[1]] *scr. supra* aotanu 260 redofenah] rodefenah *ms a. c.* 261 -quamini] -quamini nos *ms a. c.* 263 a] *lege* ad 265 a] *lege* ar -tum[2]] *lege* -tam 266 ha niseteret] ha nisetarim *ms a. c. corr. s. l.*

fol. 196r

plurale	*ad singulare*	*-quamini eum*	*ad fe. singulare*	*-quamini eam*
Rabim	le iahid̄	**ridefuhu**	linekeuah	**ridefuha**

ad -tos	*-queris eos*	*ad fe. -nas*	*-queris eas*	*et fe.*	*ad -tos*	*-quamini eos*
ha nisetarim	**Radefem**	ha nisetarot̄	**radefen**	vnekeuah	ha nisetarim	**ridefim**

et fe.	*ad -tas*	*-queris eas*	*et plurale*	*ad fe. -nas*	*-quamini eas*
v nekauah	ha nisetarot	**ridefin**	v Rabim	hanisetarot̄	**ridefun**

et plurale	*ad -tos*	*-quamini eos*	*et plurale*	*ad plurale mas.*	*-quamini*	*eos*
ve Rabim	ha nisetarim	**ridefum**	ve Rabot̄	ha nisetarim	**redofenah**	**ạot̄am**

et fe. plurale	*ad plurale fe.*	*-quamini*	*eas*
ve Rabot̄	ha nisetarot̄	**redofenah**	**ạot̄an**

presens
hovet̄

mas.	*loquens procl.*	*deseipso*	*super*	*solo*	*qui persequitur*	*pesequitur me*
zachar	medaber	behasemo	hal	ha-iahid̄	harodefo	**rodefi**

et ad fe.	*persequitur*	*me*	*et ad plurale*	*persequitur nos*	*et ad plurale fe.*	*persequitur nos*
ve ha nekeuah	**rodefeta**	aot̄i	vharabim	**rodefenu**	veharabot̄	**rodefatenu**

et singulare	*ad singulare*	*abscon-ditum*	*-quitur eum*	*et singulare*	*ad fe.*	*-tam*	*persequetur eam*
ve iahid̄	ha iahid̄	nisetar	**rodefo**	ve iahid̄	ha nekeuah	niseteret	**rodefahi**

et fe.	*ad singulare mas.*	*-quetur eum*	*et mas. singulare*	*ad plurale mas.*	*-quitur eos*
ve nekeuah	ha iahid̄	**rodefatu**	ve iahid̄	harabim	**rodefam**

et singulare fe.	*ad plurale mas.*	*pesequitur eos*	*et mas. singulare*	*ad plurale fe.*	*-quitur eas*	*et singulare fe.*	*ad fe. plurale*	*-quitur eas*
vi huadah	ha rabim	**rodefatam**	ve iahid̄	ha rabot̄	**rodefan**	vi hid̄ha	rabot̄	**rodefatan**

et singulare	*ad singulare*	*probatum*	*-sequitur te*	*et singulare*	*ad fe.*	*-quitur te*
ve iahid̄	ha iahid	nocha	**rodefecha**	ve iahid̄	ha nekeuah	**rodofen**

269 ridefuha] ridefu ha *ms* 270 -nas] *lege* -tas? 271 ha[3]] *lege* la 272 -nas] *lege* -tas (?) 273 v nekauah] *lege* venekeuah ha] *lege* la hanisetarot̄] *lege* lanisetarot̄ 275 ha[1]] *lege* la ha[2]] *lege* la ạot̄am] *punctum infra* a 277 ha] *lege* la ạot̄an] *punctum infra* a 279 hovet̄] *lege* hoveh 280 procl.] *lege* pro uel deseipso] *lege* de se ipso 282 ad[1]] *lege* ar. ad[2]] *lege* ar. ad[3]] *lege* ar. 283 rodefeta] *lege* rodefet rodefatenu] *lege* rodefotenu 285 persequetur] *lege* persequitur 286 ha[1]] *lege* la ha[2]] *lege* la rodefahi] *lege* rodefah 289 -quetur] *lege* -quitur 290 ha] *lege* la harabim] *lege* larabim 292–294 -quitur eas rodefatan] *scr. infra l.* 294 vi huadah] *lege* vi hidah (ויחידה) ha[1]] *lege* la ha[2]] *lege* la rabot̄] *lege* lerabot̄ 297 ha[1]] *lege* la nocha] *lege* nochah ha[2]] *lege* la rodofen] lege rodefech?

et fe.	*ad solum*		*-quitur te*	*et mas. solum*	*ad plures*	*-quitur vos*
v nekeuah	ha iahid̄	n{o}cha	**rodefatech**	ve iahid̄	ha rabim	**rodefechem**

et singulare	*ad pl. mas.*	*persequitur uos*	*et mas.*	*ad fe. pl.*	*persequitur uos*
vi hidah	ha rabim	**rodefatechem**	ve iahid	ha rabot̄	**rodefene**

et sola	*ad plures fe.*	*-quitur uos*
vi hidah̄	ha rabot̄	**rodefetechen**

res uel uerbum	*unius*	*operis*
hauar	ahad	pahul

loquens	*de se ipso*	*persecucio mea*	*et a plures*	*persecucio nostra*
ha medaber	behasemo	**redufati**	ve ha rabim	**redufatenu**

duas	*res*	*operatas*
senei	deuarim	pehulim

qui loquitur	*de se ipso*	*persecuciones mee*	*et ad plures*	*persecuciones nostre*
ha medaber	behasemo	**redufotai**	ve ha rabim	**redufoteinu**

quatuor	*ar. he idiomata*	*ar. mas.*	*et ar. fe.*
arebahah	ha lesonot	le zachar	ve la nekeuah

qui loquitur	*de incerto*	*operato uel opere*	*et de operatis uel operibus*	*persecu-ciones sue*	*-ciones sue*	*uel*	*persecutiones*
ha medaber	minisetar	mi pahul	v mipehulim	**redufato**	**redufotai**	ve ao	**redufo**

et de fem. incerta	*persecucio eius*	*-ciones eius*	*et de incertis*	*persecuciones eorum*	*persecuciones eorum*	*eorum*
v mi neseteret	**redufatah**	**redufotẹịha**	v minisetarim	**redufatam**	**redufotam**	**-teihen**

et de femin. incertis	*persecucio earum*	*-cuciones earum*	*-cuciones earum*
v mi nisetarot	**redufatan**	**redufotan**	**redufoteihech**

et de certa	*persecucio tua*	*-cuciones tue*	*et de fe. certa*	*persecucio tua*
v mi nocha	**redufatecha**	**redufoteicha**	v mi nochahah	**redutateche**

persecuciones tue
redufotaich

et de certis	*persecucio uostra*	*{-ciones uostre*	*et de fe. certis*	*persecuciones uostre*
u mi nochahim	**Redufateichem**	**redufoteichem**}	v mi nochahot̄	**redufatechen**

300 ha^1] *lege* la n{o}cha] *lege* nochah | o *add. s. l.* ha^2] *lege* la 302 ha^1] *lege* la ha^2] *lege* la rodefene] *lege* rodefechen (?) 304 ha] *lege* la 307 se ipso] seipso *ms* a] *lege* ad 308 ha^2] *lege* la 312 ha^2] *lege* la 315–316 persecuciones sue] *lege* persecucio sua 316 sue^2] *lege* mee? 317 redufo] *lege* redufot (?) 319 eorum^3] *lege* earum 320 redufotẹịha] *cum vocalibus hebraicis* 321 neseteret] *lege* niseteret 323 redufoteihech] *lege* redufoteihen 325 nocha] *lege* nochahat 328 persecuciones] persecucones *ms* 329–330 -ciones uostre redufoteichem] *scr. sub l.*

Grammar Textual Unit 2: The Essay on Hebrew Vowels and Accents

fol. 196v

[Col. 1] Ceteras uocales uocant heua-|-roth id est iuncturas uel iungentes; | set hebrei non habent uocales sicut | greci et latini, et quedam alie ling-|-ue, set apicibus id est punctis et lineis | quibusdam designant sonos uo-|-calium in qualibet littera. Et sunt | xii quia quamlibet uocalem sonant | dupliciter et insuper habent sextum sonum | quasi medium inter uocales et ille | quoque duobus modis profertur uel tribus | secundum quod diuersimode punctatur. | Hii omnes soni et apices sonorum | nominaque apicum patent per or-|-dinem in pagina precedente.

P-|-rimus autem representatur per vau | cum puncto ante et sonat u. Et uocatur | surik, quod interpretatur sibilus, quia | in extremo oris rotundi profertur, | sicut rotundantur labia quando homo | sibilat.

Secundus scribitur per lineam cum | puncto subtus et sonat a. Et uocatur | kames gadol, hoc est accepcio pungni | maior, quia cames significat gallice en-|-pomher, hoc est tollere cum pungno, | ac si dicerem pugillare, quia iste sonus || [Col. 2] profertur cum magna oris aperti comprehen-|-sione, sicut cum manus aperta contra-|-hitur ut aliquis tollat quemadmo-|-dum dicitur Le. 2, quod sacerdos de-|-buit tollere pugillum simile et hec | est a longa.

Tercius fit cum punc-|-to unico sub littera et sonat i. Non | solum sub iod set sub quacumque alia | littera cum sono ipsius. Vocatur autem hirek, | quod gallice dicitur rechiner, quia quando profertur | i, os aperitur et labia contrahuntur sicut | quando fit rictus, unde ab hoc ebreo dicitur fremere | et frendere, ut S. 34 et iiii 8.

Quar-|-tus habet duo puncta iacencia sub lit-|-tera, et sonat quasi inter e et i. Hoc est non | aperte e set fere i, et uocatur ca-|-mes caton, hoc est paruus cames, quia fit | cum apercione et comprehensione oris, set non | cum tanta sicut secundus supradictus.|

Quintus habet punctum in parte anteriori superius | et sonat o. Vocaturque holim quod est silere | nomini (?) sompnii. Predicti autem q<uinque> soni | dicuntur habere frenum quia sunt producti, et intra den[tes] | retardantur quasi retrahuntur.

12 significat] sigiit *ms a.c.*

Sextus habet | tria puncta subtus retro quasi caudam, et sonat | u, set interius quam primus et uicinius sono nostri ||

fol. 197r

[Col. 1] o et u breuis. Vocatur autem melophim, quod | est plenum os, quia quasi ore pleno profertur, | aliquantulum quidem aperto et rotundo, set | non sicut sibilus.

Septimus habet line-|-am solam sub littera iacentem et sonat | sicut secundus, set uelocius quasi breuis a. | Vocaturque phatha gadol id est apertura ma-|-ior ad differentiam noni ut patebit, et est | a beuis.

Octauus habet duo puncta | stancia sub littera et habet sonum medium | quia non sonat a nec e nec i nec o nec | u, set medio modo. Quem sonum non habent | latini uel greci, set alie lingue, ut gal-|-lica et anglica, et arabica et cetere. Vo-|-catur autem saba uel hateph quod significat | auferre.

Nonus habet tria puncta sub | littera et sonat sicut quartus, set | eminencius uidelicet uicinius sono | a et remocius ab i, magis autem sub | paluto quam nostrum e. Et uocatur pha-|-tha caton, id est apertura minor, quia | aperte sonat, set minus quam septimus, | et est e breuis.

Decimus habet sub littera | lineam cum puncto uno subtus et duobus | stantibus retro lineam. Sonat autem o | sicut quintus, set uelocius, quia est o bre-|-uis. Vocatur autem hateph cames for-|-te ideo quia accipit spiritum et tamen aufert, | quia non plene sonat. Hii q<uinque> posterio-|-res non habent frenum, quia sunt breues.

Undecimus habet sub littera lineam cum duo-|-bus punctis stantibus retro et sonat sicut | octauus set contractius sono a, unde interpretes || [Col. 2] sepius eum representauerunt per a. Vocatur autem | hateph phatha forte quia aperte sonat | set non plene nec ponitur nisi cum iiii litteris gut-|-talibus, aleph, heth, he, ain.

Duodecimus | habet sub littera quinque puncta scilicet duo | stancia et tria quasi triangulis. Sonat autem | sicut octauus set contractius sono e, unde interpretes | eum sonuerunt per e. Et uocatur hateph phatha | caton forte ideo quia licet aperte sonet non | tantum plene nec ponitur nisi cum quatuor litteris | predictis.

31 melophim] *lege* melophum   42 paluto] *lege* palato   53 guttalibus] *lege* gutturalibus   56 hateph] hceph *ms a. c.*

Predicti duodecim apices possunt | dici uocalicii quia nullius littere patet sonus, | nisi per aliquam istorum sibi appositorum. Et priores 10 | patent, in una dictione, nutariecon, uide | supra.

Item duo sunt alii apices modera-|-tiui siue uirtuales quia moderantur uirtutem | littere cui apponuntur. Quando in uentre littere | ponitur simplex punctus auget sonum eius, | et rigidius siue forcius sonat. Quando autem super | litteram ponitur linea iacens minuitur sonus | eius. Prior uocatur dages, secunda raphe, uide | supra. Et ibi diximus quod sex littere, scilicet beth, | gimel, daleth, chaph, phe, thau laxant | sonum suum quando eas sequitur iod uel he | uel uau uel aleph, nisi ibi fiat distinctio | *simane* uel nota cantus. Sunt autem 19 note | quasi apices que distinguunt *simanim* siue | cantu m. Sunt enim preter apices pretactas | qui sonum faciunt alii 22 sentenciales, | uidelicet 19 distinctiui, qui dicuntur reges, | et 7 coniunctiui qui dicuntur seruientes, quia duo | uerba coniungunt quasi sensui deseruiunt. Vide supra | nomina et figuras eorum. Itaque apices ebreorum sunt | 36, scilicet 12 uocalicii, duo moderatiui, 22 sentenciales.

61 moderantur] *lege* moderant   62 in] n. in *ms a. c.*   67 simane] Simane and simanim below are transliterations of Hebrew סימן, "sign, symbol." It is likely that the author intended *ṭeʿamim*, "accents, cantillation signs."   69 19] *lege* 15

Translation

fol. 196v

[Col. 1] What remains are vowels which are called heua|rot (הברות) that is "connections" or "connecting." | However, the Hebrews do not have vowels like | the Greeks and Latins, and certain other langua|ges, but mark the sounds of the vo|wels in any letter with strokes, that is with dots and lines. There are | twelve of them because every vowel sounds | double, and in addition they have a sixth sound | like intermediary between the vowels, and this one | also is pronounced in two or three ways | according to the different manners of its pointing. | All these sounds and strokes of the sounds | are laid out according to their | order on the previous page.[1]

1. Indeed, the part of the grammar in Hebrew characters ends with a list of vowels containing their graphic symbols and names; see fols. 198r–197v.

The | first one is represented by a vav | with a dot in front,[2] and it sounds *u*.[3] It is called | *shuruḳ* (שרוק), which is translated as "whistling," because | it is pronounced by the extremity of the rounded mouth, | as the lips become rounded when a man | whistles.

The second is written as a line with | a dot below[4] and sounds *ạ*. It is called | *ḳamaẓ gadol,* that is the "big seizure with a fist" | because cames means in French "en|pomher" (Modern French "empoigner"), that is "to seize with a fist" | and as if I said "to fist-clench," because this sound || [Col. 2] is pronounced with a large grasp of the mouth wide-open | as if the open palm contracted | to take something; | similarly it is said in Leviticus 2 (Leviticus 2:2)[5] that a priest had to | grab a fistful of flour. It sounds like | a long *a*.

The third is made with one single | dot under a letter and sounds *i*. Not | only under a *yod* but under any other | letter with its own sound. It is called *ḥireḳ* (חירק), | that in French is "rechiner" ("to bare one's teeth, to snarl"[6]) because when *i* is uttered | the mouth opens and the lips are contracted as | when one makes a grimace. From that it is said in Hebrew "to growl" | and "to gnash one's teeth" as in Psalm 34[7] and IIII, 8.[8]

The | fourth has two dots lying under a let|ter, and sound like between *e* and *i*. This is not | an open *e* but almost *i*, and is called *ḳa|maẓ ḳaṭan,* that is small *ḳamaẓ,* because it is made | with the opening and contracting the mouth but not | as much as the abovementioned second (vowel). |

The fifth has a dot in the upper part in front,[9] | and sounds *o*. And it is called *ḥolem* which means "to be silent," | as noun (?) "sleep." The aforementioned five sounds | are said to have a brake because they are produced and | are delayed as if drawn back between the teeth.

2. *Puncto ante*: the dot in *shuruḳ* "precedes" the body of the letter if it is considered in Latin order, from left to right: וּ.

3. The Latin spelling uses v and u interchangeably. It is therefore likely that the text refers to the pronunciation as *u*.

4. Although the printed form of the *ḳamaẓ* resembles a tiny T, in medieval manuscripts the symbol is indeed composed of a horizontal line and a detached dot below it.

5. Leviticus 2:2: וקמץ משם מלא קמצו מסלתה: "quorum unus tollet pugillum plenum similae."

6. See *AND*[2] s.v. rechiner.

7. Psalm 34:16 (MT 35:16) חָרֹק עָלַי שִׁנֵּימוֹ : "frenduerunt super me dentibus suis."

8. It is difficult to understand this reference. None of the occurences of the root חרק in the Bible corresponds to a chapter 4 verse 8.

9. "In parte anteriori superius" refers to the upper left-side part of the letter. Anterior, "in front," refers to the place of the dot from the Latin direction of reading, from left to right.

The sixth has | three dots below and behind, like a tail, and sounds | *u*, but more internally than the first one, close to our sound ||

fol. 197r

[Col. 1] short *o* and *u*. It is called *melo fum*, which | is "full mouth," because it is uttered as if with a mouth full | certainly a little open and rounded but | not like whistling.

The seventh has one single | line placed under a letter and sounds | like the second but quicker, like a short *a*. And it is called *pataḥ gadol*, that is "large | opening," apparently to differentiate from the ninth,[10] and it is | a short *a*.

The eighth has two dots | standing below a letter and has a medium sound | because it sounds neither *a* nor *e*, nor *i*, nor *o*, nor | *u* but in between. The Latins and Greeks do not have this sound | but it (exists) in other languages like French, and English, and Arabic, and others. | It is called *shva* or *ḥaṭaf*, which means | "to snatch away."[11]

The ninth has three dots under | a letter and sounds like the fourth but | clearer, apparenty closer to the sound | *a* and further from *i*, more under | the palate than our *e*. And it is called *pa|taḥ ḳaṭan*, that is "small opening" because | it sounds open but less than the seventh, | and it is a short *e*.

The tenth has, under a letter, | a line with one dot below and two (dots) | standing behind the line.[12] It sounds *o* | like the fifth but quicker because it is a short *o*. | It is called *ḥaṭaf ḳamaẓ*, pro|bably because it takes air but then takes it away | because it does not sound complete. The latter five (vowels) | do not have a brake[13] because they are short. |

The eleventh has a line under a letter with | two dots standing behind, and sounds like | the eighth but closer to the sound *a*; this is why the commentators (informers) || [Col. 2] often represented it as *a*. It is called | *ḥaṭaf pataḥ* maybe because it sounds open | but not fully, nor is it placed with any letter but four gutturals: *alef*, *ḥet*, *heh*, *ʿayin*.

10. See below; the vowel number nine, *segol*, is called *pataḥ ḳaṭan*.

11. Auferre, "take away, snatch away," translates *ḥaṭaf*.

12. Retro, "behind," means to the right of the line: the components are described from left to right.

13. Reference to *meteg*, a cantillation sign.

The twelfth | has five dots under a letter, that is two | standing and three like a triangle. It sounds in fact | like the eighth but closer to the sound *e*, that is why the commentators (informers) | made it sound like an *e*. And it is called small *ḥaṭaf pataḥ*, | probably because although it sounds open, (it sounds) | not so fully, nor is it placed but with the four letters | mentioned above.

The aforementioned twelve strokes can | be said to be vocalic because no letter will have a sound | unless through one of those attached to it. And the first 10 | are illustrated in one word "notaricon," see above.[14]

In addition, there are two other strokes moder|ating or virtual because they modify the virtue | of a letter to which they are attached. When in the belly of the letter | is placed a single dot, its sound is increased, | and it sounds harder or stronger. When however over | a letter is placed a horizontal line, its sound | decreases. The first is called *dagesh*, the second *rafeh*, see | above. And here we said that six letters, that is *bet*, | *gimel, dalet, kaf, peh, tav* weaken | their sound when they are followed by a *yod*, or *heh* | or *vav* or *alef*, unless a difference of a symbol or cantillation note is effected here |. There are in fact 19 notes | like strokes which make up different *simanim* or | cantillations. Thus, there are, besides the aforementioned strokes | which make sound, other 22 syntactic ones, | including 15 disjunctive, which are called "kings" | and 7 conjunctive, which are called "servants," because they link two | words as if they were serving the meaning. See above | their names and graphic shapes. Thus, the strokes of the Hebrew are | 36, that is 12 vowels, two moderators and 22 syntactic.

14. On fols. 197v and 198r, the word נוטריקון appears twice with vowels.

Grammar Textual Unit 3: The Hebrew Grammar in Hebrew Characters

Fol. 202v is blank.

fol. 202r

[...א]כָּל אש׳ | [...] אֵלֵךְ | [...]שן אִיקַץ | [...] אחַמֵּם [...] יֹאכַּל יִשְׁתֶה | [...י]לֵךְ יַבֹּא יִשַן | [...]ן יִשְׁכַּבֿ יְחַמֵּם | [...י]לְבַּש ״ תַּעֲשֶׂה תֹּאכַּל | תִשְׁתֶה תַּקוּם תֵּלֵךְ | תַּבֹּא תִּישַׁן תִּשְׁכַּבֿ | תְּחַמֵּם תִּלְבַּש ״ נֹאכַּל נַעֲשֶׂה נִשְׁתֶה | נַקוּם נֶלֵךְ נַבֹּא נִישַׁן | נִשְׁכַּבֿ נְחַמֵּם נִלְבַּש | נֵצֵא נֵשֵׁבֿ ״ צִיוּוּי לְאֶחַדְ ׳ אֱכוֹל | שְׁתֵה עֲשֶׂה קוּם לֵךְ || בֹּא יְשַׁן שְׁכֹּב חַמֵּם | לְבוּש צֵא שֵׁבֿ ׳ צִיוּוּי לְאִשַׁה אַחָת ׳ | עֲשִׂי אִיכְלִי שְׁתִי | קוּמִי לְכִי בֹּאִי יַשְׁנִי | שִׁכְּבִי חֲמִי לִבְשִׁי צְאִי | שְׁבִי : צִיוּוּי לִשְׁנֵי | אֲנַשִׁים ׳ עֲשׂוּ אִיכְלוּ | שְׁתוּ קוּמוּ לְכוּ בֹּאוּ | יַשְׁנוּ שִׁכְבוּ חֲמוּ | לִבְשׁוּ צְאוּ שְׁבוּ : ׳ צִיוּוּי לִשְׁתֵּי נַשִׁים | עֲשֵׂינָה אֱכֹלְנָה | שְׁתֵינָה קוּמְנָה לֵכְנָה | יְשַׁנֶּנָה שְׁכַבְנָה | חְמַמְנָה לְבַשְׁנָה | שְׁאֵינָה שַׁבְנָה ״ עֲבַר | לְאִיש אֵחַד ׳ עֲשַׂה

fol. 201v

אֲכַל שַׁתַּה קָם הַלַךְ | יָשָׁן שָׁכָבֿ חַמֵּם לָבַש | נָשָׂא שָׁבֿ ״ עָבָר | לְאִשָּׁה אַחַתֿ ׳ עַשְׂתָה | אָכְלַה שַׁתַּה קָמָה | דִּבְּרַה הַלְכַה יַשְׁנַה | שַׁכְבַה חַמְמַה לַבְּשַׁה | נַשְׂאַה שַׁבַּה ״ עֲבַר | לְעַצְמִי {ול}אַחֵר ׳ | עַשִׁינוּ אַכַּלְנוּ | שַׁתִינוּ קַמְנוּ דִּבַּרְנוּ | הַלַכְנוּ יַשַׁנְנוּ שַׁכַבְנוּ | חַמַּמְנוּ לַבַּשְׁנוּ | נַשַׂאנוּ שַׁבְנוּ : וְכֵן | לַאִשַׁה ׳ דְּבַר הוֵה | לְאֵחַד ׳ אוֹכֵל שוֹתֵה | עוֹשֵׂה מְדַבֵּר דוֹבֵר | מֵהַלֵךְ הוֹלֵךְ יַשֵׁן || שוֹכֵבֿ מְחַמֵּם לוֹבֵש | נוֹשֵׂא ״ דַּבַר הוֵה | לִשְׁנַים ׳ עוֹשִׂים | אוֹכְלִים שוֹתִים | מְדַבְּרִים הוֹלְכִים | יְשֵׁנִים שוֹכְבִים | מְחַמְמִים לוֹבְשִׁים | נוֹשְׂאִים ״ לַנְקֵיבַה |

1 [...א]כָּל אש] Anticipation of אשתה, probably written in full at the beginning of the next line, not preserved. אחַמֵּם] *lege* אֲחַמֵּם 2 יַבֹּא] *lege* יָבֹא יְחַמֵּם] *lege* יְחַמֵּם 3 תִשְׁתֶה] *lege* תִּשְׁתֶּה תַּקוּם] *lege* תָּקוּם תַּבֹּא] *lege* תָּבֹא 4 נַעֲשֶה] *lege* נַעֲשֶׂה נִשְׁתֶה] *lege* נִשְׁתֶּה נַקוּם] *lege* נָקוּם נֶלֵךְ] *lege* נֵלֵךְ נַבֹּא] *lege* נָבֹא נְחַמֵּם] *lege* נְחַמֵּם 5 צִיוּוּי] *lege* צִיּוּוִי לְאֶחַדְ] *lege* לְאֶחָד עֲשֶׂה] *lege* עֲשֵׂה 6 לְאִשַׁה] *lege* לְאִשָּׁה אַחָת] *lege* אַחַת יַשְׁנִי] *lege* יִשְׁנִי *vel* שְׁנִי חֲמִי] *lege* חַמְּמִי 7 צִיוּוּי] *lege* צִיּוּוִי אֲנַשִׁים] *lege* אֲנָשִׁים יַשְׁנוּ] *lege* יִשְׁנוּ *vel* שְׁנוּ חֲמוּ] *lege* חַמְּמוּ 8 צִיוּוּי] *lege* צִיּוּוִי נַשִׁים] *lege* נָשִׁים עֲשֵׂינָה] *lege* עֲשֶׂינָה לֵכְנָה] *lege* לֵכְנָה יְשַׁנֶּנָה] *lege* יְשַׁנָּה *vel* שְׁנָּה שְׁכַבְנָה] *lege* שְׁכַבְנָה חְמַמְנָה] *lege* חַמֵּמְנָה 9 לְבַשְׁנָה] *lege* לְבַשְׁנָה שְׁאֵינָה] *lege* צְאֶינָה שַׁבְנָה] *lege* שֵׁבְנָה עֲבַר] *lege* עָבָר אֵחַד] *lege* אֶחָד עֲשַׂה] *lege* עֲשָׂה 10 אֲכַל] *lege* אָכַל שַׁתַּה] *lege* שָׁתָה הַלַךְ] *lege* הָלַךְ יָשָׁן] *lege* יָשֵׁן שָׁכָב] *lege* שָׁכַב חַמֵּם] *lege* חִמֵּם לָבַש] *lege* לָבַש עַשְׂתָה] *lege* עָשְׂתָה 11 אָכְלַה] *lege* אָכְלָה שַׁתַּה] *lege* שָׁתְתָה קַמָה] *lege* קָמָה דִּבְּרַה] *lege* דִּבְּרָה הַלְכַה] *lege* הָלְכָה יַשְׁנַה] *lege* יָשְׁנָה שַׁכְבַה] *lege* שָׁכְבָה חַמְמַה] *lege* חִמְּמָה לַבְּשַׁה] *lege* לָבְשָׁה נַשְׂאַה] *lege* נָשְׂאָה שַׁבַּה] *lege* שָׁבָה 12 עֲבַר] *lege* עָבַר {ול}אַחֵר] וְל *add. s. l.* עַשִׁינוּ] *lege* עָשִׂינוּ אַכַּלְנוּ] *lege* אָכַלְנוּ שַׁתִינוּ] *lege* שָׁתִינוּ דִּבַּרְנוּ] *lege* דִּבַּרְנוּ הַלַכְנוּ] *lege* הָלַכְנוּ יַשַׁנְנוּ] *lege* יָשַׁנּוּ שַׁכַבְנוּ] *lege* שָׁכַבְנוּ 13 חַמַּמְנוּ] *lege* חִמַּמְנוּ לַבַּשְׁנוּ] *lege* לָבַשְׁנוּ נַשַׂאנוּ] *lege* נָשָׂאנוּ לַאִשַׁה] *lege* לָאִשָּׁה הוֵה] *lege* הֹוֶה לְאֵחַד] *lege* לְאֶחָד שוֹתֵה] *lege* שׁוֹתֶה עוֹשֵׂה] *lege* עוֹשֶׂה 14 מֵהַלֵךְ] *lege* מְהַלֵּךְ יַשֵׁן] *lege* יָשֵׁן דַּבַר] *lege* דָּבָר *uel* דְּבַר הוֵה] *lege* הֹוֶה 15 מְחַמְמִים] *lege* מְחַמְּמִים לַנְקֵיבַה] *lege* לַנְקֵבָה

אוֹכֵלֶתָ שׁוֹתַה עוֹשַׂה | מְדַבֵּרֶתָ הוֹלֶכֶתָ שׁוֹכֵבֶתָ | מְחַמֵּמֶתָ לוֹבֵשֶׁתָ | נוֹשֵׂאתָ ״ דְּבַּר הֹוֵה | לַנְקִיבוֹת ׳ אוֹכְלוֹתָ | שׁוֹתוֹת עוֹשׁוֹת | מְדַבְּרוֹתָ הוֹלְכוֹת | שׁוֹכְבוֹתָ מְחַמְּמוֹתָ | לוֹבְשׁוֹתָ נוֹשְׂאוֹתָ | שַׁבוֹתָ ״ עַבַר לְנוֹכַח

fol. 201r

לְאֶחָד ״ עַשִׂיתַ | אַכַלְתַּ שַׁתִיתַ קַמְתַּ | הַלַכְתַּ יַשַׁ{נְ}נְתַּ שַׁכַּבְתַּ | חַמַּמְתַּ לַבַּשְׁתַּ נַשַׂאתַ | נַשַׂאתַ שַׁבְתַּ ׳ עַבַּר | לְנוֹכַּח לִשְׁנַיִם | עְשִׂיתֶם אֲכַלְתֶּם | שְׁתִיתֶם קַמְתֶּם לַכְּתֶם | יְשַׁנְתֶּם שְׁכַּבְתֶּם | חֲמַמְתֶּם לְבַשְׁתֶּם | נְשַׂאתֶם שַׁבְתֶּם ״ עַבַּר לְאִשָּׁה אַחַת | לְנוֹכַחַת ׳ עַשִׂיתְ | אַכַּלְתְּ שַׁתִיתְ קַמְתְּ | הַלַכְתְּ יַשַׁנְתְּ שַׁכַבְתְּ | חַמַּמְתְּ לַבַּשְׁתְּ נַשַׂאתְ | שַׁבְתְּ ״ עַבַּר לְנוֹכַּח | לִשְׁתֵּי נָשִׁים ׳ עְשִׂיתֶן || אֲכַלְתֶּן שְׁתִיתֶן קַמְתֶּן | הֲלַכְתֶּן יְשַׁנְתֶּן שְׁכַבְתֶּן | חֲמַמְתֶּן לְבַשְׁתֶּן | נְשַׂאתֶן שַׁבְתֶּן ״ עַבַּר | לִשְׁנֵי אֲנָשִׁים לְנִסְתַּרִים ׳ | עַשׂוּ אַכְלוּ שַׁתוּ קַמוּ | הַלְכוּ יַשְׁנוּ שַׁכְבוּ | חַמְּמוּ לַבְשׁוּ נַשְׂאוּ | שַׁבוּ ׳ וְכֵן לִשְׁתֵּי נָשִׁים | לְנִסְתַּרוֹתָ ״ לְשׁוֹן עַתִיד | לְאִישׁ אֶחָד ׳ אֶעֱשֶׂה | אוֹכַל ׳ וְכֵן הַרְבֵּה | כְּשֶׁמְדַבֵּר מֵעַצְמוֹ | לְשׁוֹן עַתִיד לְאַחֵר ׳ | יַעְשֶׂה יֹאכַל יִשְׁתֶּה | יַקוּם יֵלֵךְ ׳ לַרַבִּים לְשׁוֹן | עַתִיד לְנִסְתַּרִים ׳ יַעְשׂוּ | יֹאכְלוּ יִשְׁתּוּ יַקוּמוּ

16 אוֹכֵלֶתָ] lege אוֹכֶלֶתָ שׁוֹתַה] lege שׁוֹתָה עוֹשַׂה] lege עוֹשָׂה מְדַבֵּרֶתָ] lege מְדַבֶּרֶתָ הוֹלֶכֶתָ] lege הוֹלֶכֶתָ שׁוֹכֵבֶתָ] lege שׁוֹכֶבֶתָ מְחַמֵּמֶתָ] lege מְחַמֶּמֶתָ לוֹבֵשֶׁתָ] lege לוֹבֶשֶׁתָ נוֹשֵׂאתָ] lege נוֹשֵׂאתָ הֹוֵה] lege הֹוֶה 17 לַנְקִיבוֹת] lege לַנְּקֵבוֹת מְדַבְּרוֹתָ] lege מְדַבְּרוֹתָ מְחַמְּמוֹתָ] lege מְחַמְּמוֹתָ נוֹשְׂאוֹתָ 18 שַׁבוֹתָ] lege שָׁבוֹתָ עַבַר] lege עָבָר 19 לְאֶחָד] lege לְאֶחָד עַשִׂיתַ] lege עָשִׂיתָ אַכַלְתַּ] lege אָכַלְתָּ שַׁתִיתַ] lege שָׁתִיתָ קַמְתַּ] lege קַמְתָּ הַלַכְתַּ] lege הָלַכְתָּ יַשַׁ{נְ}נְתַּ] lege יָשַׁנְתָּ || נְ add. s. l. שַׁכַּבְתַּ] lege שָׁכַבְתָּ חַמַּמְתַּ] lege חִמַּמְתָּ לַבַּשְׁתַּ] lege לָבַשְׁתָּ 20 נַשַׂאתַ] lege נָשָׂאתָ || rep. ms שַׁבְתַּ] lege שַׁבְתָּ עַבַּר] lege עָבָר עְשִׂיתֶם] lege עֲשִׂיתֶם אֲכַלְתֶּם] lege אֲכַלְתֶּם שְׁתִיתֶם] lege שְׁתִיתֶם קַמְתֶּם] lege קַמְתֶּם 21 לַכְּתֶם] lege הֲלַכְתֶּם יְשַׁנְתֶּם] lege יְשַׁנְתֶּם || יְשַׁנְנתֶּם ms a. c. שְׁכַּבְתֶּם] lege שְׁכַבְתֶּם חֲמַמְתֶּם] lege חִמַּמְתֶּם לְבַשְׁתֶּם] lege לְבַשְׁתֶּם נְשַׂאתֶם] lege נְשָׂאתֶם שַׁבְתֶּם] lege שַׁבְתֶּם 22 עַבַּר] lege עָבָר לְאִשָּׁה] lege לְאִשָּׁה עַשִׂיתְ] lege עָשִׂיתְ אַכַּלְתְּ] lege אָכַלְתְּ שַׁתִיתְ] lege שָׁתִיתְ הַלַכְתְּ] lege הָלַכְתְּ יַשַׁנְתְּ] lege יָשַׁנְתְּ שַׁכַבְתְּ] lege שָׁכַבְתְּ 23 חַמַּמְתְּ] lege חִמַּמְתְּ לַבַּשְׁתְּ] lege לָבַשְׁתְּ נַשַׂאתְ] lege נָשָׂאתְ עַבַּר] lege עָבָר נָשִׁים] lege נָשִׁים עְשִׂיתֶן] lege עֲשִׂיתֶן אֲכַלְתֶּן] lege אֲכַלְתֶּן שְׁתִיתֶן] lege שְׁתִיתֶן 24 הֲלַכְתֶּן] lege הֲלַכְתֶּן יְשַׁנְתֶּן] lege יְשַׁנְתֶּן שְׁכַבְתֶּן] lege שְׁכַבְתֶּן חֲמַמְתֶּן] lege חִמַּמְתֶּן לְבַשְׁתֶּן] lege לְבַשְׁתֶּן נְשַׂאתֶן] lege נְשָׂאתֶן שַׁבְתֶּן] lege שַׁבְתֶּן עַבַּר] lege עָבָר 25 אֲנָשִׁים] lege אֲנָשִׁים לְנִסְתַּרִים] lege לְנִסְתָּרִים עַשׂוּ] lege עָשׂוּ אַכְלוּ] lege אָכְלוּ שַׁתוּ] lege שָׁתוּ קַמוּ] lege קָמוּ הַלְכוּ] lege הָלְכוּ יַשְׁנוּ] lege יָשְׁנוּ שַׁכְבוּ] lege שָׁכְבוּ חַמְּמוּ] lege חִמְּמוּ לַבְשׁוּ] lege לָבְשׁוּ 26 נַשְׂאוּ] lege נָשְׂאוּ שַׁבוּ] lege שָׁבוּ נָשִׁים] lege נָשִׁים לְנִסְתַּרוֹתָ] lege לְנִסְתָּרוֹתָ עַתִיד] lege עָתִיד אֶחָד] lege אֶחָד אֶעֱשֶׂה] lege אֶעֱשֶׂה 27 כְּשֶׁמְדַבֵּר] lege כְּשֶׁמְּדַבֵּר עַתִיד] lege עָתִיד יַעְשֶׂה] lege יַעֲשֶׂה יִשְׁתֶּה] lege יִשְׁתֶּה יַקוּם] lege יָקוּם 28 עַתִיד] lege עָתִיד לְנִסְתַּרִים] lege לְנִסְתָּרִים יַעְשׂוּ] lege יַעֲשׂוּ יַקוּמוּ] lege יָקוּמוּ

fol. 200v

יִלְכּוּ יִשְׁנוּ יִשְׁכְּבוּ | יַחְמְמוּ יִלְבְּשׁוּ יִשְׁאוּ | יֵשְׁבוּ ׳ וְכֵן לִשְׁתֵּי נַשִׁים | לְנִסְתַּרוֹת ״ לְנוֹכַח לִשְׁנֵי | אֲנַשִׁים לְשׁוֹן עַתִּידֹ ׳ | תַּעֲשׂוּ תֹאכְלוּ תִשְׁתּוּ | תַּקוּמוּ תִּלְכוּ תִשְׁנוּ | תִשְׁכְּבוּ תְחָמְמוּ תִלְבְּשׁוּ | תִשְׁאוּ תִצְאוּ תִשְׁאוּ ״ | וְיֵשׁ דְּבַרִים שֵׁשְׁמוֹתָּם | נוֹסַף ׳ אַסַף כְּמוֹ הוֹסִיף ׳ | הֶאֱבִידֹ כְּמוֹ אַבַּדֹ ׳ הִפְּקִידֹ | כְּמוֹ פַּקַדֹ ׳ הֶאְזִין כְּמוֹ | אִיזֵן הֵשִׁיבֹ כְּמוֹ שַׁבֹ ׳ | הֵבְאִישׁ כְּמוֹ בָּאַשׁ ׳ וְכֵן | הַרְבֵּה ׳ וְהֵנַּה {הַהֵי} נִקְרַא הַנּוֹסַף | וְיֵשׁ נוֹסַף שֵׁהַמֵּם נוֹסֵפֵת | מְדַבֵּר כמו דוֹבֵר ׳ מְהַלֵּךְ || כְּמוֹ הוֹלֵךְ מְאַסֵּף | כְּמוֹ אוֹסֵף ׳ מְבַקֵּר כמו | בֹּקֵר ׳ צֵירְקוֹנֵטְ ״ וְכֵן | הַרְבֵּה ׳ וְיֵשׁ דְּבַרִים | שֵׁנִקְרַאִים מִשְׁקַל כַּבֵּדֹ | וּמִשְׁקַל קַל פַּעַל {כְּמוֹ פִּעֵל} ׳ אַבַּדֹ | כְּמוֹ אִבֵּדֹ ׳ דַּבַק כְּמוֹ | דִּבֵּק ׳ גָּבָּר כְּמוֹ גִּבֵּר ׳ | שַׁבַּר כְּמוֹ שִׁבֵּר ׳ גַּדַּל {כְּמוֹ} | גִּדֵּל ׳ שַׁמַּר כְּמוֹ שִׁמֵּר ׳ | צַדַּק כְּמוֹ צִדֵּק ׳ וְכֵן | הַרְבֵּה ׳ בְּזֵה תּוּכַל לְהַבִּין | כָּל לְשׁוֹן עִבְרִי ׳ אֵשְׁמֹר | גַּרְדְּרֵי ׳ יִשְׁמֹר גַּרְדְּרַה ׳ | תִּשְׁמֹר גַּרְדְּרַשׁ ׳ נִשְׁמֹר | גַּרְדְּרוֹמְשׁ ׳ שְׁמוֹר | גַּרְדְּא ׳ שַׁמֵּר כמו כֵּן | אֵלַא {tamen} שֵׁזֵה {istud} מִמִּשְׁקַל

fol. 200r

כַּבֵּדֹ ׳ וְזֵה מִמִּשְׁקַל | קַל ׳ שִׁמְרוּ גַּרְדֵּישׁ | שַׁמְּרוּ גַּרְדֵּירְנְט ׳ | שְׁמַרְתִּיךָ גַּרְדֵּיטֵיי ׳ | שְׁמַרְתִּיךָ פִּיט גַּרְדֵּירְ ׳ | טֵיי ׳ שְׁמַרְתַּנִי | גַּרְדַּשְׁמֵי ׳ שְׁמַרְתַּנִי | פִּישְׁ גַּרְדֵּירְמֵיי ׳ | שְׁמְרֵנִי גַּרְדְּמֵיי | שְׁמַרַנִי גַּרְדַּהְמֵיי ׳ | שְׁמַרַהוּ גַּרְדְּהַלִּי ׳ וְכֵן | שְׁמַרוֹ ״ שַׁמַּר גַּרְדַּה ׳ | שַׁמְּרוּ גַּרְדֵּירְנְט ׳ | שַׁמַּרְתִּי גַּרְדֵּי ׳ | שְׁמַרְתֵּם גַּרְדַּשְׁטְשְׁ | שְׁמַרְנוּם גַּרְדַּמְשְׁאוּשׁ ׳ | שְׁמַרְתִּיכֵם גַּרְדֵּיבוֹשׁ ׳ | שְׁמַרְתַּנוּ גַּרְדַּשְׁנוֹשׁ ׳ | שְׁמַרְנוּכֵם גַּרְדַּמְשְׁבוֹשׁ ׳ || שׁוֹמֵר גַּרְדּוֹנְטְ ״ לַנְקֵיבַה | שְׁמַרְתַּהוּ גַּרְדַּלִּי ׳ אוֹ |

29 יִלְכּוּ] *lege* יֵלְכוּ יִשְׁנוּ] *lege* יִישְׁנוּ יִשְׁכְּבוּ] *lege* יִשְׁכְּבוּ יַחְמְמוּ] *lege* יְחַמְּמוּ נַשִׁים] *lege* נָשִׁים 30 לְנִסְתַּרוֹת] *lege* לְנִסְתָּרוֹת אֲנַשִׁים] *lege* אֲנָשִׁים עַתִּידֹ] *lege* עָתִידֹ תַּעֲשׂוּ] *lege* תַּעֲשׂוּ תַּקוּמוּ] *lege* תָּקוּמוּ תִּלְכוּ] *lege* תֵּלְכוּ תִשְׁנוּ] *lege* תִּישְׁנוּ 31 תִשְׁכְּבוּ] *lege* תִּשְׁכְּבוּ תְחָמְמוּ] *lege* תְּחַמְּמוּ תִצְאוּ] *lege* תֵּצְאוּ דְּבַרִים] *lege* דְּבָרִים שֵׁשְׁמוֹתָּם] *lege* שֶׁשְּׁמוֹתָם נוֹסַף] *lege* נוֹסָף 32 אַסַף] *lege* אָסַף הֶאֱבִידֹ] *lege* הֶאֱבִידֹ אַבַּדֹ] *lege* אָבַדֹ פַּקַדֹ] *lege* פָּקַדֹ הֶאְזִין] *lege* הֶאֱזִין אִיזֵן] *lege* אִזֵּן 33 שַׁבֹ] *lege* שָׁבֹ הֵבְאִישׁ] *lege* הִבְאִישׁ הַהֵי] *scr. in marg. et s. l.* נִקְרַא] *lege* נִקְרָא הַנּוֹסַף] *lege* הַנּוֹסָף 34 נוֹסַף] *lege* נוֹסָף שֵׁהַמֵּם] *lege* שֶׁהַמֵּם נוֹסֵפֵת] *lege* נוֹסֶפֶת מְהַלֵּךְ] *lege* מְהַלֵּךְ מְאַסֵּף] *lege* מְאַסֵּף 35 מְבַקֵּר] *lege* מְבַקֵּר דְּבַרִים] *lege* דְּבָרִים שֵׁנִקְרַאִים] *lege* שֶׁנִּקְרָאִים מִשְׁקַל] *lege* מִשְׁקָל 36 וּמִשְׁקַל] *lege* וּמִשְׁקָל פַּעַל] *lege* פָּעַל פִּעֵל כְּמוֹ] *add. alia manus in marg.* אַבַּדֹ] *lege* אָבַדֹ גָּבָּר] *lege* גָּבַר 37 שַׁבַּר] *lege* שָׁבַר כְּמוֹ] *add. alia manus in marg* || ג׳ *ms a. c.* גַּדַּל] *lege* גָּדַל שַׁמַּר] *lege* שָׁמַר צַדַּק] *lege* צָדַק צִדֵּק] *lege* צִדֵּק 38 בְּזֵה] *lege* בָּזֶה תּוּכַל] *lege* תּוּכַל לְהַבִּין] *lege* לְהָבִין אֵשְׁמֹר] *lege* אֶשְׁמֹר 39 אֵלַא] *lege* אֶלָּא tamen] *scr. s. l.* שֵׁזֵה] *lege* שֶׁזֶּה מִמִּשְׁקַל] *lege* מִמִּשְׁקָל 40 וְזֵה] *lege* וְזֶה מִמִּשְׁקַל] *lege* מִמִּשְׁקָל שַׁמְּרוּ] *lege* שָׁמְרוּ שְׁמַרְתִּיךָ] *lege* שְׁמַרְתִּיךָ 41 פִּיט] *lege* פִּישׁ טֵיי] דֵּי *ms a. c.* שְׁמַרְתַּנִי] *lege* שְׁמַרְתַּנִי שְׁמַרְתַּנִי] *lege* שְׁמַרְתַּנִי 42 שְׁמַרַנִי] *lege* שְׁמָרַנִי שְׁמַרַהוּ] *lege* שְׁמָרָהוּ שְׁמַרוֹ] *lege* שְׁמָרוֹ שַׁמַּר] *lege* שָׁמַר שַׁמְּרוּ] *lege* שָׁמְרוּ 43 שַׁמַּרְתִּי] *lege* שָׁמַרְתִּי שְׁמַרְתֵּם] *lege* שְׁמַרְתֶּם שְׁמַרְתִּיכֵם] *lege* שְׁמַרְתִּיכֶם שְׁמַרְתַּנוּ] *lege* שְׁמַרְתָּנוּ 44 שְׁמַרְנוּכֵם] *lege* שְׁמַרְנוּכֶם לַנְקֵיבַה] *lege* לַנְּקֵבָה שְׁמַרְתַּהוּ] *lege* שְׁמָרַתְהוּ

שְׁמַרַתּוֹ ׳ שְׁמַרְתִּיכֶּם | גַּרְדֵיבֹּוֹש ׳ שְׁמַרְתִּינוּ | גַּרְדַּשְׁנוֹש ׳ שְׁמַרְנוּךְ {גַרְדַּמְשְׁטֵיי שִׁמַּרְנוּךְ} | פִּיש גַּרְדֵירְטֵי ׳ שְׁמַרְתִּינִי | גַרְדַּשְׁמֵיי ׳ שְׁמַרְתִּינוּ | גַרְדַּשְׁנוֹש ׳ שׁוֹמֵר | גַרְדּוֹנְטְ ׳ שִׁמְרִי גַרְדְּא | שׁוֹמֵרֶתָ גַּרְדּוֹנְטְאָה ׳ | שׁוֹמְרִים גַרְדּוֹנְש | שׁוֹמְרוֹתָ גַרְדּוֹנְטְשְׁ | שַׁמּוֹר גַרְדֵּי ׳ שִׁמְרוּ | גַרְדֵּיש ׳ שִׁימַּרְנָה | גַרְדֵּיש ׳ שְׁמַרוּן | גַרְדֵירְנְטְאוּש ׳ שְׁמַרַן | גַרְדַּהאוּש ׳ שַׁמּוֹר | גַרְדּוֹנְטְ ׳ שִׁמִירַתְּכֶם | נוֹשְׁטְרְגַרְדְּא ׳ וְכֵּן

{preceptum facere}

fol. 199v

וְכֵן מִשְׁמַרְכֶּם ׳ לְנַשִׁים | יֹאמַר שְׁמִירַתְּכֶן ׳ אוֹ | מִשְׁמַרְכֶּם ׳ שׁוֹמְרֵיכֶּן | נוֹשְׁגַרְדוֹנְשְׁ ׳ יִשְׁמֹרְכֶּם | גַרְדְרַהבֹּוֹשְׁ ׳ יִשְׁמֹרְךָ | גַרְדְרַהטֵי ׳ הַשֵּׁם דַּבָּר ׳ | מִשְׁמֵרֶתָ גַרְדְּאְ ״

{hec omnia consingnata poss[unt] reperiri in omnibus uerbis et aliis pun[ctis] prescriptis}

נוּטָרִיקְן נֻוטַרְיֵיקוֹן

שׁוּרֶק פַּתַּח חִירֶק סֶגוֹל | חוֹלֵם צֵרִי קַמֵץ ״

שֵׁם דַּבַר עְשִׂיַּה זִכְרַה | זִכַּרוֹן אֲמִירַה בִּינַה | יִרְאַה דַעַת חֹכְמַה | שְׁאֵילַה גְבֹּוּרַה תְּבֹוּנַה | חַיּוּתָ רְפוּאַה שְׁכִיבַה | קִימַה לִימוּדָ לֵקַח | יוֹשֵׁר תְּמִימוּתָ עְנוֵה | פְּקִידַּה ׳ וְכֵן הַרְבֵּה ׳ || סְלִיק ״ רֹאשׁ {chef} רֹאשִׁי | רֹאשׁוֹ רֹאשְׁךָ רֹאשֵׁ{נוּ} | רֹאשְׁכֶם רֹאשַׁם אוֹ | רַאשֵׁיהֶם ׳ חֹכְמַה {sens} | חֹכְמַתִי חֹכְמַתְנוּ | חֹכְמַתוֹ חֹכְמַתָּם | חֹכְמַתְךָ ׳ עְשִׂיַּה {feseement} אוֹ | מַעְשֶׂה מַעְשִׂי | מַעְשֵׂיהוּ מַעֲשַׂיו | מַעְשֵׂינוּ מַעְשֵׂיהֶם | מַעְשֵׂיכֶם מַעְשֵׂיךָ ״״

45 שְׁמַרַתּוֹ] lege שְׁמָרַתּוּ שְׁמַרְתִּיכֶּם] lege שְׁמַרְתִּיכֶם שְׁמַרְתִּינוּ] lege שְׁמַרְתִּינוּ גַרְדַּמְשְׁטֵיי שִׁמַּרְנוּךְ] add. alia manus in marg. cum signo correctionis || lege שִׁמַּרְנוּךְ 46 פִּיש] lege פימש שׁוֹמֵר] lege שֹׁמֵר 47 גַרְדּוֹנְטְ] rep. ms שׁוֹמֵרֶתָ] lege שׁוֹמֶרֶת שַׁמּוֹר] lege שָׁמוֹר 48 שְׁמַרוּן] lege שְׁמָרוּן שְׁמַרַן] lege שְׁמָרָן שַׁמּוֹר] lege שָׁמוֹר שִׁמִירַתְּכֶם] lege שְׁמִירַתְכֶם 49 נוֹשְׁטְרְגַרְדְּא] lege בושטרגרדא. 50 preceptum facere] add. in marg. 51 מִשְׁמַרְכֶּם] lege מִשְׁמַרְכֶם לְנַשִׁים] lege לְנָשִׁים שְׁמִירַתְּכֶן] lege שְׁמִירַתְכֶן מִשְׁמַרְכֶּם] lege מִשְׁמַרְכֶם שׁוֹמְרֵיכֶּן] lege שׁוֹמְרֵיכֶן נוֹשְׁגַרְדוֹנְשְׁ] lege בושגר־דונש יִשְׁמֹרְכֶּם] lege יִשְׁמָרְכֶם יִשְׁמֹרְךָ] lege יִשְׁמָרְךָ הַשֵּׁם דַּבָּר] lege שֵׁם דָּבָר 52 מִשְׁמֵרֶתָ] lege מִשְׁמֶרֶת 53–54 hec … prescriptis] add. in marg. 56 חוֹלֵם] lege חוֹלֶם חִירֶק] lege חִירֶק צֵרִי] lege צֵרֵי קַמֵץ] lege קָמֶץ 57 שֵׁם דַּבַר] lege שֵׁם דָּבָר עְשִׂיַּה] lege עֲשִׂיָּה זִכְרַה] lege זִכְרָה זִכַּרוֹן] lege זִכָּרוֹן אֲמִירַה] lege אֲמִירָה בִּינַה] lege בִּינָה יִרְאַה] lege יִרְאָה חֹכְמַה] lege חָכְמָה שְׁאֵילַה] lege שְׁאֵלָה 58 גְבֹּוּרַה] lege גְבוּרָה תְּבֹוּנַה] lege תְּבוּנָה רְפוּאַה] lege רְפוּאָה שְׁכִיבַה] lege שְׁכִיבָה קִימַה] lege קִימָה לִימוּדָ] lege לִימוּד לֵקַח] lege לֶקַח יוֹשֵׁר] lege יוֹשֶׁר 59 עְנוֵה] lege עֲנָוָה פְּקִידַּה] lege פְּקִידָּה chef] add. s. l. נוּ] add. alia manus 60 רֹאשְׁכֶם] lege רֹאשְׁכֶם רֹאשַׁם] lege רֹאשָׁם רַאשֵׁיהֶם] lege רָאשֵׁיהֶם חֹכְמַה] lege חָכְמָה sens] add. s. l. חֹכְמַתִי] lege חָכְמָתִי חֹכְמַתְנוּ] lege חָכְמָתֵנוּ || חֹכְמַתִינוּ ms a.c. חֹכְמַתוֹ] lege חָכְמָתוֹ 61 חֹכְמַתָּם] lege חָכְמָתָם עְשִׂיַּה] lege עֲשִׂיָּה feseement] add. s. l. מַעְשֶׂה] lege מַעֲשֶׂה מַעְשִׂי] lege מַעֲשִׂי מַעְשֵׂיהוּ] lege מַעֲשֵׂיהוּ מַעֲשַׂיו] lege מַעֲשָׂיו 62 מַעְשֵׂינוּ] lege מַעֲשֵׂינוּ מַעְשֵׂיהֶם] lege מַעֲשֵׂיהֶם מַעְשֵׂיכֶם] lege מַעֲשֵׂיכֶם מַעְשֵׂיךָ] lege מַעֲשֶׂיךָ

זֶכֶּר {remenbrance} שֵׁם דַּבַר ׳ זִכְרִי זִכְרוֹ | זִכְרְךָ זִכְרְכֶם זִכְרוֹנֵינוּ | זִכְרַם אוֹ זִכְרֵיהֶם ״ וְכֵן | זִכַּרוֹן שֵׁם דַּבַר ׳ זִכְרוֹנִי | זִכְרוֹנוֹ זִכְרוֹנַם זִכְ{רוֹ}נֵיכֶּם | זִכְרוֹנוֹ זִכְרוֹנֵיהֶם | זִכְרוֹנְךָ ״ אֲמִירַה {dite} שֵׁם | דַּבַר ׳ אֲמִירַתַם אֲמִירַתִי

fol. 199r

אֲמִירַתּוֹ אֲמִירַתָּם | אֲמִירַתְכֶם אֲמִירַתְךָ ״ | שֵׁם דַּבַר בִּינַה {auertissement} ׳ בִּינַתִי | בִּינַתֵנוּ בִּינַתְךָ בִּינַתוֹ | בִּינַתְ{כֶ}ם בִּינַתַם ׳ שֵׁם | דַּבַר יִרְאַה {creinure} יִרְאַתִי | יִרְאַתוֹ יִרְאַתְךָ יִרְאַתַם | יִרְאַתְכֶם ׳ שֵׁם דַּבַר דַּעַתָּ {sauer} | אוֹ דֵּיעָה דַּעְתִּי דַּעְתּוֹ | דַּעְתְּךָ דַּעְתְּכֶם דַּעְתַּם ׳ | שֵׁם דַּבַר שְׁאֵילַה {demaund} | שְׁאֵלַתִי שְׁאֵלַתּוֹ | שְׁאֵלַתֵּנוּ שְׁאֵילַתְךָ | שְׁאֵלַתְכֶם שְׁאֵלַתָּם | שְׁאֵלַתּוֹ ״ לְנַשִׁים | בִּמְקוֹם {en le lou} שְׁאֵלַתְךָ יֹאמַר {diras} | שְׁאֵלַתֵּךְ בִּמְקוֹם | שְׁאֵלַתְכֶם ׳ יֹאמַר || שְׁאֵלַתְּכֶן ״ סְלִיק ״ כַּלֵב מֹשֶׁה מְשַׁמְשֵׁ{י}ם {servent} | בְּרֹאשׁ {en le chef} הַתֵּיבַה {le mot} ׳ וְכֵן וַיו ״ | אֵיתַן מְשַׁמֵשׁ בְּרֹאשׁ | הַתֵּיבַה בִּפְעוּלַה {en overaigne} ׳ אֵת | כָּל עַל אֲשֶׁר הִנֵה אַף | גַּם זֶה לַזַכַר וְזֹאתָ | לִנְקֵיבַה ׳ אִם כִּי רַק אַל | לֹא ״

{non tanguntur tanguntur | *caf* ‘cum’ *la* ‘a’ *ba* ‘en’ *me* ‘de’ *se* ‘ke’ *ha* ‘le’ de[...] super *vaue* {‘et’} | *ethan* seruit factioni *essia* ‘fesement’ *misa* ‘ki sert’ *beros* | ‘en le chef’ . *hate* ‘del mot’ *bife* ‘en overaigne’ . *et* ‘a’ *col* ‘tut’ *esser* ‘ke’ *hine* ‘eke’ *af* ‘gers’ *gam* ‘gers’ *ze* ‘cest’ *laza* ‘a un | madle’ *vezo* ‘a femme’ dicitur *el* ‘a’ *im* ‘si’ *ki* ‘kar’ *rak* ‘gers’ *al* | ‘nun’ *lo* ‘nun’}

63 remenbrance] *add. s. l.* שֵׁם דַּבַר] *lege* שֵׁם דָּבָר זִכְרְכֶם] *lege* זִכְרְכֶם זִכְרוֹנֵינוּ] *debet esse* זִכְרֵנוּ זִכְרַם] *lege* זִכְרָם זִכְרֵיהֶם] *lege* זִכְרֵיהֶם 64 זִכַּרוֹן] *lege* זִכָּרוֹן דַּבַר] *lege* דָּבָר זִכְרוֹנַם] *lege* זִכְרוֹנָם זִכְ{רוֹ}נֵיכֶּם] *lege* זִכְרוֹנֵיכֶם || רוֹ *add. s. l.* זִכְרוֹנֵיהֶם] *lege* זִכְרוֹנֵיהֶם 65 אֲמִירַה] *lege* אֲמִירָה dite] *add. s. l.* דַּבַר] *lege* דָּבָר אֲמִירַתַם] *lege* אֲמִירָתָם אֲמִירַתִי] *lege* אֲמִירָתִי 66 אֲמִירַתָּם] *rep. ms* אֲמִירַתְכֶם] *lege* אֲמִירַתְכֶם דַּבַר] *lege* דָּבָר בִּינַה] *lege* בִּינָה auertissement] *add. s. l.* בִּינַתִי] *lege* בִּינָתִי 67 בִּינַתֵנוּ] *lege* בִּינָתֵנוּ בִּינַתוֹ] *lege* בִּינָתוֹ בִּינַתְ{כֶ}ם] *lege* בִּינַתְכֶם || כֶ *add. alia manus s. l.* בִּינַתַם] *lege* בִּינָתָם דַּבַר] *lege* דָּבָר יִרְאַה] *lege* יִרְאָה creinure] *add. s. l.* יִרְאַתִי] *lege* יִרְאָתִי 68 יִרְאַתוֹ] *lege* יִרְאָתוֹ יִרְאַתְךָ] *lege* יִרְאָתְךָ יִרְאַתַם] *lege* יִרְאָתָם יִרְאַתְכֶם] *lege* יִרְאַתְכֶם דַּבַר] *lege* דָּבָר sauer] *add. s. l.* 69 דַּעְתְּךָ] *lege* דַּעְתְּךָ דַּעְתְּכֶם] *lege* דַּעְתְּכֶם דַּעְתַּם] *lege* דַּעְתָּם דַּבַר] *lege* דָּבָר שְׁאֵילַה] *lege* שְׁאֵלָה demaund] *add. s. l.* שְׁאֵלַתִי] *lege* שְׁאֵלָתִי שְׁאֵלַתוֹ] *lege* שְׁאֵלָתוֹ 70 שְׁאֵלַתֵנוּ] *lege* שְׁאֵלָתֵנוּ שְׁאֵילַתְךָ] *lege* שְׁאֵלָתְךָ שְׁאֵלַתְכֶם] *lege* שְׁאֵלַתְכֶם שְׁאֵלַתַם] *lege* שְׁאֵלָתָם שְׁאֵלַתוֹ] *lege* שְׁאֵלָתוֹ לְנַשִׁים] *lege* לְנָשִׁים en le lou] *add. s. l.* 71 שְׁאֵלַתְךָ] *lege* שְׁאֵלָתְךָ diras] *lege* dira || *add. s. l.* שְׁאֵלַתְכֶם] *lege* שְׁאֵלַתְכֶם שְׁאֵלַתְכֶן] *lege* שְׁאֵלַתְכֶן 72 כַּלֵב] *lege* כָּלֵב מֹשֶׁה] *lege* מֹשֶׁה מְשַׁמְשֵׁ{י}ם] *lege* מְשַׁמְּשִׁים || י *add. s. l.* servent] *add. s. l.* en le chef] *add. s. l.* הַתֵּיבַה] *lege* הַתֵּיבָה le mot] *add. s. l.* 73 מְשַׁמֵשׁ] *lege* מְשַׁמֵּשׁ הַתֵּיבַה] *lege* הַתֵּיבָה בִּפְעוּלַה] *lege* בִּפְעוּלָּה en overaigne] *add. s. l.* אֲשֶׁר] *lege* אֲשֶׁר 74 הִנֵה] *lege* הִנֵּה זֶה] *lege* זֶה לַזַכַר] *lege* לְזָכָר לִנְקֵיבַה] *lege* לִנְקֵבָה 75–79 non tanguntur...lo ‘nun’] *scr. in margine* 75 non tanguntur tanguntur] *scr. supra alia manus* 76 {‘et’}] *add. s. l.* misa] *lege* mesames (מְשַׁמֵּשׁ) 77 hate] *lege* hatevah (הַתֵּיבָה) bife] *lege* bifeulah (בִּפְעוּלָּה) 78 madle] *lege* masle

זֵה כְּלַל {claustrura uel exemplum} גַדֹּול | בִּמְקוֹם דַגֵשׁ כְּמוֹ | יוֹדִיעֵנוּ דַגֵשׁ שַׁבְרַה | לִי וּבִמְקוֹם רַפֵּה כְּמוֹ | יוֹדִיעֵנוּ רַפֵּה שַׁבְרַה | נוֹשׁ ׳ תְּבַקְשֵׁינוּ דַגֵשׁ | רְקֵירַשְׁ לִי ׳ תְּבַקְשֵׁנוּ | רְקֵרַשְׁנוֹשׁ ׳ יַשְׁמִיעֵנוּ | דַגֵשׁ אוֹרַה לִי ׳ יַשְׁמִיעֵנוּ | רַפֵּה אוֹרַה נוֹשׁ ׳

fol. 198v

וְכֵן הַרְבֵּה ״ וַאֲדַבֵּר עַל | אוֹדוֹת הַדִּיבּוּק {כְּמוֹ} בִּמְקוֹם |{quod} שֵׁהַתֵּיבָה נִדְבֵּקֶת כְּמוֹ | חֲכְמַה בִּמְקוֹם {quod} שֵׁאֵינוֹ | נִדְבַּק לְתֵיבָה שֵׁל | אַחְרַיו אֲנִי מֵשִׂים | בַּתֵּיבַה הִי לְאַחְרֵיהַ ״

וּכְשֵׁהוּא {et quando ille} דַבּוּק לְתֵיבַה | שֵׁל אַחְרַיו כְּמוֹ אַדַם | שֵׁאמֵר חֲכְמַת אַדַם | אַז אֲנִי מֵשִׂים תַּיו ׳ | בְּסוֹפַה ״ וְכֵן הַרְבֵּה | כְּמוֹ בְּהֵמַה ׳ בְּהֵמַת | הַאַדַם ׳ בִּינַה ׳ בִּינַת | הָאַדַם דֵּיעַה דַּעַת | הַאַדַם ׳ גְבוּרַה גְבוּרַת | הַאַדַם ׳ וְכֵן הַרְבֵּה ׳ אֲבַל {tamen} | אֵין אַתַּה אוֹמֵר בְּהֵמַה || הַאַדַם מִפְּנֵי {propterea ke} שִׁיְהֵא | נִרְאֵה שֵׁהַאַדַם יִהְיֵה | בְּהֵמַה ׳ וְכֵן חכְמַה | הַאַדַם אִם תִּכְתְּבֵהוּ | בְּלֹא {sine} תַּיו בְּסוֹף הַתֵּיבַה | נִרְאֵה שִׁיְהֵיֵה הַאַדַם | שֵׁם הַחכְמַה ׳ וְכֵן בִּינַה | אִם תַּשִׂים הֵי בְּסוֹף | הַתֵּיבַה נִרְאֵה שִׁיְהֵיֵה | הַאַדַם שֵׁם הַבִּינַה | כַּאֲשֵׁר תִּדַבְּקֵנוּ לְתֵיבַה | שֵׁל אַחְרַיו בְּלֹא הַתַּיו | וְכֵן גְבוּרַה אִם תִּדַבְּקֵנוּ | לְתֵיבַה שֵׁל אַחְרַיו בְּלֹא | הַתַּיו ׳ יִהְיֶה נִרְאֵה | שֵׁהַאַדַם הוּא שֵׁם | הַגְבוּרַה ״ כַּלּוֹ אוֹדוֹת | הַדִּיבּוּק ״ וַיַּעַר הַצּוּר {excitauit creator}

80 זֵה] *lege* זֶה   claustrura uel exemplum] *add. in marg. et rep. alia manus*   גַדֹּול] *lege* גָדוֹל   דַגֵשׁ] *lege* דָגֵשׁ   יוֹדִיעֵנוּ] הוֹדִיעֵנוּ *ms a. c.*   דַגֵשׁ] *lege* דָגֵשׁ   81 רַפֵּה] *lege* רָפֶה   רַפֵּה] *lege* רָפֶה   תְּבַקְשֵׁינוּ] *lege* תְּבַקְשֵׁנוּ   דַגֵשׁ] *lege* דָגֵשׁ   82 תְּבַקְשֵׁנוּ] *lege* תְּבַקְשֵׁנוּ   דַגֵשׁ] *lege* דָגֵשׁ   רַפֵּה] *lege* רָפֶה   83 וְאַדַבֵּר] *lege* וַאֲדַבֵּר   כְּמוֹ] *add. alia manus s. l.*   quod] *add. in marg.*   שֵׁהַתֵּיבָה] *lege* שֶׁהַתֵּיבָה   נִדְבֵּקֶת] *lege* נִדְבֶּקֶת   84 חֲכְמַה] *lege* חָכְמָה   quod] *add. in marg.*   שֵׁאֵינוֹ] *lege* שֶׁאֵינוֹ   נִדְבַּק] *lege* נִדְבָּק   לְתֵיבָה] *lege* לְתֵיבָה   שֵׁל] *lege* שֶׁל   אַחְרַיו] *lege* אַחֲרָיו   מֵשִׂים] *lege* מֵשִׂים   85 בַּתֵּיבַה] *lege* בַּתֵּיבָה   לְאַחְרֵיהַ] *lege* לְאַחֲרֵיהָ   86 וּכְשֵׁהוּא] *lege* וּכְשֶׁהוּא   et quando ille] *add. in marg. et rep. alia manus*   דַבּוּק] *lege* דָבוּק   לְתֵיבַה] *lege* לְתֵיבָה   שֵׁל] *lege* שֶׁל   אַחְרַיו] *lege* אַחֲרָיו   אַדַם] *lege* אָדָם   חֲכְמַת] *lege* חָכְמַת   87 אַדַם] *lege* אָדָם   מֵשִׂים] *lege* מֵשִׂים   תַּיו] *lege* תָּיו   בְּסוֹפַה] *lege* בְּסוֹפָה   בְּהֵמַה] *lege* בְּהֵמָה   הַאַדַם] *lege* הָאָדָם   88 בִּינַה] *lege* בִּינָה   הָאַדַם] *lege* הָאָדָם   דֵּיעַה] *lege* דֵעָה   הַאַדַם] *lege* הָאָדָם   גְבוּרַה] *lege* גְבוּרָה   הַאַדַם] *lege* הָאָדָם   89 אֲבַל] *lege* אֲבָל   tamen] *add. s. l.*   אַתַּה] *lege* אַתָּה   בְּהֵמַה] *lege* בְּהֵמָה   הַאַדַם] *lege* הָאָדָם   propterea ke] *add. s. l.* ש *gallice*   שִׁיְהֵא] *lege* שֶׁיְהֵא   90 נִרְאֵה] *lege* נִרְאֶה   שֵׁהַאַדַם] *lege* שֶׁהָאָדָם   יִהְיֵה] *lege* יִהְיֶה   בְּהֵמַה] *lege* בְּהֵמָה   חכְמַה] *lege* חָכְמָה   הַאַדַם] *lege* הָאָדָם   sine] *add. in marg.*   91 תַּיו] *lege* תָּיו   הַתֵּיבַה] *lege* הַתֵּיבָה   נִרְאֵה] *lege* נִרְאֶה   שִׁיְהֵיֵה] *lege* שֶׁיִּהְיֶה   הַאַדַם] *lege* הָאָדָם   הַחכְמַה] *lege* הַחָכְמָה   בִּינַה] *lege* בִּינָה   תַּשִׂים] *lege* תָּשִׂים   92 הַתֵּיבַה] *lege* הַתֵּיבָה   נִרְאֵה] *lege* נִרְאֶה   שִׁיְהֵיֵה] *lege* שֶׁיִּהְיֶה   הַאַדַם] *lege* הָאָדָם   הַבִּינַה] *lege* הַבִּינָה   כַּאֲשֵׁר] *lege* כַּאֲשֶׁר   תִּדַבְּקֵנוּ] *lege* תִּדַבְּקֶנּוּ   לְתֵיבַה] *lege* לְתֵיבָה   93 שֵׁל] *lege* שֶׁל   אַחְרַיו] *lege* אַחֲרָיו   הַתַּיו] *lege* הַתָּיו   גְבוּרַה] *lege* גְבוּרָה   תִּדַבְּקֵנוּ] *lege* תִּדַבְּקֶנּוּ   לְתֵיבַה] *lege* לְתֵיבָה   שֵׁל] *lege* שֶׁל   אַחְרַיו] *lege* אַחֲרָיו   94 הַתַּיו] *lege* הַתָּיו   נִרְאֵה] *lege* נִרְאֶה   שֵׁהַאַדַם] *lege* שֶׁהָאָדָם   הַגְבוּרַה] *lege* הַגְבוּרָה   הַצּוּר] *lege* הַצּוּר   95 excitauit creator] *add. s. l. et rep. alia manus*

fol. 198r

אֶתּ רוּחִי לְדַבֵּר עַל | תֵּיבוֹת שֶׁפַּעְמַים {quod sepe} | מְדַבְּרִים בִּלְשׁוֹן זַכַּר | וּפְעַמִים מְדַבֵּר | בִּלְשׁוֹן נְקֵיבַּה ׳ | וְהַמַּשַל וְרוּחַ גְּדוֹלַה | בַּאַה ׳ הֵרִי {hec est} לְשׁוֹן | נְקֵיבַה ׳ וַיִּגַּע בְּאַרְבַע | פִּינוֹת הַבַּית הֵרִי | לְשׁוֹן זַכַּר {ke} שֶׁאֵינוּ {non ille}| וַתִּגַע בְּאַרְבַע פִּינוֹת | הַבַּית ׳ וְכֵן וְזַרַח {et splenduit}| הַשֵּׁמֵשׁ הֵרִי לְשׁוֹן | זַכַּר ׳ וְזַרְחַה לַכֵם | שֵׁמֵשׁ הֵרִי {here} לְשׁוֹן | נְקֵיבַה ׳ מִפְּנֵי שֶׁכָּל {quod omnis} | דַּבַר {res} שֶׁאֵין בּוֹ רוּחַ | חַיִּים [qui]bus} non est uita} תֹאמְרֵנוּ | פְּעַמִים בִּלְשׁוֹן זַכַר || וְפְעַמִים בִּלְשׁוֹן | נְקֵיבַה כְּמוֹ אֵלֵה | הַדְּבַרִיםשֵׁמֵשׁ וְרוּחָ | וְדּוּגְמַתָּם : {[du]kemat, similitudo}

{נִיקוּד}

שׁוּרֵק אוּ ׳

קַמֵּץ גַּדוֹל אָה ׳

אִי חִירֵק ׳

אֵי קַמֵּץ קַטַן ׳

אוֹ חוּלֵם ׳

אֵילוּ הֶבְרוֹת | יֵשׁ לַהֶם מֵתֵג ׳

אַךְ אֵינוּ בָא | אֶלָא בְּא׳ח׳ה׳ע׳ | וְכֵן חַטֵף פַּתַח | קַטַן אֶ ׳

מְלֹא פּוּם אְ ׳

פַּתַח גַּדוֹל אַ ׳

שְׁבַא אְ ||

אוּ חַטֵף ׳

פַּתַח קַטַן אֶ ׳

חַטֵף קַמֵּץ אֳ ׳

חַטֵף פַּתַח אֲ

96 שֶׁפַּעְמַים] *lege* שֶׁפְּעָמִים quod sepe] *add. s. l.* זַכַּר] *lege* זָכָר וּפְעַמִים] *lege* וּפְעָמִים מְדַבֵּר] *debet esse* מְדַבְּרוֹת 97 נְקֵיבַּה] *lege* נְקֵבָה וְהַמַּשַל] *lege* וְהַמָּשָׁל גְּדוֹלַה] *lege* גְּדוֹלָה בַּאַה] *lege* בָּאָה הֵרִי] *lege* הֲרֵי hec est] *add. s. l.* נְקֵיבַה] *lege* נְקֵבָה 98 בְּאַרְבַע] *lege* בְּאַרְבַּע פִּינוֹת] *lege* פִּנּוֹת Job 1:19: וְהִנֵּה רוּחַ גְּדוֹלָה בָּאָה מֵעֵבֶר הַמִּדְבָּר וַיִּגַּע בְּאַרְבַּע פִּנּוֹת הֵרִי] *lege* הֲרֵי זַכַּר] *lege* זָכָר ke] *add. s.* ש *gallice* שֶׁאֵינוּ] *lege* שֶׁאֵינוֹ non ille] *add. s. l.* 99 פִּינוֹת] *lege* פִּנּוֹת et splenduit] *add. s. l.* Kohelet 1:5: וְזָרַח הַשֶּׁמֶשׁ הֵרִי] *lege* הֲרֵי זַכַּר] *lege* זָכָר 100 Mal. 3:20: וְזָרְחָה לָכֶם יִרְאֵי שְׁמִי שֶׁמֶשׁ הֵרִי] *lege* הֲרֵי here] *add. s. l.* נְקֵיבַה] *lege* נְקֵבָה quod omnis] *add. s. l.* דַּבַר] *lege* דָּבָר res] *add. in marg.* שֶׁאֵין] *lege* שֶׁאֵין 101 [qui]bus…uita] *add. in marg.* תאמְרֵנוּ] *lege* תֹאמְרֵנוּ פְּעַמִים] *lege* פְּעָמִים זַכַר] *lege* זָכָר וְפְעַמִים] *lege* וּפְעָמִים 102 נְקֵיבַה] *lege* נְקֵבָה אֵלֵה] *lege* אֵלֶּה הַדְּבַרִים] *lege* הַדְּבָרִים שֵׁמֵשׁ] *lege* שֶׁמֶשׁ וְרוּחָ] *lege* וְרוּחַ וְדּוּגְמַתָּם] *lege* וְדוּגְמָתָם [du]kemat, similitudo] *add. in marg.* 103 נִיקוּד] *lege* נִקּוּד || *add. alia manus in marg. superiore* 104 שׁוּרֵק] *lege* שׁוּרֶק 105 קַמֵּץ] *lege* קָמֵץ 106 חִירֵק] *lege* חִירֶק 108 חוּלֵם] *lege* חוֹלֶם 109 הֶבְרוֹת] *lege* הֲבָרוֹת לַהֶם] *lege* לָהֶם מֵתֵג] *lege* מֶתֶג 110 אֵינוּ] *lege* אֵינוֹ אֶלָא] *lege* אֶלָּא חַטֵף] *lege* חָטֵף פַּתַח] *lege* פַּתָּח קַטַן] *lege* קָטָן 112 גַּדוֹל] *lege* גָּדוֹל 113 שְׁבַא] *lege* שְׁוָא 114 חַטֵף] *lege* חָטֵף 115 קַטַן] *lege* קָטָן 116 חַטֵף] *lege* חָטֵף קַמֵּץ] *lege* קָמֵץ 117 חַטֵף] *lege* חָטֵף

קַמֵץ קַטֹן אִי ׳
פַּתַח קַטֹן אֶ ׳
{אֵלוּ אֵין לַהֵם מֵתֵג ׳}
שׁוּרֵק אוּ ׳
קַמֵץ אָה ׳
חִירֵק אִי ׳
חוֹלֵם יֵשׁ מֵתֵג
נוֹטָרִיֵקוֹן
מְלֹא פוּם פַּתַח
חַטֵף חַטֵף קַמֵץ
אֲאַאְאֱ בְזֶה

fol. 197v

אֵין מֵתֵג נֹוטַרְ{יֶ}קֹן
אוֹתִיוֹת הַגַרוֹן הַחִיךְ אַחְ|הָע ׳ גִיכַּק בֵּין שֵׁנַיִם | {ו}הַלַשׁוֹן {et lingua} ׳ זַשְׁסְרָץ דַטְלָנָת | {hec x littere non form[antur] in gurgite} אוֹתִיוֹת שְׁפַתַיִם בּוּמָף {inter labia} | אֵלֵה חַמֵשׁ מוֹצַאוֹתֿ כֹּל אוֹתִיוֹת | הַמוֹצַא {que exit} מִתְחַלֶפֶת {mutat} לִפְעַמִים | כֹּל אוֹת {littera} בַּחְבֵרוֹ {pro alia} ׳ יְהוּא ׳ | בְּגַד כְּפַת ׳ דַגֵשׁ בּ רַפֵה בֿ | כְּשֵׁאוֹתִיוֹתְ יֵהוּא {quod quando littere de iehu} בַּאוֹת לִפְנֵי {ante} | בְּגַד כְּפַת מַרְפּוֹת {relaxant} בְּגַד כְּפַת ׳ אֶם | לֹא שְׁיֵשׁ {quod habet} עַל הַאוֹת שֵׁל {de} בְּגַד | כַּפַת אֶחַד {unum} מִט׳ו׳ {de xv} {טו iste due littere d[e] xv} מְלַכִים| הַפּוֹרְעִים חוֹק אוֹתִיוֹת יֶהוּא | וְאֵלֵה הֵם {isti xv reges frangunt [cons]uedudinem de iod et he et [vav] et alef} ׳ |

118 קַמֵץ] *lege* קָמֶץ קַטֹן] *lege* קָטֹן 119 קַטֹן] *lege* קָטֹן 120 לַהֵם] *lege* לָהֶם אֵלוּ אֵין לַהֵם מֵתֵג] *scr. in marg.* ||*pertinent ad* פַּתַח קַטֹן אֶ | קַמֵץ קַטֹן אִי || מֵתֵג] *lege* מֶתֶג 121 שׁוּרֵק] *lege* שׁוּרֶק 122 קַמֵץ] *lege* קָמֶץ 123 חִירֵק] *lege* חִירֶק 124 חוֹלֵם] *lege* חוֹלֶם מֵתֵג] *lege* מֶתֶג 127 חַטֵף] *lege* חָטֵף חַטֵף] *lege* חָטֵף קַמֵץ] *lege* קָמֶץ 129 מֵתֵג] *lege* מֶתֶג נֹוטַרְ{יֶ}קֹן] יֶ *add. s. l* 130 הַגַרוֹן] *lege* הַגָּרוֹן הַחִיךְ] *lege* הַחֵךְ שֵׁנַיִם] *lege* שִׁנַּיִם ו] *add. alia manus in marg.* הַלַשׁוֹן] *lege* הַלָּשׁוֹן et lingua] *add. in marg.* 131 hec x… in gurgite] *add. in marg.* שְׁפַתַיִם] lege שְׂפָתַיִם inter labia] *add. s. l.* אֵלֵה] *lege* אֵלֶּה 132 חַמֵשׁ] *lege* חָמֵשׁ מוֹצַאוֹתֿ] *lege* מוֹצָאוֹתֿ הַמוֹצַא] *lege* הַמּוֹצָא que exit] *add. in marg.* mutat] *add. s. l.* לִפְעַמִים] *lege* לִפְעָמִים 133 littera] *add. s. l.* בַּחְבֵרוֹ] *lege* בַּחֲבֵרוֹ pro alia] *add. s. l.* דַגֵשׁ] *lege* דָּגֵשׁ רַפֵה] *lege* רָפֶה בֿ] *lege* בֿ כְּשֵׁאוֹתִיוֹתְ] *lege* כְּשֶׁאוֹתִיּוֹת 134 quod quando littere de iehu] *add. in marg.* בַּאוֹת] *lege* בָּאוֹת ante] *add. s. l.* relaxant] *add. s. l.* 135 אֶם] *lege* אִם שְׁיֵשׁ] *lege* שֶׁיֵּשׁ quod habet] *add. s. l.* שֵׁל] *lege* שֶׁל de] *add. s. l.* unum] *add. s. l.* 136 xv] *add. s. l.* de] *add. s. l. manus xvi s.* {טו iste due littere d[e] xv}] *add. in marg.* מְלַכִים] *lege* מְלָכִים 137 isti] iste *ms a. c.* isti xv… et alef] *add. in marg.*

אַתְנַחְתָּא ׳ זָקֵף ׳ גָּדוֹל ׳ | זָקֵף קָטֹן ׳ זַרְקָא | יֶתִיב ׳ טְרֶם טְפְחָא || לְגַרְמֵיה | ׳ סְגוֹל | סוֹף
פַּסוּק ׳ רְבִיַע | פָּזֵר פַּשְׁטָא | שָׁלְשֶׁלֶת ׳ תְּבִיר | תְלִישָׁא גְדוֹלָה ׳ | כֹּל אֵלוּ מַבְדִּילִים בֵּין
טָעָם {sensus} | לַטַעָם {pro intelligentiam} {וְהַנִיגוּן melodiam} ׳ וְאֵלֶה הַמְשָׁרְתִים
| שֶׁמְחַבְּרִים {qui coniungunt} הַטַעַם וְהַנִיגוּן {et notam} : |
מַהְפַּךְ מוּנָח ׳ דַרְגָא ׳ | מֵרְכָא ׳ מְאַיְּלָה ׳ | תְלִישָׁא ׳ קְטַנָּה | קַדְמָה :

138 יֶתִיב] *lege* יְתִיב   טְרֶם] *lege* גֵּרֶשׁ?   טְפְחָא] *lege* טִפְחָא   139 פַּסוּק] *lege* פָּסוּק   פַּשְׁטָא] *lege* פַּשְׁטָא   שָׁלְשֶׁלֶת] *lege* שַׁלְשֶׁלֶת   תְלִישָׁא גְדוֹלָה] *lege* תְּלִישָׁא גְדוֹלָה   בֵּין] *lege* בֵּין   140 טָעָם] *lege* טַעַם   sensus] *add. s. l. manus xvi s.*   לַטַעָם] *lege* לְטַעַם   pro intelligentiam] *add. s. l. manus xvi s.*   melodiam] *add. s. l. manus xvi s.*   141 qui coniungunt] *add s.* ש   142 מוּנָח] *lege* מוּנַּח   דַרְגָא] *lege* דַּרְגָּא   מֵרְכָא] *lege* מֵרְכָא   מְאַיְּלָה] *lege* מַאיְלָא   תְלִישָׁא קְטַנָּה] *lege* תְּלִישָׁא קְטַנָּה   קַדְמָה] *lege* קַדְמָא

Grammar Textual Unit 4: The Hebrew Verb Paradigms in Latin Characters

fol. 203v

Col. 1	Col. 2	Col. 3	Col. 4
Alef	Ra[...]	[...5 ll.]	[Nur]adef
Beit	Radafet[a]?	[Ha]uar	[Tu]radefu
Gimel	Radafetem?	[Pa]ssiuum	Iuradefu
Dalet	Imp[erfectum]	Rudafeti	[...3 ll.]
He	Aeredof	Ruda[feta]	Hiteradafe[ti]
Uau	Tiredof	Rudaf	Hiteradafe[ta]
Zain	Iredof	Ruda[fe]nu	Hiterad[af]
Heit	Niredof	Ru[defu]	Hiteradafenu
Teit	Tiredefu	Passiuum	Hiteradafetem
Yu[d]	Iredefu	Earudaf	Hiteradafu
Kaf	Imperatiuum	Terudaf	Im[perfec]tum
Lamad	Redof	Ierudaf	Aeteradef Femi.
M[em]	[Ri]defu	Nerudaf	Titeradef
Mem	Passiuum	Terudefu	Iiteradef
[N]un	Raduf	Ierudefu	Niteradef
Nun	R[e]dufim	Hauar	Titeradefu
Samec	Prete[ritum]	H[ured]afeti	Iiteradefu
Hain	Ridafeti	[H]uredafet[a]	I[mperati]uum
Pe	[Ri]dafeta	Huredaf	Hiteradef
S[...]	[Ri]def	Huredafenu	Hiteradef[u]
[...]	Ridafe[nu]	Huredafet[em]	
4 illegible lines	Ri[da]fetem	Huredefu	
[Ha]uar	Ri[da]fu	I[mperfect]um	

12 femi.] *lege* masc.

Col. 1	Col. 2	Col. 3	Col. 4
R[ada]feti	Imperfectum	[. . . 2 ll.]	
Rada[fe]nu?	Aeradef		
Rada[. . .]	Teradef		
Radaf[. . .]	Ieradef		
[. . .]	Neradef		
	T[aerad]efu		
	I[era]d[efu]		
	Im[peratiuum]		
	Rade[f]		

fol. 203r

Col. 1	Col. 2	Col. 3	Col. 4
[. . .]uredaf		Tiredefi	
[. . .]uredefi	Rodefim in tribus personis	Tiredof	Passiuum
[. . .]uredaf	Hauar	Niredof	Merudaf
[. . .]urodaf	Radaffeti	Tiredefenah	Merudafim
[. . .]uredefenah	Radaffeta	I[. . .]uo	Houe fe.
[. . .]uredefu	Radaff	[Tir]edeffenah	Meradefet
	Radaffenu	Imperatiuum	Meradefot
[Preteri]tum	Radaffetem	Ridefi	Hauar
[H]iteradafeti	Radaffu	Rideffenah	Ridaffeti
[H]iteradafete	Hatid	Passiuum	Ridaffete
[H]iteradefah	Aeredof	Redufaht	Ridaf
[H]iteradafenu	Tiredof	Redufot	Ridaffenu
[H]iterafeten	Hiredof	Houe mas.	Ridaffeten

34 in] i *ms* 44 redufaht] *lege* redufah ridaf] *lege* ridafah 46 [h]iterafeten] *lege* hiteradafeten hiredof] *lege* niredof

Col. 1	Col. 2	Col. 3	Col. 4
[H]iteradafenah	Tiredefu	Meradef	Ridaffu
[Imperfect]um	Iredefu	Meradefim	Hatid
[A]eteradef	Redof	Hauar	Aeradef
[Ti]teradefi	Ridefu	Ridaffeti	Teradefi
[Tit]eradef	Passiuum	Ridaffeta	Teradef
[Niter]adef	Raduf	Ridaf	Neradef
[Titera]defenah	Radufim	Ridaffenu	Tiradefenah
[Yterade]efu	Houe mas. fe.	Ridaffetem	Teradeffenah
[. . . 2 ll.]	Houe	Ridefu	Siwi
[ ]ah	Redefet	Hatid	Radefi
[. . .]	Rodefot	Aeradef	Radeffonah
	Hauar	Teradef	Passiuum
	Radeffeti	Iradef	Merudafet
	Radeffate	Neradef	Merudafot
	Radeffah	Teradefu	Poal beloet
	Radafanu	Iradefu	Biredof
	Radaffeten	Siwi	Kiredof
	Radafu	Radef	Liredof
	[Ha]tid	Radefu	Miredof
	[A]eredef		Lezachar uel lanekeua

47 [h]iteradafenah] *lege* [h]iteradafu 50 ridaffeti] radaffeti *ms a. c.* 53 tiradefenah] *lege* teradefenah 54 mas. fe.] *lege* fe. 56 redefet] *lege* rodefet 57 radeffonah] *lege* radeffenah 59 iradef] *lege* ieradef merudafet] *lege* merudefet 62 iradefu] *lege* ieradefu

fol. 204r

Col. 1	Col. 2	Col. 3	Col. 4
Poal beloet			
Beradef	Nuradaf	Miteradef	Titeradef
Keradef	Turedefu	Miteradefim	Niteradef
Leradef	Iuredefu	Hauar	Titeradefenah
Meradef	Hauar fe.	Hiteradaffeti	Hiteradefu
Lizachar venekeua	Rudaffeti	Hiteradaffeta	
	Rudaffete	Hiteradaf	
Hauar	Rudaf	Hiteradaffenu	
Rudaffeti	Rudafenu	Hiteradaffetem	
Rudaffeta	Rudaffeten	Hiteradefu	
Rudaf	Rudeffu	Hatid	
Rudaffenu	Hatid	Aeteradef	
Rudaffetem	Aerudaf	Titeradef	
Rudaffu	Terudaf	Iteradef	
Hatid	Terudaf	Niteradef	
Aerudaf	Nerudaf	Titeradefu	
Terudaf	Terudefenah	Iteradefu	
Irudaf	Terudefenah	Siwi	
Nerudaf	Hauar fe.	Hiteradef	
Tiredefu	Huteradaffeti	Hiteradef	
Iredefu	Huteradaffeta	Hove fe.	
Hauar	Huteredaf	Miteradefet	
Huteradaffeti	Huteradaffenu	Miteradefot	
Huteradaffeta	Huteradaffeten	Hauar	

71 hauar] hanar *ms* 72 hiteradefu] *lege* iteradefu 75 rudaf] *lege* rudafah 81 terudaf] *lege* terudefi 85 irudaf] *lege* ierudaf 87 tiredefu] *lege* terudefu hiteradef] *lege* hiteradefu 88 iredefu] *lege* ierudefu huteradaffeta] *lege* huteradaffete

Col. 1	Col. 2	Col. 3	Col. 4
Huteradaf	Huteradeffu	Hiteradaffeti	
Huteradaffenu	Hatid fe.	Hiteradaffete	
Huteradaffetem	Aeuredaf	Hiteradefah	
Huteredefu	Turedefi	Hiteradaffenu	
Hatid	Turedaf	Hiteradaffeten	
Auradaf	Nuredaf	Hiteradefanah	
Turadaf	Turedefenah	Hatid	
Iuradaf	Turedefu	Aeteradef	
	Hove mas.	Titeradefi	

Fol. 204v is blank.

CHAPTER FIVE

Contents and Sources of the Longleat House Grammar

The most salient feature of all four different but related works contained in the Longleat House Grammar (see Table 1.1) is their unprecedented reliance on Jewish sources. These texts combine elements of the ancient masoretic genre devoted to the vocalization and correct reading of the Bible, in a version transmitted by French and English sages, with the morphological paradigms reflecting the Spanish-Provençal Jewish grammatical tradition. As we shall see, this originally Eastern and Andalusi tradition seems to have been accessed by Christian compilers through local channels. Indeed, some Jewish approaches to language in the Longleat House Grammar reflect contemporary masoretic and grammatical creativity in England and can be related to such works as the already mentioned *Darkhei ha-Nikḳud ve-ha-Neginot* (Ways of Vocalization and Cantillation) by Moses ben Yom Tov of London. The contents of the four units of the Longleat House Grammar are examined here in separate subsections before the general conclusions sum up their shared grammatical approaches and sources.

Grammar Textual Unit 1: The Hebrew Grammar in Latin Characters

This part of the Longleat House Grammar is a rare example of the study of the Hebrew verb conjugation by medieval Christians. While some aspects of the Hebrew language such as the alphabet and pronunciation were more popular, only rarely did Christian Hebraists reach the necessary competence to venture into the field of verb morphology. GTU 1 is an exceptional Christian work on Hebrew verb paradigms with their parsing. The forms are explained in Hebrew, using Jewish grammatical terminology and methods, all transliterated into Latin characters.

Transliteration into Latin Characters

The reason why this short Hebrew text was transliterated into Latin characters was evidently pedagogical. Indeed, numerous Latin texts contain transliterated Hebrew glosses because transliteration was valued as a method in language study. Similarly, Greek texts were copied in Latin script.[1] Transliterated Hebrew words appear in numerous glosses in the aforementioned bilingual Bible manuscripts from medieval England or in the twelfth-century theological tractate *Odonis Ysagoge in theologiam* attributed to a follower of Peter Abelard.[2] Isolated Hebrew words in Latin script are included in the manuscripts of the commentaries of Alexander Neckam, Herbert of Bosham or Andrew of Saint-Victor, as well as in the works of Roger Bacon.[3] Transcriptions of excerpts from Hebrew books were quoted in large numbers in polemical anti-Jewish writings in Europe; for instance, the dossier of documents for the Paris Talmud trial of 1240–1242 and its revision around 1245, fully preserved in Paris, BnF, MS latin 16558, contains the transliteration and translation of over 1900 passages from the Talmud (*Extractiones de Talmud*).[4]

1. For example, the bilingual Greek and Latin Psalter in Latin characters in Cambridge, CCC, MS 468, see above, p. 36.

2. Johann Fischer, "Die hebräischen Bibelzitate des Scholastikers Odo," *Biblica* 15 (1934): 50–93; Hans-Georg von Mutius, *Die hebräischen Bibelzitate beim englischen Scholastiker Odo* (Frankfurt am Main, 2006).

3. Horst Weinstock, "Roger Bacon and Phonetic Transliteration," *Folia Linguistica Historica* 12 (1992): 57–87.

4. For the Paris Talmud trial and the dossier, see esp. Isidore Loeb, "La controverse de 1240 sur le Talmud," *REJ* 1 (1880): 247–261; *REJ* 2 (1881): 248–270; *REJ* 3 (1881): 39–57; Chenmelech Merchaviah, *The Church versus Talmudic and Midrashic Literature* (Jerusalem, 1970) (Hebrew); Gilbert Dahan and Elie Nicolas, eds., *Le brûlement du Talmud à Paris, 1242–1244* (Paris, 1999); John Friedman, Jean Connell Hoff and Robert Chazan, *The Trial of the Talmud: Paris, 1240* (Toronto, 2012); Alexander Fidora and Görge K. Hasselhoff, eds., *The Talmud in Dispute During the High Middle Ages* (Bellaterra, 2019); Alexander Fidora, "The Latin Talmud and Its Translators: Nicholas Donin vs. Thibaud de Sézanne?," *Henoch* 37.1 (2015): 17–28; see Ulisse Cecini and Eulàlia Vernet i Pons, eds., *Studies on the Latin Talmud* (Bellaterra, 2017). For the edition of the *Extractiones de Talmud*, see Ulisse Cecini and Óscar Luis de la Cruz Palma, eds., *Extractiones de Talmud per ordinem sequentialem* (Turnhout, 2019). For the second translation of the anthology of Talmudic passages elaborated in the context of the Paris disputation, see Alexander Fidora, "Textual Rearrangement and Thwarted Intentions: The Two Versions of the Latin Talmud," *Journal of Transcultural Medieval Studies* 2.1 (2015): 63–78; Ulisse Cecini and Óscar Luis de la Cruz Palma, "Beyond the Thirty-Five Articles: Nicholas Donin's Latin Anthology of the Talmud (With a Critical Edition)," in *The Talmud in Dispute*, ed. Fidora and Hasselhoff, 59–100. For the transliterations, see Chenmelech Merchaviah, "Talmudic Terms and Idioms in the Latin manuscript Paris B.N. 16558," *Journal of Semitic Studies* 11 (1966): 175–201; Gilbert Dahan, "Les traductions latines de Thibaud de Sézanne," in *Le brûlement du Talmud à Paris*, ed. Dahan and Nicolas, 95–120.

The unfamiliar alphabets were the main obstacle for the study of languages, and inversely, the mastering of the alphabet was deemed to be a key to linguistic and philosophical knowledge. In the mid-twelfth century, Geoffrey of Ufford, in his compilation *Scutum Bede*, introduced a display of Hebrew, Greek, Runic and Latin alphabets by a short rhymed statement that "through the understanding of the alphabet the knowledge of a more profound doctrine stands open before him."[5] Considered a sufficient preparation to address a text, alphabets exercised a great deal of fascination among medieval Christians.[6] Thus, Christian scholars and scribes proudly displayed their knowledge of Hebrew, Greek and also other, even more exotic, alphabets such as Runic or Slavonic. Hebrew letters are mentioned in medieval commentaries, and Latin manuscripts often have the Hebrew alphabet penned on their flyleaves and margins.[7] As we saw, the Hebrew grammatical notes

5. London, BL, MS Stowe 57, fol. 2: "Scilicet per intelligentiam subtilius cogniti alphabeti est facilius, aperiatur michi profundioris doctrine scientia."

6. The genre of elementary introductions to the Hebrew alphabet and pronunciation received a renewed interest in the sixteenth century, when a number of such Hebrew alphabets were printed. The earliest is probably the *Introductio perbrevis ad hebraicam linguam* appended to Aldo Manuzio, *De literis Graecis ac diphthongis & quemadmodum ad nos ueniant* [...] (Hagenau, 1518).

7. For the study of the Hebrew alphabet and its various uses and significance in the patristic sources and the Early Middle Ages, see Matthias Thiel, *Grundlagen und Gestalt der Hebräischkenntnisse* (Spoleto, 1973); for the chart of the Latin, Greek and Hebrew alphabets from Byrhtferth's *Enchiridion* (written in 1011 at Ramsey Abbey), an introduction to his treatise on calendrical computation, *Byrhtferth's Manual*, ed. Samuel J. Crawford (repr., London, 1966), 196. For the use of Hebrew letters in the alphabetical Psalms in the Eadwine Psalter, see Sarah Larratt Keefer and David R. Burrows, "Hebrew and the Hebraicum in Late Anglo-Saxon England," *Anglo-Saxon England* 19 (1990): 67–80, at 77. For examples from later Middle Ages, see Jean Bonnard, "Un alphabet hébreu-anglais au XIVe siècle, I," *REJ* 4.8 (1882): 255–259 and Arsène Darmesteter, "Même sujet, II," *REJ* 4.8 (1882): 259–268; Judith Olszowy-Schlanger, "The Knowledge and Practice of Hebrew Grammar Among Christian Scholars in Pre-expulsion England: The Evidence of 'Bilingual' Hebrew-Latin Manuscripts," in *Hebrew Scholarship and the Medieval World*, ed. Nicholas De Lange (Cambridge, 2001), 107–128, at 118–120; Judith Olszowy-Schlanger, *Les manuscrits hébreux dans l'Angleterre médiévale: Étude historique et paléographique* (Leuven and Paris, 2003), 49. For the Runa accompanying Hebrew and Greek alphabets in Paris, BnF, MS hébreu 113 (fol. 137v), see esp. Malachi Beit-Arié, *Hebrew Manuscripts of East and West: Towards a Comparative Codicology* (London, 1992), 109; Gilbert Dahan, "Deux psautiers hébraïques glosés en latin," *REJ* 158 (1999): 61–87, at 61–79; Olszowy-Schlanger, *Les manuscrits hébreux*, 181. The Cyrillic alphabet with examples illustrating each letter in Old Russian written in Hebrew characters appears, together with Hebrew, Greek and Arabic alphabets, in Oxford, Bodl., MS Or. 3 (fol. 73v), see Olszowy-Schlanger, *Les manuscrits hébreux*, 271; Alexander Kulik, "Jews from Rus' in Medieval England," *JQR* 102 (2012): 371–403. The Hebrew alphabet was studied by Roger Bacon in his *Operis maioris* III (new edition), ed. John Henry Bridges (Turnhout, 2010), 3: 89–103, and in the Grammar, "Cambridge Hebrew Grammar," in *The Greek Grammar*

attributed to Roger Bacon discuss the Hebrew alphabet in detail but deal with the rest of the Hebrew grammar in a matter of a few brief sentences.[8]

The rationale behind GTU 1 is similar: through the skills of a scholar proficient in Hebrew, the transliterated text paves the way for the study of Hebrew for those who might have been discouraged by the intricacies of the exotic letter-shapes. It is difficult to ascertain whether the scribe of GTU 1 was the one who transliterated it. The complicated page and text layout of the GTU 1 suggests that it was copied from an earlier manuscript or at least from a draft. The transliterations contain inconsistencies, but there are no major mistakes which would unmask the scribe's total lack of understanding of the text in front of him. The most remarkable feature of this transliteration is its fidelity to the written form of the Hebrew word rather than to its pronunciation. Thus, the *shva*, both vocal and quiescent, is rendered systematically by an *e*, even in the forms where it was most probably not pronounced. One example is the ending of the perfect tense 2nd person feminine singular: רָדַפְתְ is transliterated as *radafete*, even though the *shva* at the end is normally not pronounced.

As far as the transliteration of the consonants is concerned, most are consistently transcribed by their Latin equivalents: *zayin – z*, *yod – i*, *lamed – l*, *mem – m*, *nun – n*, *samekh – s*, *ẓadi – s*, *ḳuf– k*, *resh – r*. This regular transliteration resembles that of the trilingual dictionary bound together with the grammar, whilst other transliterated texts may propose different phonetic solutions.[9]

The consonants belonging to the group *begadkefat* follow in principle the double pronunciation in the case of *bet*, *kaf* and *peh*, and sometimes also indicate a double nature of *dalet* and *tav*. They are not, however, transcribed very consistently. *Bet* at the beginning of a new word or *bet* with a *dagesh* is transliterated as *b*: e.g., *medaberim* for מְדַבְּרִים; *bet rafeh* (without *dagesh*) is often transcribed as *u*: e.g., *hauar* for עָבָר, *linekeuah* for לִנְקֵבָה, but also as *v*: e.g., *vminekevah* for וּמִנְקֵבָה, or as *w*: e.g., *linekewot* for לִנְקֵבוֹת. This transliteration of the *bet rafeh* differs from that of

of *Roger Bacon and a Fragment of His Hebrew Grammar*, ed. Edmond Nolan and Samuel A. Hirsch (Cambridge, 1902), 199–208. See Hans H. Wellisch, *The Conversion of Scripts: Its Nature, History, and Utilization* (New York, 1978), 154–161; Horst Weinstock, "Roger Bacon's Polyglot Alphabets," *Florilegium* 11 (1992): 160–178; Horst Weinstock, "Roger Bacon und das 'hebräische' Alphabet," *Aschkenas* 2 (1992): 15–48.

8. Aside from the fact that Bacon's Hebrew knowledge was probably not advanced, he deliberately insisted on the importance of the solid bases acquired through the learning of the rudiments of the language, including the alphabet, see *Compendium Studii Philosophiae*, in *Opera quaedam hactenus inedita*, ed. J.S. Brewer (London, 1859), 433–434, see above, Chapter Three.

9. See Gilbert Dahan, "Les transcriptions en caractères latins," in *Dictionnaire hébreu-latin-français de la Bible hébraïque de l'Abbaye de Ramsey (XIIIe s.)*, ed. Judith Olszowy-Schlanger and Anne Grondeux (Turnhout, 2008), xxvii–xxx.

the dictionary in LH MS 21, where it is usually transliterated as *b* with a *rafeh*-like sign – a short horizontal line above the Latin letter. However, the transliteration of *bet* without a *dagesh* by *u* (or *v* which was used interchangeably with *u* in the Latin manuscripts of the period) is found elsewhere in Latin texts containing transliterated Hebrew.[10] As for the letter *gimel*, there are only a few instances of its transcription, and it appears in them as *g*: *gunaueti* for גֻּנַּבְתִּי (in a transliterated quotation of Genesis 40:15). The use of the *rafeh*-like stroke in the transliteration to differentiate the letters with *dagesh* from those without is, however, found in the Longleat House Grammar in the case of the letter *dalet*. The *rafeh*-like sign is traced above *dalet* without *dagesh*, such as *rad̄af* for רָדַף, *hadtid̄* for עָתִיד, while *dalet* with *dagesh* is rendered by *d* without the stroke, such as *dagesh* forte of *Piʿel*: e.g., *ridafeti* for רִדַּפְתִּי. The use of the *rafeh*-like stroke is inconsistent. There are as well some errors of transcription of the *dalet* which is rendered by *t*, e.g., *hatit* versus *hadtid̄* for עָתִיד. *Kaf* (with *dagesh*) and *khaf* (without *dagesh*) are usually differentiated; *kaf* is rendered either by *c*: e.g., *col* for כֹּל or by *k*: e.g., *kiredof* for כִּרְדֹּף, while *khaf* is rendered by *ch*: e.g., *lazachar* for לַזָּכָר. The transliteration of *peh* as *p* or *f* follows the Hebrew pronunciation, e.g., *pohal* for פֹּעַל and *ridef* for רִדֵּף. *Tav* with *dagesh* is rendered as *t*, while *tav* without *dagesh* is rendered (inconsistently) as *t* with a *rafeh*-like sign above, e.g., *linekeuot̄* for לִנְקֵבוֹת.

As for the guttural consonants, *heh* and *ḥet* are both transcribed as *h*: e.g., *ha-arbahah* for הָאַרְבָּעָה and *nochah* for נֹכַח. *H* is also used to transcribe *ʿayin*: e.g., *pohal* for פֹּעַל, *behasemo* for בְּעַצְמוֹ, *hauar* for עָבָר. The transliteration of *alef* is more complicated: it is usually rendered just by its vowel sounds, e.g., *eradef* for אֲרַדֵּף (*ḥaṭaf pataḥ* is transcribed *e*, like a simple *shva*), *eleh* for אֵלֶּה, or *ha-arbahah* for הָאַרְבָּעָה. However, when *alef* is followed by the vowel *o*, it is transcribed with an a: e.g., *aoto* for אֹתוֹ.

The system of transliteration of the vowels is simple: *pataḥ* and *ḳamaẓ* are rendered by *a*, *ẓere* and *segol* as well as *shva* and the *ḥaṭafs* by *e*, *ḥireḳ* by *i*, *ḥolam* by *o* and *shuruḳ* and *ḳubbuẓ* by *u*. This simple way of rendering of the Hebrew vocalic system by five Latin sounds *a e i o u* corresponds to the pronunciation of Hebrew among French and English Jews. Unlike the vowel system recorded in the Tiberian vocalization tradition which contains seven vocalic sounds, the North European Jews distinguished only five. In Hebrew manuscripts from the Ashkenazi area, this reduced number of sounds is reflected in the spelling confusion between the graphic signs of *pataḥ* and *ḳamaẓ*, both pronounced as an identical *a*, and *ẓere* and *segol*, both pronounced *e*.[11] This simplified system found in Jewish pronunciation and manuscripts was adopted and further simplified by Christian Hebraists in

10. Dahan, "Les transcriptions en caractères latins."

11. Ilan Eldar, *The Hebrew Language Tradition in Medieval Ashkenaz* (Jerusalem, 1978), 1: 28–31 (Hebrew).

England for the vocalization of Hebrew texts. The Hebrew alphabet of Geoffrey of Ufford also includes only five vowels, omitting *ḳamaẓ* and *segol* altogether.[12] The simplified five vowels system also appears in GTU 3 (see below).

This is not to say that the Christian creators and readers of the Longleat House Grammar were not aware of the more complex graphic system of the vowels attested in the contemporary Hebrew manuscripts reflecting the masoretic tradition. On the contrary: GTU 3 contains a comprehensive list of twelve Hebrew vowels, including different *a*-s and two different *e*-s, whereas GTU 2 explains their names and describes their graphic forms and pronunciation. The scholars involved in the production and study of Longleat House Grammar were therefore familiar with the full Hebrew vocalization but did not attempt to render its nuances in their Latin transliterations.

The Structure of Grammar Textual Unit 1

Though rendered in Latin characters, the text of the GTU 1 is almost entirely in Hebrew. The Latin textual elements are limited to the interlinear translations on fol. 193v and fol. 195r, l. 15 to fol. 196r. The contents of GTU 1 consist of a list of the conjugated Hebrew verbs. The first part of GTU 1 follows the classification of the verbal derivational patterns or structures (*binyanim*). There are paradigms corresponding to five (out of seven) *binyanim*, in the following order: *Ḳal, Piʿel, Puʿal, Hufʿal, Hitpaʿel*. The *binyanim Nifʿal* and *Hifʿil* are not included. The second portion of GTU 1 contains the forms of the verb in *binyan Ḳal* with pronominal suffixes; in Hebrew, suffixes attached to the conjugated verb express the direct object.

Every conjugated form is labeled using Hebrew grammatical terminology. The term *bineian* for בִּנְיָן appears several times in GTU 1. The use of the notion of *binyanim* indicates that the underlying model is the classical grammar of the Spanish school (see below, pp. 125–126). The verb chosen to illustrate the verbal paradigms is רדף, "to pursue, chase." The same verb is used in the conjugation table in the GTU 4. The choice of רדף helps to identify a specific Jewish text which had inspired the compiler of GTU 1. The use of this root to illustrate conjugation is indeed very rare. Joseph Kimhi, for example, used the verb שמר, "to keep, guard." שמר is also used as a conjugation model in GTU 3, where it is translated into French. As for רדף, "to pursue, to chase," of GTU 1 and GTU 4, I was able to identify only one source using it as a paradigm. Interestingly, this source is the *Darkhei ha-Niḳḳud ve-ha-Neginot* of Moses ben Yom Tov of London.[13] It seems that the

12. London, BL, MS Stowe 57, fol. 3r.

13. Moses ha-Naḳdan, *Tractatio de punctis et accentibus quae a Moyse Punctatore scripta dicitur*, ed. Samuel Löwinger (Budapest, 1929).

Christian Hebraists who wrote the Longleat House Grammar were familiar with the linguistic works composed by contemporary local Jewish authors.

Like GTU 3 (see below, pp. 157–158), the grammatical terminology and concepts of GTU 1 follow the Jewish approach of the classical Spanish and Provençal school. This includes the very notion of the verbal derivation as a set of analogical "structures," *binyanim*. The compilers of the Longleat House Grammar likely learned about these linguistic ideas from the South through the works of Anglo-Jewish grammarians, lexicographers and Masoretes. Some of them quoted works of such Provençal authors as Joseph Kimhi and his son David (see pp. 69–70). However, GTU 1 is not a transliteration of any known and identifiable Hebrew grammar book. We have seen that the model verb for conjugation, רדף, was probably borrowed from a tractate on vocalization and phonetics composed by a local English Masorete rather than from a grammatical compendium in a strict sense. GTU 1 differs in scope from the works of medieval Jewish grammarians. While the latter often include long theoretical discussions, GTU 1 contains almost exclusively word paradigms with their precise grammatical identification. These paradigms may have been extracted from existing Hebrew works on grammar, maybe with the help of a Jew or a convert.

Copied from left to right, like a Latin codex, GTU 1 opens with the conjugation of רדף in *binyan Ḳal* (or *Pa'al*). The paradigm of this *binyan* occupies the first 18 lines of fol. 193r. The *Ḳal* paradigm is provided with an interlinear Latin *superscriptio*. It is relevant that, like in several bilingual Hebrew-Latin bibles discussed above, the scribe resorted to the *superscriptio* layout for this translation. As we saw, the verbal paradigms are written in four columns per page. The first and third columns contain grammatical terms which parse and describe the given form (see Table 5.1). This description contains the indication of the person, gender, and grammatical tense: each person-gender is followed by *hauar* (עבר, "past tense" or perfect) or *hatid* (עתיד, "future tense" or imperfect). The corresponding lines in columns two and four contain the actual conjugated verbs.

The *Ḳal* paradigm starts with the 1st person singular. Columns 1–2 concern the past tense and columns 3–4 the future tense. The line below contains the form of the 1st person plural, with the forms of the past and future tense placed respectively in columns 1–2 and 3–4. An additional note intercalated between these two lines explains that for the 1st person singular and plural there is no distinction between masculine and feminine forms: "col eleth [for *eleh*] haarebhah sauim lazachar ve la nekevah" (כל אלה הארבעה שווים לזכר ולנקבה). The *superscriptio* translates into Latin: "omnia hec quatuor eque masculinum et femininum," "all these four are the same for masculine and feminine."

While the paradigm for the 1st person was arranged into columns according to the grammatical tense, past-future, the remaining conjugated forms are arranged according to the gender: 3rd person masculine singular past tense in the columns 1–2 corresponds to the 3rd person feminine past tense in the facing columns 3–4, and so on. This arrangement into columns according to the grammatical gender also concerns the other categories: imperative (*siwi* for ציווי), present tense (or active participle, howet for *houeh*, הווה) and past participle (*pahul* for פעול). For the present and past participles, an interlinear Latin gloss adds that the same form applies to all three persons (*in tribus personis*).

Table 5.1 The structure and order of the grammatical categories in the paradigm of the verb *Ḳal* in GTU 1, fol. 193r

Ḳal	
Past tense	Future tense
1st person singular	1st person singular
1st person plural	1st person plural
Masculine	Feminine
3rd person masculine singular past tense	3rd person feminine singular past tense
3rd person masculine singular future tense	3rd person feminine singular future tense
3rd person masculine plural past tense	3rd person feminine plural past tense
3rd person masculine plural future tense	3rd person feminine plural future tense
2nd person masculine singular past tense	2nd person feminine singular past tense
2nd person masculine singular future tense	2nd person feminine singular future tense
2nd person masculine plural past tense	2nd person feminine plural past tense
2nd person masculine plural future tense	2nd person feminine plural future tense
Imperative	
Masculine	Feminine
Masculine singular	Feminine singular
Masculine plural	Feminine plural
Present	
Masculine	Feminine
Masculine singular	Feminine singular
Masculine plural	Feminine plural
Past participle	
Masculine	Feminine
Masculine singular	Feminine singular
Masculine plural	Feminine plural

Conjugated forms are followed by the infinitive construct with prepositions בְּ, כְּ and מִן (בִּרְדוֹף, כִּרְדוֹף and מִרְדוֹף) with an explanation that these forms concern both masculine and feminine (*lazachar velanekeuah* for לזכר ולנקבה). The information on the grammatical gender is of course irrelevant for the infinitive construct, but it follows logically from the arrangement of the forms previously listed according to their grammatical gender.

The presentation of the next *binyan*, *Piʿel*, follows an identical structure; it sets aside the 1st person placed in the columns according to the past and future tense, but the remaining conjugated forms are arranged according to their gender. Like in the *Ḳal* paradigm, the order of the persons is 1st singular-plural, 3rd singular-plural and 2nd singular-plural. The presentation of *Piʿel* matches *Ḳal* completely; the forms of the active participle are followed by passive participle, *merudaf* (מְרֻדָּף). Although this form is considered by most grammarians as the participle of the following *binyan*, *Puʿal*, the passive of *Piʿel*, David Kimhi in his *Sefer Mikhlol* does consider such forms as a passive participle (פעול) of *Piʿel*.[14] He notably describes as the passive participle of *Piʿel* a few rare forms without an initial *mem* but with a *dagesh* in the second radical letter and a *ḳubbuẓ* (or *ḳamaẓ ḳaṭan*) under the first (e.g., יֻלַּד, "was born" in Isaiah 9:5).[15] The compiler of GTU 1 assorted this form with a comment: "hoc non dicitur sine *mem* in presenti," "this cannot be said in the present without *mem*."

Since the participle of the *binyan Puʿal* was listed here, like in David Kimhi's grammar, as the past participle of *Piʿel*, the paradigm of *Puʿal* which follows immediately after that of *Piʿel* is shorter. Its arrangement is similar to that of *Ḳal* and *Piʿel*, but it contains the explanation that this *binyan* does not contain forms of the present, imperative, infinitive construct or passive participle. The text points out, however, that there is one exception: the infinitive construct of *Puʿal* is attested in one instance only: "pohal belohet nimesa hehad kigunos [for *kigunov*] gunaueti mibeit ha hiuerim" (פועל בלאת נמצא אחד כי גונב גנבתי מבית העברים), "infinitive construct: there is one: I was truly stolen from the house of the Hebrews." This transcription is reminiscent of Genesis 40:15: כִּי גֻנֹּב גֻּנַּבְתִּי מֵאֶרֶץ הָעִבְרִים (here with a variant *mibeit* for מִבֵּית instead of מֵאֶרֶץ of the Masoretic Text).

The remaining two *binyanim*, *Hufʿal* and *Hitpaʿel* follow the same general arrangement as *Ḳal*, *Piʿel* and *Puʿal*. For each of them, there are separate comments concerning the absence of certain forms: for *Hufʿal* we read: "gam bezeh habineian ein siuui vehozeh [for *houeh*] v pa{h}ul v pohal be lo hēt" (גם בזה הבנין אין ציווי והווה ופעול ופועל בלאת), "In this *binyan* either there is no imperative, present, past participle or infinitive construct." For *Hitpaʿel*, the infinitive construct is listed, but the past participle is described as never attested: "paul ein be beneian zeh le holam" (פעול אין בבנין זה לעולם).

Expecting to find the past participle, *pahul* (פעול), in the *binyanim* other than

14. David Kimhi, *Sefer Mikhlol*, ed. Isaac Rittenberg (Lyck, 1842), fol. 59r.

15. David Kimhi, *Sefer Mikhlol*, ed. Rittenberg, fol. 62r. Such forms are considered to be conjugated verbs in the perfect tense by some medieval and most modern grammarians.

Ḳal shows the interference of the Latin grammatical tradition in the otherwise Jewish morphological approach. Indeed, except David Kimhi's few examples of what he described as a past participle of *Piʿel*, only *Ḳal* contains the past or passive participle – פעול alongside its active participle. Other *binyanim* are either active, reflexive or passive by their nature. The active participle of *Ḳal* and the participles of other *binyanim* correspond to the form of the present, *houeh* (הווה). This use of the participle as the present tense in post-biblical (including modern) Hebrew is attested in the discussions by medieval Jewish grammarians. The addition of the comment on the past or passive participle shows the Longleat House Grammar's striving for coherency of the verbal paradigms – all *binyanim* are thought to include the same categories, and if these forms are not attested in the biblical text, the fact is clearly stated and commented upon. However, this artificial coherency also shows a certain lack of insights into the meaning and function of the Hebrew verbal patterns. Indeed, since, unlike Latin conjugations, the *binyanim* have by definition either an active, reflexive or passive mode, it is natural that their respective participles adopt the same modes and semantic nuances. Thus, *Puʿal* as such is a passive of *Piʿel* of the corresponding verb. Its participle will therefore often have the meaning of the passive in respect to the active participle of *Piʿel*. It is, however, unusual to classify the *Puʿal* participle – as done in the Longleat House Grammar among the forms of *Piʿel*, unless the compiler is familiar with the aforementioned discussion of some special forms by David Kimhi.

The second part of the GTU 1 opens with a slightly disorderly list of the forms of the direct object particle אֶת, transcribed as *aot-*, with personal suffixes (fol. 194v, l. 1–7). The letter *a* in these forms is often provided with a dot below, which may indicate that it is not pronounced. This mention of the direct object is followed by the paradigms of the conjugated *Ḳal* verb, again illustrated by רדף, this time with the attached object suffixes. This involves no less than 154 forms. It was a real challenge for the scribe to arrange this text. The paradigms of the *Ḳal* verb with object suffixes appear in GTU 3 as well, but with the verb שמר as the model.

The tables begin with the forms of the conjugated verbs in the past and future. For the start (fol. 194v and fol. 195r, l. 1–6), the text seems to be consistently arranged in parallel columns, columns 1–2 containing masculine forms, and columns 3–4 feminine forms of the conjugated verb with suffixes. The second subdivision concerns the suffixes: listed first are all forms with the object suffix of the 1st person singular, then of the 1st person plural. A comment at the end of this subsection explains that the forms of 1st person masculine and 1st person feminine, in singular and plural respectively, are identical: "col eleh ha arbahah sauim lazachar ve lanekeuat [for *nekeuah*]" (כל אלה הארבעה שווים לזכר ולנקבה, "All these four are equal for the masculine and feminine"). The general structure of the section of the verb *Ḳal* with 1st person suffixes is presented in Table 5.2.

Table 5.2 The structure of the presentation of the *Ḳal* verb with object suffixes of the 1st person singular and plural

Masculine	Feminine
Object suffix of 1st person singular attached to:	
3rd person masculine singular past tense	3rd person feminine singular past tense
2nd person masculine singular past tense	2nd person feminine singular past tense
3rd person masculine singular future tense	3rd person feminine singular future tense
2nd person masculine singular future tense	2nd person feminine singular future tense
3rd person masculine plural past tense	3rd person feminine plural past tense
2nd person masculine plural past tense	2nd person feminine plural past tense
3rd person masculine plural future tense	3rd person feminine plural future tense
2nd person masculine plural future tense	2nd person feminine plural future tense
Object suffix of 1st person plural attached to:	
3rd person masculine singular past tense	3rd person feminine singular past tense
2nd person masculine singular past tense	2nd person feminine singular past tense
3rd person masculine singular future tense	3rd person feminine singular future tense
2nd person masculine singular future tense	2nd person feminine singular future tense
3rd person masculine plural past tense	3rd person feminine plural past tense
2nd person masculine plural past tense	2nd person feminine plural past tense
3rd person masculine plural future tense	3rd person feminine plural future tense
2nd person masculine plural future tense	2nd person feminine plural future tense

The arrangement of the other forms is different. The second subdivision concerns the object suffixes of the 3rd person singular and plural and masculine and feminine. These suffixes are first listed attached to all the forms of the conjugated verb in 3rd person in the following order: masculine singular past tense, feminine singular past tense, masculine singular future, feminine singular future, masculine plural past, feminine plural past, masculine plural future and feminine plural future. This is followed by verbs in the 2nd person with the suffixes of the 3rd person, this time subdivided into past and future forms. In the section of the verbs in the 2nd person, two alternative forms of the direct object are given: one expressed by an object suffix attached to the verb and another – by the particle את with the corresponding suffixes. For example, the 3rd person feminine plural future tense verb with the object suffix of the 3rd person feminine plural ("nisetarot le nisetarot" for נסתרות לנסתרות) is "tiredefena aotan" for תִּרְדֹּפְנָה אֹתָן, translated into Latin as "(perse)quuntur eas uel eos" (the masculine form *eos* is incorrect as the translation of the feminine form אֹתָן, at least in classical Hebrew). The paradigms of the past and future verbs with suffixes are incomplete: there are no forms with the suffixes of the 2nd person masculine and feminine and singular and plural and no suffixed forms attached to the conjugated verb in the 1st person singular or plural.

The section of the past and future verb with object suffixes is followed by a section of imperative with object suffixes, a section of the present (active participle) with suffixes and, finally, the past participle with suffixes. In the section of the present and past participle, there are several forms with the suffixes of the second person masculine, feminine, singular and plural.

Hebrew Grammatical Terminology of GTU 1 and Its Origin

As noted above, each form of the verb is provided with its grammatical analysis expressed in transliterated Hebrew. This includes Hebrew terms for a variety of grammatical categories. The gender is expressed by *zakhar* (זכר), "masculine" (Lat. *masculinum*) and *nekeuah* (נקבה), "feminine" (Lat. *femininum*). The number is usually inherent in the description of the grammatical person in the conjugation of the verb: e.g., *nisetar* (נסתר, lit. "hidden"), "3rd person masculine singular," versus *nisetarim* (נסתרים), "hidden" (masculine plural), "3rd person masculine plural". But there are some rare cases of the use of specific terms, such as *iahid* (יחיד), "singular" (Lat. *singularis*) and *rabim* (רבים), "plural" (Lat. *pluralis*) (e.g., fol. 196r). Interestingly, plural is also expressed by the numeral "two," e.g., fol. 196r: "senei deuarim pehulim" (שני דברים פעולים, "two past participles," translated in Latin literally: "duas res operatas"): *redufotai* for רדופותי, which looks like past participle feminine plural with the possessive suffix of the 1st person singular (lit. "my persecuted ones").[16] Of course, Hebrew possesses a category of the dual for the nouns, yet the use of "two" here does not apply to the dual but indeed to the plural forms. Similar use of "two" for the plural also appears in GTU 3. The terms designating the tenses are *hauar* (עבר), "past tense" – perfect (Lat. *preteritum*), *hadtid* or *hatid* (עתיד), "future" (Lat. *futurum*) – imperfect, and *houeh* (הווה), "present" (Lat. *presens*) – participle. *Siwi* or *siuui* (ציווי) designates "imperative" (Lat. *imperatiuum*), and *pahul* (פעול) is used for "past participle" (Lat. *passiuum*). The conjugation patterns bear the generic name of *bineian* (בינין), and four *binyanim* (out of five included in GTU 1) are called by their Hebrew names: *pihel* (פִּעֵל), *puhal* (פֻּעַל), *hupehal* (הֻפְעַל) and *hitepahel* (הִתְפַּעֵל). There is no attempt to translate the names of the *binyanim* into Latin.

The grammatical persons bear names as shown in Table 5.3. These designations are used both for the description of the conjugated forms of the verb and of the

16. Unless רדופותי was intended as a dual form but the scribe omitted the final *mem*. In any case, such form is not attested in Hebrew.

object suffixes. In the description of the relationship between a verb and its object suffix (between the agent and the patient), the grammar uses the expressions such as (fol. 195r): "dauar seiaheseh nisetar lenisetarim" (דבר שיעשה נסתר לנסתרים), lit. "a thing that 3rd person masculine singular does to 3rd person masculine plural," translated in Latin: "uerbum quod faciet absconditus ad absconditos – iredefem" (יִרְדְּפֵם), or "medaberim behasemam ministar aehad" (מדברים בעצמם מנסתר אחד), lit. "1st person plural from 3rd person masculine singular" (i.e. the suffix of 1st person plural is attached to 3rd person masculine singular) – *redafanu* (רְדָפָנוּ).

Table 5.3 Designations of the grammatical persons

1st sg.	medaber behasemo	(מדבר בעצמו)	sermo pro se ipso
2nd masc. sg.	nochah	נוכח	probatus
2nd fem. sg.	nochahat	נוכחת	probata
3rd masc. sg.	nisetar	נסתר	absconditus
3rd fem. sg.	niseteret	נסתרת	abscondita
1st pl.	medaberim behasemam	מדברים בעצמם	sermo pro se ipsis
2nd masc. pl.	nochahim	נוכחים	probati
2nd fem. pl.	nochahot	נוכחות	probate
3rd masc. pl.	nisetarim	נסתרים	absconditi
3rd fem. pl.	nisetarot	נסתרות	abscondite

The Hebrew terminology transliterated and sometimes translated in GTU 1 is borrowed for its major part from the Jewish grammatical tradition of the Spanish-Provençal type. For example, the designations of the grammatical persons echo Joseph Kimhi. They were, however, also employed by Jewish grammarians in thirteenth-century England or France. The same terms appear in a list of grammatical concepts scribbled on the blank initial page of the Oxford copy of the *Sefer ha-Shoham* of Moses ben Isaac ha-Nessi'ah. They are followed by their translation in Anglo-Norman French in Hebrew characters.[17] The system of verbal patterns – *binyanim* – was first introduced by Judah Ḥayyūj at the turn of the tenth and eleventh century and became widespread among the Spanish and Provençal grammarians. It was adopted in northern Europe, and in particular in

17. Oxford, Bodl., MS Oppenheim 152, fol. 1r: מדבר עצמו פְּרְמָא פְּרִישׁוֹנָא . נכ׳ח שגודא פרשוש | נסתר טריצא פרישונא, "מדבר עצמו, "perime perisone" (mF "première personne," "first person"), נכ׳ח, "segode persos" (mF "seconde personne," "second person"), נסתר, "teriṣe perisone" (mF "troisième personne," "third person").

England, only in the thirteenth century. Indeed, while the description of the verbs' conjugation according to the *binyanim* is attested in the treatises of Joseph Kimhi or Abraham ibn Ezra which were available in twelfth- and thirteenth-century England, the first explicit mentions of the *binyanim* in the works written in England are those of Moses ben Yom Tov and Moses ben Isaac ha-Nessi'ah.

However, GTU 1 is not a word-by-word transliteration of any known Hebrew grammar. It has close affinities with the Hebrew grammar in Hebrew characters in GTU 3 but is not identical to it either; it also uses a different model verb (see below, p. 149). The use of the verb רדף, "to pursue," is particularly relevant. While the presentation of the verb conjugation in terms of *binyanim* and the meta-grammatical terminology (names of the *binyanim*, terms to designate grammatical persons) reflect the works of Spanish-Provençal authors, and chief among them Joseph Kimhi and Abraham ibn Ezra,[18] the verb רדף to illustrate the paradigms is not used by them. It does appear, together with the verb שמר, in the work of Moses ben Yom Tov of London.[19] Although his masoretic essay *Darkhei ha-Nikkud ve-ha-Neginot* is not a systematic presentation of the conjugation, there is evidence that Moses ben Yom Tov was interested in morphology in addition to the art of the reading of the Bible. His disciple, Moses ben Isaac ben ha-Nessi'ah, in his *Sefer ha-Shoham* (The Onyx Book), discussed his teacher's opinions on the conjugated verbs with object suffixes:

> And my master the Rabbi R. Moses ben *ḥaver* R. Yom Tov said that they were attached and that the object pronoun for the feminine and masculine, שמרום ("they guarded them"), are the same, as we found in the word תשמרנה אותם ("they [fem.] will guard them") – תשמרום ("they will guard them").[20]

This discussion, relevant to the grammatical description in our GTU 1 and GTU 3, is not found in the existing manuscripts of the *Darkhei ha-Nikkud ve-ha-Neginot* and might have been either included in a different version, now lost, in another lost essay by Moses ben Yom Tov or was transmitted orally to his students.

18. On the grammatical approach of Abraham ibn Ezra, see Luba R. Charlap, *Rabbi Abraham Ibn-Ezra's Linguistic System: Tradition and Innovation* (Be'er-Sheva, 1999) (Hebrew).

19. Moses ha-Naḳdan, *Tractatio*, ed. Löwinger, 13, 54.

20. Moses ben Isaac ha-Nessi'ah, *A Grammar and Lexicon of the Hebrew Language entitled Sefer Hassoham*, ed. George Wolseley Collins (London, 1882), p. 37: ומור' הר' ר' משה בן הח' ר' יו' טו' אמר כי יתחברו ושוה הכנוי לנקבות כ' לזכרים שמרום כאשר מצאנו במלת תשמרנה אותם תשמרום.

Grammar Textual Unit 2: The Essay on Hebrew Vowels and Accents

The short work on Hebrew vowels and accents was inserted on the blank pages between two booklets (and two quires) composing the Longleat House Grammar, GTU 1 and GTU 2. From the text itself, we gather that it comments, corrects and expounds upon the list of vowels and accents at the end of GTU 3, fol. 198r–197v. GTU 2 contains succinct but surprisingly complete information about the masoretic signs: vowels, *dagesh* and *rafeh* and a brief mention of the conjunctive and disjunctive accents (or cantillation signs).

The note opens with a brief definition of the Hebrew vowels. This definition is addressed to the Christian readers familiar with the Latin grammatical tradition. The Hebrew term for "vowels" used here is *heuaroth* (הברות), wrongly translated as "*iuncture*," "joinings" (see below). It differs from the usual term תנועות, lit. "movements," used in the works of most medieval Jewish grammarians, including Abraham ibn Ezra, Joseph Kimhi and his sons Moses and David, as well as by some Ashkenazi grammarians such as Yeḳutiel ha-Naḳdan.[21] The term הברה usually designates a syllable, but it designates both syllables and vowels in the *Darkhei ha-Niḳḳud ve-ha-Neginot* of Moses ben Yom Tov of London. For example, in his discussion of the *ḳamaẓ* we read: "All sages, be aware that in the whole Torah every vowel *a* (הברת אָ) should be vocalized as *ḳamaẓ gadol* with eight exceptions which exclude/cancel it [. . .]"[22] or on the *dagesh forte*: "the dagesh is found after the vowel *a* (הברת א"ה), and it is vocalized with a *pataḥ* because the *dagesh* cancels the *ḳamaẓ*."[23] Again, in the rules concerning the *ḥolam*, we read: "In all the Torah, the rule concerning the vowel *o* (הברת או) is to vocalize it as a *ḥolam*, except in seven cases of its cancellation,"[24] or "every accented vowel *o* (הברת או) in the plural form of a word, when the accent affects the end of the word, it is vocalized with *ḥataf ḳamaẓ* like קודש, חדש, which will be (in plural) קדשים, חדשים (קֳדָשִׁים, חֳדָשִׁים)."[25] הברה with the same meaning of "vowel" is found also in the *Sefer ha-Shoham* (The Onyx Book) by Moses ben Isaac ha-Nessi'ah.[26] Thus, the term הברה, meaning

21. See his *'Ein ha-Ḳore'* in London, BL, MS Add. 19776, fol. 177r.

22. Moses ha-Naḳdan, *Tractatio*, ed. Löwinger, 13: ידעו כל חכמי לב כי כל התורה משפט[ה] להנקד בכל הברת אָ קמץ גדול לולי שמנה מבטלים'.

23. Moses ha-Naḳdan, *Tractatio*, ed. Löwinger, 29: ונמצא דגש אחר הברת א"ה ולפיכך נפתח כי דגש מבטל קמץ.

24. Moses ha-Naḳdan, *Tractatio*, ed. Löwinger, 50: בכל התורה כלה בהברת או דינה להנקד בחולם לולי מבטלים והם שבעה.

25. Moses ha-Naḳdan, *Tractatio*, ed. Löwinger, 56: כל הברת א"ו אשר הנגינה בה וברבות המילה תרד הנגינה בה בחטף קמץ כמו קודש, חדש, שיאמר קדשים, חדשים.

26. Oxford, Bodl., MS Oppenheim 152, for example, fol. 78v, l. 21.

"vowel," can be traced to the *Darkhei ha-Nikḳud ve-ha-Neginot* or another work of an English Jewish grammarian. The author of GTU 2 did not follow Moses ben Yom Tov (or his disciple, Moses ben Isaac ha-Nessi'ah) exactly and wrongly translated *heuaroth* as *iuncturas* or *iungentes* ("jointure" or "joining"). This faulty translation reveals that he thought that the word הברה, "syllable," (spelled with *heh*) begins with a *ḥet* and derives from the root חבר, "to join, to link."

The compiler of GTU 2 went on warning his Latin-trained readers about the essential difference of the Hebrew vowel signs in respect to their familiar Latin vocalic system. In Hebrew, says the text, there are no vowels similar to those in Greek and Latin, but rather graphic symbols (*apices*), which are constituted of points (*puncti*) and lines (*linee*). When added to any letter, these symbols render vowel sounds in writing. To dispel any doubt about their vocalic nature, the compiler stressed that no letter can be uttered unless one of these symbols is attached to it ("Predicti duodecim apices possunt dici uocalicii quia nullius littere patet sonus nisi per aliquam istorum sibi appositorum," "The aforementioned twelve graphic symbols can be said to be vocalic because no letter will have a sound unless when one of those is attached to it"). This basic definition of vowels as sound-producing is found in the descriptions of the Latin grammar, notably in the influential encyclopaedic *Etymologies* of Isidore of Seville (c. 560–636),[27] as well as in various Jewish grammatical texts. The *Mahalakh Shevilei ha-Da'at* of Moses Kimhi, for example, opens the discussion on the vowels by stating that the consonants can be pronounced thanks to the vowels, seven in number, and to the *matres lectionis alef, vav* and *yod*, and that without the vowels the articulated sounds are not possible.[28] He was not the first: the concept of the vowels as sound producing was discussed by Oriental Hebrew masoretes as early as the tenth century. Several compilations on Hebrew phonetics found among the fragments from the Cairo Genizah call the "vowels" by a name borrowed from Arabic sources, *muṣawwitāt*, "the sounding ones" (from Ar. *ṣawt*, "sound").[29] The vowels are also

27. Isidore of Seville, *The Etymologies*, ed. and trans. Stephen A. Barney, Jennifer Beach, W.J. Lewis and Oliver Berghof (Cambridge, 2014), I.iv.3, 40: "[Vowels] are called 'vowels' (*vocalis*), because they make a complete 'vocal sound' (*vox*) on their own, and on their own they make a syllable with no adjoining consonant. [...] [Consonants] are called 'consonants' (*consonans*), because they do not produce sound by themselves, but rather 'sound together' (*consonare*)." The description of vowels as "sounding, voiced" may go back to Aristotle's *Poetics*, or Dionysius Thrax's *Techne Grammatike*; see *The Grammar of Dionysios Thrax*, trans. Thomas Davidson (St Louis, 1874), 630–632.

28. והם גם כן יסוד כי בלעדם לא ישמע קול מחותך, Moses Kimhi, *Mahalakh Shevilei ha-Da'at, Mosis Kimchi 'Οδοιπορία ad scientiam, cum exposition Doctoris Eliae* [...] (Leiden, 1631), 11.

29. See Nick Posegay, *Points of Contact: The Shared Intellectual History of Vocalisation in Syriac, Arabic, and Hebrew* (Cambridge, 2021), 26.

essential from the semantic point of view. The long version of the *Hidāyat al-Qārī'* states that if the vowels (the "seven kings") were absent, the understanding of the groups of consonants alone would not be possible.[30]

The list and description of the vowels in GTU 2 states that they are twelve in number. GTU 2 refers explicitly to the list in GTU 3 (fols. 198r–197v), first in its opening paragraph ("hii omnes soni et apices sonorum nominaque apicum patent per ordinem in pagina precedente," "All these sounds and graphic symbols of the sounds are laid out according to their order on the previous page"), and again, in the conclusion of the description, referring to the mnemonic symbol ("*notaricon*") for the vowels in the Hebrew part ("Et priores 10 patent, in una dictione, nutariecon, uide supra," "And the first 10 are illustrated in one word '*notaricon*' see above"). Indeed, the vowels listed in the Hebrew part are divided into two groups, both summarized and represented by two vocalized versions of the word *notaricon* (term designating a system of shorthand, abbreviating words by writing only their initial letter, and using these acrostics as a technique of interpretation): נוּטָרִיֵקוֹן (for the vowels "with the *meteg*" or long vowels) and נְוֹטַרְ{יֶ}קֳן (for the vowels "without the *meteg*" or short vowels). The vowels are described in detail, each description listing the Hebrew name of the vowel, the translation of this name into Latin and, in two cases, into French, the description of the graphic shape of the letter, its Latin equivalent sound and, finally, the way it is uttered (Table 5.4).

30. See Geoffrey Khan, *The Tiberian Pronunciation Tradition of Biblical Hebrew: Including a Critical Edition and English Translation of the Sections on Consonants and Vowels in the Masoretic Treatise Hidāyat al-Qārī' 'Guide for the Reader'* (Cambridge, 2020), 2: 43–44.

Table 5.4 List and description of vowels in GTU 2 and their comparison to the list in Hebrew in GTU 3

Name in MS	**Current name**	**Shape**	**Sound**	**Meaning**	**Pronunciation**	**Hebrew list in GTU 3 (fols. 198r–197v)**
5 vowels accepting a *meteg*						
surik	*shuruḳ*	*vav* with a dot on the left	*u*	sibilus, "whistling"	pronounced at the extremity of the rounded mouth, with rounded lips, like for whistling	שוּרֶק אוּ
kames gadol	*ḳamaẓ*	a line with a dot below	*a* long *a*	acceptio pungni maior, "big seizure with a fist," Fr. "enpomher"	pronounced with the mouth wide open as if the open palm contracted to grasp something	קַמֶץ גָדוֹל אָה
hirek	*ḥireḳ*	a single dot under a letter	*i*	fremere et frendere, "to growl, to gnash one's teeth," Fr. "rechiner" ("to bare one's teeth, to snarl")	pronounced with the mouth open and the lips contracted as when one makes a grimace	אִי חִירֶק
cames caton	*ẓere*	two dots lying (horizontally) under a letter	between *e* and *i*	paruus cames, "small *ḳamaẓ*"	pronounced with the opening and contracting of the mouth but not as much as for the ḳamaẓ gadol	אֵי קָמֵץ קָטֹן

Name in MS	Current name	Shape	Sound	Meaning	Pronunciation	Hebrew list in GTU 3 (fols. 198r–197v)
holim	*ḥolam*	a dot in the upper part on the left	*o*	silere, "to be silent, to sleep"		אוֹ חוֹלֵם
Vowels without a *meteg*						
melo phum	*ḳubbuẓ*	three dots below at the back, like a tail	*u* but more internally than *shuruḳ*, close to short *o* and *u*	plenum os, "full mouth"	pronounced "more internally" – at the back of the tongue, with a full mouth, a little open and rounded but not like for whistling	מְלֹא פֻּום אֻ
phatha gadol	*pataḥ*	one line under a letter	short *a*	apertura maior, "large opening"	pronounced like *ḳamaẓ gadol* but quicker	פַּתַח גַּדוֹל אַ
saba uel hateph	*shva*	two dots standing (vertically) below a letter	medium	auferre, "to snatch away" (transl. *ḥaṭaf*)	pronounced neither as *a* nor *e*, nor *i*, nor *o*, nor *u* but between these sounds	שְׁבָא אְ אוֹ חַטֵף
phatha caton	*segol*	three dots under a letter	short *e*	apertura minor, "small opening"	pronounced like *ḳamaẓ* but more clearly, closer to *a* and further from *i*, more under the palate than our *e*. It sounds open but less than *pataḥ gadol*	פַּתַח קַטֹן אֶ

Name in MS	Current name	Shape	Sound	Meaning	Pronunciation	Hebrew list in GTU 3 (fols. 198r–197v)
hateph cames	*ḥaṭaf ḳamaẓ*	a line with one dot below and two dots standing vertically to the right	short *o*		pronounced like *ḥolam* but quicker. It takes air in but then expels it out; does not sound complete	חֲטֵף קַמֵץ אֳ
hateph phatha	*ḥaṭaf pataḥ*	a line under a letter with two dots standing vertically to the right	*a*		pronounced like *shva* but closer to a. It sounds open but not fully, and is placed only with *alef, ḥet, heh, ʿayin*	חֲטֵף פַּתַח אַ (אֲ for)
hateph phatha caton	*ḥaṭaf segol*	five dots under a letter, two standing vertically and three like a triangle	*e*		pronounced like a *shva* but closer to *e*. It sounds open but not so fully, and is placed only with *alef, ḥet, heh, ʿayin*	*it should be* אֱ *but* פַּתַח קָטֹן אֶ *was repeated by mistake*

The order and names of the vowels in GTU 2 closely follow the list in Hebrew characters in GTU 3, on fol. 198r–197v, but GTU 2 corrects and improves upon it. Like in the Hebrew list, the vowels are divided into two groups: those which accept the *meteg* and those which cannot take it. *Meteg* (מֶתֶג, "brake" or "bridle") has the form of a short vertical stroke placed to the left of the vowel sign under the consonant in carefully executed Bible manuscripts (and printed editions) following the Tiberian Masorah. It is one of the symbols belonging to the so-called accents (טעמים), graphic signs which guide the chanting and rhythm of the public reading while marking the tonic stress and, to some extent, the syntactic division of the biblical text.[31] Unlike the other *ṭeʿamim* which indicate, among other functions, the primary stress on a word, the *meteg* rather supplements the accent signs by marking secondary stress.[32] Its main role in the cantillation of the Bible is to mark in writing a tenuous nuance of the orally performed reading, to slow down or to stop a precipitated utterance of a vowel, thus changing subtly the quality of its pronunciation.[33] This is why in the early masoretic texts this *ṭaʿam* is called *gaʿyah* (געיה), which means "bellowing, raising voice." In the *Hidāyat al-Qārīʾ*, Abū al-Faraj Hārūn defined the *gaʿyah*'s function in aesthetic terms as the "extension of the melody so that joy is diffused in the heart in order to conduct the reading along, animating the reader and moving him to read more."[34] The term *meteg* appears later in Hebrew masoretic and grammatical texts composed in medieval Europe. This name change reflects a different understanding of the role of this *ṭaʿam* as well: from a qualitative, musical modulation of the sound to the sound's "quantity" or length.

The term used in the Longleat House Grammar reflects this later terminological development. Here, the role of the *meteg* is described as limited to the vowels which are defined as "long." They are described as having a "brake" or "bridle" because "they are produced and delayed as if drawn back between the teeth" ("dicuntur habere frenum quia sunt producti, et intra den[tes] retardantur quasi retrahuntur"). As we shall see, the quantitative distinction of the vowels is a later development in Jewish grammatical thought, proper to the Spanish-Provençal approach in the twelfth century. In this quantitative description of the vowels, first proposed by Joseph Kimhi, the *gaʿyah/meteg* with its sense of stopping, delaying – and thus lengthening – the sound is essential. Kimhi's approach is more nuanced than the simple attribution of the *gaʿyah/meteg* to the long vowels as in the Longleat House Grammar. He describes indeed the long vowels as pronounced with "tarrying" (*ʿikuv*) and "delay" (*ʾiḥur*), whereas short vowels are "hurried" (*temaher*),[35] but also attributes to the *gaʿyah/meteg* the capacity of lengthening the pronunciation of short vowels in specific circumstances, such as *pataḥ*, short by nature, which is pronounced long if preceding a guttural consonant and bears a *meteg*, because the *meteg* "makes stand, stops" (*maʿamidan*) the syllable.[36]

31. Israel Yeivin, *Introduction to the Tiberian Masorah*, trans. E.J. Revell (Missoula, 1980), 242.

32. Geoffrey Khan, *A Short Introduction to the Tiberian Masoretic Bible and Its Reading Tradition* (Piscataway, NJ, 2013), 5.

33. Yeivin, *Introduction to the Tiberian Masorah*, 243.

34. Khan, *The Tiberian Pronunciation Tradition*, 2: 182–183, ll. 1195–1198.

35. Joseph Kimhi, *Sefer Zikkaron/Sefer Sikkaron: Grammatik der hebraïschen Sprache*, ed. Wilhelm Bacher (Berlin, 1888), 18.

36. Joseph Kimhi, *Sefer Zikkaron/Sefer Sikkaron*, ed. Bacher, 18.

The systematization of the *meteg* as a distinguishing marker of long versus short vowels in the Longleat House Grammar differs from the role of this *ṭaʿam* in the early Tiberian tradition; neither does it take aboard the nuances of the description in Joseph Kimhi's grammar. It is true that in manuscripts the *meteg* is usually placed with the vowels which will be defined as long in the Spanish-Provençal tradition and is notably used to indicate a "long" *ḳamaẓ gadol* pronounced *a* rather than *ḳamaẓ ḳaṭan* pronounced closer to an *o*, but it can also affect vowels which are defined as "short," such as *segol* (= *pataḥ ḳaṭan* in our grammar) or *pataḥ* which is followed by a *ḥaṭaf*. Despite this discrepancy, it is remarkable that the compiler of the Longleat House Grammar does attempt to understand and apply the complex concept of the Hebrew masoretic notation or *niḳḳud*. A later Christian hand, writing in Hebrew in GTU 3, defined this list using precisely this Hebrew term, נִיקּוּד, for "vocalization." Even if not completely accurate, the relationship between the *meteg* and the vowels' length reflects the approach first conceptualized by Joseph Kimhi.

The order of the vowels in GTU 2 is: *shuruḳ* (אוּ), *ḳamaẓ gadol* (אָ), *ḥireḳ* (אִ), *ḳamaẓ ḳaṭan* (= *ẓere*) (אֵ), *ḥolam* (אֹ), *melo fum* (= *ḳubbuẓ*) (אֻ), *pataḥ gadol* (אַ), *shva* (אְ), *pataḥ ḳaṭan* (= *segol*) (אֶ), *ḥaṭaf ḳamaẓ* (אֳ), *ḥaṭaf pataḥ* (אֲ), *ḥaṭaf pataḥ ḳaṭan* (= *ḥaṭaf segol*) (אֱ). Like the division into groups with and without a *meteg*, this ordering corresponds to the list in GTU 3. However, there are a few differences. The list in GTU 3 contains inconsistencies. The *ḳamaẓ ḳaṭan* (= *ẓere*) (קָמֵץ קָטֹן אֵי) was listed twice, once between *ḥireḳ* and *ḥolam*, like in GTU 2, and for the second time among the *ḥaṭafs*, after *ḥaṭaf pataḥ*. The sign which follows it in the Hebrew list is also a repetition of *pataḥ ḳaṭan* (= *segol*) placed here instead of its corresponding *ḥaṭaf segol*. GTU 2 corrects these errors by omitting the second mention of *ḳamaẓ ḳaṭan* (= *ẓere*) and by replacing the second *pataḥ ḳaṭan* (= *segol*) with the correct description of the expected *ḥaṭaf pataḥ ḳaṭan* (*ḥaṭaf segol*), placed at the end of the list after *ḥaṭaf ḳamaẓ* and *ḥaṭaf pataḥ*, and described correctly as having "five dots, i.e., two standing vertically and three like a triangle."

In GTU 2, every vowel is described from the point of view of its graphic shape. The Hebrew vowels are not graphically illustrated in GTU 2: there is no need for that; they appear in full in GTU 3. GTU 2 describes their shapes, added to the letter *alef* as an example in GTU 3, on fols. 198r–197v. The combination of dots (*puncta*) and lines (*linee*) reflects the shapes of the vowels as found in manuscripts. The letter *alef* was chosen to illustrate the vowels both in Jewish and non-Jewish tractates. Moses Kimhi, in his *Mahalakh Shevilei ha-Daʿat* chose *alef* as the model for his discussion of the graphic shapes and phonetic realization of the vowels. *Alef* is also chosen in the grammatical note attributed to Roger Bacon.[37] The description of the vowel shapes in GTU 2 is practical, matter-of-fact and devoid

37. Bacon, "Cambridge Hebrew Grammar," ed. Nolan and Hirsch.

of interpretation. The way the direction and the order of the components of the vowels is presented indicates a Christian scholar who conceived of writing as an activity running from left to right. Thus, *shuruḳ* is described as a "*vav* with a dot in front" (וּ): *ante*, "in front, before," means that the dot is placed to the left of the letter, so "before" the letter from the Latin direction of reading. Similarly, the *ḥolam* is described as "a dot in the upper part in front" of a letter ("punctum in parte anteriori superius"). *Melo fum* (= *ḳubbuẓ*) for its part is described as three dots below the letter behind, like a tail ("tria puncta subtus retro quasi caudam") (אֻ); here again, *retro*, "behind, at the back," simply means to the right of the letter, which is "behind the letter" for someone approaching the flow of the writing from the left. This is also the case of the descriptions of the *ḥaṭaf ḳamaẓ* and *ḥaṭaf pataḥ* as composed respectively of a *ḳamaẓ* (line and a dot below) or *pataḥ* and two vertical dots "standing behind the line" ("stantibus retro lineam") (אֳ and אֲ).

GTU 2 also defines every vowel phonetically, from the point of view of its production by the vocal tract and the organs of speech (Table 5.4). Although the description is practical and free of theoretical concerns, it appears that the underlying approach understands the utterance of the different vowels as the modulation of the flow of the air in the vocal tract by different degrees of the opening of the mouth, contraction of the lips and the place in respect to the palate. Thus, the *ḥaṭaf ḳamaẓ* is pronounced by inhaling air and then letting it quickly out. *Ḳamaẓ* (= *ḳamaẓ gadol*) is uttered with the mouth wide open, *ḥireḳ* with the mouth open, *ẓere* (= *ḳamaẓ ḳaṭan*) with the mouth opening and contracting, *shuruḳ* with the extremity of the rounded mouth and *ḳubbuẓ* with the "full mouth" (corresponding to the meaning of its name *melo fum* and the phonetic realization at the back of the tongue), with the airflow filling the space of the mouth but meeting with resistance of the roundedness of the lips, opening only a little towards the front. Some vowels are described according to the position of the lips. Thus, to utter *shuruḳ*, the lips are rounded "like for whistling;" they are also rounded for *ḳubbuẓ* but in a slightly different way, described as "not like whistling." For *ḥireḳ*, the lips contract baring the speaker's teeth. *Segol* (= *pataḥ ḳaṭan*) is described in relation to the palate as uttered "more under the palate than our *e*."

This qualitative phonetic description according to the shape and position of the mouth cavity and the organs of speech is followed by remarks on the length of the vowels, an approach characteristic of the Spanish-Provençal Jewish grammar. Some vowels are explicitly described as long (*ḳamaẓ*: long *a*) or short (*pataḥ*: short *a*, *segol* [= *pataḥ ḳaṭan*]: short *e*, *ḥaṭaf ḳamaẓ*: short *o*), or their length is implied (as we saw, not always in conformity with the Jewish authors) by their listing within a group of vowels with or without a *meteg*. The length of the vowels is described in terms of the rapidity of their utterance: *pataḥ* is pronounced like *ḳamaẓ* but quicker and *ḥaṭaf ḳamaẓ* like *ḥolam* but quicker.

Despite the underlying theories of both phonetics and quantity, the aim of this note on pronunciation in GTU 2 is practical: simply to teach Christian scholars how to pronounce Hebrew words. The text contains a mention of Jewish *interpretes* who provide the correct pronunciation. It seems that the author/compiler of GTU 2 consulted some unnamed Jews to learn how Hebrew vowels should be pronounced, but to convey it to his Christian audience, he introduced a comparison with the Latin vowels. He showed similarities and differences rather than a perfect equivalence between Hebrew and the five vowels of Latin. He described some letters as equivalent to the Latin sounds but with the distinction of their length, such as *ḳamaẓ gadol,* which sounds like a long *a,* while *pataḥ* is a short *a, segol* (= *pataḥ ḳaṭan*) is a short *e.* Only *ḥireḳ* is given a straightforward Latin equivalent, *i.* Other vowels are differentiated by their quality, and some are described as sounding like "in-between" different Latin vowels. *Shuruḳ* and *ḳubbuẓ* both correspond to *u,* but *shuruḳ* is uttered at the front of the mouth, like whistling (which makes it akin to the French *u*), whereas *ḳubbuẓ* (= *melo fum*) is a back vowel (like a French *ou* sound). *Ḳamaẓ ḳaṭan* (= *ẓere*) sounds like an intermediary sound between *e* and *i,* and *segol* (= *pataḥ ḳaṭan*) is a short *e,* closer to *a* and further from *i. Shva* is particularly problematic. It is described as an intermediary sound between all five Latin vowels ("et habet sonum medium quia non sonat a nec e nec i nec o nec u set medio modo"). The author states that this sound is foreign to both Latin and Greek but does exist in French, English, Arabic and other languages ("quem sonum non habent latini uel greci, set alie lingue, ut gallica et anglica, et arabica et cetere"). Whereas there is no indication that the author understood the double nature of the "silent" and "mobile" *shva* of the Hebrew vowels system and their complex role in the syllabic structure, he correctly identified the *ḥaṭaf* signs as related to the *shva* and placed only under the gutturals (*alef, heh, ḥet* and *ʿayin*). He identified *ḥaṭaf pataḥ* as a *shva* pronounced *a,* and *ḥaṭaf segol* (= *ḥaṭaf pataḥ ḳaṭan*) as a *shva* pronounced *e.*

The description of the vowels contains their Hebrew name in Latin characters and its translation into Latin and sometimes into French. *Ḳamaẓ gadol* (אָ), or *kames gadol* in the text, is translated as *accepcio pungni maior,* "a big seizure with the fist," since "*cames* means in French '*enpomher*'" (Modern French *empoigner*)," which is retranslated back into Latin as *tollere cum pungno,* "to grab with the fist." This etymology is associated with the description of how the letter is articulated: "cum magna oris aperti comprehensione, sicut cum manus aperta contrahitur ut aliquis tollat quemadmodum," "with a contraction of the mouth wide open, like when the hand contracts when someone takes something in this manner." This is also the case with *ḥireḳ* (אִ), identified with *i.* Its name is translated as "to growl, to gnash one's teeth," or as French "*rechiner,*" "to bare one's teeth, to snarl," because "when *i* is pronounced, the mouth is open and the lips contracted as when one makes a grimace" ("quia quando profertur *i* os aperitur et labia contrahuntur sicut quando fit rictus").

After the description of the vowels, GTU 2 contains a note concerning the six letters *begadkefat* and their double sound depending on whether they have a *dagesh* or a *rafeh*. These two signs are called *modertatiui*, "moderating." A short note mentions further twenty-two graphic symbols (*apices*), corresponding to the accents or cantillation signs (טעמים). They are called *sentenciales*, alluding to their role in the syntactic relationship between the words in a sentence. The *ṭeʿamim* are not enumerated: the note in GTU 2 refers to their list and graphic forms "*supra*," that is in GTU 3. GTU 2 concludes by stating that Hebrew has in total 36 graphic symbols (*apices*), which include 12 vowels, two "moderators" and 22 accents.

Sources of the Vowels' Names and Descriptions

GTU 2's reliance on Jewish phonetics is undeniable, even if it is not a translation or adaptation of a specific Jewish grammar book. This lack of one model may reflect the fact that the author did not consult Jewish books, or not exclusively, but rather learned from Jewish teachers. That he was himself a Christian and received a Latin education can be gathered from his portrayal of the graphic shape of some vowels which he perceived in the "Latin" direction, from left to right, and the fact that he refers to the Latin sounds as "our *o* or *u*" in the description of the *ḳubbuẓ* (*melo fum*) or "our *e*" for *segol* (= *pataḥ ḳaṭan*). His description of the vowel sounds seems to reflect the theoretical phonetics of Jewish grammatical and masoretic works, as well as the way he heard the vowels pronounced by his Jewish informers. It is indeed in this sense that we should understand the two references to the *interpretes*: living "intermediaries" rather than commentators consulted via a written book. While the first reference, concerning the pronunciation of the *ḥaṭaf pataḥ*, is unclear as to the oral nature of communication because the *interpretes* are said to "represent" this vowel as an *a*, the second mention, referring to the *ḥaṭaf segol*, leaves no doubt: the *interpretes* are said to "make it sound like an *e*." The note on the vowels in GTU 2 turns out to be a structured and thought-through result of lessons with Jewish teachers. It remains, however, that these teachers followed certain grammatical approaches and that their diligent student transmitted it in a form reflecting his own understanding and desire to systematize.

Hebrew pronunciation was a frequent topic in the works of medieval Christian Hebraists. In addition to GTU 2, a few other comprehensive expositions of the pronunciation of Hebrew came down to us from the period before the end of the thirteenth century: the tractate on pronunciation appended to a copy of the *Interpretation of Hebrew Names* in Paris, BnF, MS latin 36,[38] the aforementioned grammatical notes attributed to Roger Bacon in Cambridge, University Library, MS Ff. 6. 13,[39] or notes on the flyleaves of the Hebrew-Latin Psalter London, Lambeth Palace Library, MS 435.[40] The phonetic approach and the reliance on Jewish sources appear in the notes in London, Lambeth Palace Library, MS 435, but GTU 2 is more detailed and far better structured, presenting the vowels as a coherent system of 12 signs and sounds. GTU 2 differs from the descriptions in Paris, BnF, MS latin 36 and in the grammar of Roger Bacon whose aim is mainly to attempt to match Hebrew and Latin vowels. Indeed, while the study of the Hebrew consonants harks back to the patristic tradition which pre-dates the invention of the vowel signs in the early Middle Ages, the Christians who wished to study the obviously post-Jerome masoretic vowels were faced with the lack of patristic models. They could either try to match the Hebrew vowels to those of the Latin grammar or they could learn from Jewish grammarians.

As said, the author of GTU 2 chose the second way: the names and phonetic descriptions of the vowels follow Jewish grammatical thought. His immediate source was the list in GTU 3, but he added a more extensive explanation of the Hebrew names of the vowels, their articulation in specific organs of speech and their comparison with Latin. GTU 2 focuses on the vowels and accents and omits a passage of GTU 3 concerning the organs of articulation of the consonants. It also corrects the Hebrew list in one case; it places the *ḥaṭaf pataḥ ḳaṭan* (= *ḥaṭaf segol*) with the two other *ḥaṭafs* and describes it as composed of five dots, while in GTU 3 it is confused with a *pataḥ ḳaṭan* (= *segol*) (אֶ). The much broader scope of GTU 2 implies that its author had access to more information on Jewish ideas about vowels and cantillation signs than provided by GTU 3.

When compared with Jewish sources, the presentation of the vowels by the Christian author of GTU 2 appears somehow eclectic: it follows not one but two different Jewish approaches to Hebrew vowels. In addition, it reflects its author's personal understanding of the concepts transmitted by the Jewish grammarians. The names of the vowels which appear in GTU 2 are those found in the classical Tiberian tradition of vocalization. The names of two vowels, *ḳamaẓ*

38. Samuel Berger, *Quam notitiam linguae Hebraicae habuerint Christiani medii aevi temporibus in Gallia* (Paris, 1893), 21–24; Gilbert Dahan, "Lexiques hébreu-latin?: Les recueils d'interprétations des noms hébreux," in *Les manuscrits des lexiques et glossaires de l'Antiquité tardive à la fin du moyen âge*, ed. Jacqueline Hamesse (Louvain-la-Neuve, 1996), 511–521.

39. Bacon, "Cambridge Hebrew Grammar," ed. Nolan and Hirsch, 199–208. See Gilbert Dahan, *Les intellectuels chrétiens et juifs au moyen âge* (Paris, 1990), 254–255; Olszowy-Schlanger, "The Knowledge and Practice of Hebrew Grammar," 109–110.

40. Olszowy-Schlanger, "The Knowledge and Practice of Hebrew Grammar," 123.

(which may refer to a *ḳamaẓ* or a *ẓere*) and *pataḥ* (referring to either a *pataḥ* or a *segol*), go back to the early masoretic lists. The complete list of seven vowels of the Tiberian system – *ḳamaẓ, pataḥ, ḥolam, ẓere, ḥireḳ, shuruḳ* and *segol* – is included in the works of the tenth-century authors, Aharon ben Moshe ben Asher, scribe, Masorete and author of the *Diḳduḳei ha-Ṭeʿamim*, and Saʿadiah ben Joseph al-Fayyumi Gaon in his commentary on *Sefer Yeẓirah* and chapter five of his book on Hebrew grammar.[41] Various grammarians, and chief among them Abraham ibn Ezra who left a lasting impact on Jewish intellectual life in Normandy and England, also counted seven vowels (שבע מלכים, "seven kings": *ḥolem, shuruḳ, ḥireḳ, pataḥ gadol, pataḥ ḳaṭan, ḳamaẓ gadol, ḳamaẓ ḳaṭan*).[42]

An important element of the vowels' treatment in GTU 2 is the description of their phonetic realization. The phonetic description of the sounds according to to their organs of articulation is attested in Latin works on grammar, notably in medieval England, but the precise descriptions of the specific vowels differ from those in GTU 2.[43] The phonetics description in GTU 2 is strikingly similar to the treatises of the genre of the correct reading of the Bible. The phonetics of the vowels, and notably their organs of articulation, were first described in the early eleventh century, in the aforementioned *Hidāyat al-Qārīʾ*. This treatise, based on the Masorah and the Arabic genre of the guides to the reading of the Koran, considers the vowel sounds from the qualitative phonetic point of view. It describes their graphic shapes, their names and the airflow in the mouth cavity (e.g., *ḥolam* is described as "fullness" because it fills the space of the mouth), as well as the position of the lips, teeth or palate (e.g., *shuruḳ* is a round vowel uttered with lips "gathered together," the name of *ẓere* is explained as "splitting" because

41. Aron Dotan, *The Dawn of Hebrew Linguistics: The Book of Elegance of the Language of the Hebrews by Saadia Gaon* (Jerusalem, 1997) (Hebrew).

42. Abraham ibn Ezra, *Sefer Moznayim*, ed. Mordechai S. Goodman (Jerusalem, 2016), 11 (Hebrew). Abraham ibn Ezra also refers to a u-vowel *ḳubbuẓ* but, like the earlier grammarians, considers it as a purely graphic variant of the *shuruḳ*.

43. An interesting example from twelfth-century England is the aforementioned miscellaneous compilation *Scutum Bede* of Geoffrey of Ufford in London, BL, MS Stowe 57, fol. 5r. His description concerns the phonetic realisation of all the letters of the Latin alphabet. The five vowels are described as follows: "*a* directo oris fauciumque hiatu – absque ulla collisione – solo congruo profertur spiritu" ("*a* is pronounced with one regular airflow with a direct opening of the mouth and the jaws, with no obstacle [contact with the organs of speech]"); "*e* sub oris hiatu – lingua paululum pressa profertur" ("*e* is pronounced below the opening of the mouth, with the tongue slightly squeezed"); "*i* spiritu leniter procedente, dentibus prope pressis innascitur" ("*i* is born when the air flows slowly, with clenched teeth"); "*o* ore rotundo per spiritum aperto propagatur" ("*o* is produced with rounded mouth forced open by the airflow"); "*v* ore stricto, labrisque prominulis emittitur" ("*v* [= *u*] is emitted with the pursed mouth and the lips slightly protruding").

"it splits between the teeth," and *ḥireḳ*'s name derives from Psalm 37:12, "and he gnashes his teeth against him," because the teeth make a squeaking sound when it is pronounced).[44] Only *segol* is not presented from the point of view of its articulation but its graphic shape: three dots below the consonants, resembling a grape.[45] Composed in Jerusalem, the *Hidāyat al-Qāriʾ* became vastly popular across the Jewish world. In various forms and translations, based on either the long version of the work or on its abridgment (*Mukhtaṣar*) (both preserved in many Eastern Judaeo-Arabic manuscripts[46]), it spread to Byzantium[47] and Yemen.[48] Most importantly for our purpose, a Hebrew translation was also made and

44. Ilan Eldar, *The Art of the Correct Reading of the Bible* (Jerusalem, 1994), 121 (Hebrew); Khan, *The Tiberian Pronunciation Tradition*, 2: 72–75 (longer version) and 2: 246–247 (shorter version).

45. Khan, *The Tiberian Pronunciation Tradition*, 2: 246–247.

46. For the list of manuscripts and fragments, see Eldar, *Art of the Correct Reading*, 43–47, and Khan, *The Tiberian Pronunciation Tradition*, 2: 8 (long version) and 2: 9–10 (short version). For the abridgment, probably composed by Abū al-Faraj Hārūn himself, see Giulio Busi, "Sulla versione breve (araba ed ebraica) della Hidāyat al-Qāri," *Henoch* 5 (1983): 371–395; Ilan Eldar, "Mukhtaṣar *Hidāyat al-Qāriʾ*: The Grammatical Section According to Genizah Passages," *Leshonenu* 50 (1986): 214–231 (part I) and *Leshonenu* 51 (1987): 3–41 (part II) (Hebrew); Ilan Eldar, "Mukhtaṣar (an Abridgment) of Hidāyat al-Qāriʾ: A Grammatical Treatise Discovered in the Genizah," in *Genizah Research after Ninety Years: The Case of Judaeo-Arabic*, ed. Joshua Blau and Stefan C. Reif (Cambridge, 1992), 67–73; Khan, *The Tiberian Pronunciation Tradition*.

47. A Hebrew version was included together with several other masoretic works in a compendium *ʿAdat Devorim* (Swarm of Bees) by the Karaite author Joseph the Constantinopolitan (ha-Ḳustandini), probably of the late eleventh century. This work has been preserved in only one manuscript, today in St Petersburg (National Library of Russia, II Firkovitch Evr. 161), copied in 1207–1208 in Gagra (on the Black Sea shore) by Judah ben Jacob ben Judah. See M. Zislin, *Meʾor ʿAyin (The Light of the Eye): A Karaite Grammar of the Hebrew Language from a Manuscript of 1208* (Moscow, 1990), 11 (Russian); Nicholas de Lange, "Hebrew Scholarship in Byzantium," in *Hebrew Scholarship and the Medieval World*, ed. Nicholas De Lange (Cambridge, 2001), 23–37. The *Hidāyat al-Qāriʾ* was also used by Judah Hadassi in his monumental alphabetically arranged encyclopaedia of Karaite lore, the *Eshkol ha-Kofer* (Cluster of Henna), written in 1148, in Constantinople. See Busi, *Horayat ha-Qoreʾ: Una grammatica ebraica del secolo XI* (Frankfurt am Main and New York, 1984), 33. On the *Eshkol ha-Kofer* and its Judaeo-Arabic elements, see Daniel J. Lasker, Johannes Niehoff-Panagiotidis and David Eric Sklare, *Theological Encounters at a Crossroads: An Edition and Translation of Judah Hadassi's Eshkol ha-Kofer, First Commandment* (Leiden, 2019).

48. Under the name of *Maḥberet ha-Tijān* (The Booklet of the Biblical Codices), Hebrew and Arabic versions of the *Hidāyat al-Qāriʾ* circulated in Yemen, often appended to Bible codices. See Joseph Derenbourg, "Manuel du lecteur d'un auteur inconnu publié d'après un manuscrit venu du Yémen et accompagné de notes," *JA* (6e série) 16 (1870): 309–550; Wilhelm Bacher, "Une grammaire hébraïque du Yémen: Ses rapports avec le Manuel du lecteur," *REJ* 23 (1891): 238–248; Adolf Neubauer, *Petite grammaire hébraïque provenant du Yémen* (Leipzig, 1891); Shelomo Morag, *Hebrew of the Yemenite Jews* (Jerusalem, 1963), 31–37

studied among Masoretes and grammarians in Western Europe.[49] A prologue of this Hebrew version, whose relatively early extant witnesses are thirteenth-century manuscripts Oxford, Bodl., MS Oppenheim 625 and Vatican City, Biblioteca Apostolica Vaticana, MS Vat. ebr. 402, tells a story of its transmission in northern Europe: "This book is the *Guide for the Reader*, which was brought from Jerusalem and explained briefly by R. Joseph ben Ḥiyya, the scribe, who brought it from there written in Arabic as they copied it there. R. Meshullam ben R. Nathanael translated it from Arabic into the Holy Tongue in the city of Mainz."[50] The Hebrew translation circulated across northern Europe[51] and was one of the sources of masoretic and grammatical essays, such as the *ʿEin ha-Ḳoreʾ* (The Eye of the Reader) by Yeḳutiel ha-Naḳdan.[52] In Italy, a version, entitled *Tokhen Ezra*, was copied in 1145 by Menaḥem ben Solomon, together with his own grammar, *Even Boḥan*.[53]

More importantly for our purpose, the Hebrew version of the *Hidāyat al-Qāriʾ* had also reached medieval England. Moses ben Yom Tov knew the tractate in Hebrew when he wrote his *Darkhei ha-Niḳḳud ve-ha-Neginot* around 1250.[54] His description of vowels has affinities with the work of Abū al-Faraj Hārūn in its Hebrew garb, and our GTU 2, too, reflects similar ideas. The manuscript Vatican City, Biblioteca Apostolica Vaticana, MS Vat. ebr. 402 containing *Horayat ha-Ḳoreʾ* on fols. 80–89[55] is connected with England or Normandy (as discussed above, pp. 63–64) whereas Oxford, Bodl., MS Oppenheim 625 can be defined as northern French on palaeographical grounds, as well as from the presence of vernacular French glosses and quotations of Benjamin of Cambridge in the

---

(Hebrew); Busi, *Horayat ha-Qoreʾ*, 31–32; Ilan Eldar, "Recueils grammaticaux yéménites des 'Tigân' et sources du recueil hébraïque," *REJ* 151 (1992): 149–159.

49. For the critical edition of the Hebrew version, see Busi, *Horayat ha-Qoreʾ*.

50. Vatican City, Biblioteca Apostolica Vaticana, MS Vat. ebr. 402, fol. 80r: זה ספר הוריית הקורא אשר הובא מירושלים נבאר בדרך קצרה והביאו יוסף בן חייא הסופר משם מתורגם בלשון ערבי כאשר העתיקו לשם. ור׳ משלם בר׳ נתנאל הפכו מלשון ערבי ללשון הקדש בעיר מיינצא. In Oxford, Bodl., MS Oppenheim 625, fol. 241v, the name of the translator is Nathanael ben Meshullam. See also Busi, *Horayat ha-Qoreʾ*, p. 42.

51. For the list of nine manuscripts of the Hebrew translation, see Busi, *Horayat ha-Qoreʾ*, 27–31.

52. On Yeḳutiel ha-Naḳdan and his sources, see Ilan Eldar, "The Chapter 'Noaḥ ha-Tevot' from 'Ein ha-Kore': Rules of Milraʿ and Milʿel by Yequtiel ha-Kohen ben Judah the Vocalizer," *Leshonenu* 40 (1976): 190–210 (Hebrew); Ilan Eldar, "The Grammatical Literature," *Massorot*, 10–11; Olszowy-Schlanger, "The Science of Language Among Medieval Jews," in *Science in Medieval Jewish Cultures*, ed. Gad Freudenthal (Cambridge, 2011), 396.

53. Milan, Biblioteca Ambrosiana, MS A 186 Inf.

54. Moses ha-Naḳdan, *Tractatio*, ed. Löwinger. On his work, see Aron Dotan, "Moses ben Yom Tov," in *Encyclopaedia Judaica* (Jerusalem, 1971), 12: col. 427–428.

55. Benjamin Richler, ed., *Hebrew Manuscripts in the Vatican Library* (Vatican City, 2008), 348–350.

margins of the copy of the dictionary of Solomon ibn Parḥon contained in the same codicological unit.

The well-attested circulation of the Hebrew translations of the *Hidāyat al-Qārī*ʾ in thirteenth-century England explains the surprising similarity of one part of the description in GTU 2 with this Eastern work. As in this masoretic treatise, the vowels of GTU 2 are described from the point of view of their graphic shapes, names and phonetics. In particular, the description of the *shuruḳ* as uttered with the lips pursed together like for "whistling" in GTU 2 is reminiscent of the *Hidāyat al-Qārī*ʾ and *Horayat ha-Ḳore*ʾ.[56] An interesting parallel can also be drawn with the description of the *ḳamaẓ*. Not only, as in the *Hidāyat al-Qārī*ʾ/*Horayat ha-Ḳore*ʾ, is this vowel discussed in GTU 2 as pronounced with contracted lips like a "clenched fist," but also both texts refer to the etymology of the word *ḳamaẓ* by quoting a biblical verse: Leviticus 2:2 in GTU 2, and Leviticus 5:12 in *Hidāyat al-Qārī*ʾ/*Horayat ha-Ḳore*ʾ.[57] *Ḥireḳ* is also described in both GTU 2 and the *Hidāyat al-Qārī*ʾ/*Horayat ha-Ḳore*ʾ with a biblical reference explaining contextually the etymology of the name. Here again, the quotation is not the same: GTU 2 evokes Psalm 34:16 (MT 35:16) חָרֹק עָלַי שִׁנֵּימוֹ "frenduerunt super me dentibus suis," "they gnash their teeth against me," whereas the verse mentioned in the *Hidāyat al-Qārī*ʾ is Psalm 37:12: חורק עליו שניו, and in *Horayat ha-Ḳore*ʾ, Job 16:9: חרק עלי בשיניו. An interesting connection between GTU 2/ GTU 3 and the Hebrew *Horayat ha-Ḳore*ʾ is the use in both works of the mnemonic expression נוטריקון to portray all the vowels at a glance.[58]

Although the similarity of the description of specific vowels and their articulation in GTU 2 and the *Horayat ha-Ḳore*ʾ is beyond doubt, the two texts are not identical: GTU 2 lists twelve rather than seven vowels and orders them differently. While the *Horayat ha-Ḳore*ʾ and its Arabic original list the vowels in the order of their place of articulation, from the back of the throat (*ḥolam*) to the tips of the lips (*shuruḳ*), the GTU 2 introduces a division according to the vowels' length. This reflects a different strand of the Hebrew grammatical thought.

Indeed, the description of the vowels based on the masoretic tradition as represented by the *Horayat ha-Ḳore*ʾ underwent a major transformation in

56. Busi, *Horayat ha-Qore*ʾ, 152: והוא שרק, בפירוש כמ׳ לשמוע שריקות עדרים, לפי שכשאדם שרק בשפתיו ומשמיע קול, נשמע כמ׳ או, "This is *shuruḳ*, with the meaning like 'To hear whistling of the flocks' (Judges 5:16), because when a man whistles with his lips and makes a sound, it is like a *u*." A similar description is provided also by Abraham ibn Ezra; see *Sefer Moznayim*, ed. Goodman, 27–28: כאדם שהוא שורק, "like a man who is whistling…"

57. Busi, *Horayat ha-Qore*ʾ, p. 152: והמלך השני קמץ, מוציא [פירושו] מן וקמץ הכהן, לפי שהוא מקמץ את הפה, "The second king is *ḳamaẓ*; it derives its meaning from 'And the priest grasps' (Leviticus 5:12 or Numbers 5:26), because one contracts one's mouth."

58. Busi, *Horayat ha-Qore*ʾ, 152: המלכים הם ז׳, כעין נוטריקון, והם אֹ אָ אַ אֶ אֵ אִ אֻ, "There are 7 kings, as shown in the notaricon: these are אֹ אָ אַ אֶ אֵ אִ אֻ."

the twelfth century. Jewish grammarians of the Provençal school developed a quantitative approach to vowels which came to be presented as either long or short. The first author to have introduced the distinction of length to the classification of the Hebrew vowels was Joseph Kimhi, who, as we saw, was well known in medieval northern France and England. His polemics against the grammatical ideas of Rabbenu Tam and a rejoinder by Tam's English student and admirer, Benjamin of Cambridge, transmitted in Vatican City, Biblioteca Apostolica Vaticana, MS Vat. ebr. 402, give witness to intellectual contacts between England and the Sefardi circles in Provence. It is relevant that this manuscript, as well as Oxford, Bodl., MS Oppenheim 625 contain a copy of the *Horayat ha-Ḳore'* alongside the works by Joseph Kimhi. An easy flow of ideas between the South and the North is confirmed by the quotations of Sefardi grammarians by the London scholars, Moses ben Yom Tov and Moses ben Isaac ha-Nessi'ah.

The masoretic work of Moses ben Yom Tov, *Darkhei ha-Niḳḳud ve-ha-Neginot,* is crucial for our discussion, as it combines the Oriental masoretic learning with grammatical ideas of the Spanish school. According to Wilhelm Bacher, Moses ha-Naḳdan (that Bacher wrongly identified with Moses ben Yom Tov's student, Moses ben Isaac ha-Nessi'ah[59]) studied and annotated Joseph Kimhi's grammar, *Sefer Zikkaron* (The Book of Remembrance). Bacher observed that some manuscripts of the *Sefer Zikkaron* contain comments, one of which identifies its writer as the author of a work entitled *Niḳḳud* (Vocalization). The content of the gloss resembles a passage in the *Darkhei ha-Niḳḳud ve-ha-Neginot.*[60]

Bacher's study confirms that *Sefer Zikkaron* was known in thirteenth-century England. It was precisely in this book that Joseph Kimhi presented for the first time a new coherent system of ten vowels. In his approach, they have five qualities (*a, e, o, u, i*), but each has a long and a short variant. They constitute five corresponding pairs in two groups according to their length ("five large and five small," הם חמש גדולות וחמש קטנות): *ḳamaẓ gadol* – *pataḥ gadol*, *ẓere* – *segol* or *pataḥ ḳaṭan*, *ḥolam* – *ḥaṭaf ḳamaẓ*, *shuruḳ* – *ḳubbuẓ*, "long" *ḥireḳ* (followed by a *yod*) – "short" *ḥireḳ* (not followed by a *yod*) (Table 5.5).

In addition to these five corresponding pairs organised according to the vowels' length, Kimhi described the *shva* (mobile and quiescent, נע and נח) and specified that *shva* is not an independent vowel, it is not one of the "seven kings."[61]

59. In the introduction to his edition of the *Sefer Zikkaron/Sefer Sikkaron,* p. ix. As stated by Löwinger, the fact that Moses ha-Nessi'ah was Moses ben Yom Tov's disciple accounts for similarities in their explanations, Moses ha-Naḳdan, *Tractatio,* ed. Löwinger, 8.

60. Wilhelm Bacher, "Moïse ha-naqdan, glossateur de la grammaire de Joseph Kimhi," *REJ* 12 (1886): 73–79.

61. Joseph Kimhi, *Sefer Zikkaron/Sefer Sikkaron,* ed. Bacher, 17–18: השבא אינה תנועה בפני עצמה ולא המליכוה בשבעה מלכים כי לא נתן עליה הוד מלכות.

Table 5.5 Joseph Kimhi's classification of vowels

Sound equivalent	Long vowels	Short vowels
ā / a	קמץ גדול	פתח גדול
ē / e	צרי	סגול=פתח קטן
ō / o	חולם [נקודה אחת ממעלה]	חטף קמץ
ū / u	שורק בו"ו	שורק בלא ו"ו=קבוץ שפתים
ī / i	חירק ביו"ד [נקודה אחת תחת האות]	חירק בלא יו"ד

Although Kimhi followed the Tiberian tradition to a large extent and referred to the vowels as "seven kings," he built a system based on quantitative pairs. He applied it to the structure of the syllables and morphology in general. In his system of the matching pairs, he is the first to differentiate between two lengths of *u, o* and *i*. It is for the first time in the Hebrew grammatical tradition that the *u*-sound written as three dots placed obliquely under a consonant (*ḳubbuẓ*) is not considered as a mere orthographic variant of the *shuruḳ* (וּ) but as an independent vowel defined as a short *u*.[62]

The list of vowels in the Longleat House Grammar, at the end of GTU 3[63] and in GTU 2, which translates and describes in Latin the list in GTU 3 (the 11 vowels of GTU 3 plus *ḥaṭaf pataḥ ḳaṭan* [= *ḥaṭaf segol*] which was forgotten in GTU 3), contains many similarities to the list in Joseph Kimhi's book. It includes all the vowels from Kimhi's list except for the "short" *ḥireḳ*. But it adds to the list of the vowels the *shva* and the *ḥaṭaf pataḥ*, described as "intermediary sounds," which are not considered as proper vowels by Kimhi. The description of some vowels in GTU 2 contains information about their length, and GTU 2 distinguishes the groups of vowels accepting the *meteg* and those which do not as equivalent to long and short vowels, like in Kimhi's vowels' classification.

Thus, as Jewish linguistic models go, GTU 2 integrates some elements of the Spanish-Provençal school of Joseph Kimhi together with the Oriental approach of the Masorah-based *Guide of the Correct Reading of the Bible*, as transmitted in the local English masoretic writings. Indeed, unlike GTU 2 and the Eastern tradition, Kimhi did not describe the vowels from the point of view of phonetics or their graphic shapes (except for *shuruḳ* and "long" *ḥireḳ*).

In addition to these two Jewish models, the author of GTU 2 shows a degree of independence, sometimes resulting in confusion. For example, GTU 2 (following GTU 3), uses the masoretic name *melo fum*, "fullness of the mouth," for the

62. Abraham ibn Ezra follows the Tiberian tradition considering both as graphic variants which reflect the same sound: *shuruḳ* is for him "a dot in the middle of the letter *vav* or three dots below the letter," Abraham ibn Ezra, *Sefer Moznayim*, ed. Goodman, 7a.

63. The list in GTU 3 is slightly confused: some of the vowels are mentioned twice.

kubbuẓ. The term *melo fum* appears as well in a Hebrew adaptation of the *Hidāyat al-Qāriʾ* (in the *Hidāyat al-Qāriʾ* itself it is expressed by the verbal form of the root, "it fills the mouth") but as an alternative name for a *ḥolam* rather than *kubbuẓ*.[64] Surprisingly, in GTU 2, the pronunciation of the *ḥolam* is not described, the letter being presented only from the point of view of its graphic form and etymology of its name, which differs from the etymology given in the *Hidāyat al-Qāriʾ*. The alternative name of the *ḥolam* in the masoretic tradition, *melo fum*, appears in GTU 2 immediately after the discussion of the *ḥolam*, but is attributed to a different vowel. It may not be irrelevant that the name *shuruk*, which in the masoretic tradition is interchangeable with *kubbuẓ*, is sometimes described as קבוץ פום, "a contraction of the mouth" – the opposite to מלא פום, containing, however, the same component, פום, "mouth." Maybe an oral explanation given to the Christian compiler comparing the two vowels and discussing their alternative names led to the confusion in the Longleat House Grammar?

While he adheres to at least two Jewish sources, the author of GTU 2 shows some degree of creativity. The description of *u*-sounds is interesting despite the terminological confusion mentioned above. Instead of accepting Kimhi's distinction between *shuruk* and *kubbuẓ*, understood as long *u* versus short *u*, GTU 2 gives a qualitative phonetic description which differs from that of Jewish sources. Whereas Jewish authors such as Abraham ibn Ezra discuss the phonetic difference between *shuruk* and *ḥolam*, GTU 2 discusses a phonetic difference between *shuruk* and *melo fum* (= *kubbuẓ*). *Shuruk* is described as uttered by the extremity of the mouth, with the lips rounded as for whistling, whereas *melo fum* is uttered with the full mouth slightly opened and rounded "but not like whistling." According to GTU 2, the two vowels are two different *u* sounds, maybe like the French *ou* and *u* respectively.

Thus, the approach to the vowels reflected in GTU 2 shows an original understanding by its Christian author of the different strands of the Jewish description of the vowels: Oriental description based on masoretic phonetics on the one hand and the differentiation between long and short vowels as first elaborated by Joseph Kimhi in Provence on the other. As stated, the two approaches could have been easily transmitted through the teaching of the Jewish scholars in medieval England. Indeed, as we saw, the writings of Moses ben Yom Tov of London, his *Darkhei ha-Nikkud ve-ha-Neginot* and his glosses on the *Sefer Zikkaron*, constitute a bridge between Oriental Masorah and Spanish-Provençal grammar. The connection between the works of Moses ben Yom Tov or of Moses ben Isaac ha-Nessiʾah and GTU 2 is confirmed by the use in the latter of the same idiosyncratic term הברה understood as "vowel."

64. Eldar, *Art of the Correct Reading*, 121.

Grammar Textual Unit 3: The Hebrew Grammar in Hebrew Characters

The longest of the four textual units, GTU 3, was probably also the core component of the Longleat House Grammar. It differs from the other three textual units by its alphabet and the direction of writing; it is written in Hebrew characters like a Hebrew book, from right to left. The overwhelming majority of the text consists of verbal paradigms and lists of nouns with possessive suffixes. There are only a few comments and metalinguistic discussions. Some textual elements, such as the addition of vernacular French translations and inconsistencies in grammatical definitions, suggest that GTU 3 is not a copy of a known Jewish tractate but rather a new compilation based on Jewish sources.

The text gives little information about its authorship and production. A few times we hear the voice of the author of GTU 3, in the first person. On fol. 198v, he announces: ואדבר על אודות הדיבוק, "and (now) I will speak about the construct state," and then addresses his reader directly by stating: אני משים בתיבה הי לאחריה, "I put a *heh* at the end of the word" when explaining the *status constructus*, and on fol. 198r: ויער הצור את רוחי לדבר על תיבות, "and the Rock (God) has awoken my spirit to speak about the words [. . .]." The latter sentence, a vaguely paraphrased biblical verse (e.g., Haggai 1:14), was used by medieval Jewish authors as an expression of God's inspiration for writing. A similar declaration is found, for example, in the author's preface to the comprehensive grammar (*Sefer Mikhlol*) of David Kimhi.[65]

Despite a few clumsy Hebrew formulations, the author of GTU 3 was probably a Jew or a convert. It is possible that he was also the scribe of the text, and, as pointed out earlier, he certainly trained in Jewish scribal tradition. The contents of GTU 3 indicate that he was familiar with various works of Jewish grammarians. However, some inconsistencies in his grammatical definitions, such as listing a verb belonging to the *binyan Pi'el*, חִמֵּם, with a series of *Ḳal* verbs, indicate that he may not have been a dedicated grammarian.

Even stronger doubts about the grammatical proficiency of the maker or makers of GTU 3 are raised by the way in which the consonantal forms were vocalized. Whilst the last part of GTU 3 is dedicated to the Tiberian vowels and accents and their graphic forms, the consonantal text of the GTU 3 was provided with a simplified vowel system. In the majority of cases, *pataḥ* replaced the expected *ḳamaẓ* to render the sound *a*, and *ẓere* replaced *segol* for *e*. However, unlike most texts vocalized by Christian Hebraists in medieval England where the

65. ויער ייי את רוחי ויאמץ את לבי לכתוב . . . , ed. Isaac Rittenberg (Lyck, 1842), fol. אr.

system is coherent in having only one sign for *a* (*pataḥ*) and one for *e* (*ẓere*),[66] in GTU 3 *ḳamaẓ* and *segol* appear too, albeit infrequently. Thus, it cannot be said that the system of vocalization in GTU 3 has strictly one sign for *a* and one for *e*. Rather than a consistent system of five sounds expressed by five vowels plus a *shva*, the vocalization of the grammar reflects confusion between two *a* and two *e* sounds. Such confusion is frequent in Jewish non-biblical manuscripts, such as liturgical texts, and reflects the underlying pronunciation of the northern European Jews, notably those whose vernacular tongue was French.[67] The underlying French pronunciation in GTU 3 is probably also the reason for a frequent presence of a *dagesh* in the *yod* at the beginning of words. Foreign to the Tiberian rules, this phenomenon is found in the vocalization of another manuscript of English origin, a Psalter, Paris, BnF, MS hébreu 113. This *dagesh* may reflect a pronunciation of *yod* similar to French *j*. The fact that all Tiberian vowels were used in GTU 3 shows that it follows a non-standard, and maybe careless vocalization rather than a Christian simplified convention of only five vowel signs.

It is surprising that non-standard vocalization had been applied to a linguistic text, in the morphological paradigms for which vowels are so pertinent. Who was the text's vocalizer? As observed, the palaeographical analysis of the consonants reveals that their scribe trained in Jewish tradition. GTU 3 contains other conventions of Jewish scribes, such as the justification of the left-hand margins through the abbreviated anticipation of the first word of the next line, or ending the paragraphs with the common explicit formula, סליק. Of course, a Christian scribe might have learned such graphic devices, but together with the characteristic ductus of the letters his Jewish training is very likely. Was this reasonably well-trained scribe also the one who added the vowels? Similar ink used for the consonants and vowels suggests that both text components may have been written at the same time and place but cannot confirm the identity of the writers. If we assume that the scribe and vocalizer was one and the same person, was this Jew or convert unaware of the intricacies of the masoretic vocalization? Was he unable to apply the theory (represented by the list on fols. 198r–197v) to the practice of vocalizing the actual grammatical forms? It cannot be excluded that the vowels resulted from another person's attempt to capture the pronunciation following oral instruction.

66. See Judith Olszowy-Schlanger, "A Christian Tradition of Hebrew Vocalisation in Medieval England," in *Semitic Studies in Honour of Edward Ullendorff*, ed. Geoffrey Khan (Leiden and Boston, 2005), 126–146.

67. Ilan Eldar, *The Hebrew Language Tradition in Medieval Ashkenaz* (Jerusalem, 1978), 1: 28–31 (Hebrew). For the liturgical texts, see e.g., Ilan Eldar, "The Vocalization of the Passover Haggadah in Maḥzor Vitry," *Leshonenu* 39 (1975): 192–216 (Hebrew). For the confusion of the vowels in the Hebrew-Old French glossary of Basel, see Menahem Banitt, *Le glossaire de Bâle* (Jerusalem, 1972), 1: 12.

The Structure of Grammar Textual Unit 3

In conformity with the unanimous tradition of medieval Jewish grammarians, GTU 3 distinguishes three parts of speech: verb, noun and particle. This division is not stated explicitly but is inherent in the structure of GTU 3. The treatment reserved for the three parts of speech is unequal: verbs represent the lion's share of the text, while the description of the particles is limited to their list. Syntax receives very little attention. GTU 3 ends with a list of vowels (discussed above, under GTU 2) and *ṭeʿamim* (cantillation signs).

The preserved part of GTU 3 begins with the verb conjugation in *binyan Ḳal*. The forms are listed first according to the tense and then according to the grammatical person. For each person, several so-called weak verbs – or verbs presenting a certain irregularity – are conjugated simultaneously. The verbs in question are: ישב, יצא, לבש, חמם, שכב, ישן, בוא, הלך, אכל, עשה. Their particular irregularity is not discussed. The preserved text begins with the future (imperfect), with the persons in the following order: 1st person singular, 3rd person masculine singular, 2nd person masculine singular, 1st person plural. The list of the future forms stops abruptly, and the text enumerates the four forms of the imperative: 2nd person masculine singular, 2nd person feminine singular, 2nd person masculine plural and 2nd person feminine plural. It is worth noting that the imperative of the verb לבש, "to dress, wear clothes," is formed according to the pattern *ḳeṭol* (לְבוֹשׁ) as in rabbinic Hebrew rather than the biblical *ḳeṭal* form (לְבַשׁ). Then, the past (perfect) is listed but includes only 3rd person masculine singular, 3rd person feminine singular, and 1st person plural. This is followed by the present (active participle), which is also incomplete: it lists masculine plural, feminine plural, feminine singular, and again, by mistake, feminine plural. Immediately after, the text returns to the past tense, with the forms of the 2nd masculine singular, 2nd masculine plural, 2nd feminine singular, 2nd feminine plural and 3rd masculine plural, the latter described as corresponding to the 3rd person feminine plural. Quite inconsistently, the examples go back to the forms of the future tense for 1st person singular, 3rd person masculine singular, 3rd person masculine plural and 2nd person masculine plural. The 3rd person masculine plural is described as identical to the 3rd person feminine plural; although in Hebrew there exists a specific feminine form, the two are indeed often confused, the masculine form being used with the feminine subject. Interestingly, the identical forms for masculine and feminine in the case of object suffixes were commented upon by Moses ben Yom Tov of London, as attested by the aforementioned quotation in his student's dictionary, the *Sefer ha-Shoham*.[68] As for the

68. See above, note 19.

paradigms of the future tense, 1st person singular and 3rd person masculine singular are here conjugated twice.

Unlike GTU 1 and GTU 4 which give forms of several *binyanim*, GTU 3 focuses on *Ḳal*. The other verbal structures are described briefly. They are described as forms with additions (ויש דברים ששמותם נוסף, "and there are forms whose name is 'additional'") and illustrated with examples of what corresponds to *Hifʿil*, i.e., forms with an additional *heh* (והנה ההי נקרא הנוסף), e.g., האביד כמו אבד, and the forms with an additional *mem*, corresponding to *Piʿel* participle (ויש נוסף שהמם נר־ספת), e.g., מדבר כמו דובר. A distinction is also made between verb *Ḳal*, "light" and *Kaved*, "heavy"; the examples of the latter correspond to *Piʿel*.

The next part of the GTU 3 contains the conjugation of the verb שמר, "to guard." The conjugation is incomplete, many forms have been omitted, and their order is sometimes confused. It contains the forms of שמר in *Ḳal* (future singular, past singular and plural, imperative and active participles) and a few forms in *Piʿel*. Some forms are conjugated with object suffixes. Despite a certain disorder and omissions, these paradigms are of particular interest: Hebrew verb forms are translated into French written in Hebrew characters and vocalized with Hebrew vowels. Only one other example of conjugated Old French verbs in Hebrew characters is known: the paradigm of the root פקד, translated into French as קוֹנְטַא, qonṭa (mF "*il compta*"), "he counted," in Turin, Biblioteca Nazionale e Universitaria, MS A IV 13. In this manuscript, the Hebrew-Old French grammar, entitled *Maʿayan Ḳodesh* (The Fountainhead of Holiness) followed a Hebrew-Old French glossary arranged alphabetically.[69] Unfortunately, this precious manuscript perished in the conflagration of the Turin library in 1904.[70] As such, the GTU 3 contains not only the paradigm of the Hebrew verb but also a very early example of the paradigm of a French verb, the translation of שמר ("to guard, keep") – "*garder*." The forms of *Piʿel* immediately follow the corresponding *Ḳal* forms and are translated as causative or factitive verbs, with the French auxiliary "*faire*." In Table 5.6 below, the forms in French in Hebrew characters in their order of appearance, with their Hebrew equivalents (vocalized as they appear in the text[71]) and their parsing, are followed by their transliteration and Modern French equivalents.

69. Arsène Darmesteter, "Rapport sur une mission en Italie: Gloses et glossaires hébreux-français, notes sur des manuscrits de Parme et de Turin," *Archives des missions scientifiques et littéraires*, 3rd series, 4 (1877): 426–432.

70. Georges Bourguin, "L'incendie de la Bibliothèque nationale et universitaire de Turin," *Bibliothèque de l'École des Chartes* 65 (1904): 132–140.

71. For the standard vocalization, see the critical apparatus in the edition in Chapter Four.

Table 5.6 Form of שמר translated into French written in Hebrew characters

אֶשְׁמֹר	Ḳal 1st sg. fut.	גַּרְדְּרֵי	garderei	je garderai
יִשְׁמֹר	Ḳal 3rd sg. masc. fut.	גַּרְדְּרַה	gardera(h)	il gardera
תִּשְׁמֹר	Ḳal 2nd sg. masc. fut.	גַּרְדְּרַש	garderas	tu garderas
נִשְׁמֹר	Ḳal 1st pl. fut.	גַּרְדְּרוֹמְש	garderomes	nous garderons
שְׁמוֹר	Ḳal 2nd sg. masc. imp.	גַּרְדְּא	garde	garde!
שִׁמְרוּ	Ḳal 2nd sg. masc. imp.	גַּרְדֵּיש	gardeis	gardez!
שָׁמְרוּ	Ḳal 3rd pl. past	גַּרְדֵּירְנְט	gardeirent	ils gardèrent
שְׁמַרְתִּיךָ	Ḳal 1st sg. past + suffix 2nd sg. masc.	גַּרְדֵּיטֵיי	gardeiteiy	je te gardai
שִׁמַּרְתִּיךָ	Pi'el 1st sg. past + suffix 2nd sg. masc	פִּיט גַּרְדֵּירְ טֵיי	fit [probably an error for fis] gardeir teiy	je te fis garder
שְׁמַרְתַּנִי	Ḳal 2nd sg. masc. past + suffix 1st sg.	גַּרְדַּשְׁמֵי	gardasmei	tu me gardas
שִׁמַּרְתַּנִי	Pi'el 2nd sg. masc. past + suffix 1st sg.	פִּיט גַּרְדֵּירְמֵיי	fit [probably an error for fis] gardeirmeiy	tu me fis garder
שׇׁמְרֵנִי	Ḳal 2nd sg. masc. imp + suffix 1st sg.	גַּרְדְּמֵיי	gardemeiy	garde-moi!
שְׁמָרַנִי	Ḳal 3rd sg. masc. past + suffix 1st sg.	גַּרְדַהמֵיי	garda(h)meiy	il me garda
שְׁמָרַהוּ	Ḳal 3rd sg. masc. past + suffix 3rd sg. masc.	גַּרְדְּהַלִי	garada(h)li	il le garda
שָׁמַר	Ḳal 3rd sg. masc. past	גַּרְדַּה	garada(h)	il garada
שָׁמְרוּ	Ḳal 3rd pl. past	גַּרְדֵּירְנְט	gardeirent	ils gardèrent
שָׁמַרְתִּי	Ḳal 1st sg. past	גַּרְדֵּי	gardei	je gardai

שְׁמַרְתֶּם	Ḳal 2nd pl. masc. past	גַּרְדַּשְׁטְשְׁ	gardastes	vous gardâtes
שְׁמַרְנוּם	Ḳal 1st pl. past + suffix 3rd pl. masc.	גַּרְדַּמְשְׁאֵוּש	gardames(e)us	nous les gardâmes
שְׁמַרְתִּיכֶם	Ḳal 1st sg. past + suffix 2nd pl. masc.	גַּרְדֵּיבֿוֹש	gardeivos	je vous gardai
שְׁמַרְתַּנוּ	Ḳal 2nd sg. masc. past + suffix 1st pl.	גַּרְדַּשְׁנוֹש	gardasnos	tu nous gardas
שְׁמַרְנוּכֶם	Ḳal 1st pl. past + suffix 2nd pl. masc.	גַּרְדַּמְשְׁבֿוֹש	gardamesvos	nous vous gardâmes
שׁוֹמֵר	Ḳal sg. masc. present	גַּרְדּוֹנְטְ	gardont	gardant
שְׁמַרַתְּהוּ	Ḳal 3rd sg. fem. past + suffix 3rd sg. masc.	גַּרְדַּלִי	gardali	elle le garda
שְׁמַרְתִּיכָם	Ḳal 1st sg. past + suffix 2nd pl. masc.	גַּרְדֵּיבֿוּש	gardeivus	je vous gardai
שְׁמַרְתִּינוּ	Ḳal 2nd sg. fem. past + suffix 1st pl.	גַּרְדַּשְׁנוּש	gardasnus	tu nous gardas
שְׁמַרְנוּךְ	Ḳal 1st pl. past + suffix 2nd sg. masc.	גַּרְדַּמְשְׁטֶיי	gardamesteiy	nous te gardâmes
שְׁמַרְנוּךְ [for שִׁמַּרְנוּךְ (שְׁמַרְנוּךָ)]	Pi'el 1st pl. past + suffix 2nd sg. masc.	פִּיש גַּרְדֵּירְטֵי	fis [should be fimes] gardeirtei	nous te fîmes garder
שְׁמַרְתִּינִי	Ḳal 2nd sg. fem. past + suffix 1st sg.	גַּרְדַּשְׁמֶיי	gardasmeiy	tu me gardas
שְׁמַרְתִּינוּ	Ḳal 2nd sg. fem. past + suffix 1st pl.	גַּרְדַּשְׁנוּש	gardasnus	tu nous gardas
שׁוֹמֵר	Ḳal sg. masc. present	גַּרְדּוֹנְטְ	gardont	gardant

שִׁמְרִי	Ḳal 2nd sg. fem. imp.	גַרְדְא	garde	garde!
שׁוֹמֶרֶת	Ḳal sg. fem. present	גַרְדוֹנְטְאָה	gardonte(h)	gardante
שׁוֹמְרִים	Ḳal pl. masc. present	גַרְדוֹנְש	gardons	gardants
שׁוֹמְרוֹת	Ḳal pl. fem. present	גַרְדוֹנְטְשְׁ	gardontes	gardantes
שָׁמוּר	Ḳal sg. masc. passive participle	גַרְדֵי	gardei	gardé
שִׁמְרוּ	Ḳal 2nd pl. masc. imp.	גַרְדֵיש	gardeis	gardez!
שִׁימַרְנָה	Ḳal 2nd pl. fem. imp.	גַרְדֵיש	gardeis	gardez!
שְׁמָרוּן	Ḳal 3rd pl. past + suffix 3rd pl. fem.	גַרְדֵירְנְטְאוּש	gadreirenteus	ils les gardèrent
שְׁמָרָן	Ḳal 3rd sg. masc. past + suffix 3rd pl. fem.	גַרְדַהאוּש	garada(h)eus	il les garda
שָׁמוֹר	Ḳal inf. absolutus	גַרְדוֹנְטְ	gardont	gardant
שְׁמִירַתְכֶם	verbal noun	נוֹשְׁטְרְגַרְדְא [should be בושטרגרדא: Hebrew word is a noun with the possessive suffix of the 2nd person masculine plural]	nostregarde [should be vostregarde]	notre garde
שׁוֹמְרֵיכֶן	Ḳal pl. masc. present + suffix 2nd pl. masc.	נוֹשְׁגַרְדוֹנְשְׁ [should be בושגרדונש: Hebrew word is a noun with the possessive suffix of the 2nd person feminine plural]	nosgardons [should be vosgardons]	nous gardant (pl.)

יִשְׁמׇרְכֶם	Ḳal 3rd sg. masc. fut. + suffix 2nd pl. masc.	גַּרְדְּרַהבּוֹשְׁ	gardera(h)vos	il vous gardera
יִשְׁמׇרְךָ	Ḳal 3rd sg. masc. fut. + suffix 2nd sg. masc.	גַּרְדְּרַהטֶי	gardera(h)tei	il te gardera
מִשְׁמֶרֶת	verbal noun	גַּרְדְּא	garde	une garde

The Hebrew transliteration, even when vocalized as here, does not precisely render the French sounds. Some Hebrew consonants appear as *matres lectionis* to ascertain the pronunciation of the preceding vowel, such as *heh* at the end of the 3rd person singular future tense ending: e.g., גַּרְדְּרַה rendering "*(il) gardera*." The *heh* firmly establishes the pronunciation of the long *a*. One observes that the short *e* (*e* "*muet*") at the end of a word is followed by an *alef* in the transliteration: e.g., the imperative of the 2nd person singular masculine *Ḳal*: גַּרְדְּא rendering "*garde*"!, or the feminine singular active participle: גַּרְדוֹנְטְאָה, rendering a gerundive form with *e* "*muet*" – feminine marker at the end – "*gardante*." The conjugated forms are standard Old French forms, with some elements which may indicate a northern dialect, such as *–oms* or *-omes* (instead of the more frequent *–ons*) ending of the 1st person plural: e.g., גַּרְדְּרוֹמְש "*garderom(e)s*" for "*nous garderons*," "we will guard."[72]

Pertinent features are the forms of the personal pronouns with their direct object function. The forms are *mei, tei, li, nos* (or *nus*), *vos* (or *vus*), *eus*. The forms of the first and second person are transliterated with a *yod*, and often with a double *yod* at the end. This transliteration may indicate a strong pronunciation, *mei, tei,* and suggests an accented form of the accusative of the personal pronoun (versus the weak forms *me, te*). The accented forms *mei* and *tei* are attested in particular in Anglo-Norman, while other dialects of the *langue d'oïl* rather have *moi, toi* (mF *moi, toi* versus the weak forms *me, te*).[73] The form of the 3rd person plural, *eus*, is also the accented form of the pronoun (versus the weak form *les*, mF *eux* versus *les*). The form of the 3rd person singular *li* (or *ly*) also seems to be an accented form (a more frequent accented form is *lui*, mF *lui*), while the weak form is *le*. The choice of the accented forms of the accusative of the personal pronoun in the translation in GTU 3 is justified by their place after the verb. Indeed, only accented object pronouns in French can be placed after the verb, while the weak object pronoun precedes the verb. The place of the pronoun as following the verb corresponds to the Hebrew syntax, where the object suffix is attached at the end of the verb.

72. For the North and North-East form of the 1st person plural ending –omes, see for example Frédéric Duval, *Le français médiéval* (Turnhout, 2009), 134.

73. *AND2*, s.v. mei.

The writing of the French pronoun as attached to the end of the verb shows an attempt to reflect the Hebrew grammatical form as closely as possible, even if it is artificial according to the rules of the French syntax.

In addition to this conjugation, a few other Judeo-French terms appear in GTU 3. On fol. 200v, בִּקֵּר is translated (not altogether correctly, as one would expect a *Piʿel* form) as צֵירְקוֹנֶט, "ṣeyreqoneṭe" (mF *cherchant*), "searching," and on fol. 199r, Old French is used to explain a special case of an object suffix.

The part on verbs in GTU 3 is followed by an explanation concerning the noun, designated by the term שם דבר, lit. "name of a thing." First, there is a brief list of examples of nouns, followed by nouns with possessive suffixes. The chosen examples are translated into French in a gloss written in Latin characters between the lines: רֹאשׁ – *chef*[74] (mF *tête*, "head"), חָכְמָה – *sens*[75] (mF *sagesse*, "wisdom"), עֲשִׂיָּה – *feseement*[76] (mF *fait, action*, "action, doing"), זֶכֶר – *remenbrance*[77] (mF *souvenir*, "remembrance"), אֲמִירָה – *dite*[78] (mF *dicton, parole*, "saying"), בִּינָה – *avertissement*[79] (mF *discernement*, "awareness"), יִרְאָה – *creinure*,[80] (mF *crainte*, "fear"), שְׁאֵלָה – *demaund*[81] (mF *demande*, "question").

The discussion on folio 199r concerning the third part of speech, the particle, is slightly inconsistent: it includes a list of the particles and prepositions but also some observations on the sounds and function of the consonants. It contains a mention of the so-called servile letters arranged in two groups and expressed by two respective mnemonic formulae: כַּלֵּב מֹשֶׁה, gathering consonants which, placed before a noun, have a function of prepositions (כְּ, "as," לְ, "to, towards," בְּ, "in," מִן, "from"), serve as a relative pronoun (שֶׁ) or as a definite article (הַ), and אֵיתָן which, placed before a verb, have a grammatical function of the prefixes of the future tense.[82] This is followed by a list of particles (אֶת כָּל עַל אֲשֶׁר הִנֵּה אַף גַּם זֶה לְזַכֵּר וְזֹאת

74. *DEAF*, s.v. *chief.*
75. *DEAF*, s.v. *sens.*
76. *DEAF*, s.v. *faire* (spelling: *faisement*).
77. *DEAF*, s.v. *remembrer* (spelling: *remembrance*).
78. *DEAF*, s.v. *dire.*
79. *DEAF*, s.v. *avertir.*
80. This form of the noun is not listed. It is derived from *criembre* (mF *craindre*).
81. *DEAF*, s.v. *demander.*
82. The classification of the Hebrew consonants according to their capacity of being a part of the derivational base or "radicals" (יסוד) only, or of serving as grammatical additions too, "servile letters" (משרתים) is attested already in masoretic tractates such as the *Diḳduḳei Ṭeʿamim*, and was accepted by most later grammarians. Medieval grammarians listed the "radical" and "servile" consonants using mnemonic formulae. For a general discussion of such formulae, see for example Wilhelm Bacher, David Kaufmann, Gruenwald, and Nathan Porgès, "Les signes mnémotechniques des lettres radicales et serviles," *REJ* 16 (1888): 286–291; Joseph Derenbourg, "Les signes mnémotechniques des lettres radicales et serviles," *REJ* 16 (1888): 57–60; David Rosin, "The Meaning of the Mnemonic Formulae for the Radical and Servile

לֹא לְנְקֵיבָה אִם כִּי רַק אַל). The list of the particles is transliterated and provided with French translations in a note in Latin characters written by a slightly later hand in the upper margin of the same folio. There follows a short note described as כלל גדול, "a major rule," concerning the presence or absence of a *dagesh* in the object suffix נּוּ versus נוּ, which differentiates between the 3rd person masculine singular (in the first case) and the 1st person plural (in the second case). To explain this rule, the scribe translated the Hebrew examples into French written in Hebrew characters (fol. 199r). The Old French verbs *saveir*, "to know," *requerir*, "to ask," and *oir*, "to hear" are used to illustrate the nuances of the object suffix נו respectively with or without dagesh: שַׁבְּרָה לִי, *savra(h) li*, "he will know him" versus שַׁבְרָה נוֹשׁ, *savra(h) nos*, "he will know us"; רְקֵירַשׁ לִי, *requeir(r)as li*, "you will ask him" versus רְקֵירַשׁ נוֹשׁ, *requeir(r)as nos*, "you will ask us"; אוֹרָה לִי, *or(r)a li*, "he will hear him" versus אוֹרָה נוֹשׁ, *or(r)a nos*, "he will hear us".

The treatment of the syntax is limited to two remarks. The first is the mention of the Hebrew possessive construction of the nouns: the so-called *status constructus*, expressed in GTU 3 through different terms from the root דבק, "to adhere," which expresses the possession through the apposition of two nouns, of which only the second can bear the marks of definition (definite article or possessive suffix), while the first takes the "construct" form, which in most cases differs from the "absolute" or basic form of the noun. GTU 3 comments notably on the feminine nouns ending with a *heh* in absolute singular form, in which, in the construct state, *heh* is replaced by *tav*. The comment conveys the importance of the use of the construct form for a correct syntactic relationship and meaning of the phrase (fol. 198v):

> I am going to speak about the *status constructus* (דיבוק), namely about the places where the word adheres (נדבקת), for example, חכמה, "wisdom." When it does not adhere (שאינו נדבק) to the word which follows it, I put a *heh* at the end of this word but when this word adheres to the word which follows it, for example, אדם, "man," when I say חכמת אדם, "a man's wisdom," I put a *tav* at its end. There are many examples such as בהמה, "beast" – בהמת האדם, "the man's beast," בינה, "discernment" – בינת האדם, "the man's discernment," דיעה, "knowledge" – דעת האדם, "the man's knowledge," גבורה, "fortitude" – גבורת האדם, "the man's fortitude," and many others. But you don't say בהמה האדם, lit. "a beast the man," because it would look as if the man were a beast. Similarly, with חכמה האדם, lit. "wisdom the man," if you write it without *tav*, it would look as if man was a designation for wisdom [...].

Letters in Hebrew," *JQR* 6 (1894): 475–501; Nadia Vidro, "Mnemonic: Medieval Period," in *Encyclopedia of Hebrew Language and Linguistics*, ed. Geoffrey Khan et al. (Leiden and Boston, 2013), 2: 650–653.

The second remark on syntax concerns the nouns which can be either feminine or masculine, like שמש, "sun" or רוח, "wind." After several contextual examples of the change of the gender, the text explains that this is characteristic of inanimate Hebrew nouns (fol. 198r):

> And the Rock (God) has awoken my spirit to talk about the words which sometimes "speak" in masculine and sometimes in feminine. For example, ורוח גדולה באה, "and a great wind came" (Job 1:19), in feminine, and ויגע בארבע פינות הבית, "and it (verb in masc.) smote the four corners of the house" (Job 1:19), in masculine, since it is not ותגע בארבע פינות הבית, "and it (verb in fem.) smote the four corners of the house," and similarly, וזרח השמש, "and the Sun shone (verb in masc.)" (Kohelet 1:5), in masculine and וזרחה לכם שמש, "and the Sun shone (verb in fem.) for you" (based on Malachi 3:20), in feminine, because any thing which does not have the spirit of life in it, you may express it sometimes as masculine and sometimes as feminine (מפני שכל דבר שאין בו רוח חיים תאמרנו פעמים בלשון זכר ופעמים בלשון נקיבה).

GTU 3 ends with a list of *ṭeʿamim*. While the Hebrew masoretic tradition distinguishes between *ṭeʿamim* of three poetic books (Job, Proverbs and Psalms) and the remaining 21 books, the Longleat House Grammar lists only the accents used in non-poetic texts. They are divided into two groups, and their names, in Hebrew characters, are provided with graphic signs for the relevant *ṭeʿamim*. First are listed 16 "disjunctive accents" or, in the words of our Grammar, those "which separate between meanings for the sake of the understanding and melody" (כל אלו מבדילים בין טעם לטעם והניגון). The first occurrence of טעם is glossed in Latin as "*sensus*" and the second as "*intelligentia*." "*Melodia*" translates ניגון. Second, the text enumetares eight "conjunctive accents," described as the "servants linking the meaning and the melody" (ואלה המשרתים שמחברים הטעם והניגון). Here too, some terms are provided with a Latin *superscriptio* translation: שמחברים as "*qui coniungunt*" and ניגון as "*nota*." The names of the *ṭeʿamim* follow the tradition attested in Ashkenazi sources. The order of the *ṭeʿamim* in the lists contained in different works may vary a great deal from one manuscript to another. The order of the disjunctive *ṭeʿamim* in the Longleat House Grammar is very close to the list of the *Darkhei ha-Nikḳud ve-ha-Neginot*: the only difference is the mention of *zaḳef gadol* and *zaḳef ḳaṭan* in our Grammar, whereas the critical edition of the *Darkhei ha-Nikḳud ve-ha-Neginot* mentions only one undifferentiated *zaḳef*, and the *sof pasuḳ*, which appears in our Grammar where the *Darkhei ha-Nikḳud ve-ha-Neginot* has a *silluḳ*.[83]

83. Moses ha-Naḳdan, *Tractatio*, ed. Löwinger, 61.

Grammatical Terminology and Jewish Sources of GTU 3

Hebrew grammatical concepts used in GTU 3 can be divided into three groups: 1. Terms commonly found in Jewish grammatical (and other) literature of various origins (Oriental, Spanish or Ashkenazi); 2. Terms reflecting one specific tradition of the Hebrew grammar: Jewish grammatical approaches of a classical type as elaborated by Andalusi grammarians of the late tenth and eleventh century and transmitted in Provence; 3. Unusual terms and expressions which cannot be traced to any specific Jewish source.

1. To the first group belong terms such as זכר, "masculine"; נקבה, "feminine"; תיבה, "word"; עבר, "past"; עתיד, "future"; ציווי, "imperative." The use of these metalinguistic terms is already attested in the early masoretic texts. Some grammatical terms in GTU 3 are found in the eleventh-century commentary of Rashi of Troyes: דבוק, "attached," for "*status constructus*," or שם דבר, "name of a thing," for "noun" are found alongside masoretic terms and vowel names (similar to GTU 2) in various passages of Rashi's biblical exegesis.[84]

2. The second group is relevant for the identification of the sources of GTU 3 (but also GTU 1 and GTU 4). It reflects a linguistic approach first proposed by Judah Ḥayyūj in Cordoba by the end of the tenth century. One of its main characteristics is the classification of verbs into conjugation patterns: *binyanim*, "structures." Only two *binyanim* are referred to explicitly in GTU 3: פַּעַל (for פָּעַל), *Paʿal* and פִּעֵל, *Piʿel* (וְיֵשׁ דְּבָרִים שֶׁנִּקְרָאִים מִשְׁקַל כָּבֵד וּמִשְׁקַל קַל פַּעַל כְּמוֹ פִּעֵל, "And there are forms [lit. 'things'] which are called 'heavy pattern' and 'light pattern,' *Paʿal* as well as *Piʿel*"), but three others appear in GTU 1. GTU 3 further differentiates between the "light" and "heavy" patterns (משקל קל, lit. "light verbal pattern" and משקל כבד, lit. "heavy verbal pattern"), and verbal patterns which contain additional prefixes: וְיֵשׁ דְּבָרִים שֶׁשְּׁמוֹתָם נוֹסָף, "and there are forms (lit. 'things') which are called 'additional, augmented.'" Two such forms are listed, but without a detailed discussion or examples: וְהִנֵּה הַהֵי נִקְרָא הַנּוֹסָף וְיֵשׁ נוֹסָף שֶׁהַמֵּם נוֹסֶפֶת, "and behold the *heh* called 'additional,' and there is 'addition' in which there is an additional *mem*." Furthermore, the terms which designate the grammatical person reflect the classical Spanish tradition: מדבר בעצמו for 1st person singular – מדברים בעצמם for 1st person plural, נוכח\נוכחת for 2nd person singular masculine/feminine – נוכחים\נוכחות for 2nd person plural masculine/feminine, and נסתר\נסתרת for 3rd person singular masculine/feminine – נסתרים\נסתרות for 3rd person plural masculine/feminine.

While the broadly defined classical Spanish origin of the grammatical terminology is beyond doubt, it is more difficult to pinpoint a particular Jewish source.

84. For example, Rashi on Exodus 15:2: זמרת הוא דבוק לתיבת השם.

Indications of the grammatical person, for example, are in most cases – but not always – consistent with those found in the *Sefer Zikkaron* of Joseph Kimhi. The similarity with this particular grammarian is further stressed by the choice of the verb שמר as the model of conjugation with object suffixes: שמר is indeed the model used in the *Sefer Zikkaron*. However, the verb שמר was also used as a paradigm by Abraham ibn Ezra, whose terminology too bears some similarity to our grammar. שמר also appears in several masoretic tractates. The *Hidāyat al-Qārī*[85] and the *Darkhei ha-Niḳḳud ve-ha-Neginot* of Moses of London often illustrate specific issues with this verb, the latter interchangeably with the verb רדף.

The use in GTU 3 of the term שם דבר, lit. "name of a thing" to designate the noun, and of the root דבק, "to cling, adhere" to express the *status constructus* of the nouns, is analogous to the *Sefer Zikkaron*.[86] However, these terms used in the *Sefer Zikkaron* are also found "closer to home," in the texts from northern France and England. As we saw, דבוק, "attached," for *status constructus* or שם דבר for "noun" appear in Rashi's biblical exegesis. *Darkhei ha-Niḳḳud ve-ha-Neginot* also refers to the nouns by the term שם דבר[87] and to the *status constructus* as דבקות.[88] However, unlike Rashi or the earlier masoretic works, the Longleat House Grammar, just like Moses ben Yom Tov of London, had also integrated the concept of *binyanim* and used their names to discuss conjugation.[89] Like the Spanish-Provençal grammarians, the author of our grammar also referred to משקל נוסף, "additional, augmented pattern," to designate *binyanim* involving the addition of a prefix (such as *heh* in *Hif'il* and *mem* in *Pi'el*).[90]

An interesting case is a short discussion on the nouns which can be either masculine or feminine, notably "wind" and "sun," with biblical quotations to prove this point. The grammatical gender incongruency of several nouns in the biblical text had been observed and discussed by most medieval grammarians and exegetes, chief among them Dunash ibn Labrāṭ, Jonah ibn Janāḥ, Moses ben Samuel ha-Kohen ibn Giḳaṭilla (who authored an alphabetically organized composition on masculine and feminine[91]), Abraham ibn Ezra and David Kimhi in the Spanish-Provençal school, and Rashi in France. While most agree that some

85. See as an example, Khan, *The Tiberian Pronunciation Tradition*, 2: 43–44.

86. Joseph Kimhi, *Sefer Zikkaron/Sefer Sikkaron*, ed. Bacher, 14.

87. Moses ha-Naḳdan, *Tractatio*, ed. Löwinger, 17: שם דבר בסופו כמו דבר, בקר, בשר, אדם, מקדש, מלאך...

88. Moses ha-Naḳdan, *Tractatio*, ed. Löwinger, e.g. 13.

89. Moses ha-Naḳdan, *Tractatio*, ed. Löwinger, e.g. 13, 14: בנין נפעל.

90. Moses ha-Naḳdan, *Tractatio*, ed. Löwinger, 59: משקל נוסף העלומי העין.

91. This *Kitāb al-tadhkīr wal-ta'nīth*, inspired by Jonah ibn Janāḥ, was preserved only in fragments, see Nehemiah Allony, "Fragments of the Book on Masculine and Feminine, *Kitāb al-tadhkīr wal-ta'nīth* by R. Moshe ha-Kohen Ibn Gikitilla," *Sinai* 24 (1949): 34–67 (Hebrew).

words can be either feminine or masculine, the formulation found in our grammar is more specific. It postulates that this interchangeable grammatical gender affects inanimate nouns only. The wording of this rule in our grammar (מפני שכל דבר שאין בו רוח חיים תאמרנו פעמים בלשון זכר ופעמים בלשון נקיבה) is reminiscent of the expression כל דבר שאין בו רוח חיים זכרהו ונקבהו, "every inanimate noun, make it masculine and feminine." This expression, with some variations, is known from citations in the works by later grammarians, such as Profiat Duran (c. 1350–1415), or Abraham de Balmes (1440–1523), who attributed it to Abraham ibn Ezra.[92] The exact quotation does not figure in Ibn Ezra's known works, although the analysis of Ibn Ezra's interpretation of different instances of grammatical gender incongruency in the Bible shows that this rule does agree with his general approach to the topic.[93]

3. The third group contains some unusual terms, notably the expressions designating singular and plural for both genders: לאחד, lit. "for one," for masculine singular, לאשה אחת, lit. "for one woman," for feminine singular, לשני אנשים, lit. "for two men," for masculine plural (alongside the more traditional לרבים) and לשתי נשים, lit. "for two women," for feminine plural.

This incongruous and often clumsy terminology, together with the formulation of the text in the 1st person singular, strengthens our hypothesis that GTU 3 was a personal work of an author who certainly benefitted from Jewish education and had access to the main works of the Hebrew Masorah and grammar but was not himself a trained grammarian.

92. Michel Wilensky, "La source de la proposition כל דבר שאין בו רוח חיים זכרהו ונקבהו," *REJ* 98 (1934): 66–71. Wilensky considers that the expression goes back to Solomon Yarḥi (of Lunel) whom he places in the fourteenth century. For a detailed analysis of the saying and tracing it back to the eleventh century and to Arabic sources, see Esther Goldenberg, "Medieval Linguistics and Good Hebrew," *Leshonenu* 54 (1990): 183–216 at 190–216 (Hebrew). See also Luba R. Charlap, "Three Views Regarding the Gender of Biblical Nouns in the Works of Medieval Hebrew Grammarians," in *Jewish Studies at the Turn of the Twentieth Century: Proceedings of the 6th EAJS Congress, Toledo, July 1998*, ed. Judit Targarona Borrás and Angel Sáenz Badillos (Leiden, 1999), 1: 17–25.

93. This view was expressed by Goldenberg, "Medieval Linguistics and Good Hebrew," but was argued against by Charlap, "Three Views," 22–24. More recently, Hanokh Gamaliel argued in favour of the compatibility of Abraham ibn Ezra's views with the saying, see "More on Congruency in the Language of the Bible," *Da'at Lashon* 2 (2016): 35–45 (Hebrew).

Grammar Textual Unit 4: The Hebrew Verb Paradigms in Latin Characters

The last textual unit of the Longleat House Grammar is a simple table designed to convey the intricacies of the Hebrew verb conjugation, structured as a list of verbal forms. In addition, the list contains the names of the Hebrew consonants written in Latin characters. While Jewish grammarians had included lists of verbal paradigms in their works of pedagogical nature from the early stages of development of this linguistic genre, GTU 4 is the unique known example of such a list of paradigms produced by Christian scholars in the Middle Ages.[94]

As already mentioned, GTU 4 has palaeographical and textual affinities with GTU 1. Both units were copied by the same scribe; both are in Hebrew language but in Latin characters. They both deal with paradigms of the Hebrew verb and use the root רדף as their model. Like GTU 1, GTU 4 deals only with five out of seven *binyanim*: *Ḳal, Piʿel, Puʿal, Hufʿal* and *Hitpaʿel*. Unlike GTU 1, here only the conjugated verbs are listed, without the metalinguistic parsing and mentions of their person and number. The names of the *binyanim* are not indicated. There are, however, headings of *hauar* (for עבר) or *preteritum* for the past tense, *hatid* (for עתיד) or *imperfectum* for the future, *houeh* (for הווה) for the present (active participle), as well as occasional mentions of masculine and feminine. The *binyanim* with a passive meaning (*Puʿal, Hufʿal*) are all introduced as *passiuum*. The imperative is introduced as *imperatiuum* or its Hebrew equivalent *siwi* (for צווי). GTU 4 contains a conjugation of "*hutradef*" in the past tense as well. Such a *binyan* does not exist in Hebrew and seems to be a confused hybrid between *Hufʿal* and *Hitpaʿel*. The future forms of this *binyan* correspond to those of the *Hufʿal*, and the place in the logical arrangement of the list suggests that the author may have wanted to write past tense *Hufʿal* masculine (fol. 204r, col. 1) and then feminine (fol. 204r, col. 2), and included a superfluous formant "*te*" after the prefix "*hu*" by mistake.

In addition to this confused *Hufʿal/Hitpaʿel* form, the transcriptions and specific verbal forms contain several errors, whose corrections are systematically suggested in the critical apparatus of the text edition (see pp. 108–112). Some of the masculine forms on fol. 203v are repeated on fols. 203r and 204v. Spelling is inconsistent, including an occasional doubling of the letter *f* of *radaf*, the third letter of this root, which could be motivated by an erroneous understanding of the grammatical doubling of the second (not third) radical required in the "strong" *binyanim* (*Piʿel, Puʿal* and *Hitpaʿel*). However, this double *f* is not written

94. For the paradigms in the works of Saʿadiah Gaon, see Esther Goldenberg, "The First Hebrew Table of Paradigms," *Leshonenu* 43 (1979): 83–99 (Hebrew); Esther Goldenberg, "שמע [Shemaʿ] as Representing the Paradigm in Saadiah's Inflectional Table," *Leshonenu* 55 (1991): 323–326 (Hebrew).

systematically and may be also due to the scribe's wish to render a strongly pronounced *f*. As for the required grammatical doubling of the second consonant of the root in these strong *binyanim*, it is not reflected at all in the transliterations in GTU 4. The poor state of preservation of GTU 4 adds to the confusion: folio 203 became detached and was rebound incorrectly so that the recto – and the beginning of the text – was placed and marked as the verso of the page. Our edition in Chapter Four (above) restores the correct order of the text (see pp. 108–109). However, despite errors and repetition of several paradigms, the grammatical material does follow an internal and relatively coherent logic, quite consistent on fols. 203r–204r, which shines through the mapping of the list of paradigms below (Table 5.7).

GTU 4 is written like a Latin work, from left to right, and covers three pages, fols. 203v–203r–204r. It is laid out in four columns per page, whose reading order also follows from left to right, vertically. The tabular layout is misleading. Unlike in GTU 1, there is no connection between horizontally parallel items; these are not "double entry" tables but simply such narrow columns that the scribe had accommodated four of them per page.

The text opens with a list of Hebrew consonants. It is damaged, and the last four names are illegible. The remaining text of this folio (203v) was also affected: large portions of the columns have been erased and the writing is almost invisible. I was able to read the text with the help of ultraviolet light. As far as we can judge, the alphabet is followed by masculine forms of *Ḳal* (past, future, imperative and past participle), *Pi'el* (past, future, imperative), *Pu'al* (past, future), *Huf'al* (past, future), and finally *Hitpa'el* (past, future and imperative). The next page, fol. 203r, begins with the list of feminine forms of *Huf'al* (past) and *Hitpa'el* (past, future) as a direct continuation of the previous page. From that point, however, the paradigms are repeated, and placed in a coherent order, with separate conjugation for masculine and feminine forms for every *binyan*, listing first the two active *binyanim*, *Ḳal* and *Pi'el*, and then the *binyanim* which are described here as passive (*passiuum*). Thus, *Ḳal* masculine (present, past, future, imperative, past participle) is repeated and followed by the corresponding *Ḳal* feminine forms; masculine *Pi'el* forms in the same order as *Ḳal* are followed by their feminine equivalents, with what looks like the participle of *Pu'al* listed as the past participle of *Pi'el* (see above). *Ḳal* and *Pi'el* infinitive construct with prepositions close the list of the forms of the active *binyanim*. The section on passive *binyanim* opens with masculine forms of *Pu'al* (past, future), followed by the erroneous hybrid *binyan* (past), then by *Huf'al* (future), followed by the corresponding feminine forms. The list of the paradigms ends with the repetition of the forms of *Hitpa'el*, first masculine (present, past, future, imperative) and then the corresponding feminine forms. The grammatical concepts implied in GTU 4 reflect the morphological approach of the Spanish-Provençal school.

Table 5.7 The mapping of the verb paradigms in GTU 4

col. 1	**col. 2**	**col. 3**	**col. 4**
	Fol. 203 verso		
Hebrew Alphabet: names of the consonants in Latin script (4 illegible lines) Ḳal: past tense (masc. ?)	Ḳal: past tense masc. (end) Ḳal: future tense masc. Ḳal: imperative masc. sg. and pl. Ḳal: passive participle masc. sg. and pl. Piʿel: past tense masc. Piʿel: future tense masc. Piʿel: imperative masc.	(5 illegible lines) Puʿal: past tense masc. Puʿal: future tense masc. Hufʿal: past tense masc. Hufʿal: future tense masc. (2 illegible lines)	Hufʿal: future tense masc. (end) (3 illegible lines) Hitpaʿel: past tense masc. Hitpaʿel: future tense masc. Hitpaʿel: imperative masc. sg. and pl.
	Fol. 203 recto		
Hufʿal: past tense fem. Hitpaʿel: past tense fem. Hitpaʿel: future tense fem. (2 illegible lines)	Ḳal: present masc. pl. Ḳal: past tense masc. Ḳal: future tense masc. Ḳal: imperative masc. sg. and pl. Ḳal: past participle masc. sg. and pl. Ḳal: present fem. sg. and pl. Ḳal: past tense fem. Ḳal: future tense fem.	Ḳal: future tense fem. (end) Ḳal: imperative fem. sg. and pl. Ḳal: past participle fem. sg. and pl. Piʿel: present masc. sg. and pl. Piʿel: past tense masc. Piʿel: future tense masc. Piʿel: imperative masc. sg. and pl.	Piʿel/Puʿal: past participle masc. sg. and pl. Piʿel: present fem. sg. and pl. Piʿel: past tense fem. Piʿel: future tense fem. Piʿel: imperative fem. sg. and pl. Piʿel/Puʿal: past participle fem. sg. and pl. Ḳal: infinitive construct with prepositions

Fol. 204 recto

Piʿel: infinitive construct with prepositions Puʿal: past tense masc. Puʿal: future tense masc. *Hybrid 'huteradaffeti': past tense masc.* Hufʿal: future tense masc.	Hufʿal: future tense masc. (end) Puʿal: past tense, fem. Puʿal: future tense fem. *Hybrid 'huteradaffeti': past tense fem.* Hufʿal: future tense fem. Hitpaʿel: present masc. sg. and pl.	Hitpaʿel: present masc. sg. and pl. (end) Hitpaʿel: past tense masc. Hitpaʿel: future tense masc. Hitpaʿel: imperative masc. sg. and pl. Hitpaʿel: present fem. sg. and pl. Hitpaʿel: past tense fem. Hitpaʿel: future tense fem.	Hitpaʿel: future tense fem. (end)

Conclusions

The four units of the Longleat House Grammar have a clear pedagogical purpose. They are rudimentary, but they certainly represent the most complete introduction to the Hebrew grammar produced and used by Christian scholars in medieval Europe. The evident reliance of the Longleat House Grammar on Jewish grammatical tradition attests to the familiarity of their Christian authors with Jewish linguistic writings, and indeed to their unprecedented philological curiosity and openness to the unfamiliar linguistic tradition.

The grammatical concepts underlying this work, created for Christian readership, reflect to some extent the state of Jewish linguistic scholarship in medieval England. Whereas the influence of the Spanish-Provençal tradition, and in particular of Joseph Kimhi, is evident, notably in the field of verb morphology and in the classification of the vowels according to their length, this knowledge was transmitted to our Christian Hebraist authors in a form elaborated in England, in such works as the *Darkhei ha-Nikḳud ve-ha-Neginot* of Moses ben Yom Tov of London or the *Sefer ha-Shoham* of his disciple Moses ben Isaac ha-Nessi'ah. These writings of Jewish grammarians and Masoretes of medieval England combined the achievements of the Spanish-Provençal school and the ancient Oriental masoretic tradition.

The analysis of the Longleat House Grammar reveals, however, that none of its four textual units is a direct copy of any identifiable grammatical or masoretic tractate. Rather, it seems to be an independent work, so far known only from this unique manuscript, LH MS 21. This grammar provides for the learning needs of the students proposing a simplified version of the theoretical discussions on the parts of speech found in Jewish grammar books. It also assists the beginners by introducing and clearly presenting the verbal paradigms, laid out in a tabular form and marked by blue and red initials for easy reference and memorization. Given its roots in Jewish grammatical thought, this work invites its Christian readers to abandon the familiar terminology and categories of the Latin grammar and to embrace instead the Jewish modes of understanding and describing linguistic phenomena.

The precise identity of the author(s), scribes and readers of the Longleat House Grammar remains unknown, although our current analysis allows us to hypothesize that these were monks of the Ramsey Abbey. They undertook the study of Hebrew, possibly aided by contacts with Jewish neighbours or converts. The familiarity of these Benedictine monks with the Hebrew language and with Jewish texts has no known parallels in Christian scholarship before the Renaissance.

The author(s) of the Longleat House Grammar praised this booklet and set for it an ambitious aim: בְּזֶה תּוּכַל לְהָבִין כֹּל לְשׁוֹן עִבְרִי, "with that, you can grasp all the Hebrew language." This statement is undoubtedly overly optimistic, insofar as the Longleat House Grammar is not a comprehensive treatment of the *lingua sacra*. It is, however, a promise and a bold declaration that it is through the understanding of Jewish linguistic approaches that the Christian students can successfully master the Hebrew language and partake in its literary and exegetical heritage. It is surely telling that this exhorting sentence was written... in Hebrew.

Bibliography

Primary Sources

Abraham ibn Ezra. "'Iggeret ha-Shabbat." Ed. M. Friedlander. *Transactions of the Jewish Historical Society of England* 2 (1894–1895): 61–75.

—. *Sefer Moznayim.* Ed. Mordechai S. Goodman. Jerusalem: Mossad Harav Kook, 2016. Hebrew.

Bacon, Roger. "Cambridge Hebrew Grammar." In *The Greek Grammar of Roger Bacon and a Fragment of His Hebrew Grammar*, ed. Edmond Nolan and Samuel A. Hirsch, 199–208. Cambridge: Cambridge University Press, 1902.

—. *The Greek Grammar of Roger Bacon and a Fragment of His Hebrew Grammar.* Ed. Edmond Nolan and Samuel A. Hirsch. Cambridge: Cambridge University Press, 1902.

—. *Operis maioris partes I–VI.* Ed. John Henry Bridges. 3 vols. Oxford: Clarendon Press, 1897–1900. New online edition: Library of Latin Texts, Series B. Turnhout: Brepols, 2010.

—. *Opera quaedam hactenus inedita.* Ed. J.S. Brewer. Rerum Britannicarum medii aevi scriptores 15. London: Longman, Green, Longman, and Roberts, 1859.

Baḥya ibn Paḳuda. *Sefer Torat Ḥovot ha-Levavot* (The Duties of the Heart). Ed. Joseph Kafiḥ. Repr., New York: Feldheim, 1984. Hebrew.

Berekhiah ben Natronai ha-Naḳdan. *A Commentary on the Book of Job from a Hebrew Manuscript in the University Library, Cambridge.* Ed. William Aldis Wright. Trans. S.A. Hirsch. Text and Translation Society 6. London: Williams & Norgate, 1905.

Byrhtferth. *Byrhtferth's Manual (A.D. 1011).* Ed. Samuel J. Crawford. Early English Text Society, Original Series. Oxford: Oxford University Press, 1929. Repr., London: Oxford University Press, 1966.

Cecini, Ulisse, and Óscar Luis de la Cruz Palma, eds. *Extractiones de Talmud per ordinem sequentialem.* Corpus Christianorum, Continuatio Mediaevalis 291. Turnhout: Brepols, 2019.

Dionysius Thrax. *The Grammar of Dionysios Thrax.* Trans. Thomas Davidson. St Louis: R.P. Studley, 1874.

Dunash ibn Labrāṭ (Dunash ben Labrat). *Sefer Teshuvot Dunash ben Labrat: ʿIm Hakhraʿot Rabbenu Yaʿakov Tam.* Ed. Herschell Filipowski, Leopold Dukes and Raphael Kircheim. London and Edinburgh: Meʿorerei Yeshanim, 1855.

—. *Teshuvot.* Ed. Ángel Sáenz-Badillos. Granada: Universidad de Granada, 1980.

Friedman, John, Jean Connell Hoff and Robert Chazan. *The Trial of the Talmud: Paris, 1240.* Mediaeval Sources in Translation 53. Toronto: Pontifical Institute of Mediaeval Studies, 2012.

Hardy, Thomas D., ed. *Rotuli litterarum clausarum in Turri Londinensi asservati*. 2 vols. London: G. Eyre and A. Spottiswoode, 1833–1844.

Isidore of Seville. *The Etymologies*. Ed. and trans. Stephen A. Barney, Jennifer Beach, W.J. Lewis and Oliver Berghof. Cambridge: Cambridge University Press, 2014.

Jerome. "Liber interpretationis nominum Hebraicorum." In *Hebraicae Quaestiones in Libro Geneseos* […], ed. Paul de Lagarde, 57–161. S. Hieronymi Presbyteri Opera, pars 1: Opera Exegetica 1. Corpus Christianorum Series Latina 72. Turnhout: Brepols, 1959.

Kimhi, David. *Mikhlol*. Ed. and trans. William Chomsky. New York: Bloch, 1952.

—. *Sefer Mikhlol*. Ed. Isaac Rittenberg. Lyck: Pettsal, 1842. Repr., Jerusalem: Pettsal, 1966. Hebrew.

—. *Sefer ha-Shorashim: Radicum Liber sive Hebraeum Bibliorum Lexicon cum animadversionibus Eliae Levitae*. Ed. Fürchtegoff Lebrecht and Johann Heinrich Raphael Biesenthal. Berlin: G. Bethge, 1847.

Kimhi, Joseph. *Sefer ha-Galui*. Ed. H.J. Mathews. Sifriyah le-Toldot ha-Lashon ha-ʿIvrit 1. Berlin: Ittskovski, 1887. Repr., Jerusalem, 1967.

—. *Sefer Zikkaron/Sefer Sikkaron: Grammatik der hebraïschen Sprache*. Ed. Wilhelm Bacher. Berlin: Mekiẓe Nirdamim, 1888.

Kimhi, Moses. *Mahalakh Shevilei ha-Daʿat: Mosis Kimchi Ὀδοιπορία ad scientiam, cum expositione Doctoris Eliae* […]. With comments by Constantin l'Empereur. Leiden: Ex officina Bonaventurae et Abraham Elzevir, 1631.

Leland, John. *De uiris illustribus (On Famous Men)*. Ed. and trans. James P. Carley, with the assistance of Caroline Brett. Toronto: Pontifical Institute of Mediaeval Studies; Oxford: Bodleian Library, 2010.

Matthew Paris. *Monachi Sancti Albani Chronica Majora*. Ed. Henry Richards Luard. Rerum Britannicarum medii aevi scriptores 57. 7 vols. London: Longman, 1872–1883.

Meʾir ben Elijah of Norwich. *Haruzim: Hebräische Poesien des Meir ben Elia aus Norwich*. Ed. Abraham Berliner. London: David Nutt, 1887. Hebrew.

Menaḥem ben Saruḳ. *Maḥberet: Edición crítica e introducción*. Ed. Ángel Sáenz-Badillos. Granada: Universidad de Granada, 1986.

Moses ben Isaac ha-Nessiʾah. *A Grammar and Lexicon of the Hebrew Language entitled Sefer Hassoham*. Ed. George Wolseley Collins. London: Trübner, 1882.

—. *The Sefer ha-Shoham* (The Onyx Book). Ed. Benjamin Klar. With introduction by Cecil Roth. London: Jewish Historical Society of England, 1947. Hebrew.

Moses ha-Naḳdan. *Tractatio de punctis et accentibus quae a Moyse Punctatore scripta dicitur*. Ed. Samuel Löwinger. Budapest: Kohn Mor, 1929. Hebrew.

Patrologiae cursus completus, Series Latina. Ed. J.-P. Migne. 221 vols. Paris, 1844–1855.

Richard de Bury. *Ricardi de Bury Philobiblon ex optimis codicibus recensuit versione anglica necnon et prolegomenis adnotationibusque auxit Andreas Fleming West*. Ed. Andrew Fleming West. 3 vols. New York: Grolier Club, 1889.

Salomon ben Abraham ibn Parḥon. *Mahberet he-ʿArukh: Salomonis ben Abrahami Parchon Aragonensis Lexicon Hebraicum*. Ed. Salomo Gottlieb Stern. Pressburg: Anton von Schmid, 1844.

Samuel ben Me'ir. *Dayyaqut me-Rabbenu Semuel [Ben Meir (Rashbam)]: Critical Edition with an Introduction and a Detailed Table of Contents.* Ed. Ronela Merdler. Jerusalem: Hebrew University, 1999. Hebrew.

Sefer Yeẓirah (The Book of Creation). "A Preliminary Critical Edition of *Sefer Yezira.*" Ed. Ithamar Gruenwald. *Israel Oriental Studies* 1 (1971): 135–177.

Trivet, Nicholas. *Annales sex regum Angliae, qui a comitibus andegavensibus originem traxerunt.* Ed. Thomas Hog. Publication of the English Historical Society. London: Sumptibus Societatis, 1845.

Yehudah ibn Bal'am. *Sefer Ta'amei ha-Mikra' [Liber de accentibus scripturae].* Ed. Jean Mercier. Paris: Robert Estienne, 1565.

Zislin, M.N., ed. *Me'or 'Ayin (The Light of the Eye): A Karaite Grammar of the Hebrew Language from a Manuscript of 1208.* Pamâtniki Pis'mennosti Vostoka 96. Moscow: Nauka, 1990. Russian.

Secondary Sources

Allony, Nehemiah. "Fragments of the Book on Masculine and Feminine, *Kitāb al-tadhkīr wal-ta'nīth* by R. Moshe ha-Kohen Ibn Gikitilla." *Sinai* 24 (1949): 34–67. Hebrew.

Anglo-Norman Dictionary Online. 2nd edition. http://www.anglo-norman.net.

Anheim, Étienne, Benoît Grévin and Martin Morard. "Exégèse judéo-chrétienne, magie et linguistique: Un recueil de *Notes* inédites attribuées à Roger Bacon." *AHDLMA* 68 (2001): 95–154.

Auroux, Sylvain. "Grammatisation." *HEL* 11.1 (1995): 5–6.

Bacher, Wilhelm. "Une grammaire hébraïque du Yémen: Ses rapports avec le Manuel du lecteur." *REJ* 23 (1891): 238–248.

—. "Moïse ha-Nakdan, glossateur de la grammaire de Joseph Kimhi." *REJ* 12 (1886): 73–79.

—. "Salomon Ibn Parhon's hebräisches Wörterbuch: Ein Beitrag zur Geschichte der hebräischen Sprachwissenschaft und der Bibelexegese" (Part I). *Zeitschrift für die Alttestamentliche Wissenschaft* 10 (1890): 120–156.

—. "Aus Salomon Ibn Parchon's Machberet." *Zeitschrift für hebräische Bibliographie* (1896): 57–61.

Bacher, Wilhelm, David Kaufmann, Gruenwald, and Nathan Porgès. "Les signes mnémotechniques des lettres radicales et serviles." *REJ* 16 (1888): 286–291.

Banitt, Menahem. "L'étude des glossaires bibliques des juifs de France au moyen âge: Méthode et application." In *Proceedings of the Israel Academy of Sciences and Humanities,* 2.10: 189–190. Jerusalem: Israel Academy of Sciences and Humanities, 1967.

—. "Fragments d'un glossaire judéo-français du moyen âge." *REJ* 120 (1961): 259–296.

—. *Le glossaire de Bâle.* Corpus Glossariorum Biblicorum Hebraico-Gallicorum Medii Aevi I. 2 vols. Jerusalem: Israel Academy of Sciences and Humanities, 1972.

—. *Le Glossaire de Leipzig*. 4 vols. Jerusalem: Israel Academy of Sciences and Humanities, 1995–2005.

Barbour, Ruth. "A Manuscript of Ps.-Dionysius Areopagita Copied for Robert Grosseteste." *The Bodleian Library Record* 6.2 (1958): 401–416.

Beit-Arié, Malachi. *Catalogue of the Hebrew Manuscripts in the Bodleian Library: Supplement of Addenda and Corrigenda to Vol. 1 (A. Neubauer's Catalogue)*. Oxford: Clarendon Press, 1994.

—. *Hebrew Manuscripts of East and West: Towards a Comparative Codicology*. Panizzi Lectures 8. London: British Library, 1992.

—. "MS Oxford, Bodleian Library, Bodl. Or. 135." *Tarbiz* 54 (1985): 631–634. Hebrew.

—. "The Valmadonna Pentateuch and the Problem of Pre-expulsion Anglo-Hebrew Manuscripts – MS London, Valmadonna Trust Library 1: England (?), 1189." In *The Makings of the Medieval Hebrew Book: Studies in Palaeography and Codicology*, ed. Malachi Beit-Arié, 129–151. Jerusalem: Magnes Press, 1993. First published as *The Only Dated Medieval Hebrew Manuscript in England (1189 CE) and the Problem of Pre-expulsion Anglo-Hebrew Manuscripts*. London: Valmadonna Trust Library, 1985.

Ben-Yehudah, Eliezer. *Thesaurus totius Hebraitatis et veteris et recentioris (Milon ha-Lashon ha-ʿIvrit)*. 17 vols. Berlin and Jerusalem: Langenscheidt, 1908–1959.

Berger, Samuel. *Quam notitiam linguae Hebraicae habuerint Christiani medii aevi temporibus in Gallia*. Paris: Hachette, 1893.

Berndt, Rainer. *André de Saint-Victor (1175): Exégète et théologien*. Bibliotheca victorina 2. Turnhout: Brepols, 1991.

Bischoff, Bernhard. "The Study of Foreign Languages in the Middle Ages." *Speculum* 36 (1961): 209–224.

Blondheim, David S. "Le glossaire d'Oxford." *REJ* 57 (1909): 1–18.

Boehmer, Eduard. "De vocabulis Francogallicis Judaice transcriptis." *Romanische Studien* 1.2 (1872): 197–220.

Bonnard, Jean. "Un alphabet hébreu-anglais au XIVe siècle, I." *REJ* 4.8 (1882): 255–259.

Boulhol, Pascal. *La connaissance de la langue grecque dans la France médiévale, VIe–XVe s*. Textes et documents de la Méditerranée antique et médiévale. Aix-en-Provence: Publications de l'Université de Provence, 2008.

Bourguin, Georges. "L'incendie de la Bibliothèque nationale et universitaire de Turin." *Bibliothèque de l'École des Chartes* 65 (1904): 132–140.

Burnett, Charles, and James P. Carley, eds. *Hebraism in Sixteenth-Century England: Robert and Thomas Wakefield*. Toronto: Pontifical Institute of Mediaeval Studies, forthcoming.

Busi, Giulio. *Horayat ha-Qoreʾ: Una grammatica ebraica del secolo XI*. Judenthum und Umwelt 11. Frankfurt am Main and New York: Peter Lang, 1984.

—. "Sulla versione breve (araba ed ebraica) della Hidāyat al-qāri." *Henoch* 5 (1983): 371–395.

Callus, D.A. "William de la Mare." In *New Catholic Encyclopaedia*, 14: 928B–929A. New York: McGraw Hill, 1967.

Carley, James P. "Religious Controversy and Marginalia: Pierfrancesco di Piero Bardi, Thomas Wakefield, and Their Books." *TCBS* 12 (2002): 206–245.

—. "Thomas Wakefield, Robert Wakefield and the Cotton Genesis." *TCBS* 12 (2002): 246–265.

Carruthers, Mary J. *The Book of Memory: A Study of Memory in Medieval Culture.* Cambridge Studies in Medieval Literature 10. Cambridge: Cambridge University Press, 2008. First ed., 1992.

Cecini, Ulisse, and Óscar Luis de la Cruz Palma. "Beyond the Thirty-Five Articles: Nicholas Donin's Latin Anthology of the Talmud (With a Critical Edition)." In *The Talmud in Dispute During the High Middle Ages,* ed. Alexander Fidora and Görge K. Hasselhoff, 59–100. Documents (Universitat Autònoma de Barcelona, Servei de Publicaciones) 116. Bellaterra: Universitat Autònoma de Barcelona, Servei de Publicaciones, 2019.

Cecini, Ulisse, and Eulàlia Vernet i Pons, eds. *Studies on the Latin Talmud.* 1st ed. Documents (Universitat Autònoma de Barcelona, Servei de Publicaciones) 113. Bellaterra: Universitat Autònoma de Barcelona, Servei de Publicaciones, 2017.

Charlap, Luba R. *Rabbi Abraham Ibn-Ezra's Linguistic System: Tradition and Innovation.* Be'er-Sheva: Ben Gurion University of the Negev Press, 1999. Hebrew.

—. "Three Views Regarding the Gender of Biblical Nouns in the Works of Medieval Hebrew Grammarians." In *Jewish Studies at the Turn of the Twentieth Century: Proceedings of the 6th EAJS Congress, Toledo, July 1998,* vol. 1, ed. Judit Targarona Borrás and Angel Sáenz-Badillos, 17–25. Leiden: Brill, 1999.

Cohen, Jeremy. *The Friars and the Jews: The Evolution of Medieval Anti-Judaism.* Ithaca: Cornell University Press, 1984.

—. *Living Letters of the Law: Ideas of the Jew in Medieval Christianity.* The S. Mark Taper Foundation Imprint in Jewish Studies. Berkeley: University of California Press, 1999.

Costambeys, Marios. "Gregory [Gregory of Huntingdon]." In *Oxford Dictionary of National Biography.* Oxford University Press, 2004; online edition, 2011. https://doi.org/10.1093/ref:odnb/11454.

Creytens, Raymond. "Autour de la littérature des correctoires." *Archivum Fratrum Praedicatorum* 12 (1942): 313–330.

Dahan, Gilbert. "Deux psautiers hébraïques glosés en latin." *REJ* 158 (1999): 61–87.

—. "L'enseignement de l'hébreu en occident médiéval (XIIe–XIVe siècles)." *Histoire de l'éducation* 57 (1993): 3–22.

—. *Les intellectuels chrétiens et juifs au moyen âge.* Patrimoines, Judaïsme. Paris: Éditions du Cerf, 1990.

—. "Juifs et chrétiens en Occident médiéval: La rencontre autour de la Bible (XIIe–XIVe siècles)." *Revue de Synthèse* 110 (1989): 3–31.

—. "Lexiques hébreu-latin?: Les recueils d'interprétations des noms hébreux." In *Les manuscrits des lexiques et glossaires de l'Antiquité tardive à la fin du moyen âge,* ed. Jacqueline Hamesse, 481–526. Textes et études du moyen âge 4. Louvain-la-Neuve: Fédération internationale des instituts d'études médiévales, 1996.

—. "Les traductions latines de Thibaud de Sézanne." In *Le brûlement du Talmud, 1242–1244*, ed. Gilbert Dahan and Elie Nicolas, 95–120. Nouvelle Gallia Judaica. Paris: Éditions du Cerf, 1999.

—. "Les transcriptions en caractères latins." In *Dictionnaire hébreu-latin-français*, ed. Olszowy-Schlanger and Grondeux, xxvii–xxx.

Dahan, Gilbert, and Elie Nicolas, eds. *Le brûlement du Talmud à Paris, 1242–1244*. Nouvelle Gallia Judaica. Paris: Éditions du Cerf, 1999.

Darmesteter, Arsène. (Review of J. Bonnard, "Un alphabet hébreu-anglais au XIVe siècle, I.") "Même sujet, II." *REJ* 4.8 (1882): 259–268. Reprinted in *Reliques scientifiques recueillies par son frère*, vol. 1, 204–216. 2 vols. Paris: Cerf, 1890.

—. "Rapport sur une mission en Italie: Gloses et glossaires hébreux-français, notes sur des manuscrits de Parme et de Turin." *Archives des missions scientifiques et littéraires*, 3rd series, 4 (1877): 383–432.

Davis, Myer David. *Hebrew Deeds of English Jews before 1290*. Publications of the Anglo-Jewish Historical Exhibition 2. London: Office of the *Jewish Chronicle*, 1888.

De Lange, Nicholas. "Hebrew Scholarship in Byzantium." In *Hebrew Scholarship and the Medieval World*, ed. Nicholas De Lange, 23–37. Cambridge: Cambridge University Press, 2001.

De Visscher, Eva. "An Ave Maria in Hebrew: The Transmission of Hebrew Learning from Jewish to Christian Scholars in Medieval England." In *Christians and Jews in Angevin England: The York Massacre of 1190, Narratives and Contexts*, ed. Sarah Rees Jones and Sethina Watson, 174–183. Cambridge: Cambridge University Press and Suffolk: Boydell and Brewer, 2013.

—. "'Closer to the Hebrew': Herbert of Bosham's Interpretation of Literal Exegesis." In *The Multiple Meaning of Scripture: The Role of Exegesis in Early-Christian and Medieval Culture*, ed. Ienje Van't Spijker, 249–272. Commentaria Brill 2. Leiden: Brill, 2009.

—. "Cross-religious Learning and Teaching: Hebraism in the Works of Herbert of Bosham and Contemporaries." In *Crossing Borders: Hebrew Manuscripts as a Meeting-place of Cultures*, ed. Piet van Boxel and Sabine Arndt, 123–132. Oxford: Bodleian Library, 2009.

—. "Putting Theory into Practice?: Hugh of St Victor's Influence on Herbert of Bosham's Psalterium cum commento." In *Bibel und Exegese in der Abtei Saint-Victor zu Paris: Form und Funktion eines Grundtextes im europäischen Rahmen*, ed. Rainer Berndt, 491–502. Corpus Victorinum 3. Münster: Aschendorff, 2009.

—. *Reading the Rabbis: Christian Hebraism in the Works of Herbert of Bosham*. Leiden: Brill, 2014.

Denifle, Heinrich. "Die Handschriften der Bibel-Correctorien des 13. Jahrhunderts." *Archiv für die Literatur- und Kirschengeschichte des Mittelalters* 4 (1888): 263–311 and 471–601.

Derenbourg, Joseph. "Manuel du lecteur d'un auteur inconnu publié d'après un manuscrit venu du Yémen et accompagné de notes." *JA* (6e série) 16 (1870): 309–550.

—. "Les signes mnémotechniques des lettres radicales et serviles." *REJ* 16 (1888): 57–60.

Dictionnaire Etymologique de l'Ancien Français. http://www.deaf-page.de/fr/.

Dolbeau, François. "Les textes latins du volume." In *Dictionnaire hébreu-latin-français*, ed. Olszowy-Schlanger and Grondeux, xiv–xv.

Dotan, Aron. *The Awakening of Word Lore: From the Massora to the Beginnings of Hebrew Lexicography*. Jerusalem: The Academy of the Hebrew Language, 2005. Hebrew.

—. *The Dawn of Hebrew Linguistics: The Book of Elegance of the Language of the Hebrews by Saadia Gaon*. 2 vols. Jerusalem: World Union of Jewish Studies, 1997. Hebrew.

—. "De la Massora à la grammaire: Les débuts de la pensée grammaticale dans l'hébreu." *JA* 278 (1990): 13–30.

—. "Moses ben Yom Tov." In *Encyclopaedia Judaica*, 12: cols. 427–428. Jerusalem: Keter, 1971.

—. "The Origins of Hebrew Linguistics and the Exegetic Tradition." In *History of the Language Sciences: An International Handbook on the Evolution of the Study of Language from the Beginnings to the Present*, ed. Sylvain Auroux, E.F.K. Koerner, Hans-Josef Niederehe and Kees Versteegh, 1: 215–244. Handbücher zur Sprach- und Kommunikationswissenschaft 18. 3 vols. Berlin: De Gruyter, 2000–2006.

—. "Saadia Gaon: A Master Linguist." In *Jewish Studies at the Turn of the Twentieth Century: Proceedings of the 6th European Association of Jewish Studies Congress, I: Biblical, Rabbinical and Medieval Studies, Toledo, July 1998*, ed. Judit Targarona Borrás and Angel Sáenz-Badillos, 26–30. Leiden: Brill, 1999.

Drory, Rina. *The Emergence of Jewish Arabic Literary Contacts at the Beginning of the Tenth Century*. Tel Aviv: Ha-Kibbutz ha-Me'uḥad, 1988. Hebrew.

Duval, Frédéric. *Le français médiéval*. Atelier du médiéviste 11. Turnhout: Brepols, 2009.

Einbinder, Susan. "Meir b. Elijah of Norwich: Persecution and Poetry Among Medieval English Jews." *Journal of Medieval History* 26 (2000): 145–162.

Eldar, Ilan. "The Andalusian School of Grammar: The First Period." *Pe'amim* 38 (1989): 21–33. Hebrew.

—. *The Art of the Correct Reading of the Bible*. Jerusalem: Academy of the Hebrew Language, 1994. Hebrew.

—. "The Chapter 'Noaḥ ha-Tevot' from 'Ein ha-Kore': Rules of Milra' and Mil'el by Yekutiel ha-Kohen ben Judah the Vocalizer." *Leshonenu* 40 (1976): 190–210. Hebrew.

—. "È davvero Yehudah ibn Bal'am l'autore della Hidāyat al-Qāri?" *Henoch* 7 (1985): 301–324.

—. "The Grammatical Literature of Medieval Ashkenazi Jewry." *Massorot* 5–6 (1991): 1–34. Hebrew.

—. "The Grammatical Literature of Medieval Ashkenazi Jewry." In *Hebrew in Ashkenaz: A Language in Exile*, ed. Lewis Glinert, 26–45. New York: Oxford University Press, 1993.

—. *The Hebrew Language Tradition in Medieval Ashkenaz*. Edah ve-Lashon 04–05. 2 vols. Jerusalem: Publications of the Hebrew University Language Tradition Project, 1978. Hebrew.

—. "Hebrew Philology Between the East and Spain: The Concept of Derivation as a Case Study." *Journal of Semitic Studies* 43 (1998): 49–61.

—. "Ḥayyūj's Grammatical Analysis." *Leshonenu* 54 (1990): 169–181. Hebrew.

—. "Mukhtaṣar *Hidāyat al-Qāri:* The Grammatical Section According to Genizah Passages with Introduction and Hebrew Translation." *Leshonenu* 50 (1986): 214–231 (part I) and *Leshonenu* 51 (1987): 3–41 (part II). Hebrew.

—. "'Mukhtaṣar (an Abridgment) of Hidāyat al-Qāri': A Grammatical Treatise Discovered in the Genizah." In *Genizah Research after Ninety Years: The Case of Judaeo-Arabic,* ed. Joshua Blau and Stefan C. Reif, 67–73. University of Cambridge Oriental Publications 47. Cambridge: Cambridge University Press, 1992.

—. "Recueils grammaticaux yéménites des 'Tigân' et sources du recueil hébraïque." *REJ* 151 (1992): 149–159.

—. "The Vocalisation of the Passover Haggadah in Maḥzor Vitry." *Leshonenu* 39 (1975): 192–216. Hebrew.

Englander, Henry. "Grammatical Elements and Terminology in Rashi's Biblical Commentaries." Part I: *HUCA* 11 (1936): 367–389; Part II: *HUCA* 12/13 (1937–1938): 505–21; Part III: *HUCA* 14 (1939): 387–429.

—. "Rabbenu Jacob ben Meir Tam as Grammarian." *HUCA* 15 (1940): 485–495.

—. "Rashi's View on the Weak ʿayin-ʿayin and peh-nun Verbs: With Special Reference to the Views of Menaḥem b. Saruk and Dunash b. Labrat." *HUCA* 7 (1930): 399–437.

Esneval, Amaury d'. "Le perfectionnement d'un instrument de travail au début du XIIIe siècle: Les trois glossaires bibliques d'Etienne Langton." In *Culture et travail intellectuel dans l'Occident médiéval,* ed. Geneviève Hasenohr and Jean Longère, 163–175. Paris: Centre national de la recherche scientifique, 1981.

Fidora, Alexander. "The Latin Talmud and Its Translators: Nicholas Donin vs. Thibaud de Sézanne?" *Henoch* 37.1 (2015): 17–28.

—. "Textual Rearrangement and Thwarted Intentions: The Two Versions of the Latin Talmud." *Journal of Transcultural Medieval Studies* 2.1 (2015): 63–78.

Fidora, Alexander, and Görge K. Hasselhoff, eds. *The Talmud in Dispute During the High Middle Ages.* Documents (Universitat Autònoma de Barcelona, Servei de Publicacions) 116. Bellaterra: Universitat Autònoma de Barcelona, 2019.

Fischer, Johann. "Die hebräischen Bibelzitate des Scholastikers Odo." *Biblica* 15 (1934): 50–93.

Flahiff, George B. "Ralph Niger: An Introduction to His Life and Works." *Mediaeval Studies* 2 (1940): 104–126.

Fontaine, Resianne. "Between Scorching Heat and Freezing Cold: Medieval Jewish Authors on the Inhabited and Uninhabited Parts of the Earth." *Arabic Sciences and Philosophy* 10 (2000): 101–137.

Gamaliel, Ḥanokh. "More on Congruency in the Language of the Bible." *Daʿat Lashon* 2 (2016): 35–45. Hebrew.

Garel, Michel. *D'une main forte: Manuscrits hébreux des collections françaises.* Paris: Seuil, Bibliothèque Nationale, 1992.

Gibson, Margaret T. *The Bible in the Latin West.* Notre Dame: University of Notre Dame, 1993.

Glorieux, Palémon. *Répertoire des maîtres en théologie de Paris au XIIIe siècle,* vol. 2. Études de philosophie médiévale 18. Paris: Vrin, 1934.

Golb, Norman. *The History and Culture of the Jews of Rouen in the Middle Ages*. Tel Aviv: Devir, 1976. Hebrew.

—. *The Jews in Medieval Normandy: A Social and Intellectual History*. Cambridge: Cambridge University Press, 1998.

—. *Les juifs de Rouen au moyen âge: Portrait d'une culture oubliée*. Publications de l'Université de Rouen 66. Mont Saint-Aignan: Publications de l'Université de Rouen, 1985.

Goldenberg, Esther. "The First Hebrew Table of Paradigms." *Leshonenu* 43 (1979): 83–99. Hebrew.

—. "Medieval Linguistics and Good Hebrew." *Leshonenu* 54 (1990): 183–216. Hebrew.

—. "שמע [Shemʿa] as Representing the Paradigm in Saadiah's Inflexional Table." *Leshonenu* 55 (1991): 323–326. Hebrew.

Goodwin, Deborah L. *Take Hold of the Robe of a Jew: Herbert of Bosham's Christian Hebraism*. Leiden: Brill, 2006.

Grabois, Aryeh. "The Hebraica Veritas and Jewish-Christian Intellectual Relations in the Twelfth Century." *Speculum* 50 (1975): 613–634.

Grévin, Benoît. "L'hébreu des Franciscains: Nouveaux éléments sur la connaissance de l'hébreu en milieu chrétien au XIIIe siècle." *Médiévales* 20.41 (2001): 65–82.

—. "Systèmes d'écriture, sémiotique et langage chez Roger Bacon." *HEL* 24.2 (2002): 75–111.

Harris, Kate. "An Augustan Episode in the History of the Collection of Medieval Manuscripts at Longleat House." In *The English Medieval Book: Studies in Memory of Jeremy Griffiths*, ed. Anthony Stockwell Garfield Edwards, Vincent Gillespie and Ralph Hanna, 233–247. British Library Studies in the History of the Book. London: The British Library, 2000.

van der Heide, Albert. *Hebrew Manuscripts of Leiden University Library*. Codices Manuscripti, Bibliotheca Universitatis Leidensis 18. Leiden: Universitaire Pers, 1977.

Hillaby, Joe and Caroline Hillaby. *The Palgrave Dictionary of Medieval Anglo-Jewish History*. Basingstoke: Palgrave Macmillan, 2013.

Hirschfeld, Hartwig. *Literary History of Hebrew Grammarians and Lexicographers Accompanied by Unpublished Texts*. Jews' College Publications 9. London: Oxford University Press, H. Milford, 1926.

James, Montague Rhodes. *The Ancient Libraries of Canterbury and Dover: The Catalogues of the Libraries of Christ Church Priory and St Augustine's Abbey at Canterbury and St Martin's Priory at Dover*. Cambridge: Cambridge University Press, 1903. Repr., Cambridge: Cambridge University Press, 2011.

—. *A Descriptive Catalogue of the Manuscripts in the Library of Corpus Christi College, Cambridge*. 2 vols. Cambridge: Cambridge University Press, 1912.

—. *The Western Manuscripts in the Library of Trinity College, Cambridge: A Descriptive Catalogue*. 4 vols. Cambridge: Cambridge University Press, 1900.

James, Montague Rhodes, and Claude Jenkins. *A Descriptive Catalogue of the Manuscripts in the Library of Lambeth Palace*. 5 parts in 1 vol. Cambridge: Cambridge University Press, 1930–1932.

Kaufmann, David. "Les juifs et la Bible de l'abbé Etienne de Cîteaux." *REJ* 18 (1889): 131–133.

—. "Three Centuries of Genealogy of the Most Eminent Anglo-Jewish Family Before 1290." *JQR* 3 (1891): 550–566.

Kearney, Jonathan. *Rashi Linguist Despite Himself: A Study of the Linguistic Dimension of Rabbi Solomon Yishaqi's Commentary on Deuteronomy*. Library of Hebrew Bible/ Old Testament Studies 532. New York: T&T Clark, 2010.

Keefer, Sarah Larratt and David R. Burrows. "Hebrew and the Hebraicum in Late Anglo-Saxon England." *Anglo-Saxon England* 19 (1990): 67–80.

Kessler-Mesguich, Sophie. "L'étude de l'hébreu et des autres langues orientales à l'époque de l'humanisme." In *History of the Language Sciences: An International Handbook on the Evolution of the Study of Language from the Beginnings to the Present*, ed. Sylvain Auroux, E.F.K. Koerner, Hans-Josef Niederehe and Kees Versteegh, 1: 673–680. Handbücher zur Sprach- und Kommunikationswissenschaft 18. 3 vols. Berlin: De Gruyter, 2000–2006.

—. *Les études hébraïques en France de François Tissard à Richard Simon (1508–1680)*. Introduction by Max Engammare. Travaux d'humanisme et Renaissance 517. Geneva: Droz, 2013.

Khan, Geoffrey. *A Short Introduction to the Tiberian Masoretic Bible and Its Reading Tradition*. Piscataway, NJ: Gorgias Press, 2013.

—. *The Tiberian Pronunciation Tradition of Biblical Hebrew: Including a Critical Edition and English Translation of the Sections on Consonants and Vowels in the Masoretic Treatise Hidāyat al-Qāriʾ 'Guide for the Reader'*. Semitic Languages and Cultures 1. 2 vols. Cambridge: Open Book Publishers, 2020.

Kiwitt, Marc. *Les gloses françaises du glossaire biblique B.N. hébr. 301*. Romanische Texte des Mittelalters 2. Heidelberg: Universitätsverlag Winter, 2010.

—. "Les glossaires hébreu-français du XIIIe siècle et la culture juive en France du nord." In *Cultures et Lexikographies (sic!): Actes des "Troisièmes Journées Allemandes des Dictionnaires" en l'honneur d'Alain Rey*, ed. Michaela Heinz, 113–125. Metalexikographie 2. Berlin: Frank and Timme, 2010.

Klein, S. "The Letter of Rabbi Menaḥem of Hebron." *Bulletin of the Jewish Palestine Exploration Society* 6 (1939): 19–30. Hebrew.

Kleinhans, Arduin. "Nicholas Trivet OP Psalmorum interpres." *Angelicum* 20 (1943): 219–236.

Kraml, Hans. "Guillaume de la Mare, theologian." In *Lexikon des Mittelalters*, 9: 174–175. Munich: J.B. Metzler, 1998.

Kroemer, Georg Heinrich. *Johanns von Sancto Paulo: Liber de simplicium medicinarum virtutibus und ein anderer Salernitaner Traktat; quae medicinae pro quibus morbis donandae sunt nach dem Breslauer Codex herausgegeben*. Borna-Leipzig: Druck von Robert Noske, 1920.

Kulik, Alexander. "Jews from Rus' in Medieval England." *JQR* 102 (2012): 371–403.

Kushelevsky, Rella. *Tales in Context: Sefer ha-Ma'asim in Medieval Northern France.* Raphael Patai Series in Jewish Folklore and Anthropology. Detroit: Wayne State University Press, 2017.

Lambert, Bernard. *Bibliotheca Hieronymiana Manuscripta: La tradition manuscrite des oeuvres de Saint Jérôme.* 7 vols. Instrumenta Patristica 4. Steenbrugis: Abbatia S. Petri, 1969–1972.

Lambert, Mayer, and Louis Brandin. *Glossaire hébreu-français du XIIIe siècle: Recueil de mots hébreux bibliques avec traduction française.* Paris: E. Leroux, 1905.

Landgraf, Artur Michael. *Écrits théologiques de l'école d'Abélard: Textes inédits. Spicilegium Sacrum Lovaniense, Études et Documents* 14. Leuven: Peeters, 1934.

Langmuir, Gavin I. "The Knight's Tale of Young Hugh of Lincoln." *Speculum* 47 (1972): 459–482.

Lasker, Daniel J., Johannes Niehoff-Panagiotidis and David Eric Sklare. *Theological Encounters at a Crossroads: An Edition and Translation of Judah Hadassi's Eshkol ha-Kofer, First Commandment.* Karaite Texts and Studies 11. Leiden: Brill, 2019.

Levy, Raphael. *Trésor de la langue des juifs français au moyen âge.* Austin: University of Texas Press, 1964.

Lieftinck, Gerard I. "The Psalterium Hebraycum from St Augustine's Canterbury Rediscovered in the Scaliger Bequest at Leyden." *TCBS* 2 (1955): 97–104.

Light, Laura. "French Bibles c. 1200–30: A New Look at the Origin of the Paris Bible." In *The Early Medieval Bible: Its Production, Decoration and Use,* ed. Richard Gameson, 155–176. Cambridge Studies in Palaeography and Codicology. Cambridge: Cambridge University Press, 1994.

—. "The New Thirteenth-Century Bible and the Challenge of Heresy." *Viator* 18 (1987): 275–288.

—. "Versions et révisions du texte biblique." In *Le Moyen Âge et la Bible,* ed. Pierre Riché and Guy Lobrichon, 55–93. Bible de Tous les Temps 4. Paris: Beauchesne, 1984.

Linde, J. Cornelia. *How to Correct the Sacra Scriptura?: Textual Criticism of the Latin Bible between the Twelfth and Fifteenth Century.* Medium Aevum Monographs 29. Oxford: Society for the Study of Medieval Languages and Literature, 2012.

—. "Notandum duas hic litteras, phe et ain, ordine praeposteratas esse: Rupert of Deutz, Guibert of Nogent and the Glossa Ordinaria on the Incorrect Order of the Hebrew Alphabet." *Archa Verbi* 7 (2010): 68–78.

Lipman, Vivian David. *The Jews of Medieval Norwich.* London: Jewish Historical Society of England, 1967.

Loeb, Isidore. "La controverse de 1240 sur le Talmud." *REJ* 1 (1880): 247–261; *REJ* 2 (1881): 248–270; *REJ* 3 (1881): 39–57.

Loewe, Raphael. "Alexander Neckam's Knowledge of Hebrew." In *Hebrew Study from Ezra to Ben-Yehuda,* ed. William Horbury, 207–223. Edinburgh: T&T Clark, 1999.

—. "Hebrew Books and 'Judaica' in Mediaeval Oxford and Cambridge." In *Remember the Days, Essays on Anglo-Jewish History Presented to Cecil Roth,* ed. John M. Shaftesley, 23–48. London: Jewish Historical Society of England, 1966.

—. "Herbert of Bosham's Commentary on Jerome's Hebrew Psalter." *Biblica* 34 (1953): 44–77, (II) 159–192, (III) 275–298.
—. "Jewish Scholarship in England." In *Three Centuries of Anglo-Jewish History*, ed. Vivian D. Lipman, 125–148. Cambridge: Jewish Historical Society of England, 1961.
—. "Latin Superscriptio MSS on Portions of the Hebrew Bible Other than the Psalter." *Journal of Jewish Studies* 9 (1958): 63–71.
—. "The Medieval Christian Hebraists of England: Herbert of Bosham and Earlier Scholars." *Transactions of the Jewish Historical Society of England* 17 (1953): 225–249.
—. "The Medieval Christian Hebraists of England: The Superscriptio Lincolniensis." *HUCA* 28 (1957): 205–252.
—. "The Medieval History of the Latin Vulgate." In *The Cambridge History of the Bible*, vol. 2: *The West from the Fathers to the Reformation*, ed. G.W.H. Lampe, 102–154. Cambridge: Cambridge University Press, 1969.
Longpré, Ephrem. "la Mare, Guillaume de." In *Dictionnaire de théologie catholique*, 8: 2467–2470. Paris: Letouzey et Ané, 1924.
Luncz, A.M. *Hameamer: Letters of Travellers, Inscriptions on Graves, Testimonials, Rules, Memorials and Other Documents Concerning the Middle Ages, vol.* 3. Jerusalem: Luncz, 1919. Hebrew.
Luscombe, D.E. "The Authorship of the *Ysagoge in theologiam*." *AHDLMA* 35 (1968): 7–16.
Maman, Aharon. *Comparative Semitic Philology in the Middle Ages from Saʿadiah Gaon to Ibn Barūn*. Trans. David Lyons. Studies in Semitic Languages and Linguistics 40. Leiden and Boston: Brill, 2004.
Manuzio, Aldo. *De literis Graecis ac diphthongis & quemadmodum ad nos ueniant [...]*. Hagenau: Thomas Anshelm, 1518.
Marenbon, John. "Mare, William de la" (William de Mara). In *Oxford Dictionary of National Biography*. Oxford University Press, 2004; online edition, 2011. https://doi.org/10.1093/ref:odnb/18025.
Marsden, Richard. "L'anglais du dictionnaire." In *Dictionnaire hébreu-latin-français*, ed. Olszowy-Schlanger and Grondeux, xli–xlvii.
Merchavia, Chenmelech. *The Church versus Talmudic and Midrashic Literature (500–1248)*. Jerusalem: Mosad Bialik, 1970. Hebrew.
—. "Talmudic Terms and Idioms in the Latin Manuscript Paris B.N. 16558." *Journal of Semitic Studies* 11 (1966): 175–201.
Moore, Rebecca. *Jews and Christians in the Life and Thought of Hugh of St Victor*. South Florida Studies in the History of Judaism 138. Atlanta: Scholars Press, 1998.
Morag, Shelomo. *Hebrew of the Yemenite Jews*. Jerusalem: Akademiah le-Lashon ha-ʿIvrit, 1963. Hebrew.
Murano, Giovanna. "Chi ha scritto le Interpretationes Hebraicorum Nominum?" In *Étienne Langton: Prédicateur, bibliste, théologien*, ed. Louis-Jacques Bataillon, Nicole Bériou, Gilbert Dahan and Riccardo Quinto, 353–371. Turnhout: Brepols, 2010.
Mutius, Hans-Georg von. *Die hebräischen Bibelzitate beim englischen Scholastiker Odo*. Judentum und Umwelt 78. Frankfurt am Main: Peter Lang, 2006.

Neubauer, Adolf. "Abraham ha-Babli: Appendice à la notice sur la lexicographie hébraïque." *JA* (6e série) 2 (1863): 195–216.

—. *Catalogue of the Hebrew Manuscripts in the Bodleian Library and in the College Libraries in Oxford*. Catalogi codicum manuscriptorum Bibliothecae Bodleianae 12. 2 vols. Oxford: Clarendon Press, 1886–1906.

—. "Menahem Vardimas." *REJ* 17 (1888): 151–154.

—. "Analecta I: English Massorites." *JQR* 2 (1890): 322–333.

—. *Petite grammaire hébraïque provenant du Yémen*. Leipzig: Harrassowitz, 1891.

—. "Un vocabulaire hébraïco-français." *Romanische Studien* 1.2 (1872): 163–196.

Nisse, Ruth. *Jacob's Shipwreck: Diaspora, Translation, and Jewish-Christian Relations in Medieval England*. Ithaca: Cornell University Press, 2017.

Olsson, J.T. "The World in Arab Eyes: A Reassessment of the Climes in Medieval Islamic Scholarship." *Bulletin of the School of Oriental and African Studies* 77 (2014): 487–508.

Olszowy-Schlanger, Judith. "Christian Hebraism in Thirteenth-Century England: The Evidence of Hebrew-Latin Manuscripts." In *Crossing Borders: Hebrew Manuscripts as a Meeting-place of Cultures*, ed. Piet van Boxel and Sabine Arndt, 115–122. Oxford: Bodleian Library, 2009.

—. "A Christian Tradition of Hebrew Vocalisation in Medieval England." In *Semitic Studies in Honour of Edward Ullendorff*, ed. Geoffrey Khan, 126–146. Studies in Semitic Languages and Linguistics 47. Leiden and Boston: Brill, 2005.

—. "Le dictionnaire, Ramsey et Robert Wakefield." In *Dictionnaire hébreu-latin-français*, ed. Olszowy-Schlanger and Grondeux, xxii–xxiii.

—. *Hebrew and Hebrew-Latin Documents from Medieval England: A Diplomatic and Palaeographical Study*. Monumenta palaeographica medii aevi. Series Hebraica. Cartae Hebraicis litteris exaratae quo tempore scriptae fuerint exhibentes 2. 2 vols. Turnhout: Brepols, 2015.

—. "The Knowledge and Practice of Hebrew Grammar Among Christian Scholars in Pre-expulsion England: The Evidence of 'Bilingual' Hebrew-Latin Manuscripts." In *Hebrew Scholarship and the Medieval World*, ed. Nicholas De Lange, 107–128. Cambridge: Cambridge University Press, 2001.

—. *Les manuscrits hébreux dans l'Angleterre médiévale: Étude historique et paléographique*. Collection de la Revue des études juives 29. Leuven and Paris: Peeters, 2003.

—. "'My Silent Teachers': Hebrew Manuscripts as the Source of Robert Wakefield's Hebraism." In *Hebraism in Sixteenth-Century England: Robert and Thomas Wakefield*, ed. Charles Burnett and James P. Carley. Toronto: Pontifical Institute of Mediaeval Studies, forthcoming.

—. "Provenance et histoire du dictionnaire." In *Dictionnaire hébreu-latin-français*, ed. Olszowy-Schlanger and Grondeux, xvi–xxiii.

—. "Rachi en latin: Les gloses latines dans un manuscrit du commentaire de Rachi et les études hébraïques parmi des chrétiens dans l'Angleterre médiévale." In *Héritages de Rachi*, ed. René-Samuel Sirat, 137–150. Bibliothèque des Fondations. Paris: Éditions de l'Éclat, 2006.

—. "Robert Wakefield and His Hebrew Manuscripts." *Zutot* 6.1 (2009): 25–33.

—. "Robert Wakefield and the Medieval Background of Hebrew Scholarship in Renaissance England." In *Hebrew to Latin Latin to Hebrew: The Mirroring of Two Cultures in the Age of Humanism* (Colloquium held at the Warburg Institute, London, October 18–19, 2004), ed. Giulio Busi, 61–87. Berlin Studies in Judaism 1. Berlin: Institut für Judaistik, Frei Universität Berlin, 2006.

—. "The Science of Language Among Medieval Jews." In *Science in Medieval Jewish Cultures*, ed. Gad Freudenthal, 359–424. Cambridge: Cambridge University Press, 2011.

—. "Sefer ha-Shoham ('Le Livre d'Onyx'): Dictionnaire de l'hébreu biblique de Moïse ben Isaac ben ha-Nessiya (Angleterre, vers 1260)." In *En Mémoire de Sophie Kessler-Mesguich*, ed. Jean Baumgarten, José Costa, Jean-Patrick Guillaume and Judith Kogel, 183–198. Paris: Presses Sorbonne Nouvelle, 2012.

—. "The Study of the Aramaic Targum by Christians in Medieval France and England." In *A Jewish Targum in a Christian World*, ed. Alberdina Houtman, Eveline van Staalduine-Sulman and Hans-Martin Kirn, 233–249. Jewish and Christian Perspectives Series 27. Leiden: Brill, 2014.

—. "'With That, You Can Grasp all the Hebrew Language': Hebrew Sources of an Anonymous Hebrew-Latin Grammar from Thirteenth-Century England." In *A Universal Art: Hebrew Grammar across Disciplines and Faiths*, ed. Nadia Vidro, Irene E. Zwiep and Judith Olszowy-Schlanger, 179–195. Studies in Jewish History and Culture 46. Leiden and Boston: Brill, 2014.

Olszowy-Schlanger, Judith, and Anne Grondeux, eds. *Dictionnaire hébreu-latin-français de la Bible hébraïque de l'Abbaye de Ramsey (XIIIe s.)*. Corpus Christianorum. Lexica Latina medii aevi 4. Turnhout: Brepols, 2008.

Poleg, Eyal. "The Interpretations of Hebrew Names in Theory and Practice." In *Form and Function in the Late Medieval Bible*, ed. Eyal Poleg and Laura Light, 217–236. Library of the Written Word 27. The Manuscript World 4. Leiden and Boston: Brill, 2013.

Pormann, Peter E., ed. *A Descriptive Catalogue of the Hebrew Manuscripts of Corpus Christi College, Oxford*. Cambridge: D.S. Brewer, 2015.

—. "Hebrew Manuscripts." In *A Descriptive Catalogue of Oriental Manuscripts at St John's College, Oxford*, ed. Emilie Savage-Smith and G.J.H. van Gelder, 98–103. Oxford: Oxford University Press, 2005.

Poznański, Samuel. "Un commentaire sur Job de la France septentrionale." *REJ* 52 (1906): 51–70 and 198–214.

Posegay, Nick. *Points of Contact: The Shared Intellectual History of Vocalisation in Syriac, Arabic, and Hebrew*. Cambridge: Cambridge University Press and Open Book Publishers, 2021.

Reiner, Elchanan. "'Oral versus written': The Shaping of Traditions of Holy Places in the Middle Ages." In *Ve-Zot le-Yehudah: Studies in the History of Eretz Israel presented to Yehuda ben Porat*, ed. Yehoshua Ben-Arieh and Elchanan Reiner, 308–345. Jerusalem: Yad Ben-Zvi Press, 2003. Hebrew.

—. "A Travelogue and Its Fate: The Lost Travel Account of Menahem ha-Hevroni, 'The Knowledge of the Land,' and the Beginning of the Jewish Research on the Land of Israel." *Gilyon* 133–134 (2016): 33–46. Hebrew.

Richler, Benjamin, ed. *Hebrew Manuscripts in the Vatican Library*. Studi e Testi 438. Vatican City: Biblioteca Apostolica Vaticana, 2008.

Rigg, James Macmullen. *Select Pleas, Starrs and Other Records from the Rolls of the Exchequer of the Jews, AD 1220–1284*. Publications of the Selden Society 15. London: B. Quaritch, 1902.

Robinson, J. Armitage, and Montague Rhodes James. *The Manuscripts of Westminster Abbey*. Cambridge: Cambridge University Press, 1909.

Rosier-Catach, Irène. "La Grammatica practica du ms. British Museum V A IV: Roger Bacon, les lexicographes et l'étymologie." In *L'étymologie de l'Antiquité à la Renaissance*, ed. Claude Buridant, 97–125. Lexique 14. Lille: Presses Universitaires du Septentrion, 1998.

—. "Roger Bacon and Grammar." In *Roger Bacon and the Sciences: Commemorative Essays*, ed. Jeremiah Hackett, 67–102. Studien und Text zur Geistesgeschichte des Mittelalters 57. Leiden and New York: Brill, 1997.

Roth, Cecil. *The Intellectual Activities of Medieval English Jewry*. British Academy Supplemental Papers 8. London: Geoffrey Cumberlege, 1949.

Rothschild, J.P. "Enek: targum araméen?" In *Dictionnaire hébreu-latin-français*, ed. Olszowy-Schlanger and Grondeux, lxxxi–lxxxv.

—. "Les sources du dictionnaire." In *Dictionnaire hébreu-latin-français*, ed. Olszowy-Schlanger and Grondeux, lxi–lxxxvi.

Rosin, David. "The Meaning of the Mnemonic Formulae for the Radical and Servile Letters in Hebrew." *JQR* 6 (1894): 475–501.

Russell, J.C. "The Preferments and 'Adiutores' of Robert Grosseteste." *Harvard Theological Review* 26 (1933): 161–172.

Saltman, Avrom. "Gilbert Crispin as a Source of the Anti-Jewish Polemic of the *Ysagoge in theologiam*." In *Confrontation and Coexistence*, ed. Pinḥas Artzi, 89–99. Bar Ilan Studies in History 2. Ramat Gan: Bar Ilan University Press, 1984.

—. "Odo's *Ysagoge*: A New Method of Anti-Jewish Polemic." *Criticism and Interpretation* 13–14 (1979): 265–280. Hebrew.

—. "Supplementary Notes on the Works of Ralph Niger." In *Bar-Ilan Studies in History*, ed. Pinḥas Artzi, 103–113. Ramat-Gan: Bar Ilan University Press, 1978.

Sandler, Lucy Freeman. "Christian Hebraism and the Ramsey Abbey Psalter." *Journal of the Warburg and Courtauld Institutes* 35 (1972): 123–134.

—. "The Historical Miniatures of the Fourteenth-Century Ramsey Psalter." *Burlington Magazine* 111 (1969): 605–611.

Savage-Smith, Emilie. *A Descriptive Catalogue of Oriental Manuscripts at St John's College, Oxford*. Oxford: Oxford University Press, 2005.

Sed-Rajna, Gabrielle, and Sonia Fellous. *Les Manuscrits hébreux enluminés des bibliothèques de France*. Leuven: Peeters, 1994.

Sela, Shlomo. *Abraham ibn Ezra and the Rise of Medieval Hebrew Science.* Brill Series in Jewish Studies 32. Leiden and Boston: Brill, 2003.

Shapira, Anat. *Midrash ʿAseret ha-Dibrot: Text, Sources and Commentary.* Sifriyat Dorot 70. Jerusalem: Mosad Bialik, 2005. Hebrew.

Sharpe, Richard, J.P. Carley, R.M. Thomson and A.G. Watson. *English Benedictine Libraries: The Shorter Catalogues.* Corpus of British Medieval Library Catalogues 4. London: British Library and British Academy, 1996.

Shinan, Avigdor. "Divrei ha-Yamim shel Moshe Rabbenu: Contribution to the Question of the Date, Sources and Nature of the Hebrew Tale in the Middle Ages." *Hasifrut* 24 (1977): 100–116. Hebrew.

Sinclair, Keith V. "The Manuscript Evidence for the 'Dedicatio Ecclesie' of Ramsey Abbey: A Re-examination." *Scriptorium* 38 (1984): 305–309.

Singer, Michael A. "Polemic and Exegesis: The Varieties of Twelfth-Century Hebraism." In *Hebraica Veritas?: Christian Hebraists and the Study of Judaism in Early Modern Europe,* ed. Alison P. Coudert and Jeffrey S. Shoulson, 21–32. Jewish Culture and Contexts. Philadelphia: University of Pennsylvania Press, 2004.

Sirat, Colette. "Notes sur la circulation des livres entre juifs et chrétiens au Moyen Âge." In *Du copiste au collectionneur: Mélanges d'histoire des textes et des bibliothèques en l'honneur d'André Vernet,* ed. Donatella Nebbiai-Dalla Guarda and Jean-François Genest, 383–403. Bibliologia 18. Turnhout: Brepols, 1999.

Smalley, Beryl. "Andrew of Saint Victor, Abbot of Wigmore: A Twelfth-Century Hebraist." *RTAM* 10 (1938): 358–373.

—. "A Commentary on the Hebraica by Herbert of Bosham." *RTAM* 18 (1951): 29–65.

—. *Hebrew Scholarship among Christians in XIIIth Century England as Illustrated by Some Hebrew-Latin Psalters.* Lectiones in Vetere Testamento et Rebus Iudaicis 6. London: Society of Old Testament Studies, 1939.

—. *The Study of the Bible in the Middle Ages.* Notre Dame Paperbacks 39. Notre Dame: University of Notre Dame Press, 1964. 3rd ed., Oxford: Blackwell Publishing, 1983.

Stacey, Robert C. "The Conversion of Jews to Christianity in Thirteenth-Century England." *Speculum* 67 (1992): 263–283.

Stadler, Hubert M. "Textual and Literary Criticism and Hebrew Learning in English Old Testament Scholarship, as Exhibited by Nicholas Trevet's Expositio Litteralis Psalterii and by MS. Corpus Christi College (Oxford) 11." MLitt Thesis, University of Oxford, 1990.

Stegmüller, Friedrich, and Nikolaus Reinhardt. *Repertorium Biblicum Medii Aevi.* 11 vols. Madrid: Consejo Superior de Investigaciones Centificas, Instituto Francisco Suarez, 1950–1980. http://repbib.uni-trier.de/cgi-bin/rebihome.tcl.

Stein, J.T. "The Grammar of R. Shemuel and His Grammatical Commentary on the Torah." In *Jahrbuch des Traditionstreuen Rabbinerverbandes in der Slowakei,* ed. M. Stein, 33–59 and i–vii. Trnava, 1923. Hebrew.

Steiner, Richard C. "Emphatic p in the Massoretic Pronunciation of ʾappaḏno (Dan. 11:45)." In *Hebrew and Arabic Studies in Honour of Joshua Blau,* ed. Moshe Bar Asher,

Z. Ben Hayyim, M.J. Kister, A. Levin, S. Shaked and A. Tal, 551–561. Tel Aviv: Tel Aviv University; Jerusalem: Hebrew University, 1993.

Steinschneider, Moritz. *Verzeichnis der hebräische Handschriften der Königlichen Bibliothek zu Berlin.* 2 vols. Berlin: Konigliche Akademie der Wissenschaft (G. Vogt), 1878–1897.

Stirnemann, Patricia. "Le manuscrit." In *Dictionnaire hébreu-latin-français,* ed. Olszowy-Schlanger and Grondeux, x–xiv.

Szerwiniack, Olivier. "Les interprétations des noms hébreux dans le Liber glossarum." *HEL* 36.1 (2014): 83–96.

—. "Des recueils d'interprétations de noms hébreux chez les Irlandais et le Wisigoth Théodulf." *Scriptorium* 48 (1994): 187–258.

Thiel, Matthias. *Grundlagen und Gestalt der Hebräischkenntnisse des Frühen Mittelalters.* Biblioteca degli Studi Medievali 4. Spoleto: Centro Italiano di Studi Sull'alto Medioevo, 1973.

Thomson, Rodney M. "England and the Twelfth-Century Renaissance." *Past & Present* 101 (1983): 3–21.

Thorndike, Lynn. *A History of Magic and Experimental Science.* Publications History of Science Society, new series 4. 8 vols. New York: Columbia University Press, 1923–1958.

Tolmacheva, Marina. "Ptolemaic Influence on Medieval Arab Geography." In *Discovering New Worlds: Essays on Medieval Exploration and Imagination,* ed. Scott D. Westrem, 125–141. Garland Reference Libraray of the Humanities 1436. Garland Medieval Casebooks 2. New York: Garland, 1991.

Van Liere, Frans. "Gamaliel, Twelfth-Century Christian Scholars, and the Attribution of the Talmud." *Medieval Perspectives* 17.2 (2002): 93–104.

Vidro, Nadia. "Mnemonic: Medieval Period." In *Encyclopedia of Hebrew Language and Linguistics,* ed. Geoffrey Khan et al., 2: 650–653. 4 vols. Leiden and Boston: Brill, 2013.

Vidro, Nadia, Irene E. Zwiep and Judith Olszowy-Schlanger, eds. *A Universal Art: Hebrew Grammar across Disciplines and Faiths.* Studies in Jewish History and Culture 46. Leiden and Boston: Brill, 2014.

Visi, Tamás. "Berechiah ben Natronai ha-Naqdan's Dodi ve-Nekdi and the Transfer of Scientific Knowledge from Latin to Hebrew in the Twelfth Century." *Aleph* 14.2 (2014): 9–73.

Warner, George F. and Julius P. Gilson. *Catalogue of Western Manuscripts in the Old Royal and King's Collections.* 4 vols. London: British Museum, 1921.

Wasserstein, David J. "Grosseteste, the Jews and Medieval Christian Hebraism." In *Robert Grosseteste: New Perspectives on His Thought and Scholarship,* ed. James McEvoy, 357–376. Instrumenta Patristica 27. Turnhout: Brepols, 1995.

Weinstock, Horst. "Roger Bacon und das 'hebräische' Alphabet." *Aschkenas* 2 (1992): 15–48.

—. "Roger Bacon and Phonetic Transliteration." *Folia Linguistica Historica* 12 (1992): 57–87.

—. "Roger Bacon's Polyglot Alphabets." *Florilegium* 11 (1992): 160–178.

Weiss, Roberto. "The Study of Greek in England during the Fourteenth Century." *Rinascimento* 2 (1951): 209–239. Repr. in *Medieval and Humanist Greek: Collected Essays*. Ed. Roberto Weiss. Medioevo e Umanesimo 8. Padova: Antenore, 1977.

Wellisch, Hans H. *The Conversion of Scripts: Its Nature, History, and Utilization*. Information Sciences Series. New York: Wiley, 1978.

Wilensky, Michel. "La source de la proposition כל דבר שאין בו רוח חיים זכרהו ונקבהו." *REJ* 98 (1934): 66–71.

—. "R. Moshe al-Roṭi (אלרוטי)." *HUCA* 11 (1936): 647–649.

Wilkins, Nigel. *Catalogue des manuscrits français de la bibliothèque Parker (Parker Library)*. Corpus Christi College, Cambridge, Parker Library Publications. Cambridge: Corpus Christi College, 1993.

Yassif, Eli. "'Leisure' and 'Generosity': Theory and Practice in the Creation of Hebrew Narratives in the Late Middle Ages." *Kiryat Sefer* 62 (1990): 887–905. Hebrew.

—. "Sefer ha-Ma'asim: Character, Origins and Influence of a Collection of Folktales from the Time of the Tosafists." *Tarbiz* 53 (1984): 409–429. Hebrew. Repr. in *Ke-Margalit be-Mishbetzet: Collection of the Hebrew Tales in the Middle Ages*. Tel Aviv: Ha-Kibbutz ha-Me'uḥad, 2004. Hebrew.

Yeivin, Israel. *Introduction to the Tiberian Masorah*. Trans. E.J. Revell. Masoretic Studies 5. Missoula: Scholars' Press for the Society of Biblical Literature, 1980.

Zotenberg, Hermann. *Catalogue des manuscrits hébreux et samaritains de la Bibliothèque Impériale*. Manuscrits orientaux 1. Paris: Imprimerie impériale, 1866.

Index of Quotations

Hebrew Bible
Genesis
18–19 : 49
40:15 : 117, 121
Exodus
9:31 : 77
13:4 : 77
16:15 : 66
Leviticus
2:2 : 96, 142
5:12 : 142
Numbers
5:26 : 142 n57
Deuteronomy
33:7 : 53 n44
Joshua
17:11 : 64
Job
1:19 : 105, 156
16:9 : 142
Psalms
2:9 : 72
5:7 : 72
18:4 : 73
18:22 : 73
20:9 : 73
21:5 : 73
24 (23):1 : 53
34:16 (MT 35:16) : 96 n7, 142
37:12 : 140, 142
48:3 : 64, 65
Kohelet
1:5 : 105, 156
Isaiah
9:5 : 121
Jeremiah
25:26 : 48
Daniel
11:45 : 49
Haggai
1:14 : 146
Malachi
3:20 : 105, 156

Babylonian Talmud
bHagigah
3b : 66
bMegillah
6a : 48 n27
bRosh ha-Shanah
26a : 64 n81

Index of Manuscripts

Berlin, Deutsche Staatsbibliothek zu Berlin – Preussischer Kulturbesitz
Or. Qu. 648: 61 n69
Cambridge, Corpus Christi College
CCC 468: 22, 36, 38, 39, 44, 114 n1
Cambridge, St John's College Archive
D.56.140: 37
D.56.180: 37
Cambridge, Trinity College
B.14.33: 1 n2
R. 8. 6: 2 n7
Cambridge, University Library
Dd. 8. 53: 63
Ff. 1. 24: 43 n5
Ff. 6. 13: 44, 55, 138
Einsiedeln, Stiftsbiblithek
28: 50 n35
Florence, Biblioteca Medicea Laurenziana
Santa Croce Pl. XXV sin. 4: 50 n35
Leiden, Bibliotheek der Rijksuniversiteit
Or. 4725: 8 n20
Leipzig, Universitätsbibliothek
Vollers 1099: 67
Lincoln, Cathedral Chapter Library
15: 50 n34, 71 n103
London, British Library
Add. 19776: 127 n21
Arundel 165: 43 n5
Cotton Rolls II 16/3: 35
Royal 12 D. XIII: 14 n7
Stowe 57: 76 n109, 115 n5, 118 n12, 139 n43
V A IV: 4 n13
London, Lambeth Palace Library
435: 2 n7, 32, 33, 72, 73, 74, 138
585: 35
London, Westminster Abbey Library
1: 72 n105
2: 2 n7
London, Westminster Abbey Muniments
WAM 6799: 63 n77
Longleat House, Library of the Marquess of Bath
21: *passim. See also the General Index*
Manchester, John Rylands Library
A 694: 60 n66
Milan, Biblioteca Ambrosiana
A 186 Inf: 141 n53
New York, Pierpont Morgan Library
M. 302: 39 n26
Oxford, Bodleian Library
Arch. Selden A. 3: 2 n7, 31, 32, 34, 76, 77
Bodl. 738: 72 n105
Bodl. Or. 3: 115 n7
Bodl. Or. 46: 2 n7, 23, 30, 33
Bodl. Or. 62: 2 n7, 23, 24, 31, 32, 33, 75, 76
Bodl. Or. 135: 59, 67, 71, 72
Oppenheim 152: 68, 70, 125 n17, 127 n26
Oppenheim 625: 67, 141, 143
Oxford, Corpus Christi College
5: 2 n7
6: 2 n7, 31, 32, 33
8: 2 n7
9: 2 n7, 23, 30, 32, 33

10: 2 n7, 32, 34
11: 2 n7, 53, 54 n46, 72 n105
Oxford, St John's College
143: 2 n7, 23, 31, 32, 33
Paris, Bibliothèque nationale de France
hébreu 113: 2 n7, 48, 75, 115 n7, 147
hébreu 1221: 60 n66
latin 36: 49, 138
latin 16558: 114
St Paul in Lavantthal, Stiftsbibliothek
Cod. XXV/2.19: 39 n26
St Petersburg, National Library of Russia
Firkovicz Evr II A 34: 68
Toulouse, Bibliothèque municipale
402: 50 n35 and n37
Turin, Biblioteca Nazionale e Universitaria
MS A IV 13: 149
Vatican City, Biblioteca Apostolica Vaticana
Vat. ebr. 402: 63, 64 n80, 65 n83, 66 n87, 141, 143

General Index

Abelard, Peter 114
Abraham bar Ḥiyya 65
Abraham ben Ḳamniel 70
Abraham ha-Bavli 59 n64, 60 n65
Abraham ibn Ezra 65, 67, 69, 126, 127, 139, 142 n56, 144 n62, 145, 158, 159; *Iggeret ha-Shabbat* 65; *Sefer Moznayim* 139 n42, 142 n56, 144 n62
Abū al-Faraj Hārūn 57, 60, 133, 140 n46, 141; *Hidāyat al-Qāriʾ* 60, 61 n66, 68, 76, 129, 133, 139–142, 145, 158
Abū Zakariyyā Yaḥyā Ibn Daʾūd: *see* Judah Ḥayyūj
adab 66
Aharon (scribe) 69
Aharon ben Moshe ben Asher 139
al-Fāsī, David ben Abraham: *Kitāb jāmiʿ al-ʾalfāẓ* 59 n64, 60, 71
Al-Kindi 64
Almohads 62, 66
alphabet 18; Arabic 115 n7; Greek 115; Hebrew 1, 41, 45, 46, 48, 49, 52, 67 n90, 74, 113, 115, 116, 118, 146, 161, 162; Latin 49, 76 n109, 115, 139 n43; Runic 115; Slavonic 115
analogy 58, 77
Andalusia, Andalusian authors 57, 62, 65, 66, 67
Andrew of Saint-Victor 3, 114
Anglo-Norman French 5, 6, 8, 12, 14, 69, 72, 76, 125, 153. *See also* French, Old
Arab: astronomers 65; grammarians 57
Arabic: Benjamin of Cambridge's hostility towards its use in understanding Hebrew Bible 64, 66–67; grammar and lexicography 59 n64, 60 n66, 67, 70, 128, 139, 159 n92; importance of in the comparative approach of Spanish grammarians 64, 67; in the Longleat Hebrew Grammar 94, 97, 136; "sapiential" language for Bacon 2 n5, 5 n16, 54, 55 n49; science and scientific discourse and its translation into Hebrew 1, 64–65, 141; use of by Moses ben Isaac ha-Nessiʾah 70. *See also* Abū al-Faraj Hārūn; *Horayat ha-Ḳoreʾ*
Aramaic 48, 54, 58, 64, 69. *See also* Targum
Aristotle: *Categories* 14 (see also *Predicamenta Augustini*); *Poetics* 128 n27
article: definite 43, 52, 53–54, 154, 155
Athens 43 n5

Bacon, Roger 3, 42–43, 44, 70, 74–75, 77, 114, 116, 134, 138; alphabet 115 n7; *Compendium Studii Philosophiae* 4 n13, 44, 54–55; Hebrew grammar (Cambridge, University Library, MS Ff. 6. 13) 4 n13, 44–56, 134, 138; *Opus Maius* 4 n13, 5 n16, 44–48; *Opus Tertium* 4 n13, 44; *Summa Grammatica* 44. See also *Epistle on the Secrets of the Art and of Nature and on the Invalidity of Magic*; *Notabilia extraordinaria*
Baḥyạ ibn Paḳūda: *Sefer Torat Ḥovot ha-Levavot* 66

Benedictine(s): Abbey of Ramsey 8, 9 n21, 14, 22, 27, 29, 35–40, 43, 44, 115 n7, 165. *See also* Ramsey
Benjamin of Cambridge 63, 64, 66, 67, 141, 143
Ben Sira: *Alphabet of Ben Sira* 15, 59 n64
Berekhiah ben Natronai Naḳdan 69; commentary on Job 63, 67; *Mishlei Shuʿalim* 59 n64
Bible: Hebrew 2, 4 n14, 5, 6, 7, 14, 15, 29, 30, 34, 35, 55, 56, 57, 64, 66, 68, 71, 96 n8, 113, 114, 126, 132, 133, 139, 140 n48, 144, 159; Latin Vulgate 2, 3 n9, 5, 7, 15, 16, 30 n2, 31 n4, 114; Paris Bible 2 n6, 41 n1
binyanim 25, 58, 69, 77, 118, 119, 121, 122, 124, 125, 126, 146, 148, 149, 157, 158, 160, 161
Byrhtferth: *Enchiridion, Manual* 115 n7

Cairo Genizah 128
calendar 36, 39
cantillation signs: see *ṭeʿamim*
Christian Hebraism: in medieval England 1–10, 11, 29, 31 n6, 34, 40 n26, 45; in the Renaissance 32 n11, 39, 43, 58, 166
Chronicles of Moses: see *Liber dierum Mose*
chronology, biblical 31 n4, 32, 33
Church Fathers 1, 54
clime(s) 64–66
conjugation (Hebrew) 13, 18, 58, 62, 73, 76, 113, 118, 119, 124, 125, 126, 148, 149, 154, 157, 158, 160, 161, 162, 163. See also *binyanim*
Constantina 43 n5
converts 30, 31 n6, 69, 71, 119, 146, 147, 166. *See also* Philip (Jewish convert to Christianity), Yoḥannan (Christian convert to Judaism)
correctoria 2 n6, 4 n14, 53
cryptography: and Roger Bacon 46, 47–48; and *atbash* 48

Darkhei ha-Niḳḳud ve-ha-Neginot: *see* Moses ben Yom Tov ha-Naḳdan
declension 52, 53, 56
derivation, derivational base 56, 57, 58, 62, 64, 69, 73, 119, 154 n82; and *binyanim* 69, 119
dibbuḳ: see *status constructus*
dictionary (dictionaries): Hebrew 5, 9 n21, 37, 55, 67, 68, 71, 72, 77; Hebrew-Arabic 59 n64. *See also* Moses ben Isaac ha-Nessiʾah: *Sefer ha-Shoham*; Solomon ben Abraham ibn Parḥon: *Maḥberet he-ʿArukh*. *See also under* Longleat House, MS 21: contents
Dionysius Thrax 43 n5, 128 n27
Donatus: 9, 44, 55; in Greek (*Donatus grece*) 43 n5
dual (grammatical number) 43, 52, 124
Dunash ibn Labrāṭ 57, 58, 62, 64–68, 76, 158

Eadwine Psalter 115 n7
Edward I 39
Eliezer of Beaugency 69
Eliyahu Menaḥem 69
"*enek.*" group of manuscripts 30, 32–34. *See also* Targum
England (Hebrew grammar and manuscripts) 2–10, 15–16, 58, 63, 67, 70, 113, 125, 143, 158
Epistle on the Secrets of the Art and of Nature and on the Invalidity of Magic (attributed to Roger Bacon) 47
Extractiones de Talmud 114

France (Hebrew grammar and manuscripts) 41 n1, 52 n42, 58, 61, 62, 63, 67, 69, 70, 113, 125, 141, 143, 158
French, Old 11, 29, 30, 53, 58, 59 n64, 64 n81, 67, 69, 71, 72, 73, 75, 76, 96, 97, 118, 125, 129, 136, 141, 146, 147, 149, 150–155. *See also* Anglo-Norman French

Gamaliel 15
gaʿyah 133
Geoffrey of Ufford: *Scutum Bede* 75, 76 n109, 115, 118, 139 n43
glossaries: biblical 58, 67; Hebrew-Old French 58, 59 n64, 67, 147 n67, 149
grammar (Hebrew): 1, 4 n13, 5, 6, 8 n21, 40, 44, 45, 51, 52, 54, 55, 56, 57–78, 135–146, 148, 154 n82, 157–159, 160, 165; and Greek grammar 36, 43, 44, 46 n16, 55, 56, 57; and Latin grammar 42–56, 75 n109, 128, 138, 139, 165. See also *binyanim*; dual (grammatical number); root (consonantal); *status constructus*; suffix
grammatization: of European vernaculars 42; of Hebrew 57
Grandisson, John 72
Gregory of Huntingdon 35, 36, 38, 39, 44
Grosseteste, Robert: knowledge of Greek and Hebrew 2 n7, 3, 4 n12, 43

Hebraica Psalter 39 n26, 53, 72 n105
Hebrei: *see* Jews
Hebrew (language): study of in the middle ages 1–2 *et passim*; study, translation, and learning of in England 2–5; the use of manuals for learning 5–6. *See also* alphabet: Hebrew; conjugation (Hebrew); dictionary: Hebrew; grammar (Hebrew); lexicography (Hebrew); Longleat House, MS 21; pronunciation: of Hebrew; vowels: Hebrew
Herbert of Bosham 3, 4, 39 n26, 53, 114
Hidāyat al-Qārīʾ: *see* Abū al-Faraj Hārūn. See also *Horayat ha-Ḳoreʾ*
Holbeach, Lawrence 9 n21, 37–38
Horayat ha-Ḳoreʾ 60 n66, 61, 63, 68, 140–143; circulates in Italy as *Tokhen Ezra* or *Sefer Ṭaʿamei ha-Miḳraʾ* 60 n66, 61, 68
Hugh of Lincoln 39
humoral pathology 65
Huntingdon 38–39

Iggrot shel Dibrot 60 n64
Interpretation of Hebrew Names 41, 49, 50, 71, 138
Iohannes Infantius 37
Isaac ha-Levi 70
Isidore of Seville: *Etymologies* 75–76, 128
Iudei: *see* Jews

Jacob ben Meʾir: *see* Rabbenu Tam
Jacob ben Menaḥem ha-Vardimasi 63 n77
Jacob of Tchernichov 69
Jerome 15, 41 n1, 48, 49, 50, 72 n105, 138
Jerusalem 50, 60, 65, 140, 141
Jews (Hebrei, Iudei) 1, 3 n9, 46, 48, 50, 51, 53 n45, 57, 58, 69, 71, 72, 74, 93, 136, 137, 140, 146, 147, 159; Arabic-speaking Iberian 71, 76, 117, 119, 136, 137, 139, 165; in England 1, 2, 5, 6 n17, 9, 38, 39, 67, 68, 70; French 67, 117, 147; Italian 67 n90; Spanish Jews in Provence 65, 66
"Johannes Marti" (March?) 72
John, king of England 63
John of Basingstoke 43
John of Saint Paul 14
Jonah ibn Janāḥ 67, 68, 70, 158; *Kitāb al-mustalḥaq* 70; *Maḥberet he-ʿArukh* as Hebrew adaptation of *Kitāb al-mustalḥaq* 67; *Sefer ha-Hassagah* (Hebrew translation of *Kitāb al-mustalḥaq*) 67
Joseph ben Ḥiyya (scribe) 141
Joseph Kara 69
Joseph the Constantinopolitan: *ʿAdat Devorim* 140 n47
Judah Hadassi: *Eshkol ha-Kofer* 140 n47
Judah Ha-Levi 67
Judah Ḥayyūj (Abū Zakariyyā Yaḥyā Ibn Daʾūd Ḥayyūj) 57–58, 62, 67 n90, 68, 69, 125, 157
Judah ibn Tibbon 66

Karaite(s) 57, 59 n64, 60, 140 n47. *See also* Abū al-Faraj Hārūn; al-Fāsī, David ben Abraham; Joseph the Constantinopolitan
Kimhi, David 69, 70, 76, 119, 121, 122, 127, 146, 158; *Sefer Mikhlol* 69, 70, 76, 121, 146; *Sefer Shorashim* 70
Kimhi, Joseph 62–66, 68, 69, 76, 118, 119, 125, 126, 127, 133, 134, 143–145, 158, 165; *Sefer ha-Galui* 62–66; *Sefer Zikkaron* 68, 70 n99, 133, 143, 145, 158
Kimhi, Moses 69, 128, 134
Koran 139

Langue d'oïl 8, 153. *See also* French, Old
Leland, John 37–39
Leshon Limmudim: *see* Moses ben Isaac ha-Nessi'ah
lexicography (Hebrew) 6, 14, 15, 16, 35, 36, 40, 42, 49, 56, 57, 58, 60, 62, 63, 67 n90, 68, 69, 70, 71, 72, 75, 76, 119
Liber de simplicium medicinarum uirtutibus 14
Liber dierum Mose (*Chronicles of Moses*) 15
Liber interpretationis Hebraicorum nominum: see *Interpretation of Hebrew Names*
London 61, 65, 67, 68, 69, 113, 118, 126, 127, 143, 145, 148, 158, 165
Longleat House, MS 21
—, manuscript: codicological units and composition 13–14, 17–19; page layout 24–27; scribes of 19–22; scripts in 22–24; texts in 14–17
—, Hebrew grammar (the Longleat House Grammar): and Hebrew scholarship at Ramsey Abbey 29–40; and Jewish linguistic traditions 56–78; and Latin linguistic approaches to grammar 41–56
—, contents: Hebrew grammar in Hebrew characters 99–107, 146–160; Hebrew grammar in Latin characters 81–92, 113–127; essay on Hebrew vowels and accents 93–98, 127–146; Hebrew verb paradigms in Latin characters 108–112, 160–161; Latin and Anglo-Norman French dictionary of biblical Hebrew 6, 8, 11, 13, 14, 15, 16, 19, 20, 21, 22, 29, 30, 32, 33, 34, 35, 36, 37, 69, 70, 73, 77, 116, 117

Ma'ayan Ḳodesh 149
Maḥberet ha-Tijān 140 n48. *See also* Abū al-Faraj Hārūn; *Horayat ha-Ḳore'*
Maḥberet he-'Arukh: *see* Solomon ben Abraham ibn Parḥon
Maḥberet Menaḥem: *see* Menaḥem ben Saruḳ
Mainz 60, 141
manuscripts, bilingual: Hebrew-Latin 4, 7, 8, 9, 23, 29–34, 49 n30, 53 (psalter), 72 n105 (psalter), 75 (book of Ezekiel), 77, 114, 115 n7, 119
Manuzio, Aldo 115 n6
Mare, William de la: *see* William de Mara
Masorah 57, 59, 62, 71, 132, 139, 144, 145, 159
Masoretes 61, 62, 67, 68, 70, 119, 128, 139, 141, 165
matres lectionis 74, 128, 153
Matthew Paris 43 n5
Meir ben Elijah of Norwich 63, 64 n78
Menaḥem ben Pereẓ ha-Ḥebroni 60 n64
Menaḥem ben Pereẓ Vardimas 63
Menaḥem ben Saruḳ 57, 58, 62, 64, 65, 67 n90, 68, 69, 71, 76; *Maḥberet Menaḥem* 68 n90, 71
Menaḥem ben Solomon: *Even Boḥan* 141
Meshullam ben Nathanael 141
meteg 97, 129, 130, 131, 132–135, 144
Midrash 'Aseret ha-Dibrot 60
Midrash va-Yosha' 60 n64
mishḳalim 69
mnemonics 41 n1, 45 n13, 74, 129, 142, 154

morphology 7, 10, 23, 27, 52, 56, 57, 61, 68, 72, 77, 113, 122, 126, 144, 147, 161, 165
Moses ben Isaac ha-Nessi'ah 68, 69, 70, 76, 125–126, 127, 128, 143, 145, 165; *Leshon Limmudim* 70; *Sefer ha-Shoham* 67–70, 76, 125–127, 148, 165
Moses ben Yom Tov ha-Naḳdan 61, 68, 69, 126, 143, 145, 148, 158; *Darkhei ha-Niḳḳud ve-ha-Neginot* 61, 68, 113, 118, 126, 127, 128, 141, 143, 145, 157, 158, 165
Moses ibn Ezra: *Sefer he-ʿAnak* (*Sefer Tajnis*) 59 n64, 71
Moses of London: *see* Moses ben Yom Tov ha-Naḳdan
Moses Roti 68, 69
muṣawwitāt 128

naḳdan: *see* Masoretes
Narbonne 62
Nathanael ben Meshullam 141 n50
Nathan ben Yeḥiel of Rome 67 n90, 71; *Sefer he-ʿArukh* 71
Neckam, Alexander 3, 114
Nicolas of Lyre 72 n105
niḳḳud: *see* vocalization
Normandy 59, 139, 141
Notabilia extraordinaria (attributed to Roger Bacon) 4 n13, 50–51
notaricon 98, 129, 142 n58

organs of articulation 75–76, 135, 138–142
Otot ʿEser Milḥamot Melekh ha-Mashiaḥ 60 n64
ʿOvadiah ha-Sefaradi 70

palimpsest 73
parts of speech 14, 44, 54–55, 68, 148, 165
Pater Noster (Hebrew) 31 n4
Philip (Jewish convert to Christianity) 71
phonetics 10, 68, 75, 80, 119, 128, 136, 137, 139, 142, 144, 145. *See also* organs of articulation

piyyutim 32, 76
polemics 47, 48, 62, 114, 143
Predicamenta Augustini 11, 12, 14, 19–21, 35, 36
Prior Gregory: *see* Gregory of Huntingdon
Priscian 9, 42, 44, 55–56
pronunciation: of Hebrew 7, 13, 46, 49–52, 54, 59 n64, 71, 73–75, 113, 115 n6, 116–118, 133, 136–138, 145, 147, 153
Provence 66, 143, 145, 157
psalter: Greek-Latin 36, 38–39, 44; Hebrew with Latin gloss 2 n7, 4 n12, 6–8, 11–13, 15–16, 19–21, 23–24, 29, 32–34, 48, 72–73, 138, 147; Hebrew with Old French gloss 75. See also *Eadwine Psalter*; Hebraica Psalter; *superscriptio*
Pseudo-Dionysius 43 n5
Ptolemy: *Almagest* 64

Rabbenu Tam (Jacob ben Me'ir): *Hakhraʿot* 61–63, 64, 69, 143
Ralph Niger: *Philippicus* 15 n11, 50, 71. See also *Interpretation of Hebrew Names*
Ramsey: Abbey 8, 9 n21, 14, 22, 27, 29, 35–40, 43–44, 53, 56, 77, 78, 115 n7, 165; Hebraists 37–40, 43, 56, 77; Psalter 39 n26
Rashbam (Samuel ben Me'ir) 61–62, 66, 68, 69; *Dayyḳot* (or *Dayyaḳut*) *le-R. Shemuel* 61
Rashi (Solomon ben Isaac) 2 n7, 5, 6, 15, 29, 31, 48 n27, 58, 61, 62, 64 n81, 65, 68, 69, 157, 158
Richard of Bury: *Philobiblon* 8 n21
Robert (de) Dodeford 35, 36, 38, 39
root (consonantal) 14, 56, 57–58, 61, 62 n72, 67 n90, 69, 73, 77, 96 n8, 118, 128, 145, 149, 155, 158, 160, 161, 165
Rouen 63, 67

Saʿadiah ben Joseph Gaon 57, 139, 160 n94
St Augustine's Abbey, Canterbury 8 n20, 43 n5
Saint-Victor (Paris) 3 n9, 114
Salerno, school of: medical corpus 11, 14 n7, 67
Samuel (scribe) 59 n64
Samuel ben Meʾir: *see* Rashbam
scribe(s): 4, 7–8, 9, 14–40, 72, 75, 77, 79, 80, 115–117, 119, 122, 124 n16, 139, 146, 147, 155, 160, 161, 165. *See also* Aharon (scribe); Joseph ben Ḥiyya (scribe); Samuel (scribe)
Sefer ha-Hassagah: *see* Jonah ibn Janāḥ
Sefer ha-Maʿasim 59–60 n64
Sefer ha-Shoham: *see* Moses ben Isaac ha-Nessiʾah
Sefer he-ʿArukh: *see* Nathan ben Yeḥiel of Rome
Sefer Ṭaʿamei ha-Miḳraʾ: see *Horayat ha-Ḳoreʾ*
Sefer Yeẓirah 76, 139
servile letters 154
Sindbad (Hebrew): see *Sindebar*
Sindebar (*Mishlei Sendebar*) 15, 60 n64
Solomon ben Abraham ibn Parḥon 67, 69, 70; *Maḥberet he-ʿArukh* 5, 15, 29, 59 n64, 61 n69, 67, 71, 77, 142
Solomon ben Isaac of Troyes: *see* Rashi
Spain 43, 57, 62
Spelman, Henry 11
Stamford 38, 39
status constructus 104, 146, 155, 157, 158
suffix 43, 47, 54, 56, 72, 73, 118, 122–126, 146, 148–155, 158
superscriptio 2, 4 n12, 7, 8, 9, 12, 15–16, 19, 20, 29, 30–31 nn2–7, 32, 34, 53, 79, 119, 156
syntax 148, 153, 154, 155, 156

Talmud 15, 58, 62; trial of 114. See also *Extractiones de Talmud*
Targum 5, 30, 74; Targum Jonathan 48 n27; Targum Onkelos 30
ṭeʿamim 95, 97 n13, 98, 113, 127, 133, 137, 138, 139, 148, 154 n82, 156
Thynne, Thomas, first viscount of Weymouth 11
Tokhen Ezra 61, 141
Tosafists 62, 63 n77
transliterations 22, 95, 114–118, 119, 126, 149, 153, 161
Trivet, Nicolas 3 n12, 72 n105
trivium 42, 56
Twelfth-Century Renaissance 1, 43

vocalization: Tiberian 16, 47, 51, 52 n42, 79, 117, 132, 133, 134, 138–139, 144–147. *See also* vowels: Hebrew
vowels: Hebrew 7, 16, 18, 19, 20, 22, 25, 27, 31 n7, 45–49, 56, 63, 69, 74–75, 79, 93–98, 117–118, 127–145, 146, 147, 148, 149, 165

Wakefield, Robert 21, 32, 33, 34, 36–37
Wakefield, Thomas 32 n11, 37 n19
William de Mara 4, 50; *Correctorium Vaticanum* 4 nn13–14, 53

Yeḳutiel ha-Kohen ben Judah: *ʿEin ha-Ḳoreʾ* 61, 127, 141
Yeḳutiel ha-Naḳdan: *see* Yeḳutiel ha-Kohen ben Judah
Yemen 140
Yoḥannan (Christian convert to Judaism) 69
Yūsuf ibn Nūḥ 57